SOVEREIGN WOMEN IN A MUSLIM KINGDOM

SOVEREIGN WOMEN IN A MUSLIM KINGDOM

The Sultanahs of Aceh, 1641–1699

Sher Banu A.L. Khan

Southeast Asia Program Publications

an imprint of
Cornell University Press
Ithaca and London

Copyright © 2017 Sher Banu A.L. Khan

All rights reserved. Except for brief quotations in a review, this book, or parts thereof, must not be reproduced in any form without permission in writing from the publisher. For information, address Cornell University Press, Sage House, 512 East State Street, Ithaca, New York 14850.

First published in Singapore in 2017 by NUS Press
First published in the United States of America in 2017 by Cornell University Press
First printing, Cornell Paperbacks, 2017

Printed in the United States of America

Library of Congress Cataloging-in-Publication Data

Names: Khan, Sher Banu A.L., author.
Title: Sovereign women in a Muslim kingdom: the sultanahs of Aceh, 1641–1699 / Sher Banu A.L. Khan.
Description: Ithaca: SEAP Publications, an imprint of Cornell University Press, 2017. | Includes bibliographical references and index.
Identifiers: LCCN 2017009177| ISBN 9781501713842 (cloth: alk. paper) | ISBN 9781501713859 (pbk.: alk. paper)
Subjects: LCSH: Queens--Indonesia--Aceh (Sultanate)--History--17th century. | Muslim women--Indonesia--Aceh (Sultanate)--History--17th century. | Women in Islam--Indonesia--Aceh (Sultanate)--History--17th century. | Aceh (Sultanate)--Kings and rulers.
Classification: LCC DS646.15.A8 K49 2017 | DDC 959.8/110209252--dc23
LC record available at https://lccn.loc.gov/2017009177

Cornell University Press strives to use environmentally responsible suppliers and materials to the fullest extent possible in the publishing of its books. Such materials include vegetable-based, low-VOC inks and acid-free papers that are recycled, totally chlorine-free, or partly composed of nonwood fibers. For further information, visit our website at www.cornellpress.cornell.edu.

Cover image: Imaginative portrayal of the Queen of Sumatra Island, circa 1375, by Abraham Cresques, Map of the World/Asia. This queen, in all probability, is Queen Nur Ilah, who had rights over Pasai, the antecedent of Aceh dar al-Salam whose pair of gravestones—found in the village of Minye Tujoh in Aceh—were inscribed with the dates of death 1380 or 1390 AD. (Image used with permission from the Bibliothèque Nationale de France, courtesy of Dr. Peter Borschberg, National University of Singapore)

This book is dedicated to the women of Aceh Dar al-Salam:

May you draw courage and inspiration from your own history.

Contents

List of Illustrations	viii
List of Abbreviations	ix
Acknowledgements	x
Preface	xiii
Introduction	1
1. The Succession of the First Female Ruler of Aceh	27
2. Sultanah Safiatuddin's Early Years: Keeping Afloat	57
3. Sultanah Safiatuddin's Maturing Years: Politics of Consolidation	93
4. Ties That Bind? Aceh's Overlord-Vassal Relations	129
5. Female Rulers Negotiating Islam and Patriarchy	171
6. The Practice of Queenship	210
7. The End of Female Rule and Its Legacy	248
Glossary	276
Bibliography	281
Index	306

List of Illustrations

Figure 1   A Dutch engraver's image of Iskandar Thani's funeral in 1641   60

Figure 2   Seventeenth-century drawing of the VOC factory at Aceh   65

Figure 3   Map of Sumatra, West Java and the Malay Peninsula, c. 1700   129

Figure 4   The seal of the Sultanah of Aceh Dar al-Salam with her name and title   181

List of Abbreviations

BKI   Bijdragen tot de Taal-, Land- en Volkenkunde [Journal of Humanities and Social Sciences of Southeast Asia]

EIC   English East India Company

KITLV   Koninklijk Instituut voor Taal-, Land- en Volkenkunde [Royal Netherlands Institute of Southeast Asian and Caribbean Studies]

NA   Nationaal Archief [Dutch National Archives, The Hague]

OBP   Overgekomen Brieven en Papieren uit Indie [Briefs and Papers Received from the Indies] (in the Dutch National Archives)

SWC   Sumatra West Coast

TBG   Tijdschrift voor Indische Taal-, Land- En Volkenkunde [Journal of Indonesian Linguistics and Anthropology]

VOC   Verenigde Oostindische Compagnie [Dutch United East India Company]

Acknowledgements

I would like to express my heartfelt gratitude and thanks to the following institutions and people who have helped me throughout my journey to complete this book.

To the people who formed the backbone of my book. My deepest gratitude goes to Emeritus Professor Anthony Reid, who is the inspiration for this book, who first introduced me to the world of Aceh and women in pre-colonial Southeast Asia, for his generosity in sharing his ideas and the continual discussions we have had over many years, across different places and time zones. To Professor Dr Leonard Blussé, for his unfailing support and faith in me. To Professor Dr Jan van der Putten, who generously spent many hours of his time with me deciphering the intricacies of Old Dutch. To Dr Ito Takeshi, for granting access to his invaluable transliterations of VOC materials, and his research on Aceh. The VOC materials are now published in *Aceh Sultanate: State, Society, Religion and Trade: The Dutch Sources, 1636–1661* in two volumes (Leiden: E.J. Brill, 2015). To Professor Felipe Fernández-Armesto, for his support and patience.

I am indebted to the Centre for Editing Lives and Letters, Queen Mary University of London and University of London Postgraduate Research Studentship funding which I received from 2004 to 2007. I am grateful to Universities UK for giving me the Overseas Research Students Award. I am thankful to the organisers of the TANAP (Towards an Age of Partnership) programme, Leiden University, in particular to Professor Leonard Blussé, for supporting my Advanced Master of Arts. My thanks also go to my current university, the National University of

Singapore, for granting me the start-up funding and for a semester's writing leave.

I extend my utmost appreciation to all the staff in the various institutions and libraries, generously extending their help, who went beyond the call of duty to help me locate materials and resources for my research. I thank all my friends in the Netherlands, at Leiden University, Universiteit Bibliotheek, KITLV and Nationaal Archief. In the United Kingdom, the British Library. My friends in Aceh at the Pusat Dokumentasi dan Informasi Aceh, Yayasan Hasjmy and Museum Aceh. In Kuala Lumpur, at the Universiti Kebangsaan Malaysia and Perpustakaan Negara. In Jakarta, at Arsip Negara and KITLV Jakarta. Special thanks to Paul Kratoska and Lena Qua at NUS Press, Singapore, and Emma Coupland for her expert copyediting. Last but not least my former institution, the National Institute of Education and Nanyang Technological University.

I thank all the generous scholars who have shared their expertise, thoughts and materials with me, namely Peter Borschberg, Radin Fernando, Geoff Wade, Annabel Teh Gallop, Michael Laffan, Leonard and Barbara Andaya, and the late Professors Dr Ali Hasymi, Dr Ibrahim Alfian and Dr Teuku Iskandar.

My deepest appreciation goes to my friends, colleagues and all the well-wishers I have met in the course of my research and writing this book. To Associate Professor Noor Aisha, head of the Malay Studies Department at the National University of Singapore, whose support I truly value, and to Professor Malcolm Murfett, for his concern and constant advice. Those who extended their generosity and hospitality, opening their homes to make me feel welcome when I was away from home, especially Professor Salleh Yaapar and his wife Kak Timah while they were in Leiden, Brother Feng and Anna in Leiden, the late Ami Farouk and Amati in Amsterdam, and Bhai Khaled and Kak Safiah in Dulwich, London. To my other friends, Cynthia and Marijke at Leiden University, Rosemary at KITLV, Roksana at the National Institute of Education, Saira Begum in Johor Baru and Kak Zunaima in Aceh.

I am especially beholden to my family for bearing with me on the long journey towards the completion of this book. My thanks to my parents, Abdul Latiff Khan and Noorjan, my in-laws, Abdul Rahim and Sapiah, for their supplications, my sister, Shahmim Banu, who has kept my spirits high and, most of all, my gratitude goes to my husband, Aidi, who has stood by me throughout this undertaking.

May God bless all who have helped me in one way or another, and for those whose names I may have inadvertently overlooked, thank you!

Preface

The remarkable fact that a succession of not one but four women rulers of the sultanate of Aceh Dar al-Salam in the second half of the seventeenth century has remained largely inexplicable spurred me to undertake an in-depth investigation to explain this phenomenon. Women sovereigns ruling Muslim kingdoms are few and far between, and usually unknown. Fatima Mernissi's book, *The Forgotten Queens of Islam*, attempted to rescue and to recognise them in history. However, even Mernissi had forgotten the numerous Muslim queens in Southeast Asia, despite the fact that—besides the sultanahs of Aceh—there were indeed many other Muslim queens in Patani, Sukadana, Bone, Jambi, among others. One possible reason for this neglect is the lack of records these women left, compared to the letters and diaries of European queens, and the lack of indigenous records about these Muslim queens in Southeast Asia.

To undertake such a study, one must rely on the European records to supplement the indigenous ones. In the course of the seventeenth century, the Dutch and English East Indies Companies recorded the histories of the individual Malay polities they encountered. These are the most voluminous and invaluable records—especially from the Dutch as they were the most dedicated recorders—and these are largely intact in the *Nationaal Archief* in The Hague. Although these sources are available, they are not accessible to those who do not know Dutch, especially classic Dutch, and are unable to read the beautifully written manuscripts by official scribes, illegible to the untrained eye. It took me about a year of intensive training in Old Dutch and palaeography under the TANAP programme at Leiden University before I could transliterate, translate and glean information from these records.

In the course of mining the Dutch and English company records, I was struck by the detailed reports of the company officials relating the vivid happenings at the Aceh court and was intrigued by the role the queens played, especially Sultanah Safiatuddin. The narratives gleaned from these sources not only enabled me to reconstruct a more detailed picture of the reigns of these queens but continue and deepen the conversation begun by earlier scholars. New evidence has allowed me to demonstrate that these women rulers were not mere puppets but ruled in their own right, albeit with serious challenges. Sultanah Safiatuddin nearly lost her life defending her honour when she was accused of committing adultery with an *ulama* (a religious scholar). The detailed narratives reveal interesting aspects of the queen's relations with her male elite (*orang kaya*) and the foreign envoys, and provide a more nuanced picture of royal-elite relations under female rule, where power was more fluid and contested rather than reflecting the view that power mainly tilted towards the male elite. I gained considerable insight into the male elite and demonstrate that there were many factions among them and much intrigue as they vied for power. The detailed information even described the personal relations between the Dutch, the English and the Acehnese male elite, considerably enriching the narratives, and showed that these personal relations mattered in the bigger scheme of politics and diplomacy, and the contestations for power.

However, one of the difficulties I faced in writing this book was how much of the rich narratives I should leave out—given the word limits of a book publication—without sterilising the narratives, while allowing enough space for my own observations and analysis. In the end, I adopted both a descriptive and an analytical approach. In Chapters 2, 3 and 4, the descriptive narrative illuminates the intimate, at times, emotional relations between the Acehnese elite and the company officials, and the rich discussions—even the dance Commissar Vlamingh had to perform for Safiatuddin—reported from audience days that determined how events unfolded and the actions both powers took. The other chapters provide the analytical perspective, explaining why a woman ruler was crowned for the first time in Aceh in 1641 when Southeast Asia was experiencing what

Anthony Reid termed as the "age of commerce", and why female rule was accepted for 59 years in a Muslim kingdom when it seemed an anathema to Islam. The analysis revisits the notion of the *kerajaan* (kingdom, state of having a *raja*), which characterised contemporary Malay polities, centring on male rulers despite the preponderance of female rulers in the Malay world. As the "verandah of Mecca", Aceh was plugged into the global Muslim networks and adopted many features from the Ottoman and Mughal Empires. And yet the rule of women in Aceh illustrates a significant difference from mainstream global Islamic thought, when these ideas were localised by *ulama* (a group of religious scholars) in this region, and Malay political-religious treatises reflect local understandings of statecraft, gender and Islamic authority.

This investigation allows me to compare critically the leadership styles between the queens and their male predecessors, and I illustrate that, to a large extent, these women rulers emphasised different bases of legitimacy and had differing ideas on the conceptions and practice of power and authority. However, I do not wish to suggest that political leadership style is necessarily gendered, and a more benevolent, consensual and protective rule is the prerogative of women sovereigns. Nevertheless, these Acehnese women rulers did have a unique relationship with their male elites, which set them apart from their male contemporaries.

From this investigation, I conclude that there is no universally acceptable theory and practice of women in leadership and authorial roles in Islam, but they are constructed by the power holders, depending on their own contemporary cultural and political contexts. This Acehnese case can serve as a basis of comparison to investigate other possible diversities or commonalities of women rulers/leaders in this region and the wider Muslim world in general. In this regard, I hope to facilitate research by illuminating and informing more general studies on why there was a preponderance of women rulers in the Malay/Muslim region and to further studies on Islamic female leadership in general.

The current intense often regressive debates on the role of women in Islam, the increased policing of women's actions, and the expansion of the spheres forbidden to women in the name of Islam by some groups must not be the dominant narratives among Muslims and the pervasive perception of non-Muslims. This book shows that about

500 years ago women were accepted as sovereign rulers. Lineage and the personal and political acumen of these women to maintain themselves at the helm of power and authority were important, so were other factors, such as male attitude, historical-cultural tradition and gender norms. The diversity and richness of Muslim women's experiences in history allow for a more balanced and comprehensive picture of women's roles in Islam, and can perhaps serve as a heartening example, even an inspiration, for women today.

Introduction

In the seventeenth century, Aceh Dar al-Salam was best known as a staunchly Islamic kingdom in the north of the island of Sumatra and a major trading centre for pepper. Pepper had propelled Aceh's ascendancy in the sixteenth century, making it Melaka's successor as the main Muslim commercial centre supplying the Mediterranean, through the Red Sea, rivalling the Portuguese.[1] Sultan Iskandar Muda (r. 1607–36) ushered in what was deemed as the "golden age" in Acehnese history, when Aceh's influence expanded and reached as far south as Padang in Sumatra and Johor on the Malay Peninsula.[2] His daughter, Sultanah Safiatuddin Syah, (r. 1641–75) ruled Aceh for 34 years—even longer than her father—but very little is known about her. Widowed at the age of 29 when her husband, Sultan Iskandar Thani (r. 1636–41) died unexpectedly, she succeeded her late husband when she was inaugurated as Sultanah Tajul Alam Safiatuddin Syah three days later. In an unprecedented and

---

[1] Anthony Reid, *An Indonesian Frontier: Acehnese and Other Histories of Sumatra* (Singapore: Singapore University Press, 2004), p. 6; Charles Boxer, "A Note on Portuguese Reactions to the Revival of the Red Sea Spice Trade and the Rise of Aceh, 1540–1600", *Journal of Southeast Asian History* 10, 3 (1969): 415-28. There are numerous studies that explain the rise of Aceh after the fall of the Sultanate of Melaka in 1511, such as those by Jorge Alves and Paulo Pinto. See A.K. Dasgupta, "Aceh in Indonesian Trade and Politics 1600–1641", PhD thesis, Cornell University, 1962.

[2] Aceh's purported "golden age" under the rule of Iskandar Muda (1607–36) was also well explicated: Denys Lombard, *Le Sultanat d'Atjeh au Temps d'Iskandar Muda (1607–1636)* [The Sultanate of Aceh in the Time of Iskandar Muda (1607-1636)], trans. Winarsih Arifin as *Kerajaan Aceh, jaman Sultan Iskandar Muda (1607–1636)* (Jakarta: Balai Pustaka, 1986).

never repeated episode in Acehnese history she was succeeded not by one woman ruler, but by three in succession: Sultanah Nur Alam Naqiatuddin Syah (r. 1675–78); Sultanah Inayat Zakiatuddin Syah (r. 1678–88) and; Sultanah Kamalat Zainatuddin Syah (r. 1688–99).

The main question this book seeks to answer is how these queens ruled Aceh for half a century when female rule seemed an anathema in a Muslim and largely patriarchal state, such as Aceh. Furthermore, this unique episode in Aceh's history happened when the Dutch VOC, *Veerinigde Ooost-Indische Compagnie* (United East India Company), and the English East India Company were gradually increasing their commercial hold and flexing their military muscles in the region by interfering in the affairs of indigenous polities. It is curious that in such perilous times Aceh's male elite placed the fate of the kingdom in the hands of women. Surprisingly, this remains a little known episode in Aceh's history despite these historical anomalies, and that in the same period the Acehnese kingdom was fending off European interventions as other polities, such as Makassar and Bantam, fell to the Dutch in 1669 and 1682 respectively.

There has been almost nothing written on the four sultanahs since Denys Lombard's 1967 study on the reign of Iskandar Muda, and Amirul Hadi (2004) focused on the roles of *adat* (customs) and Islam in seventeenth-century Aceh.[3] Scholarly articles by Anthony Reid on Aceh in the seventeenth century and Leonard Andaya on Sultanah Safiatuddin provided interesting insights into the origin and nature of female rule.[4] There are three unpublished studies—Takeshi Ito (1984),[5] Auni Luthfi

---

[3] Amirul Hadi, *Islam and State in Sumatra: A Study of Seventeenth-Century Aceh* (Leiden: Brill, 2004).
[4] Anthony Reid, "Female Roles in Pre-Colonial Southeast Asia", *Modern Asian Studies* 22, 3 (reprint 1998): 629–45. Leonard Y. Andaya, "'A Very-Good Natured but Awe-Inspiring Government': The Reign of a Successful Queen in Seventeenth-Century Aceh", in *Hof en Handel: Aziatische Vorsten en de VOC, 1620–1720* [Court and Trade: Asian Rulers and the VOC, 1620–1720], ed. Elsbeth Locher-Scholten and Peter Rietbergen (Leiden: KITLV Press, 2004), p. 81.
[5] Takeshi Ito, "The World of the Adat Aceh: A Historical Study of the Sultanate of Aceh", PhD thesis, Australian National University, 1984. Available at https://digitalcollections.anu.edu.au/handle/1885/10071 [accessed 24 June 2015].

(1993)⁶ and Mulaika Hijjas (2001).⁷ Ito's valuable doctoral study did not focus on the queens directly but on the role of adat in seventeenth-century Aceh. Luthfi's and Hijjas's master theses, though focusing on these women monarchs, did not purport to study female rule in Aceh comprehensively and did not base their studies on archival materials.

The Origin, Nature and Impact of Female Rule

Although generally under-researched, these Acehnese queens have fascinated many enquirers, past and present, prompting a range of comments—from hearsay to scholarly works—as varied as those making them.⁸ Various accounts of the origin, nature and impact of female rule, though valuable, raised more questions by flagging contradictions that will be explained below.

Reid argued that female rule in Aceh originated as a deliberate experiment conducted by the *orang kaya* (rich nobles who were also state officials). This experiment was a response to the absolutism of Iskandar Muda, and the choice of successors to Iskandar Muda was indicative of the court elite's ambivalent attitude towards his reign.⁹ Reid explained that female rule was one of the few devices available to a commercially-oriented aristocracy to limit the despotic powers of kings and to make the state safe for international commerce.¹⁰ Reid concluded that having experimented with the female alternative, these aristocrats sought to perpetuate it.¹¹

---

⁶ Auni Luthfi, "The Decline of the Islamic Empire of Aceh, 1641–1699", MA thesis, McGill University, 1993. Available at http://digitool.library.mcgill.ca/R/?func=dbin-jump-full&object_id=26066&local_base=GEN01-MCG02 [accessed 24 June 2015].
⁷ Mulaika Hijjas, "The Woman Raja: Female Rule in Seventeenth Century Aceh", MPhil thesis, University of Oxford, 2001.
⁸ For full citations, see the bibliography.
⁹ Anthony Reid and Takeshi Ito, "From Harbour Autocracies to 'Feudal' Diffusion in Seventeenth-Century Indonesia: The Case of Aceh", in *Feudalism: Comparative Studies*, ed. E. Leach, S.N. Mukherjee and J. Ward (Sydney: Sydney Association for Studies in Society and Culture, 1985), p. 14.
¹⁰ Reid, "Female Roles in Pre-Colonial Southeast Asia", p. 641.
¹¹ Ibid.

Inherent in this explanation is the idea that the orang kaya were supreme in Aceh and ruled as a unified oligarchy. Based on Reid's arguments, the orang kaya might have opted for female rule because a woman ruler might have been more compliant and reliant on the orang kaya, whose members sought to secure their positions and share the kingdom's wealth. But why did the orang kaya not choose a weak male ruler or, better still, a minor with one of the elite acting as a regent? Furthermore, why choose a woman in 1641, not earlier or later? Indeed, why choose a woman—something never ventured before in the dynastic succession of the Acehnese Sultanate—at such a critical juncture, when Portuguese Melaka had just succumbed to the VOC? A strong leader, à la Iskandar Muda, would perhaps be a more appropriate response to this threat.

The nature of female rule in Aceh is even more problematic. In the early nineteenth century, the East India Company (EIC) official William Marsden described it as "a new era in the history of the country", and noted that female rule in Aceh had attracted much notice in Europe.[12] Fifty years later another EIC official, Thomas Braddell, hailed the institution of female rule in Aceh as "a most singular revolution".[13] Agreeing, Iljas Sutan Pamenan, writing in the twentieth century, felt that female rule was *ganjil* (strange) and asserted that the people did not accept this institution because the subjects only recognised the rule of males. Pamenan argued that female rule was not only unacceptable but also inappropriate, especially as Aceh was not economically secure at that time. He contended that Aceh needed a strong hand to earn the respect of foreigners, and a woman would have been unable to carry out such heavy and important responsibilities.[14]

On the other hand, P.J. Veth saw female rule in Aceh as neither aberrant nor revolutionary, but as part of the indigenous practice of Southeast Asian states. He cited other examples of *vrouwenregeeringen*

---

[12] William Marsden, *The History of Sumatra*, introduction by John Bastin (Singapore: Oxford University Press, 3rd ed., 1986), pp. 447, 454.

[13] Thomas Braddell, "On the History of Acheen", *Journal of the Indian Archipelago and Eastern Asia* 5 (1851): 19.

[14] Iljas Sutan Pamenan, *Rentjong Aceh di Tangan Wanita* [Aceh's Dagger in a Woman's Hands] (Jakarta: D.J. Waringin, 1959), pp. 35–6.

(government by women) in Patani, Borneo, Palembang and Celebes.[15] Mohammad Said also maintained that female rule in Aceh was part of adat, not an aberration. He argued that a few centuries previously, Aceh had had a female admiral, and this was acceptable in Acehnese custom as women could be considered as powerful and capable as men.[16]

Despite the disagreements over the origin and nature of female rule, most of the earlier writing in the nineteenth and twentieth centuries appears to agree on the unfavourable impact of these female rulers on Acehnese history. One of the most striking and popular perceptions of Aceh's women sovereigns was that they were weaklings, mere ceremonial rulers propped up by the male elite, and responsible for the decline of the monarchy and royal power by the end of the seventeenth century. Braddell, for instance, wrote that in 1641, 12 orang kaya seized the reins of power and in order to carry on the government without opposition from the people, they placed the widow of the late king on the throne but without the power to interfere in the management of affairs.[17] Marsden noted that "the nobles finding their power less restrained ... than when ruled by kings ... supported these pageants whom they governed as they thought fit". Marsden viewed the queens as ceremonial rulers with no power to appoint or remove any of the orang kaya.[18] Veth's slightly different yet nuanced explanation was that the nobility favoured female rule because it provided a means for the nobles to exercise their power and personal influence, but Veth did not assert that these queens were powerless. Early twentieth-century scholars, such as Snouck Hurgronje and T.J. Veltman, were considerably more scathing, with Hurgronje going so far as to claim that Aceh's weak female governments were responsible for undermining the monarchy.[19] Veltman saw all Aceh's female sovereigns as manipulated by the orang

---

[15] P.J. Veth, "Vrouwenregeeringen in den Indischen Archipel" [Government by Women in the Indies Archipelago], *Tijdschrift voor Nederlandsch Indie* 2 (3 & 4) (1870): 362–5.
[16] Mohammad Said, *Aceh Sepanjang Abad* [Aceh through the Century] (Medan: Penerbit Pengarang Sendiri, 1961), p. 379.
[17] Braddell, "On the History of Acheen", p. 19.
[18] Marsden, *The History of Sumatra*, pp. 447, 454.
[19] Christiaan Snouck Hurgronje, *The Acehnese*, trans. A.W.S. O'Sullivan, with index by R.J. Wilkinson (Leiden: Brill, 1906), p. 94.

kaya and concluded that Sultanah Safiatuddin's reign contributed little to the greatness of the realm.[20] More recent historians, such as Amirul Hadi and Auni Luthfi, saw the "rise of the orang kaya" during the reigns of female rulers and the transition of power from royalty to nobility as "possibly due to the mildness of the queen in governing the state".[21]

Strangely, although the above writers concluded that the women monarchs were mere figureheads, they actually praised the governments that operated during their reigns. Braddell expressed his bewilderment by exclaiming that:

> [I]n a rude state of society and among a people like the Achinese, one is not prepared to hear of such a refinement in the art of government; and surprise is increased by learning that this government lasted for upwards of sixty years, and examination will prove that the affairs of the nation were better administered during this period than at any other time before or since.[22]

Marsden commented that Sultanah Safiatuddin Syah "reigned with a degree of tranquillity little known in these countries, upwards of thirty-four years".[23] Thus, while these writers admitted that the governments under these female rulers were actually stable and peaceful, none attributed this good governance to the queens but implied that this was owing to the orang kaya's skill, unfettered by royal power. Indeed, the orang kaya had dominated politics from the 1570s to the 1590s when kings became mere pawns in their game, but this was one of the more disastrous periods in Aceh's history. The inability to recognise that a woman ruler might actually be successful in her own right smacks more of a biased patriarchal sentiment than an informed judgement.

In fact there is little evidence to support the assertion that the female sovereigns of Aceh were mere figureheads, and the orang kaya

---

[20] T.J. Veltman, "Nota over de Geschiedenis van het Landschap Pidie" [Notes on the History of Pidie], *Tijdschrift voor Indische Taal-, Land- en Volkenkunde* 58 (1919): 66–7.
[21] Luthfi, "The Decline of the Islamic Empire", p. 124.
[22] Braddell, "On the History of Acheen", p. 20.
[23] Marsden, *The History of Sumatra*, p. 449.

held the reins of power. Advocates of this line of argument seem to suggest that the nobles formed a unified, powerful, homogeneous group that promoted and prolonged female rule for their own interests. And yet, apart from Takeshi Ito's detailed study of the world of adat which offers insights into the Acehnese Sultanate in the seventeenth century, very little is known about these orang kaya who were said to have wielded so much power. Who were they? What was their basis of power and authority? More importantly, and the focus of this book, what was their relationship with the women sultanahs? Thomas Bowrey, William Dampier and Jacob de Roy, traders present in Aceh during the reigns of these female monarchs, actually noted opposition by some orang kaya to female rule, which nonetheless lasted for 58 years!

In contrast to the aforementioned nineteenth- and twentieth-century perspectives, contemporary commentaries on the reigns of these female rulers were more favourable. These include accounts written by indigenous court chroniclers, such as Nuruddin al-Raniri, European officials, such as the employees of the Dutch and English East Indies Companies, merchants and travellers, such as Bowrey, Dampier and Wouter Schouten, among others. Bowrey, who was in Aceh from about 1675 to 1689, noted that the orang kaya, the *shahbandar*s (administrative officials) and the queen's greatest eunuchs were all very submissive to her and respected her, not daring to do any business of importance before they had thoroughly acquainted her with the matter at hand. If she agreed, she would send down her seal to show that she had granted their request. If she withheld the seal, the orang kaya had to desist from the business and do something else.[24] VOC records also reveal that the Dutch favoured female rule. They hoped that the queen would safeguard their privileges,[25] and reported that she was a better ruler than her predecessor husband, Iskandar Thani, as she was able

---

[24] Thomas Bowrey, *A Geographical Account of Countries Round the Bay of Bengal 1669–1679*, ed. Lt.-Col. Sir Richard Carnac Temple (London: The Hakluyt Society, 1905), pp. 299–300.

[25] J.A. van der Chijs et al., ed., *Dagh-Register Gehouden int Casteel Batavia vant Passerende daer ter plaetse als over Geheel Nederlandts-India Anno 1624–1682* [The Daily Journals of Batavia Castle] 31 vols ('s-Gravenhage: Martinus Nijhoff, Batavia: G. Kolff, 1887–1931), p. 423.

to maintain peace and control outright the rivalries among her nobles.²⁶ Indigenous literature corroborates the positive point of view. *Bustan us-Salatin*, written by the famous seventeenth-century *ulama* (religious scholar) Nuruddin al-Raniri, depicts Sultanah Safiatuddin as a great and generous queen.²⁷

Most recent writing, especially by those referring to contemporary accounts and archival records, tended to adopt a slightly more favourable view of these monarchs. Mulaika Hijjas, like Marsden, concluded that these Acehnese women rulers were pageant queens. However, unlike Marsden, she asserted that owing to the Malay sense of the importance of these spectacles and theatre in state power, the queens who presided over the rituals and ceremonies were not frail, but were successful exponents of traditional kingship.²⁸ Ito, Reid and Andaya believed that as the kingdom of Aceh declined in the latter half of the seventeenth century, so did royal power. But in his most recent article, Andaya described Sultanah Safiatuddin's government as humane and successful. She held the reins of government with great skill and adapted to the aggressive policies of the Dutch.²⁹ Reid asserted that under the queens:

> [T]he orangkaya found that they could govern collectively with the queen as sovereign and referee and there was something of the quality of Elizabethan England in the way they vied for her favour but accepted her eventual judgement between them.³⁰

---

²⁶ Ibid., p. 123.
²⁷ Siti Hawa Haji Salleh, ed., *Bustan al-Salatin* (Kuala Lumpur: Dewan Bahasa dan Pustaka, 1992), p. 44. Paul Wormser concluded that, faced with the important differences between Chapters 11, 12, 13, the rest of Book II, and Raniri's work as a whole, these chapters of the *Bustan al-Salatin* were not written by Raniri. Although this is plausible, I contend that al-Raniri would not disagree with the contents of these chapters as the *Bustan* was written in his name, and Iskandar Thani commissioned him to write it. See Paul Wormser, *Le Bustan al-Salatin de Nuruddin ar-Raniri: Réflexions sur le Rôle Culturel d'un Étranger dans le Monde Malais au XVIIe Siècle* (Paris: Cahiers d'Archipel, 2012), p. 210.
²⁸ Hijjas, "The Woman Raja", p. 89.
²⁹ Andaya, "A Very-Good Natured but Awe-Inspiring Government", p. 81.
³⁰ Reid, "Female Roles in Pre-Colonial Southeast Asia", p. 641.

Ito claimed that despite the decline of royal authority after the reign of Iskandar Muda, Sultanah Safiatuddin was still able to maintain integrity and respect for the monarchy.[31]

The variety of interpretations and debates and the shifts in views about these enigmatic women are the inspiration for this book. Thus far, no comprehensive in-depth study directly focusing on these female rulers has been undertaken on the basis of both European and indigenous contemporary sources. Many questions remain to be answered. What was the socio-economic context that enabled a female to be chosen to lead Muslim Aceh in 1641? Why did three more succeed her? Was this a deliberate experiment, temporary political expediency or merely an accident of history? To what extent were the latter queens so weak that they were unable to hold the monarchy and kingdom together?

These questions need to be investigated. By transliterating, translating and mining the Dutch VOC treaties, diplomatic correspondence between Aceh and the governor generals in Batavia, and the daily registers from Dutch envoys stationed for months in Aceh, this study reconstructs and provides a vivid picture of key turning points in the Acehnese court. It illustrates a more complex and complicated picture than the rather biased assumption that because they were women they knew nothing about governance, so it was the male elite who actually ruled Aceh. This monograph demonstrates that Sultanah Safiatuddin and her male elite constantly negotiated for power, and relations between royalty and elite need not be viewed as a zero-sum game. Sultanah Safiatuddin had to manoeuvre between the needs of the ruler, the elite and the European representatives who were constantly pushing for new concessions. Although she started her rule as young and inexperienced, perhaps without any expectation of becoming the ruler of her father's kingdom, she held her own and eventually managed to handle not only her own fractious male elite but accommodate the pressures and demands of foreign diplomats and merchants alike. As a result of having real power and ruling in her own right, she successfully steered the kingdom through

---

[31] Ito, "The World of the Adat Aceh", p. 120.

tumultuous times and kept Aceh independent while most Malay/Muslim coastal polities, such as Bantam and Makassar, fell to European intruders. As the first female ruler of Aceh, reigning for 34 years, she provided an exemplary model that was followed by her three female successors.

The other important question addressed here is why female rule ended in 1699, never to be repeated. Reid explained that female rule eventually failed when Aceh ran out of credible candidates who still had the charisma of the monarchy about them. Veth, on the other hand, placed much more emphasis on the Islamic factor which ended female rule.[32] He claimed that towards the end of Kamalat Syah's rule, a *priester partij* (a group of ulama, or a body of religious scholars) armed with a letter from Mecca issued by a certain Kadhi Maliku'l Adil made a strong bid to get rid of the female ruler, and in 1699 this faction won. Kamalat Syah had to step down because this letter stated that Islam forbade female rule. And if female leadership was forbidden in Islam, and Aceh was famously known as a staunchly Islamic state—the *Serambi Mekah* (Veranda of Mecca)—how was it possible that the kingdom had four female sovereigns? It would be strange indeed if, after having respected female rulers for almost 60 years, the Acehnese elite suddenly realised that Islam forbade this.

Women, Islam and Adat

Islam, some have argued, demands the seclusion of women and relegates them to the realm of the private and the domestic. The political sphere—a public domain—is generally seen as a prerogative of men, rarely encroached upon by the female; political and religious leadership in the hands of women is almost unthinkable. And yet studies by Fatimah Mernissi on Muslim queens in history and Muhamad Akram Nadawi on women religious scholars and narrators of *hadith al-Muhaddithat* (female scholars of *hadith*—sayings of the Prophet) show that there are examples in Muslim history of women exercising political and religious

---

[32] Veth, "Vrouwenregeeringen", pp. 368–9.

authority.³³ This phenomenon, however, appears to be confined to the period of early Islam, and these women leaders were exceptions rather than the norm until recently. As Islam spread and consolidated, it was interpreted and executed by males, and power and authority began to be constructed and defined as necessarily male. Only in recent years, with a more feminist reading of the Qur'an, have women begun to interpret the religion themselves in ways that have resulted in redefining ideas of power, authority and leadership.³⁴

In contrast, in insular Southeast Asia, spatially and culturally removed from the heartlands of Islam, there was a preponderance of Muslim women rulers in the early modern period as in Patani, Sukadana, Jambi, and Solor.³⁵ Indeed the tradition of Muslim women leaders continues till today with the likes of Megawati Sukarno Putri in Indonesia and Wan Azizah in Malaysia. However, there has been very little research on these women Muslim leaders as studies on gender and women in Southeast Asia have tended to focus on ordinary women, and debates regarding women's positions have centred on the tensions between adat and religion. While Anthony Reid and Wazir Jahan Karim argued that adat accorded women greater status and power, Carol Laderman, Aihwa Ong and Michael Peletz concluded that adat beliefs and practices favoured men. Others, like Barbara Andaya and Jahan Karim, argued that the spread of world religions, such as Hinduism, Buddhism, Christianity and Islam, to this region had a direct bearing on the construction of gender, and in stressing the behaviour of "good" women, they presented persuasive models of female modesty and submissiveness, relegating women to domestic space, thereby reducing their power and their public roles.³⁶ Both religion and

---

[33] Fatima Mernissi, *Forgotten Queens of Islam*, trans. Mary Jo Lakeland (Minneapolis: University of Minnesota Press, 1993); Muhammad Akram Nadawi, *Al-Muhaddithat: The Women Scholars in Islam* (Oxford: Interface Publications, 2007).

[34] Muslim feminist writings by: Fatima Mernissi, *Women's Rebellion and Islamic Memory* (London: Zed Books, 1996); Mernissi, *Forgotten Queens of Islam*; Amina Wadud, *Qur'an and Woman: Rereading the Sacred Text from a Woman's Perspective* (New York: Oxford University Press, 1999); Amina Wadud, *Inside the Gender Jihad: Women's Reform in Islam* (Oxford: Oneworld Publications, 2006).

[35] Reid, "Female Roles in Pre-Colonial Southeast Asia".

[36] Barbara W. Andaya, *The Flaming Womb: Repositioning Women in Early Modern Southeast Asia* (Honolulu: University of Hawai'i Press, 2006), p. 230.

adat are seen as disempowering women. There are recent studies on female political leaders, such as Trudy Jacobsen's *Lost Goddesses* in Cambodia and Jessica Harriden's study on women and authority in Burma, in the context of Buddhism. Jacobsen's study suggested that Buddhist traditions and patriarchy tend to frown on women holding political power but certain exceptions occurred, especially during the middle period when, perhaps in a process of localisation of Buddhism in the Cambodian context, the sister of Buddha Tibangkar earned the status of female *bodhisattva* (an enlightened being).[37] Harriden's study suggested that female monarchy was contrary to Buddhist notions of statecraft, but Viharadevi rule in Pegu from 1453–72 was an exception.[38]

In this book, I do not attempt to examine the features of female rule of Muslim polities in this region during the pre-colonial era—more research is needed. Instead, this monograph provides a detailed case study of female rule in Aceh. Contrary to Rusdi Sufi's claim that a separation of secular and religious powers enabled the queens to be accepted as temporal rulers, the sultanahs saw themselves as the *khalifah* (God's shadow or representative on earth) and took the title of caliphs just as their male predecessors did. I want to show that the ways in which women's roles were interpreted in Islam depended largely on the socio-historical context of the time and the attitude of the male elite, and there was no universal injunction upon which all Muslims agreed. Furthermore, when global Islam spread to other parts of the world and was localised and practised according to the normative values and culture of the locale, there arose many varieties of Islamic practice. As far as the Acehnese sultanahs were concerned, we do not need to look for tension between Islam and adat with regard to women's political roles and positions. Indeed, the contexts surrounding the reign of Sultanah Safiatuddin illustrate that the legitimacy of her rule and the allegiance of her subjects depended on both Islam and adat.

---

[37] Trudy Jacobsen, *Lost Goddesses: The Denial of Female Power in Cambodian History* (Denmark: NIAS Press, 2008), p. 78.

[38] Jessica Harriden, *The Authority of Influence: Women and Power in Burmese History* (Denmark: NIAS Press, 2012), p. 71.

Men of Prowess and Women of Piety—Revisiting "Kingship" in Southeast Asia

Interest in the queens of medieval Europe has been an outgrowth of feminist historical studies since the 1960s. However, it is only in recent decades that the institution of "queenship" per se has begun to attract attention. A renewed interest in women first produced accounts of prominent women—nobles, abbesses and saints, including some medieval queens that excited popular interest, such as Eleanor of Aquitaine, Blanche of Castile, Margaret of Anjou and Isabella of Castile. These works were limited because of a tendency to depict the queens as moral pendants to husbands or sons and dwell on their lives rather than their offices. Then, in the 1980s, the study of queenship fell into disrepute when political history was passed over in favour of socio-economic history, shifting the focus from elite political female roles to their less well-known and less fortunate sisters. A distaste for administrative and institutional histories also impeded investigations into queenship.

Recent publications suggest a renewed interest in the institution and workings of queenship.[39] The disentanglement of history from political history and power from political power has opened fresh approaches to discussions of gender and power in the Middle Ages. Recent studies do not focus on biographical studies of individual queens but instead have sought to dissect the ways in which queens pursued and exploited the means to power and how others interpreted their actions.[40]

By contrast, it was only in the 1980s that women were included in the historical picture by Southeast Asian historians, such as Anthony

---

[39] For a list of these publications, see John Carmi Parsons, "Family, Sex and Power: The Rhythms of Medieval Queenship", in *Medieval Queenship*, ed. John Carmi Parsons (New York: St. Martin's Press, 1993), pp. 1–2.

[40] Ibid., p. 2.

Reid[41] and later Barbara Andaya.[42] However, historical studies on elite women and female rulers in the early modern era have begun to emerge only recently, and this study hopes to contribute to this fledgling literature.[43] Stefan Amirell's and Francis Bradley's respective studies of the Patani queens, especially Raja Ijau (r.1584–1616), demonstrated that they were not mere figureheads and that they contributed to the political stability and economic prosperity of the kingdom.[44] Douglas Kammen, in his study "Queens of Timor", contended that it would be a mistake to assume that the reigning queens in nineteenth-century Timor were simply figureheads, with a male relative exercising real power as regent.[45] Jacobsen's *Lost Goddesses* in Cambodia and Harriden's studies on women and authority in Burma argued that royal women were powerful in the Cambodian and Konbaung courts before the nineteenth century. Exigent circumstances at times enabled some of them, such as Jayadevi and Sambhupura, to rule in the Cambodian case, and Supalayat, the wife of King Thibaw, became a powerful queen though she ruled behind the scenes. However, both stated that women's power and authority declined during the colonial and modern period.[46] Jacobsen cited texts, such as the *Cbpab Srei* (Code of Conduct for Women), which regard female sexuality as dangerous and female autonomy anathema.[47] Harriden stated that Burmese notions of *hpoun* (glory, innate spiritual superiority possessed by men only) legitimises the spiritual and social

---

[41] Reid drew attention to the high status of women in the early modern era as part of the defining regional or Southeast Asian characteristic. Anthony Reid, *Southeast Asia in the Age of Commerce, 1450–1680:* Vol. 1: *The Lands below the Wind* (New Haven: Yale University Press, 1988), pp. 146, 162.

[42] Barbara Watson Andaya, ed., *Other Past: Women, Gender and History in Early Modern Southeast Asia* (Honolulu: Center of Southeast Asian Studies, 2000), pp. 25–6.

[43] Recent study by Andrea Fleschenberg and Claudia Derichs, eds., *Women and Politics in Asia: A Springboard for Democracy?* (Singapore: Institute of Southeast Asian Studies, 2012).

[44] Stefan Amirell, "The Blessings and Perils of Female Rule: New Perspectives on the Reigning Queens of Patani, c. 1584–1718", *Journal of Southeast Asian Studies* 42, 2 (2011): 303–23; Francis Bradley, "Moral Order in a Time of Damnation: The *Hikayat Patani* in Historical Context", *Journal of Southeast Asian Studies* 40, 2 (2009): 267–93.

[45] Douglas Kammen, "Queens of Timor", *Archipel* 84 (2012): 149–73.

[46] Jacobsen, *Lost Goddesses*, pp. 284–5; Harriden, *The Authority of Influence*, pp. 108–9.

[47] Jacobsen, *Lost Goddesses*, p. 285.

hierarchies in which men exercised formal authority over women. Although female royal lineages, marriage alliances and patron-client relationships enabled queens to exercise political influence through familial connections, women who overtly challenged men's authority were criticised by male elites for threatening to upset the "natural" social order. This meant that women could exercise influence within the private domain of the family and household economy, but they could only exercise public power through men.[48]

How did the Acehnese queens negotiate these traditional and religious values in conducting daily political affairs with men of power? What was the nature of the relationship between the queens and the predominantly male elite within the patriarchal and Islamic context of the Acehnese court? Other aspects worth exploring are the implications of female rule in regard to the issue of political power and state formation. What was the basis of their power and authority—who were their supporters—the orang kaya or the ulama? Which factions supported the queens, when and why? By examining the Acehnese queens, this book shows how by transgressing "feminine roles", these females injected or integrated new elements or features into the largely masculine concept of the traditional monarch, kingship and the realm.

The *Bustan us-Salatin* reveals that Sultanah Safiatuddin conducted her daily audience at the *balai* (audience hall) as a shadowy figure behind a golden brocade curtain. At the same time, Dutch officials described the many outings and hunting expeditions in which the sultanah and her entourage participated with the foreign envoys. These contradictory records merely add to the intrigue and point to the need to investigate how these purportedly "forbidden" and "invisible queens"—behind the golden curtain—ruled.

Studies on leadership in Southeast Asia's early modern era tended to centre on kingship—leadership that was necessarily male. According to Wolters, "men of prowess" endowed with an abnormal amount of "personal and innate soul stuff" enabled them to distinguish their performance from their kinsmen and others in their generation. In his revised edition to *History, Culture and Region in Southeast Asian*

---

[48] Harriden, *The Authority of Influence*, pp. 305–6.

Perspectives, however, Wolters considered the roles and positions of women, and questioned whether they too should be attributed with this "vastly energetic role of women of prowess", wondering what their relationship with "men of prowess" would have been.[49] Despite his invitation for further research and new studies in gender relations in early Southeast Asia, the concept of female leadership is still little researched. In spite of the preponderance of female rulers during what Reid called the "age of commerce", their roles and contributions to the history of early modern Southeast Asia have not been adequately researched.

So, what would a study focussing on "queenship" in early modern Malay/Muslim insular polities reveal about these women rulers and the socio-cultural contexts in which they operated, and how would queenship differ from the model of Islamic kingship in Malay Sultanates? This book provides some insights into women's participation in politics at the highest level, and may inform studies on power and gender in Southeast Asia in general. Contrary to the received view that successful leadership tended to be male (men of prowess), this book demonstrates that under women sovereigns, the justification for the ruler's position relied less on notions of sacral and charismatic power based on prowess but instead shifted to Muslim notions of piety and the just ruler. These sultanahs also adopted leadership styles that differed from their male counterparts—namely being more collaborative, institutional, economically pragmatic, protective of private property and security, and placing emphasis on social welfare. Whether this constitutes a parading of "female leadership" is still debatable (and needs more research), but the sultanahs certainly provide different models of leadership, and thus they should be assessed employing criteria different from those used to judge "men of prowess" in the early modern period.

Female leadership deserves more research to understand the diverse picture of statehood and governance during early modernity in insular Malay/Muslim Southeast Asia. Female leadership under the Acehnese sultanahs, founded on moral force, consensual style of decision making

---

[49] O.W. Wolters, *History, Culture and Region in Southeast Asian Perspectives* (Singapore: Institute of Southeast Asian Studies, 2nd ed., 1999), p. 169.

based on *musyawarah* (consensus building), sanctioned by adat and Islam, provides a different model to the charismatic and absolutist models of kingship that characterised their male predecessors. The sultanahs also provide a model of royal-elite relations different from the male-centred examples of Iskandar Muda and Iskandar Thani, characterised by jealousies, rivalries, competition, hierarchical relations and absolutist control.[50] I suggest that this female model of leadership was better suited to facilitating peace, commerce and diplomacy in the age of commerce, and it was a key reason that helped Aceh to remain independent and economically autonomous in the seventeenth century.

This monograph proceeds to show why and how these queens were able to maintain their positions for 59 years, and how they dealt with challenges from their own local male elite and the European foreign envoys. The main reason these queens were accepted by the male elite was because they adopted a different leadership style from that of their male predecessors—Sultan Iskandar Muda and Sultan Iskandar Thani. The sultanahs of Aceh chose to be more collaborative than coercive, preferring to gain the loyalty and respect of the elites rather than their fear. This monograph states that this certainly *limited* royal power but, contrary to popular belief, this did not lead to its decline; rather Aceh experienced its longest period of political stability to date.

Ties That Unbind

Barbara Andaya claimed that with Aceh's decline in the mid-seventeenth century and the slow crumbling of the relationship with the VOC, Aceh lost its useful vassal state—Perak. Vassalage had brought no benefits to Perak and now Aceh could no longer enforce its former control.[51]

---

[50] Recent studies indicate transformational leadership as characteristic of a feminine model that focuses on cooperation, lower levels of control, collaboration and collective decision making while transactional leadership is characteristic of male leaders, identified with competition, hierarchical authority and greater leader control. A.H. Eagly and M.C. Johannesen-Schmidt, "The Leadership Styles of Women and Men", *Journal of Social Issues* 57, 4 (2001): 787–8.

[51] Barbara W. Andaya, *Perak, the Abode of Grace: A Study of an Eighteenth Century Malay State* (Kuala Lumpur: Oxford University Press, 1979), p. 48.

According to Jeyamalar Kathirithamby-Wells, the decline of Aceh made the VOC protectorate of the Sumatra West Coast (SWC) possible. She argued that the Dutch capture of Melaka in 1641 severely eroded Acehnese commercial supremacy and political importance, boosted Dutch prestige and damaged Aceh's bargaining powers to such an extent that Sultanah Safiatuddin Syah was obliged to adopt a conciliatory policy.[52]

If we adopt the above view, Sultanah Safiatuddin does appear weaker than her male predecessors. In 1650, the VOC succeeded in pressuring the sultanah to sign a treaty agreeing to divide Perak's tin between Aceh and the VOC. The Treaty of Painan of March 1663 and another treaty signed in April 1668 placed a number of SWC states under Dutch protection.[53] The question we have to ask is *how real* were the losses? What was the nature of ties that bound Aceh's vassal states to her, and to what extent were the sultanah's male predecessors successful in controlling these vassals? A more accommodative and peaceful diplomacy did not necessarily entail a weakening of control and power. This book examines Aceh-Perak-VOC relations and illustrates that as late as the 1670s, Aceh had important leverage over the company for the trade in Perak on the basis of its overlord rights. The VOC's unwillingness to go to war with Aceh meant the Dutch had to continue negotiating for concessions and accepting compromises. The patron-client relationship Sultanah Safiatuddin conducted with Perak was symbiotic and mutually beneficial, unlike the more predatory vassal-overlord relations enacted under her predecessors. Perak invoked the traditional overlord-vassal relationship and used Aceh as a protector not because Perak was forced to submit to Aceh, but because Aceh was useful to protect the tin trade, and this symbiotic relationship largely worked.

In examining Aceh-Perak-SWC-VOC relations, I argue that in this regard the narrative of east-west interactions in the Straits of Melaka and along the SWC was not simply one of western ascendancy and indigenous decline. Power was constantly contested and shifting, and the VOC's

---

[52] J. Kathirithamby-Wells, "Acehnese Control over West Sumatra up to the Treaty of Painan, 1663", *Journal of Southeast Asian History* 10, 3 (1969): 465.
[53] Ibid., pp. 473, 478.

increased influence and intervention in the SWC polities were the result of the initiatives and negotiations of *both* the Dutch and the local elites to advance mutual interests.

If this is the case, the question becomes when did the Europeans gain ascendency? Moving forward from the Euro-centric and Asia-centric perspectives and the narrative of the European advance and Asian decline binary, this study on Aceh illustrates that the "long drift to European hegemony in Asia in the early modern era could be seen to be less over-determined, less a foregone conclusion and much more multi-causal and contingent to specific contexts".[54]

As the connective centre between Europe, the Middle East, and India in the north, and Melaka, Java and the rest of the Indonesian archipelago in the south, Aceh was very much a part of global maritime networks. Indeed, Aceh's position as the entrepôt port for pepper, gold and Indian textiles allowed the kingdom to thrive economically for much of the seventeenth century. Aceh's interactions with the European powers was characterised less by asymmetrical relations than by interdependency, and the result was one of mutual heritage, which requires understanding of the inputs of both external and local powers.[55]

This study explores Aceh-VOC relations not in terms of an analytic separation of European intrusion and Asian response, but with a view to placing the interaction in a mutually adaptive perspective.[56] Following the argument of J.C. van Leur that Western dominance was not yet in place in the seventeenth century and Aceh remained largely unmolested by the Dutch, one could posit that there was a high degree of interaction and Dutch supremacy was not a foregone conclusion by the mid-seventeenth century—indeed that the complex and multifaceted nature of Aceh-VOC interaction depended on specific contexts.

---

[54] John E. Wills Jr, "Maritime Asia, 1500–1800: The Interactive Emergence of European Domination", *The American Historical Review* 98, 1 (1993): 83–4.

[55] Ernst van Veen and Leonard Blussé, "Introduction", in *Rivalry and Conflict: European Traders and Asian Trading Networks in the 16th and 17th Centuries*, ed. Ernst van Veen and Leonard Blussé, Studies in Overseas History, Vol. 7 (Leiden: CNWS, 2005), p. 4.

[56] Wills, "Maritime Asia", pp. 84–5.

Did Aceh Decline under Female Sovereigns?

Although in 1600 Southeast Asians interacted as equals with Europeans, Reid maintained that the inequalities were already manifesting themselves a century later.[57] "The end of commerce" in Southeast Asia came in 1680, when indigenous states retreated from international trade. A primary reason Reid cited was the critical military encounters with Europeans, which eclipsed some local ethnic shipping, caused trade to decline, the loss of revenue and defeat of the last stand of Islamic commerce.[58] What about Aceh? This raises another important question regarding the nature and impact of female rule in the latter half of the seventeenth century. In this regard, both Indonesian and European writers contended that Aceh's power dipped after the glorious reign of Iskandar Muda (1607–36). Mohammad Said,[59] Iljas Sutan Pamenan,[60] Reid,[61] Merle C. Ricklefs[62] and Leonard Andaya all concur.[63] But did Aceh *really* decline, in either relative or absolute terms? And if Aceh did decline, was it because of female rule? Reid argued that the reduced skill and authority of the rulers who succeeded Iskandar Muda and the growing power of the Dutch led to the decline of royal power.[64] Pressured by a Dutch blockade in 1647–50, Aceh could not prevent the VOC from gaining control of the dependencies that produced the pepper and tin on which its prosperity was based.[65] In line with his

---

[57] Anthony Reid, *Charting the Shape of Early Modern Southeast Asia* (Singapore: Institute of Southeast Asian Studies, 2000), p. 12.
[58] Anthony Reid, *Southeast Asia in the Age of Commerce, 1450–1680:* Vol. 2: *Expansion and Crisis* (New Haven: Yale University Press, 1993), pp. 268–325.
[59] Said, *Aceh Sepanjang Abad*, p. 377.
[60] Pamenan, *Rentjong Aceh di Tangan Wanita*, pp. 35–6.
[61] Reid, "Female Roles in Pre-Colonial Southeast Asia", p. 641.
[62] Merle C. Ricklefs, *A History of Modern Indonesia since c. 1300* (Basingstoke: McMillan, 2nd ed., 1993), p. 36.
[63] Leonard Y. Andaya, *The Kingdom of Johor, 1641–1728* (Kuala Lumpur: Oxford University Press, 1975), p. 56.
[64] Anthony Reid, "Trade and the Problem of Royal Power in Aceh, c. 1550–1700", in *Pre-Colonial State Systems in Southeast Asia: The Malay Peninsula, Sumatra, Bali-Lombok, South Celebes* (Kuala Lumpur: Monograph 6 of the Malaysian Branch of the Royal Asiatic Society, 1975), p. 52.
[65] Reid, *Southeast Asia*, Vol. 2, p. 266.

argument about the seventeenth-century crisis in Southeast Asia, during which most states experienced the end of the age of commerce, Reid indicated that Aceh too suffered and fell into disunity after its brief golden age.[66] In the standard history of Indonesia, Ricklefs depicted Aceh as entering a long period of internal disunity and ceasing to be significant outside northern Sumatra. From 1641 to 1699, royal authority was restricted to Aceh itself, and the sultanate became a weak, symbolic institution.[67]

This widely accepted view has its dissenters. G.W. Irwin maintained that the VOC's attempt to engross the tin trade of western Malaya failed by the end of the seventeenth century. He suggested that the Dutch were defeated partly by the superior resources, tactics and persistence of their rivals, but even more by the rigidity of their own economic policies.[68] It appears that Aceh was unique as it had to be treated with caution by the Dutch, who preferred persuasion to force lest too much pressure provoke retaliation and the Acehnese make it difficult to gain access to pepper on the SWC. This contrasts with many writers' picture of a weak Malay polity, dominated by the VOC's might. Takeshi Ito's study of seventeenth-century Aceh showed that the elephant trade thrived under Sultanah Safiatuddin. Not only had the VOC failed to gain a toehold in the elephant trade, Aceh was successful in actually increasing this trade from the 1640s to the 1660s.[69] In 1650, the VOC representative, J. Truijtman, reported that "Sultanah Safiatuddin did not consent for the VOC to buy even one head of an animal".[70]

This book re-examines the view that Aceh declined from the mid-seventeenth century and questions the role of the female rulers in

---

[66] Ibid., pp. 303–4.
[67] Ricklefs, *A History of Modern Indonesia since c. 1300*, p. 36.
[68] Graham W. Irwin, "The Dutch and the Tin Trade of Malaya in the Seventeenth Century", in *Studies in the Social History of China and South-East Asia: Essays in the Memory of Victor Purcell*, ed. Nicholas Tarling and Jerome Ch'en (Cambridge: Cambridge University Press, 1970), p. 287.
[69] Ito, "The World of Adat Aceh", p. 415.
[70] W.Ph. Coolhaas, ed., *Generale Missieven van Gouveneurs-Generaale en Raden aan Heren XVII der Verenigde Oostindische Compagnie* [General Correspondence of the Governor Generals and Council to the Seventeen Gentlemen of the Dutch East Indies Company] Vol. 2 ('s-Gravenhage: Martinus Nijhoff, 1964), p. 461.

bringing this about. Sultan Iskandar Muda's expansion of Aceh's power through conquests was deemed as the "golden age" in Acehnese history. In contrast, his successors, the sultanahs, were seen as weaklings: Aceh was believed to have fallen into disunity, and their influence was limited to only northern Sumatra by the end of female rule in 1699. However, this monograph argues that this prevalent view should be revised. Should rulers be measured only by the extent of their borders and how much power they could accumulate in their own hands? It is difficult to agree with the assessment that the "absolute" and tyrannical rule of Iskandar Muda constituted a "golden age" in Aceh's history. Iskandar Muda used his army to subjugate the peoples as far south as Johor on the Malay Peninsula and depopulated these areas. He eliminated potential rivals at will, at times with extreme cruelty, just because they angered him. In a region where politics were fluid, powers transient and the balance of power precarious, no state or ruler could exercise hegemony, much less absolute rule. This monograph argues that in the Malay world where soft power could be as potent as hard power, where the good behaviour and moral conduct of the ruler are important criteria in determining a good ruler, the military might and expansionist policies of Iskandar Muda should neither be the main criteria in determining the success of the ruler nor should they be the standard against which to measure his successors. Indeed, it can be argued that maintaining peace and stability so commerce could thrive was an even bigger challenge. During the time of the queens, contrary to the narrative of decline, this monograph shows that although the VOC might have controlled a larger share of the international trade in this region by the end of the century, Aceh's regional trade continued to thrive and, as a trading port which served private traders from all over the world, Aceh's international commercial networks continued to be resilient. By the end of the reigns of these women sovereigns, Malay writing and literature in Aceh had developed to a height unrivalled till today: this could be said to constitute the real golden age in Acehnese history. It is about time different standards are used to evaluate the success of rulers and statecraft in pre-colonial Southeast Asia. This monograph illustrates that under female sovereigns the success of the ruler relied less on notions of sacral and charismatic power based on prowess but more on Muslim notions of piety and the just ruler.

The question of why Aceh remained politically and economically autonomous by the end of the seventeenth century is an important one and points to a more stable period of Acehnese history than is commonly believed. This book shifts the narrative of Aceh's decline to one that focuses more on Van Leur's observations on the importance of continuity, the strategies of survival, and the resilience of indigenous political and economic institutions, and their ability to absorb and adapt new influences to meet the European challenge.

Sources

This study uses four core groups of sources:

1. Dutch VOC documents;
2. English East India Company records;
3. Malay indigenous published manuscripts; and
4. Contemporary travellers' accounts

Dutch VOC Documents

The VOC documents relating to Aceh deposited in the *Nationaal Archief* are in the *Overgekomen brieven en papieren* (OBP) *uit Indie aan de Heren XVII en de kamer Amsterdam, 1614–1794*. Before 1660, the documents on Aceh are in a separate section under "Atchin". In post-1660 there is no longer any "Atchin" section, and most reporting about Aceh is found scattered through documents in the sections on the SWC, Melaka, Batavia, and Jambi and Palembang. There is no specific Aceh *Dagh-Register* (daily reports on Aceh) because the Dutch East India Company did not have a permanent factory there after 1663. However, political and economic news about Aceh was subsequently reported in the Batavia and Melaka *Dagh-Register* and the *Generaal Missiven* or general correspondence from the governor general in Batavia to the *Heren Zeventien* (literally, Seventeen Gentlemen, the VOC Board of Directors). The most useful and richest sources of information used for this study are the correspondence between the envoys and senior traders appointed to serve in Aceh for periods of about three months at a time and the governor general in Batavia, and the daily registers kept by these officials describing the company's day-to-day affairs in Aceh. After the closure of its factory, there was no need to appoint envoys and senior traders in Aceh. Reports on Aceh become harder to find and details on the court proceedings and internal developments are lacking. This unfortunate gap affects this study, tilting coverage in favour of the reign of the first sultanah, Safiatuddin Syah.

Another important source of information found in the VOC records are the letters exchanged between the indigenous rulers and the governors in Melaka and Batavia. Most of these original letters, written in *jawi* (Malay in Arabic script) have perished and very few remain. Only one original letter from Sultanah Safiatuddin to King Charles II remains. However, much of the correspondence survives in Dutch translations filed with the other papers in the OBP. These letters are invaluable because they constitute the indigenous perspective on events and are critical in writing an autonomous history of Aceh. Although these courtly letters served in part as tools of diplomacy and propaganda, read with caution they provide helpful insights into understanding the institution of monarchy in the Malay world. Major limitations arise from the Dutch translators' tendency to interpret the original text freely, with inadvertent mistranslations owing to linguistic and cultural differences. In most cases, the important first section of the letter—the *puji-pujian* (compliments), which praises the sender, the royal person—is omitted, summarised or standardised. The VOC copiers saw these exaggerated praises as unnecessary distractions from the business at hand. On the contrary, this carefully crafted *puji-pujian* represented what the ruler and his realm stood for, thus providing important insights into understanding forms of power and royal ceremony in the Malay world.

English East India Company Records

The English East India Company (EIC) documents are found in the India Office Records of the British Library. The EIC records are not as rich as those of the VOC because the EIC's emphasis was on India rather than

Aceh and Sumatra.⁷¹ The missions sent to Aceh were sporadic, and the English were unable to establish a more permanent settlement in Aceh or the SWC owing to intense competition from the Indian traders and the VOC. Although it might be a useful future research agenda, it is beyond the scope of this book to study English sources about Aceh found in other Indian port records, or indeed other European sources, such as Portuguese, French and Danish.

Malay Indigenous Published Manuscripts

Classical Malay writings are essential to a proper understanding of the metaphysics of indigenous society. There are several major indigenous chronicles and a range of religious treaties written under the queens that help us reconstruct the cultural dimension of female rule in Aceh at a time of cultural renaissance in a major Malay polity. These manuscripts are found in the *Universiteit Bibliotheek, Leiden Universiteit*.

The Malay records include:

1. *Kitab-sejarah* (chronicles) written in the sixteenth and seventeenth centuries, such as the *Taj us-Salatin*, *Bustan us-Salatin* and *Sulalat us-Salatin*
2. The *hikayat* (folklore) and adat, such as the *Hikayat Aceh* and *Adat Aceh*
3. *Qanun* (laws), such as *Qanun Meukota Alam* and *Qanun al-Asji Darussalam*

Contemporary Travellers' Accounts

A fourth body of information is the accounts of contemporary European visitors, primarily English and Dutch, but also other Muslim travellers, such as those from Iran and Mecca, who had close links with the ruling elite and conducted business in Aceh for a length of time. Among the Europeans, these include the accounts given by Frederik de Houtman, John Davis, Augustine de Beaulieu, Nicolaus de Graaff, Peter Mundy,

---

⁷¹ Nevertheless, English activities on the SWC are detailed in Chapter 4.

Wouter Schouten, Thomas Bowrey, William Dampier, Jacob de Roy and others. For the Muslims, these constitute the Iranian and Mekkan delegations, which visited Aceh in the 1680s.

Corroboration of Sources

The VOC documents are the backbone of this study as the meticulous record keeping of the VOC officials provides detailed information on the politics of Aceh and the economic background. The English East India Company records supplement information from the VOC documents to establish the research framework and to countercheck the information whenever possible. Accounts of country traders, travellers and residents in Aceh complement the information given by both companies' officers.

This book attempts a more comprehensive and focused study of these sultanahs of Aceh than has previously been available. Given new evidence that hints at a different picture of Aceh under its female rulers, the clues have to be pieced together to obtain a fuller representation of this past to see how aptly they have been judged in history. Given the current debate on the role and status of Acehnese women in a newly emergent autonomous Aceh, gaining a better understanding of women's roles and contributions in the past—especially at the helm of power—can serve as a source of inspiration, or at the very least, as a lesson in history. Given that there have been Muslim female leaders in Muslim Asia in contemporary times—the late Benazir Bhutto (Pakistan), Khaleda Zia and Sheikh Hasina Wajed (Bangladesh), and Megawati Sukarno Putri (Indonesia) and Wan Azizah Ismail (Malaysia)—a study of these Acehnese Muslim female rulers may provide some insights into the factors that enable women to reach the highest political office: whether they do so thanks to male invitation, history, tradition, institutional structures, the ability to adapt and localise global influences or their own extraordinary abilities.

chapter

1 The Succession of the First Female Ruler of Aceh

Criteria for Political Succession in Aceh

Few realms in the seventeenth century had written succession laws, at least not in the Malay world. The closest indication of any prerequisites for a candidate to be appointed sultan of Aceh was written in the *Kanun Syarak Kerajaan Aceh* [Aceh Canonical Laws] based on *sharia* (Islamic law).[1] According to these laws, the candidate had to be a Muslim of good lineage, an adult (that is, he or she had to have reached puberty), an Acehnese citizen, courageous, wise, just, loving and soft-hearted or merciful (*lembut hati*), conversant with the nuances of language, a keeper of promises, not physically handicapped, truthful, loving, patient, restrained (keeping anger in check, controlling baser instincts), forgiving, firm and yet submissive to Allah's will, and thankful to Allah.[2]

Most rulers could not satisfy all these qualifications. Nevertheless, they prompt the following questions—to what extent were the laws followed, what were the factors that determined political succession

---

[1] The *Kanun Syarak Kerajaan Aceh* was written in 1853 by Tengku di Meulek, a descendant of Aceh's Arab Jamal al-Din dynasty during the reign of Sultan Alauddin Mansur Syah. The *Kanun Syarak Keajaan Aceh* was believed to be based on an earlier kitab, *Tazkirah Tabakah*, written in 1507 during the reign of Sultan Ali Mughayat Syah. See Abdullah Sani Usman, *Nilai Sastera Ketatanegaraan dan Undang-undang dalam Kanun Syarak Kerajaan Aceh dan Bustanus Salatin* [Value of Literature on Governance and Law in the Canon Law of the Kingdom of Aceh and Garden of Kings] (henceforth *Kanun Syarak Keajaan Aceh*) (Bangi, Selangor: Penerbit Universiti Kebangsaan Malaysia, 2005), p. 18.

[2] Usman, *Kanun Syarak Kerajaan Aceh*, p. 38.

in the kingdom, and why was a woman ruler chosen in 1641, an unprecedented event in the kingdom's history and, after 1699, never again? In order to analyse the factors governing succession, a brief overview of the *silsilah* or genealogy is necessary, looking at the rulers from the kingdom's founder, Ali Mughayat Syah, in the sixteenth century to the reign of Sultan Badr al-Alam Syariff Hashim Jamal al-Din at the end of the seventeenth century.[3]

The origins of the kingdom of Aceh and its sultans are still mired in confusion. However, the sultanate of Aceh Dar al-Salam, which began in the sixteenth century, is believed to be the result of unifying two small kingdoms, Aceh in Dar al-Kamal and Lamuri in Mahkota Alam, both at the northern tip of the island of Sumatra, separated by a river.[4] Constant rivalry between these two kingdoms ended when Munawwar Syah, king of Lamuri, attacked and defeated Inayat Syah, king of Aceh, and united the two realms. Sultan Shams Syah, son of Munawwar Syah, then ruled this united kingdom. To strengthen his position, Shams Syah married his son, Ali Mughayat Syah, to the daughter of Inayat Syah. Ali Mughayat Syah (r. 1514–28)[5] expanded the kingdom by conquering neighbouring Daya (1520), Pidie (1521) and Pasai (1524).[6] After his death, the entire northern tip of Sumatra came under the dominion of the sultanate, thus making Ali Mughayat Syah the founder and first sultan of Aceh Dar al-Salam.[7]

---

[3] The historical survey given below draws largely from the indigenous chronicle, the *Bustan us-Salatin*: Nur al-Din Raniri, *Bustan us-Salatin,* ed. Teuku Iskandar (Kuala Lumpur: Dewan Bahasa dan Pustaka, 1966) and the study by Djajadiningrat—see footnote 5.

[4] Teuku Iskandar, ed., *De Hikajat Atjeh* ('s-Gravenhage: Martinus Nijhoff, 1958), p. 72.

[5] Raden Hoesein Djajadiningrat, "Critisch overzicht van de in Maleische werken vervatte gegevens over de geschiedenis van het Soeltanaat van Atjeh", *Bijdragen tot de Taal-, Land- en Volkenkunde* 8, 1 (1911): 212. Lombard, in Arifin, *Kerajaan Aceh*, p. 247, did not give the start date of his reign, only the end date of 1530.

[6] K.F.H. van Langen, *De Inrichting van het Atjehsche Staatsbestuur onder het Sultanaat* [The Organisation of the Aceh State Administration under the Sultanante] ('s-Gravenhage: KITLV Monograph, 1888). Translated by Aboe Bakar as *Susunan Pemerintahan Aceh Semasa Kesultanan* (Banda Aceh: Pusat Dokumentasi dan Informasi Banda Aceh, 1997), p. 14.

[7] The *Bustan us-Salatin* describes Ali Mughayat Syah as the first sultan of Aceh Dar al-Salam, defender of Islam and a fine warrior, p. 31. The date of his reign in the *al-Salatin*

When the first sultan died, Ali Mughayat Syah's son, Salah al-Din (r. 1528–37), succeeded him.[8] Known as a weak leader, he was challenged by his younger brother, Ala al-Din al-Qahar, who took power and ruled from 1537 to 1568.[9] After his death, he was succeeded by his son, Sultan Husayn, who assumed the title Sultan Ali Riayat Syah (r. 1568–75).[10] A wise ruler revered by his people and the ulama, Sultan Ali Riayat Syah ruled for eight years.[11] His death in 1575 was followed by a period of political instability: he was succeeded by his four-month-old son, who died seven months later. The next ruler was his uncle, Abangta Abdul al-Jalil, who took the title Sultan Sri Alam,[12] but was assassinated within a year,[13] allegedly because of his bad temper.[14] The *Hikayat Aceh* depicts Sultan Sri Alam as extravagant as he had depleted the kingdom's treasury by giving expensive gifts to certain soldiers and elites from Fansur (Baros). The *Hikayat* relates that the orang kaya and ulama in Aceh gathered and decided this state of affairs was injurious to the kingdom, and the sultan must be deposed.[15] However, the *Hikayat* is silent on how this was done merely mentioning that he was replaced, in contrast to the *Bustan*'s account that the sultan was killed. Zayn al-Abidin, grandson of al-Qahar, became the next ruler, but he too was murdered after a few months, supposedly because of his murderous and bloodthirsty nature.[16] The *Hikayat Aceh* also relates that Sultan Zayn al-Abidin was a bad ruler, extremely bad

---

is 913-28 H (1507–22). Djajadiningrat, "Critisch", p. 212, places him at r. 1514–28; and Lombard, in Arifin, *Kerajaan Aceh*, p. 247, at r. ?–1530.

[8] Djajadiningrat, "Critisch", p. 212. The *Bustan al-Salatin*, however, states that he ruled for 17 years: Iskandar, ed., *Bustan us-Salatin*, p. 31. Lombard stated that he ruled from 1530–39: Lombard in Arifin, *Kerajaan Aceh*, p. 247.

[9] Djajadiningrat, "Critisch", p. 212. Lombard put Ala-al Din's reign as 1539–71: Lombard in Arifin, *Kerajaan Aceh*, p. 248.

[10] Djajadiningrat, "Critisch", p. 212. Lombard said Ali Riayat's reign was 1571 to 1579: Lombard in Arifin, *Kerajaan Aceh*, p. 248.

[11] Iskandar, ed., *Bustan us-Salatin*, p. 32.

[12] Ibid., pp. 32-3.

[13] Djajadiningrat, "Critisch", p. 212.

[14] Iskandar, ed., *Bustan us-Salatin*, p. 32.

[15] Iskandar, ed., *De Hikajat Atjeh*, p. 96.

[16] Djajadiningrat, "Critisch", p. 212. See a differing account in H.M Zainuddin, *Tarich Atjeh dan Nusantara* [History of Aceh and Nusantara], Vol. 1 (Medan: Pustaka Iskandar Muda, 1961), p. 399.

tempered and bloodthirsty. Again the elites of the kingdom felt that if this sultan was not stopped, it would spell disaster for them; thus they decided to depose the sultan. The *Hikayat Aceh* is again mysteriously silent on how this was done, merely stating that after the sultan's two-year rule he died.[17]

These indigenous chronicles are silent on how the sultans were deposed or killed, and they reveal next to nothing about the identities and rights of the orang kaya and court officials, except for mentioning the highest titles. Significantly, however, the chronicles show that the elites played an important role in appointing and demoting rulers: weak rulers—those who possessed unacceptable personality traits injurious to the kingdom—were removed. This means that the nobility's consent and acceptance of a candidate was a vital condition for a ruler's succession.

After this period of violent successions, there ensued an era of "foreign-born rulers"—those not belonging to the lineage of Munawwar Syah, king of Lamuri, and Inayat Syah, king of Aceh. Sultan Ala al-Din, known as Mansur Syah, of Perak origin succeeded to the throne and reigned from 1577 to 1586.[18] Again, the sources offer no account of the circumstances of his succession or why a foreigner was chosen to rule Aceh. The *Bustan* describes him as a pious and just ruler who upheld Islamic law, but he was also killed for reasons unknown.[19] Next in line was Sultan Mahkota Buyung from Inderapura, who took the title Sultan Ala al-Din Riayat Syah.[20] He reigned from 1586 to 1588 and, again for unknown reasons, was killed.[21]

---

[17] Iskandar, ed., *De Hikajat Atjeh*, p. 98.
[18] Djajadiningrat, "Critisch", pp. 159–60.
[19] Iskandar, ed., *Bustan us-Salatin*, pp. 33–4. Djajadiningrat mentioned that he was killed by his soldier but no reason was given: Djajadiningrat, "Critisch", p. 213. Zainuddin suggested that he was killed because the elites of Aceh wanted to return to their own native royal lineage of Mughayat Syah: Zainuddin, *Tarich Atjeh*, p. 400.
[20] Iskandar, ed., *Bustan us-Salatin*, p. 34. Sultan Mahkota Buyong went to Aceh to look for his sister, married to the late Sultan Sri Alam. When Sri Alam was killed, he was said to have been asked to succeed the Acehnese throne: J. Kathirithamby-Wells, "The Inderapura Sultanate: The Foundations of Its Rise and Decline, from the Sixteenth to Eighteenth Centuries", *Indonesia* 21 (Apr. 1976): 68; Hadi, *Islam and State in Sumatra*, p. 69.
[21] Iskandar, ed., *Bustan us-Salatin*, p. 34. Zainuddin ventured that during this sultan's reign, Zayn al-Abidin returned to claim the throne. He was supported by the Acehnese elites

Another important factor in the criteria for succession was the royal dynastic line should preferably come from the Munawwar Syah and Inayat Syah lineage, and the candidate be born in Aceh itself, though other foreign-born rulers were legitimate candidates if they were related by marriage to Aceh's royal house. This is elaborated upon in the following section where it is shown that another foreign-born Sultan, Iskandar Thani (r.1637–41) also died in mysterious circumstances.

After a decade of reigns by foreign sultans, the succession returned to the Aceh's Dar-al-Kamal dynasty. Sultan Ala-Addin Riayat Syah, son of Firman Syah, descendant of Inayat Syah of the Dar al-Kamal dynasty, was installed on the throne in 1588, taking the title Sultan Ali Mughayat Syah al-Mukammil.[22] The orang kaya were said to have chosen him based on his advanced years when he ascended the throne, but after becoming king, he was alleged to have killed many of the orang kaya who had supported him.[23] His eldest son, the ambitious Sultan Muda, ruler of Pidie, deposed him in 1604, and took the title Sultan Ali Ri'ayat Syah.[24] Sultan Ali Ri'ayat Syah's brother, Hussain Syah, then took over as ruler of Pidie. Supported by Iskandar Muda, his nephew, Hussain Syah opposed his brother's overthrow of their old father, but their rebellion against Ali Ri'ayat Syah failed. Hussain Syah refused to surrender Iskandar Muda to his brother, and instead they fled to Pidie to avoid punishment. Ali Ri'ayat Syah, therefore, attacked Pidie, defeating Hussain Syah, and Iskandar Muda surrendered to Sultan Ali Ri'ayat Syah.[25] However, he was released in 1606 when the sultan needed Iskandar Muda's services to repel a Portuguese attack, a task in which he was successful, but immediately after, the sultan himself died of unknown causes. Iskandar Muda lost

---

and the army, so Ala al-Din Riayat Syah of Inderapura had to rely on his soldiers. In the ensuing struggles between these two factions, Sultan Ala al-Din Riayat Syah was killed: Zainuddin, *Tarich Atjeh*, p. 401.

[22] Djajadiningrat, "Critisch", pp. 162–3, 213.

[23] See Djajadiningrat, "Critisch", pp.162–3. The *Hikayat Aceh* reveals that this person was the descendant of Inayat Syah from the Dar al-Kamal Dynasty, see Iskandar, ed., *De Hikajat Atjeh*, p. 99. The *Bustan* states that he is the son of Firman Syah; see Iskandar, ed., *Bustan us-Salatin*, p. 34.

[24] Iskandar, ed., *Bustan us-Salatin*, p. 34; Djajadiningrat, "Critisch", p. 213.

[25] Djajadiningrat, "Critisch", p. 174; Zainuddin, *Tarich Atjeh*, p. 403.

no time in getting the support of the orang kaya to place him on the throne, and his uncle from Pidie was duly captured and executed.[26]

The above events show that power was highly contested and diffused. Power was not necessarily contested between royalty and nobility but also internally within the groups themselves. Royalty and elite were not homogeneous, and they did not necessarily need to be in opposition where power swung from one to the other but were inter-dependent. A royal candidate who was militarily strong, such as Iskandar Muda, could capture power and put himself on the throne without being nominated by the elite, but he still needed the support of the orang kaya to maintain his place on the throne.

Iskandar Muda ruled from 1607 until his death in 1636.[27] The *Bustan* considers him a great ruler and conqueror: under him, Aceh expanded its territories and continued attacks against the Portuguese in Melaka.[28] Iskandar Muda died without leaving any direct heir of his own as he is believed to have had his only legitimate son killed a few weeks before his own death.[29] He named his son-in-law, Sultan Iskandar Thani, as his successor, who became the third foreign-born ruler of Aceh. Iskandar Thani was the son of the Pahang ruler named Ahmad Syah. He was brought to Aceh at the age of seven when Iskandar Muda conquered Pahang in 1618, and was married to Iskandar Muda's daughter, Puteri Seri Alam. Iskandar Thani died of unknown causes and childless in 1641 at the young age of 31.

There is the suspicion that Sultan Iskandar Thani might also have been killed as he was still young, and his death came so unexpectedly.[30] The Dutch officials reported that Iskandar Thani was not loved by the

---

[26] Djajadiningrat, "Critisch", p. 175. Zainuddin did not mention what happened to Hussain Syah.

[27] Both Lombard and Djajadiningrat placed his reign from 1607 to 1636 illustrating that the information on the historical succession of the sultans of Aceh in the seventeenth century is more definite than in the century before. See Djajadiningrat, "Critisch", p. 213; Lombard in Arifin, *Kerajaan Aceh*, p. 249.

[28] Iskandar, ed., *Bustan us-Salatin*, p. 35.

[29] Lombard in Arifin, *Kerajaan Aceh*, p. 236.

[30] The *Bustan al-Salatin* reveals a plot hatched by those against Iskandar Thani who poisoned his food. However, this plot was foiled, and the conspirators were executed: Iskandar, ed., *Bustan us-Salatin*, p. 46.

Acehnese both because he was a foreigner, and he was wasteful, depleting the treasury.[31] There had also been tensions between the VOC and Iskandar Thani in 1640—a year before his death—when he suddenly refused to help the Dutch conquer Melaka, despite his promise to do so. This was his way of registering his displeasure at the company's decision to ally itself secretly with his vassal, Johor, without first asking for his permission.[32] When the VOC conquered Melaka with Johor's help in 1641, the regional balance of power tipped away from Aceh. Furthermore, Aceh had recently lost another vassal, Pahang (Iskandar Thani's own birthplace), to Johor in 1638. These circumstances, plus the weakened state of the Acehnese military after the 1629 failed attempt to conquer Portuguese Melaka added to the Acehnese sense of insecurity. It is no surprise then that the elites got rid of Iskandar Thani: besides being foreign, he was a bad ruler and becoming a liability to the kingdom.

With no apparent male heir, his widow, Iskandar Muda's daughter, succeeded him and became the first female ruler of Aceh. She took the title Taj al-Alam Safiatuddin Syah, enjoying a long reign of 35 years until her death in 1675.[33] She was succeeded by another woman, Sri Sultanah Nur al-Alam Naqiyyat al-Din Syah, who ruled for three years until her death.[34] According to Zainuddin, she was the daughter of Hussain Syah, ruler of Pidie and uncle of Iskandar Muda.[35] Apart from this claim, there is no other information about her origin or the circumstances under which she became the sultanah. Sultanah Inayat Syah Zakiyyat al-Din Syah followed, and ruled for a decade, but again, her origins cannot be verified.[36] The *Bustan* states that she was the daughter of a certain

---

[31] *Nationaal Archief* [hereafter NA], Dagh-Register van Pieter Sourij, May–August 1642, f. 572R.

[32] For a detailed picture on why Iskandar Thani failed to help the Dutch conquer Melaka, see Sher Banu A.L. Khan, "Ties That Unbind: The Abortive Aceh-VOC Alliance for the Conquest of Melaka 1640-1641", *Indonesia and the Malay World* 38, 111 (2010): 303-21.

[33] Djajadiningrat, "Critisch", p. 214; Lombard in Arifin, *Kerajaan Aceh*, p. 249.

[34] Djajadiningrat, "Critisch", p. 214. Lombard's study stops at this first Sultanah Taj al-Alam.

[35] Zainuddin, *Tarich Atjeh*, p. 408. He provided no evidence for this claim.

[36] Djajadiningrat, "Critisch", p. 214.

Sultan Muhammad Syah.[37] Zainuddin claimed that she was either the daughter of Mahmud Syah or Sultan Ali Ri'ayat Syah (r. 1604–07).[38] After her death in 1688, the last of four queens—Kamalat Syah—was installed; her origin seems to be totally obscure. She ruled until 1699, when she was deposed by a male challenger of Arab descent, Sultan Badr al-Alam Syariff Hashim Jamal al-Din (r. 1699–1702).[39]

In his analysis of the factors governing succession in Aceh in the sixteenth and seventeenth centuries, Amirul Hadi stated that the procedure for succession was less structured in Aceh than in other Malay sultanates, and concluded that the rules were, at best, obscure. This very obscurity surrounding the rules ensured that the Acehnese approach to this issue was flexible and pragmatic. On the other hand, he saw this pragmatism as constrained by ideology, and asserted that at the core an Islamic-moral paradigm prevailed.[40]

An examination of the events surrounding the succession of Acehnese sultans does not clarify the "rules of succession" and it cannot be seen as conforming to an "Islamic paradigm", though all the rulers were Muslim. However, a few salient factors can be identified as important in governing succession. One factor that seems constant is that power was contested and diffused, and the ruler could not maintain his throne without the explicit or tacit consent and acceptance of the majority of the orang kaya. Powerful sultans who were assets to the kingdom, such as Ali Mughayat Syah, Ala al-Din al-Qahar, Ala-Addin Riayat Syah and Iskandar Muda, were able to gain acceptance from the majority of the orang kaya and ruled till their deaths. Rulers who were not strong enough to dominate the nobility and deemed unacceptable owing to their bad nature, such as Sultan Sri Alam and Sultan Zayn al-Abidin, were deposed or assassinated, and the nobility installed a new candidate. Another reason for a ruler to be deemed unacceptable was because of his "foreign" origin. In sum, the prerequisites for a candidate to be chosen as a ruler were Acehnese lineage, good conduct, being an asset to the kingdom

---

[37] Iskandar, ed., *Bustan us-Salatin*, p. 74. There was no explanation of who Sultan Muhammad Syah was.
[38] Zainuddin, *Tarich Atjeh*, p. 409.
[39] Djajadiningrat, "Critisch", p. 192.
[40] Hadi, *Islam and State in Sumatra*, p. 65.

and accepted by the majority of the orang kaya. These conform quite closely to the prerequisites laid out in the *Kanun Syarak Kerajaan Aceh*.

The significant question here is how did this practice of political succession unfold when a new criterion was introduced into the equation—the female factor in 1641? It appears that in the case of a female succession, royal lineage applied, certainly for the first sultanah, Safiatuddin Syah. This is consistent with earlier practices of male succession in which it is believed that most rulers were of royal blood. Granted that there are some inconsistencies regarding the identity of the sultans and their succession in the sixteenth century, most accounts do corroborate the dynastic lineage of the Aceh sultans, especially in the seventeenth century. The kingdom of Aceh was founded on unifying the Dar al-Kamal and Mahkota Alam dynasties, and rulers from Mughayat Syah to Zayn al-Abidin sprang from these two dynastic lines. In 1589, after the era of foreign-born rulers, al-Mukammil restarted the Dar-al-Kamal line, which ended with his son, Ali Ri'ayat Syah, in 1607. The two dynastic lines were then reunited in the person of Iskandar Muda, whose father was Mansur Syah, grandson of al-Qahar of the Mahkota Alam dynasty. His mother was Putri Raja Indra Bongsu, daughter of al-Mukammil of Dar al-Kamal.[41] Safiatuddin Syah was Iskandar Muda's daughter, clearly from a royal mother: a son of Iskandar Muda from a non-royal mother was disqualified from succeeding him.[42] According to Zainuddin, Safiatuddin's mother was Putri Sani, the daughter of Daeng Mansur while her half brother was the son of a concubine from Lam Si.[43] He became the *panglima* (governor) of one of Aceh's provinces instead and took the title *Panglima Polem*.[44] Very little is known about her other legitimate siblings except for the brother who was killed on the orders of their own father, Iskandar Muda, a few weeks before his

---

[41] Lombard in Arifin, *Kerajaan Aceh*, pp. 248-9; Djajadiningrat, "Critisch", p. 216.

[42] Ali Hasjmy also identified the mother of this princess. She was said to be royal and her title was *Puteri* (Princess) Ratna Indra. The evidence is rather vague though because the *naskah tua* (tr. old manuscript) Hasjmy mentioned could not be properly identified. Ali Hasjmy, *59 Tahun Aceh Merdaka di bawah Pemerintahan Ratu* [59 Years of Aceh's Independence under Female Rule] (Jakarta: Penerbitan Bulan Bintang, 1977), p. 33.

[43] Zainuddin, *Tarich Atjeh*, p. 426.

[44] Van Langen in Aboe Bakar, *Susunan Pemerintahan*, p. 15.

own death.⁴⁵ There was indeed a dearth of other suitable royal male heirs with impeccable lineages as Iskandar Muda had killed many royal males during his reign. He killed his own nephew, the son of the sultan of Johor (Iskandar Muda's brother-in-law), because he was jealous that his own mother favoured his nephew. His mother, whom he suspected of being engaged in a conspiracy against him, was tortured and imprisoned. He also put to death other royal relations, such as the respective sons of the sultans of Bantam and Pahang.⁴⁶ Likewise, Iskandar Thani contributed to the shortage of royal male heirs: according to Peter Mundy, he killed about 400 people including Iskandar Muda's other daughters and their sons who, he alleged, had tried to usurp his throne.⁴⁷ Thus, at the time of Iskandar Thani's death, it appears that the person with the best royal lineage was Safiatuddin Syah. Under the circumstances, she was the person qualified to succeed, and the most likely to be accepted by all as legitimate.

Unfortunately, the origins of the other three sultanahs are still inconclusive. A search of the VOC sources confirmed the accession dates of these queens but not their identities and origins. Of the indigenous chronicles, only the *Bustan* mentions the female rulers: it gives the identity of the first queen but that of her immediate successor, Naqiatuddin Syah, is unreported. According to Zainuddin, Naqiatuddin Syah was the cousin of Iskandar Muda, as she was Hussain Syah's daughter, ruler of Pidie and Iskandar Muda's uncle.⁴⁸ Teuku Iskandar stated that the second queen was another daughter of Iskandar Muda, but provided no evidence for this speculation.⁴⁹ The *Bustan* identifies the third queen, Zakiatuddin Syah, as the daughter of a certain Sultan Muhammad Syah, but did not elaborate on the identity of either one. Djajadiningrat suggested that the third

---

⁴⁵ According to Zainuddin, this son, Merah Pupok, was also not from a royal mother but the son of another concubine from Pasai: Zainuddin, *Tarich Atjeh*, p. 426.
⁴⁶ Marsden, *The History of Sumatra*, p. 446.
⁴⁷ Peter Mundy arrived in Aceh in February 1638, four months after Iskandar Thani ordered the reported executions: Peter Mundy, *The Travels of Peter Mundy in Europe and Asia, 1608–1667*, Vol. III, Part II, No. XLVI, ed. Lt.-Col. Sir Richard Carnac Temple (Cambridge: The Hakluyt Society, 1919), p. 330.
⁴⁸ Zainuddin, *Tarich Atjeh*, p. 408. He provided no evidence for this claim.
⁴⁹ Iskandar, ed., *Bustan us-Salatin*, p. 13.

queen might be the daughter of the second,[50] while Zainuddin claimed that Zakiatuddin Syah was another cousin of Iskandar Muda, as she was either Mahmud Syah or Sultan Ali Ri'ayat Syah's daughter.[51] The origins of the fourth queen, Kamalat Syah, remain a complete mystery.[52] And yet while we remain in doubt as to their origins, it is hard to imagine that they were not of royal lineage as their succession would surely have been opposed otherwise, and, so far as we know, no one contested their succession on the grounds of illegitimacy. The three foreign-born rulers who preceded them—Ala al-Din of Perak, Ala al-Din Riayat Syah of Inderapura and Iskandar Thani—were all royal themselves who married into the Acehnese royal line, so it appears that royal lineage was an essential prerequisite of succession in Aceh, even in the context of a female succession. Furthermore, it seems that as long as they were of royal lineage, the order in which progeny appeared did not matter: primogeniture did not necessarily guarantee succession. Other sons or brothers or, for that matter, daughters or sisters, of previous rulers could succeed to the throne.

Another important condition that can help explain the elites' choice of Safiatuddin Syah is that the elites were determined that no foreign-born ruler would succeed the Acehnese throne, even though Aceh faced a similar situation in 1575. After the death of Sultan Ali Riayat Syah in 1575, Aceh was faced with a dearth of suitable native-born heirs, which was why the elites felt they needed to look elsewhere for a successor. Although they were legitimate, as they were of royal blood and related to the Acehnese dynasty by marriage, the first two foreign rulers ended up being killed. It was not until 1636 that Aceh again came under a foreign ruler, Iskandar Thani. Unlike his predecessors, who were chosen and placed on the throne by the elites of Aceh, Iskandar Thani was appointed

---

[50] Djajadiningrat, "Critisch", p. 189. Djajadiningrat based this claim on some written manuscripts by Snouck Hurgronje, the details are unknown.

[51] Zainuddin, *Tarich Atjeh*, p. 409.

[52] According to Ali Hasjmy, based on the genealogy given in the *naskah tua* the origins of these female rulers could be traced back to the same family dynasty, that is, the founder of the Sultanate of Aceh's grandfather, Ali Mughayat Syah, whose name was Sultan Alauddin Abdullah Malikul Mubin. However, the evidence here is inconclusive: Hasjmy, *59 Tahun*, p. 39.

by the reigning sultan, Iskandar Muda, which was an exception in Acehnese historical succession as a ruler was always elected rather than designated. Partly because Iskandar Muda was a powerful ruler, the orang kaya did not resist or challenge Iskandar Thani's appointment at that time.

When Iskandar Thani died mysteriously without a male heir, the choice of a foreign ruler would have been a logical one. It would also have been in keeping with the sultanate's customary succession practices, rather than choosing a woman. The elites certainly had some legally possible contenders: as a result of relations by marriage, they were from Perak, Pahang and Johor.

Indeed, when news of Iskandar Thani's death reached the neighbouring Malay polities, rumours were rife as to who would go to Aceh to succeed to the throne. The Dutch records reveal that the sultan of Johor, Sultan Abdul Jalil (r. 1623–77), was in Patani, in what is now southern Thailand, and wanted to stop in Aceh to succeed Iskandar Thani en route home.[53] In 1613, when Aceh razed Johor to the ground, its ruler, Sultan Alaudin, managed to escape with his son, Abdul Jalil. Alaudin's brother, Sultan Ma'yat Syah, was carried off to Aceh to be married to Iskandar Muda's sister, thus securing the sultan of Johor a legitimate claim to the throne based on marriage ties. Sultan Abdul Jalil succeeded Sultan Ma'yat Syah when he died in 1623.

Unlike in 1579, in 1641 the elites preferred a female with Acehnese lineage to a foreign-born successor. Owing to the bad experience with Iskandar Thani, a Pahang-born ruler, the orang kaya were determined to keep out foreigners. The Acehnese elite were even wary of attempts at marrying Iskandar Thani's widow, daughter of Iskandar Muda, to a foreign prince who could later claim the throne; indeed, they jealously guarded against their queen marrying again. Thus the Acehnese orang kaya made a secret pact never to allow a foreign prince to claim the throne.[54] It is significant to note that given the elites' fears that the throne could fall into foreign hands, they accepted that Iskandar Thani's widow could rule in her own right.

---

[53] Chijs, *Dagh-Register*, 1640–41, p. 362.
[54] Batavia's Uitgaande Briefboeken, R0010236, 1634–49, Justus Schouten and Johan van Twist in Malacca, 1641, f. 343V.

In sum, as an adult, with royal Acehnese lineage as the daughter of Iskandar Muda and widow of Iskandar Thani, Safiatuddin met the prerequisites of a ruler. Still, the woman factor was unprecedented and there is still the question of whether a woman ruler is acceptable in a Muslim state, such as Aceh. The following sections deal with these concerns and explain the circumstances leading to the accession of Safiatuddin Syah in 1641.

Circumstances Leading to the Succession of the First Female Ruler of Aceh

Let us first examine both contemporary and more recent accounts on the first female succession in Aceh. In the main, these accounts differ on two major questions—whether her succession was smooth and peaceful or problematic, and whether she was installed immediately on the death of her husband or some days after. Another significant question—which will be dealt with in greater detail in the next section—is the alleged debate that took place at court among the ulama over whether a woman could be allowed to lead or rule an Islamic kingdom.

The contemporary account of Nicolaus de Graaff, a Dutch surgeon who was in Aceh at the time of Iskandar Thani's death, described a problematic succession. He wrote about an *opschudding* (state of commotion) among the orang kaya in which many people lost their lives and the company's lodge was closed for four to five days because each of the orang kaya desired to be king.[55] As a result of this chaotic situation, it took three days before Safiatuddin was installed.[56]

---

[55] Nicolaus de Graaff, *Reisen van Nicolaus de Graaff: gedaan naar alle gewesten des Werelds beginnende 1639 tot 1687 incluis* [Travels of Martinus Nicolaus de Graaff round the World from 1639-1687], ed. J.C.M. Warnsinck ('s-Gravenhage: Martinus Nijhoff, 1930), p. 13; Raden Hoesein Djajadiningrat, *Kesultanan Aceh*, trans. Teuku Hamid of "Critisch...", No. 12 (Aceh: Departemen Pendidikan dan Kebudayaan: Proyek Pengembangan Permuseuman, 1982–83), p. 56.

[56] Djajadiningrat stated that it took three days before the queen was installed. Djajadiningrat quoted Nicolaus de Graaff (1701), p. 9: Djajadiningrat, "Critisch", p. 188. However, in the Warnsinck 1930 edition of *Reisen van Nicolaus de Graaff* there was no mention of how long it took before the queen was enthroned.

No other contemporary account, either Dutch or indigenous, mentions any disturbances. The *oppercoopman* (senior trader) Jacob Compostel, who resided in Aceh, wrote in a letter dated 26 February 1641 that the king of Aceh had departed this world on 15 February without leaving any children to succeed and thereafter, after a lapse of three days, his widow was crowned as queen and assumed duties of administration.[57] Similarly, the *Bustan us-Salatin* relates that Iskandar Muda's daughter was chosen as the successor and was enthroned as Paduka Seri Sultan Safiatuddin Syah Berdaulat zillu' l-Lah fil 'alam ibnat Sultan Raja Iskandar Muda Johan Berdaulat without any opposition. But, unlike the Dutch reports, the *Bustan* states that the sultanah's reign started on the very same day of her husband's death.[58]

Modern historians tend to agree with contemporary accounts that describe a peaceful succession, though some point out that initially some difficulties and opposition arose because of her sex. While Mohammad Said claimed that her sex did not matter as Aceh already had a tradition of women holding high positions (though never a ruler), others like Ali Hasjmy and Rusdi Sufi argued that her succession was problematic as there was the question of whether a female ruler was legal in Islam.[59] Sufi claimed that just before her coronation there was some opposition in the court over the legality of a woman becoming the head of the Muslim kingdom: a woman could not even be appointed as an *imam* (head of congregational prayers) or *wali* (a bride's legal guardian).[60]

So, how does one reconcile these inconsistencies to explain the first female succession in Aceh's history? In weighing the above accounts, that of De Graaff is the most immediate and neutral. It appears that Iskandar Thani's death was certainly unexpected, for it caused uproar among the orang kaya, and no apparent successor was in sight. In an unprecedented move, some of the orang kaya appeared to have tried to put themselves

---

[57] Chijs, *Dagh-Register*, 1640–41, p. 322.
[58] Iskandar, ed., *Bustan us-Salatin*, p. 58.
[59] Said, *Atjeh Sepanjang Abad*, pp. 377–9; Ali, *59 Tahun*, p. 49.
[60] Rusdi Sufi, "Sultanah Safiatuddin Syah", in *Wanita Utama Nusantara dalam Lintasan Sejarah* [Prominent Women of the Archipelago in the Course of History], ed. Ismail Sofyan, M. Hasan Basry and Ibrahim Alfian (Jakarta: Jayakarta Agung Offset, 1994), p. 43.

up as candidates but others vehemently opposed, splitting the nobility into factions. Whether the claims were opposed because of the issue of legitimacy, as the previous rulers had royal blood, or out of sheer jealousy, none of the orang kaya wanted to pay allegiance to their own kind. None of the orang kaya factions were perhaps strong enough to support their candidates, and to force the issue might have brought Aceh to a civil war. None of the orang kaya could afford this, especially given the uncertain external condition, specifically the VOC's recent conquest of Melaka, with the help of Aceh's enemy Johor. Both the VOC and Johor representatives were on their way to Aceh to discuss peace. There was a rumour that the sultan of Johor was also on his way to Aceh to claim the throne, which was legitimately his owing to marriage ties between the Johor and Aceh royal families. He might even marry Iskandar Thani's royal widow and daughter of Iskandar Muda to confirm his right to the throne. Therefore, the initial commotion De Graaf reported did not erupt into violence, and the scramble for power did not last longer than a few days. Thus, the peaceful succession reported by most other accounts.

The other point of debate is whether Safiatuddin was crowned three days after, and was the reason why because of the alleged problem that she was a woman and that this was forbidden in Islam? To what extent is this true and, if so, why then did the elites elect her?

Is Female Rule Allowed in Islam? The "Female" Factor in Royal Succession

One finds only a handful of female Muslim sovereigns in other parts of the world. The neglect, sometimes silence, in mainstream Islamic discourses on women rulers perhaps reflects the insignificant numbers of these female sovereigns in Islamic history. The few women rulers who have been recognised and recorded in history include Sultanah Radiyya, who ruled Delhi in 1236.[61] Tindu ruled the Mongol Jallarid dynasty of Iraq

---

[61] Peter Jackson, "Sultan Radiyya bint Iltutmish", in *Women in the Medieval Islamic World: Power, Patronage, Piety,* ed. Gavin R.G. Hambly (New York: St. Martin's Press, 1998), pp. 181–2.

from 814 to 822, while some centuries later the Kutlugh-Khanid dynasty produced Kutlugh Khatun (r. 1257–82), and her daughter, Padishah Khatun (r. 1282–95). The latter's niece, Absh Khatun, ruled the Atabek dynasty from 1263 to 1287, and Sati Bek became Ilkhan sultanah in 1339.[62] The Fatimids, who established an Ismai'li Shi'i caliphate in Yemen to rival the Sunni Abbasids, placed two queens on the throne, Malika Asma and Arwa, who between them held power from 1019 to 1038.[63] In the Maldives, three queens—Sultanah Khadijah, Sultanah Myriam and Sultanah Fatima—ruled from 1347 to 1388.[64] Fatima Mernissi's survey of Muslim sovereigns shows that of the number of Muslim women who ruled in their own right, most are found in the peripheral areas of Islam.[65] The very fact that the number of such politically active and prominent women is very small, even though Islam has been established in the world for the past 14 centuries, shows that women holding high positions in the world of politics are the exception rather than the rule.

Spatially and culturally remote from the heartland of Islam in the far-flung regions of insular Southeast Asia, the ulama found themselves faced with a wholly different political reality on the new frontier, namely a tradition of strong women in general, and high-born women who played important roles at court in particular. Aceh was not unique in having women rulers. The Malay Muslim polity of Patani was governed by four women in succession from c.1584 to 1718. The *Hikayat Patani* relates that when Sultan Bahadur died with no male heir to succeed him, the orang kaya appointed his daughter, Raja Ijau, as Patani's next ruler.[66] Similarly, there were instances of women rulers in Sukadana between

---

[62] Hambly, *Women in the Medieval Islamic World*, pp. 13–7.
[63] Farhad Daftary, "Sayyida Hurra: The Isma'ili Sulayhid Queen of Yemen", in *Women in the Medieval Islamic World*, ed. Hambly, p. 118.
[64] Fatima Mernissi, *Hidden from History: Forgotten Queens of Islam* (Lahore: ASR Publications, 1994), pp. 89, 107–8.
[65] Ibid., pp. 107–8. Of the 13 female Muslim sovereigns holding the official insignia of Muslim states between the thirteenth and seventeenth centuries, 2 were Turkish, 6 Mongolians, 2 Yemenis and 3 were from the Maldives.
[66] Siti Hawa Haji Salleh, ed., *Hikayat Patani* (Kuala Lumpur: Dewan Bahasa dan Pustaka, 1992), p. 28.

1608 and 1622, in Jambi between 1630 and 1655, and in Solor from 1650 to 1670.[67]

Female rule in Aceh Dar al-Salam was unprecedented in 1641, and while this female factor must have concerned the elites of that time, it appears to have bothered recent Acehnese male historians more: they place so much emphasis on the alleged religious debate over whether a female could succeed as a ruler in Islam. This was no trivial matter—the last queen was deposed, allegedly because of a *fatwa* (religious decree) from Mecca stating that Islam forbade female rule. And yet an excellent political pedigree would not have guaranteed the succession if there was still the question of whether female leadership was legal in a Muslim state.[68] As mentioned by Hasjmy and Sufi, the sultanah was only enthroned after three days, and they conjectured that this delay was owing to a debate that took place as to whether female rule was allowed in Islam. Sufi claimed that a section of the orang kaya opposed her succession on the basis that Islamic law did not even allow a woman to be an imam or even a wali, let alone a ruler. This view, however, was opposed by another group of ulama headed by Nuruddin al-Raniri[69] and Abdul Rauf al-Singkel,[70] two of the most prominent ulama in Aceh in the seventeenth century. Al-Raniri came from Gujarat and was appointed by Iskandar Thani as *Sheikh al-Islam*, the chief religious judge, and remained as such under the first sultanah until he left Aceh in 1643. Al-Singkel was born in West Sumatra and was appointed as the Sheikh al-Islam in 1661 upon his return to Aceh from studies in the Middle East. Sufi suggested that

---

[67] Reid, "Females Roles in Pre-Colonial Southeast Asia", pp. 640–1; Cheah Boon Kheng, "Power behind the Throne: The Role of Queens and Court Ladies in Malay History", *Journal of the Malaysian Branch of Royal Asiatic Society* 66, 1 (1993): 1–2. It is beyond the scope of this book to compare these female rulers in the region. This invites further research.

[68] Sufi, "Sultanah Safiatuddin Syah", p. 43.

[69] This ulama's full name is Nur al-Din Muhammad, bin Ali al-Hamid al-Shafi'i al-Asha'ri al-Aydarusi al-Raniri al-Surati: Peter G. Riddell, *Islam and the Malay-Indonesian World: Transmission and Responses* (London: C. Hurst, 2001), pp. 116–8.

[70] Abd al-Rauf b.Ali al-Fansuri al-Singkili (c. 1615–93) was born in Singkel. He was *Sheikh al-Islam* until his death in 1693: Riddell, *Islam and the Malay-Indonesian World*, pp. 125–8; Azyumardi Azra, *The Origins of Islamic Reformism in Southeast Asia: Networks of Malay-Indonesian and Middle Eastern 'Ulama' in the Seventeenth and Eighteenth Centuries* (Australia / Honolulu: Allen and Unwin / University of Hawai'i Press, 2004), p. 71.

this difficulty was resolved when al-Singkel proposed the separation of politics and governance from religion, thus absolving a female ruler from performing the rituals expected of a Muslim leader, such as leading men in congregational prayers in mosques on Fridays.[71] Many scholars expressed the opinion that because of the intervention and support from these two ulama, a female successor was enthroned.[72]

Little information is available on the religious debates that seemed to have put the politics of the kingdom in such a state of indecisiveness. Jacob Compostel, the VOC oppercoopman in Aceh at that time, made no mention of any religious debate, and those scholars who mentioned the role these ulama had played in the presumed debate did not offer any evidence. However, it is not surprising that the issue of whether a female was allowed to rule would attract controversy in a Muslim polity, such as Aceh. Although not much information is available to confirm that such a debate took place, it is safe to conclude that without the concurrence of one of the leading ulama of that day, namely al-Raniri, the first sultanah could not have been enthroned. However, it is difficult to agree with Hadi when he claims "an orthodox (ulama) like al-Raniri should have approved a legal ruling allowing for a queen to take the throne reveals an unexpected tolerance of female rule within religious circles".[73] No such legal ruling or fatwa allowing a female to rule a Muslim polity was mentioned in al-Raniri's works. As Hadi himself pointed out, nowhere in the *Bustan* does al-Raniri seek to explain why a female ruler was allowed to rule in the first place. Nothing is said of whether her sex qualified or disqualified Safiatuddin from being a legitimate successor. Indeed, the *Bustan* merely states that her rule was accepted and justified because she had the qualities of a good ruler, that is, she was just, generous, loving, caring and pious, and exhorted her subjects to do good.[74] The possession of these virtues determined rightful

---

[71] Sufi, "Sultanah Safiatuddin Syah", p. 44.
[72] Sufi, "Sultanah Safiatuddin Syah", p. 43; Cheah, "Power behind the Throne", p. 11; Hadi, *Islam and State in Sumatra*, pp. 83–5. As mentioned earlier, Ali Hasjmy claimed that because the ulama, headed by al-Raniri, deemed that a female could rule in Islam, she was enthroned.
[73] Hadi, *Islam and State in Sumatra*, p. 83.
[74] Iskandar, ed., *Bustan us-Salatin*, p. 73.

rulers regardless of their sex, and the *Bustan* describes good male rulers in much the same way.

In contrast to Sufi's assertion that Safiatuddin was accepted as the temporal ruler of the kingdom only after the separation of politics and religion, Safiatuddin assumed the title of *khalifah* just as her male predecessors did. Although this will be discussed in greater detail in Chapter 5, it is important to highlight here that Islam was the basis of these female rulers' legitimacy and authority and, in continuing the practice of earlier Acehnese kings, there was no separation of politics and religion under the women monarchs. Indeed, in her letters to foreign powers, such as the Dutch, Sultanah Safiatuddin emphasised that she was chosen by God, and her role was to uphold Allah's laws. The issue of whether females could be an imam or wali was essentially religious in nature with little bearing on the issue of political succession. Furthermore, the *Adat Aceh*, an indigenous text covering rules and regulations for kings in the seventeenth century, states that the religious duties of an imam and a wali were not actually carried out even by a male monarch, but by the *kadhi* or religious judge, thus these so-called objections are irrelevant.

Regarding Hadi's argument about al-Singkel's role and his works[75] supporting Safiatuddin's succession, it must be noted that the *Mir'at al-Tullab* (a book on canon law), was written after he returned to Aceh in 1661.[76] While his role and work would be important in the perpetuation of female rule to enthrone the next three queens, as his *Mir'at al-Tullab*—completed in 1663—left open the possibility of women being in leadership positions, for example, as judges, it could neither be used nor should it be confused to justify the first sultanah's accession in 1641. It may be probable, based on Sufi's account that al-Singkel was one of those ulama who supported her accession to the throne in 1641, even before his appointment as the Sheikh al-Islam, and before he was commissioned to write the *Mir'at al-Tullab*. Whether he was the key to the installation of the first sultanah is still a matter of debate as he was fairly young, about 26 years old, in 1641. Furthermore, he only went to the Middle East to further his studies in 1642, which might have affected his stature as an

---

[75] Abd al-Rauf al-Singkel wrote about 22 works ranging from law, Qu'ranic exegesis, theology and mysticism: Hadi, *Islam and State in Sumatra*, pp. 85-6.
[76] Ibid., p. 85.

experienced ulama compared to the older and more authoritative al-Raniri, who held the position of Sheikh al-Islam in 1641.

Acehnese Perceptions of Power and Rulers—Islam as the Basis of Legitimacy

The question here is why the ulama accepted these queens? It is important at this juncture to draw on pre-modern sixteenth- and seventeenth-century Malay/Islamic political treatises that lay out the theories of kingship. In the context of Muslim Southeast Asia, the religious scholars in Aceh might well have referred to these contemporary religious and other writings that touched on the issue of female participation in politics and governance.

As mentioned earlier, the *Kanun Syarak Kerajaan Aceh* does not consider being male a prerequisite to becoming a ruler. The *Taj us-Salatin*, a political treatise written in Aceh in 1603 by al-Jauhari,[77] views female rule as legal in the absence of a male heir. One could argue that this treatise was decades ahead of its time and a reflection of the local religious scholars' attitude towards leadership and women in general. In Chapter Five of the *Taj us-Salatin*, under the heading of *kerajaan* (a state of having a king) and the *hukumat* (laws) regarding the sultan, the writer stated, albeit reluctantly,[78] that a female could succeed a male king but only in the event of no male heir in the royal family and to prevent a *darurat* (crisis) in the country.[79] Although he placed caveats on female leadership, the very discussion of the legality of female leadership puts this indigenous scholar's thesis in sharp contrast with the views held by more mainstream Islamic scholars of the time. Islamic doctrines formulated in the Middle East implied that a leader should necessarily be male: Islamic scholar, al-Ghazali, cited manliness, good horsemanship and skills

---

[77] Khalid M. Hussain, ed., *Taj us-Salatin* (Kuala Lumpur: Dewan Bahasa dan Pustaka, 1992), p. xiv.

[78] I suggest that al-Jauhari reluctantly agreed to female rule because, in his explication of the ten prerequisites to good leadership, he advised kings to spend less time with women because according to him, they lacked good deeds. He also stated that a king, by right, should be a male because a king is also an imam and a woman can never be an imam: Hussain, ed., *Taj us-Salatin*, p. 60.

[79] Hussain, ed., *Taj us-Salatin*, p. 60.

in bearing arms as necessary qualities a ruler should possess.[80] Following the tradition set by scholar al-Mawardi, he was severe towards women, for, according to him, they should be barred from holding even subordinate positions, such as those of a vizier, minister or judge. In contrast, the *Taj us-Salatin*'s explication of female leadership theories had, unconsciously or inadvertently perhaps, taken on a distinctly local interpretation of Islamic doctrine to explain and reflect a local political reality, that is, the existence of female rulers in the archipelago well before the issue of female succession arose in Aceh.

The *Sulalat-us-Salatin*, commonly known as *Sejarah Melayu* and believed to have been written in 1612, does not seem to object to either female rule or the involvement of powerful aristocratic women behind the throne during the Melakan sultanate; in some instances it even judges their influence as positive.[81] Tun Sri Lanang informed his readers that a woman, Sikadar Syah, ruled the kingdom of Bentan, and he described in great detail the greatness and prosperity of Bentan under her rule. For example, she bestowed upon Sang Sapurba and Sang Nila Utama, emissaries from Palembang, two crowns so decorated with precious stones that one could not even glimpse the gold underneath.[82]

As mentioned earlier, the *Taj* places two caveats to female succession. It appears that the first condition—absence of a suitable male heir—fitted Aceh's situation in 1641. The second was to avoid darurat: Hadi contended "the emergence of the first queen should be seen in the context of a political crisis that came to represent a serious threat to the social order, a circumstance that was used to justify her rule".[83] The unexpected death of Iskandar Thani, leaving Aceh with no apparent male heir, constituted a crisis in succession. The ensuing panic, coupled with the uncertain external situation, needed a speedy solution. It does appear at that juncture a female ruler was preferable to anarchy. The ulama in Aceh could have

---

[80] Ann K.S. Lambton, *State and Government in Medieval Islam: An Introduction to the Study of Islamic Political Theory: The Jurists* (Oxford: Oxford University Press, 1981), p. 121.
[81] Cheah Boon Kheng, ed., *Sejarah Melayu. The Malay Annals* (Kuala Lumpur: Malaysian Branch of the Royal Asiatic Society, 1998), pp. 10–20.
[82] Ibid., p. 25.
[83] Hadi, *Islam and State in Sumatra*, pp. 81–2.

used the *Taj* to justify their choice; however, it appears that the elite in Aceh did not see the need to justify her rule with regards to her sex. That the *Bustan* mentions the sultanah was enthroned on the very day of the previous ruler's death demonstrated that her succession was not at all problematic.[84] Sultanah Safiatuddin's succession, deemed smooth in the *Bustan*, probably reflects the concept/belief that female rule could be accepted even under less exceptional critical situations. Hadi showed very convincingly that al-Singkel had no objections to women taking the mantle of power *regardless*, whether out of necessity or in crisis, and al-Singkel even saw female rule as nothing exceptional or strange but as a "normal phenomenon".[85] This explains why three more female sovereigns ascended the throne up to 1699.

I venture that this non-gendered approach suggests a localised and contextual interpretation of Islamic leadership where a good leader must be Muslim and display exemplary behaviour but need not be male. This also reflects a local, non-gendered, pre-modern conception of rule and power, which will be illustrated in the next section. It demonstrates a respect for *daulat* (sovereignty or authority of a ruler: when uttered by the sultanah's subjects, it meant acceptance of her sovereignty or command), regardless of the sex of the person in whom it was manifested. The silence on the question of female rule reflects a normal and valid acceptance of the varied potentialities of women, instead of the more modern emphasis on masculinity and the concomitant unease with a woman who is not subordinate to a man. The fact that there is no evidence of religious debates delaying the sultanah's succession suggests that the question of whether a woman ruler was acceptable in Islam was not one asked by the elites of Aceh in 1641.

Acehnese Conceptions of Kingship/Queenship—Adat as the Basis of Legitimacy

More queens ruled in earlier times when conceptions of power and authority were not defined in terms of sex. Dean Miller argued that early

---

[84] Iskandar, ed., *Bustan us-Salatin*, p. 58.
[85] Hadi, *Islam and State in Sumatra*, p. 85.

European and Byzantine concepts of the ruler were of a hermaphroditic being, uniting masculine and feminine principles and implied that the concentration on masculinity was a modern phenomenon. In ancient and pre-colonial Africa, women held power in the phenomenon of *queen mother*. Early Islam gave women a much more prominent position compared to the latter years when religion became institutionalised and bureaucratised by male elites. Most of the writing favourable towards women's contributions in public affairs belongs to the earlier period of Islam; that is, from the eighth to the ninth centuries. This is when Islamic societies generally appear to have allowed women a great deal of prominence and in the arena of politics in particular. Some examples of the classical religious histories that recorded women's involvement in historical events are works by Ibn Saad, Shaikh Ibn Hajar and Abi Ja'afar Mohammed Ibn Jarir, better known as Tabari. During the latter period, especially from the seventeenth century, women's involvement in politics was viewed derisively, and women were seen as a factor contributing to the decline of the Ottoman and other Islamic dynasties, such as the Safavids and Mughals.[86] In Southeast Asia, ancient and pre-colonial concepts of power and authority were defined in terms of dualities of male/female with implications of fertility and complementariness.[87] According to traditional Malay ideas of political leadership as found in indigenous chronicles and *hikayat* (folklore), the ruler, or raja, had a central role as the state or government was constructed around his person. A country and people without its raja would be one that was in a state of disorder and loss. So central was his role that customs, ceremonies and laws of the land were said to be in his hands.[88] Despite this central role, the raja was not directly involved in ruling the kingdom. Like the ruler portrayed in the *Hikayat Pahang*, he was valued more for his manners than his practical skills.[89] The mark of a true king lay in his behaviour: an

---

[86] Mernissi, *Women's Rebellion*, pp. 96–8.
[87] Leonard Y. Andaya, "The Stranger-King Complex in Bugis-Makassar Society", paper presented at the Stranger-Kings in Southeast Asia and Elsewhere Workshop, Jakarta, Indonesia, 5–7 June 2006, p. 1.
[88] Anthony Crothers Milner, "The Malay Raja: A Study of Malay Political Culture in East Sumatra and the Malay Peninsula in the Early Nineteenth Century", PhD thesis, Cornell University, 1977, p. 196.
[89] Ibid., p. 198.

exemplary raja should exhibit *batik budi bahasanya* (excellent manners) and speak in a *manis* (graceful/sweet), *lemah lembut* (gentle and polite) way. One of the most important duties of a raja was to bestow titles, gifts and honours to his subjects according to their rank.[90] A raja should behave with *patut* (propriety) and if he did not, he would be considered *tiada adil* (unjust). Good manners and the ability to treat his subjects with appropriate formality were the raja's most valuable attributes. Manliness and prowess did not seem to factor at all in Malay conceptions of successful leadership: indeed, from the perspective of adat, neither did the leader's sex. A female could be as well suited to being an exemplary raja as a male.

According to Reid, "Austronesian societies ... which include Polynesia and Madagascar as well as Indonesia and the Philippines have been more inclined than perhaps any other major population group to place highborn women on the throne."[91] Indeed, the elites of Aceh needed only to look back in history to consent to the succession of a female ruler. Prior to the foundation of the Acehnese kingdom, in northern Sumatra female rulers appear not only to have already existed, but were highly honoured and commemorated. A pair of gravestones, one written in old Javanese and one in Arabic characters, found in the village of Minye Tujoh in Aceh, were inscribed with the dates of death 781 or 791 AH (1380 or 1390 AD) respectively.[92] According to Ibrahim Alfian,[93] the stones mark the grave of a Queen Nur Ilah, with the appellation "Queen of the Faith ... who has rights on Kadah [Kedah] and Pase [Pasai]."[94] In what is now the district of North Aceh, another marble gravestone with exquisite Arabic calligraphy and Qur'anic verses was also found. The Arabic translates it as "this is the grave of a brilliant holy woman, a queen respected by all ... Nahrasiyah ... who died on 17 Zulhijah 823 (1428)".[95] Although only male sultans had ruled the

---

[90] Ibid., p. 196.
[91] Reid, "Female Roles in Pre-Colonial Southeast Asia", p. 639.
[92] W.F. Stutterheim, "A Malay Sha'ir in Old-Sumatran Characters of 1380 A.D.", *Acta Orientalia* 14 (1936): 276–7.
[93] Ibrahim Alfian, "Ratu Nur-Ilah", in *Wanita Utama Nusantara*, ed. Sofyan, p. 2.
[94] Translated from old Javanese by C. Hooykaas, quoted in Alfian, "Ratu Nur-Ilah", p. 3.
[95] Alfian, "Ratu Nahrasiyah", in *Wanita Utama Nusantara*, ed. Sofyan, p. 16.

kingdom of Aceh since its founding, Aceh appears to have continued the example of powerful women rulers found in the older Muslim kingdom of Pasai and other Muslim polities, such as Patani, Sukadana, Jambi and Solor.[96] It is beyond the scope of this book to undertake a comparative study of these queens, however the preponderance of these female rulers shows that being male was not necessarily a primary criterion for succession.

Many scholars have drawn attention to the prominence of women at the Acehnese court as one explanation for why female leadership was accepted.[97] Although not necessarily holding the highest positions in the kingdom, they were nevertheless powerful in their own right. Said argued that female rule was not an aberration in Aceh, as the kingdom had a female *laksamana* (admiral of the navy), and historically Acehnese women took up positions of power.[98] Contemporary European travellers visiting the royal courts of the Acehnese sultans reported that palace women served as emissaries, advisors and guards. John Davis, who visited Aceh in 1599, claimed that Sultan Ala al-Din Riayat Shah al-Mukammil's (r. 1589–1604) "chiefest counsellers" were women.[99] Al-Mukammil also had a woman as laksamana as "hee will trust no men".[100] Even Iskandar Muda relied on female guards for his protection.[101]

Conclusion—Why Female Rule in 1641?

Reid argued that the commercially oriented aristocrats, who made every effort to maintain political control in the interests of mercantilism, prompted the rise of female rule in the age of commerce.[102] Given the common role

---

[96] Cheah, "Power behind the Throne", pp. 1–2. This invites further research.
[97] Such as Veth, Reid, Cheah and Said.
[98] Said, *Aceh Sepanjang Abad*, p. 379. Only Pamenan argued that female leadership was a strange phenomenon in Aceh: Pamenan, *Rentjong Aceh di Tangan Wanita*, pp. 34–5.
[99] A.H. Markham, ed., *The Voyages and Works of John Davis the Navigator* (London: The Hakluyt Society, 1880), p. 150.
[100] Ibid., p. 150.
[101] Augustine de Beaulieu, "The Expedition of Commodore Beaulieu to the East Indies", in *Navigantium atque Itinerarium Bibliotheca. Or a Complete Collection of Voyages*, trans. M. Thevenot, ed. John Harris (London: printed for T. Woodward, et al., revised ed., 1744), p. 744.
[102] Reid, "Female Roles in Pre-Colonial Southeast Asia", p. 641; Hadi, *Islam and State in Sumatra*, p. 81.

of Southeast Asian women as household managers, and as petty traders and money changers in the market place, a woman ruler would be more appealing as women were commonly perceived as having a tighter grip on the purse-strings and being shrewd in matters of business. In Aceh's case, Reid ventured that the orang kaya's aversion to absolutism was the reason they chose a female ruler. Iskandar Muda "had been a particularly frightening example of the dangers of absolutism, seeking to monopolize trade with the English and the Dutch while killing, terrorizing and dispossessing his own orangkaya".[103] These were indeed plausible reasons for choosing a female candidate. Nevertheless, this does not explain why the orang kaya chose a female candidate in 1641. If commercial reasons prompted the orang kaya to choose a female candidate, this could have been done perhaps decades earlier. If it was an aversion to absolutism, then the orang kaya should have appointed a female candidate in 1604 after the death of the tyrannical al-Mukammil. Furthermore, the orang kaya would have had no way of knowing beforehand whether the chosen candidate would serve their ends. As mentioned earlier, the orang kaya was thought to have chosen al-Mukammil because he was very old, but once in power he decimated their ranks. I suggest that the orang kaya who put a female on the throne did not choose her because she was a woman. Rather, they chose Safiatuddin Syah, who happened to be a woman. Nevertheless, by the unprecedented action of accepting a female candidate, the orang kaya were, in a sense, taking a gamble.

No one reason really explains the beginning of female rule in Aceh; rather the succession of the first woman ruler was the result of a unique confluence of events and personalities. It was largely internally motivated—a function of circumstances facing the kingdom at the time. A response to uncertain external circumstances in the form of increasing European incursions would logically necessitate the choice of a strong king, such as Iskandar Muda. As in the case of Safiatuddin, most women became rulers because of special circumstances, such as the death of a husband or father, rather than by laws or customs of succession. Indeed, laws or customs made by men, and male opposition motivated by religion or misogyny, were the main obstacles and only exceptional

---

[103] Reid, "Female Roles in Pre-Colonial Southeast Asia", p. 641.

queens survived. Some of these exceptional queens survived despite male opposition motivated by religion or misogyny. Some women had to devise elaborate processes of legitimation, and imperial and coronation rituals, and a few even had to declare a new dynasty. A striking example comes from Africa, where Queen Njinga of Ndongo-Matamba (r. 1624–63) overcame the illegitimacy of her sex by trying to become a man. To meet her rivals' contentions that she could not rule as a woman, Njinga acted like a man. She had many dependent husbands who became her concubines, and she required that they dress in women's clothes and sleep among her maids-in-waiting. She engaged in virile pursuits by personally leading her troops to battle.[104] Chinese sources condemned the imperial ambitions of women as unnatural calamities. Traditional Chinese historians condemned Empress Wu Zetian (r. 686–93) as an anomaly, a gender reversal and a violation of nature comparable to having hens instead of roosters crowing at dawn.[105] In Aceh, the sudden death of her predecessor husband and the absence of any male heir propelled Safiatuddin to power, and Islam as interpreted by the elite and adat, which allowed women to assume positions of power, enabled the first female ruler to succeed.

The accession of the first female ruler set a new tradition in the succession history of the Acehnese kingdom as three more female rulers followed. The option to place the first female on the throne was a deliberate albeit a cautious one, dictated by circumstances. This was no mere accident of history and, as I will show in later chapters, the success of the first sultanah paved the way for her three successors. Thereafter, the idea of a woman ruling this Muslim kingdom became widely acceptable. Little information is available on these three other rulers, but the fact that indigenous chronicles and VOC sources agree that all three were replaced after they died from natural causes and not because they were killed or deposed (except for the last queen) shows that the course of succession over these six decades of female rule was peaceful. This was in contrast to the earlier period of violent and unstable historical

---

[104] John K. Thornton, "Legitimacy and Political Power: Queen Njinga, 1624–1663", *Journal of African History* 32, 1 (1991): 38-9.
[105] Jennifer W. Jay, "Imagining Matriarchy: 'Kingdoms of Women' in Tang China", *Journal of the American Oriental Society* 116, 2 (1996): 228.

successions in the 1570s and 1580s. The only mention of a problematic succession in 1688, quickly resolved in favour of female rule, comes from William Dampier, who related that "all the orangkaya were not for the election; many of them were for choosing a king".[106] This episode however, illustrates that the option of female successors was not the dictate of a homogenous group of orang kaya but a contested one. Female rule was not simply a device of the male elite who sought to weaken royal power in order to promote and perpetuate their own interests.

In conclusion, although Aceh had no fixed rules or laws of succession in the sixteenth and seventeenth centuries, there were some identifiable preconditions for qualification before a candidate was accepted as a legitimate successor to the throne. These prerequisites were that the candidates had royal lineage as well as the consent and support of at least the majority of the orang kaya and ulama. As ruler of a Muslim kingdom, the ruler also had to be a Muslim. These prerequisites took precedence over the practice of designation by the reigning ruler: in Iskandar Thani's case an appointed heir could not survive without the consent and support of the elite. The reasons for consent and support were, however, changeable, determined by the attitudes and perceptions of the elites and the political and religious milieu of the time. During the time of the first female succession in 1641, the sex of the candidate seems not to have factored too heavily for the elites. Other considerations, such as being a Muslim with an impeccable lineage, took precedence as Safiatuddin was an adult closest in consanguinity to her predecessors, considering the lack of a suitable royal male heir. In Aceh, unlike France, there was no Salic law forbidding the succession of a female ruler. Furthermore, unlike Queen Mary Tudor and Queen Elizabeth in England, Sultanah Safiatuddin did not have a John Knox to contend with. In his treatise, *The First Blast of the Trumpet*, Knox stated that a woman had no natural right to rule any realm, even when the royal line of succession included no male heir.[107] On the contrary, the ulama in Aceh at that time

---

[106] William Dampier, *Voyages and Discoveries*, Intro. and Notes by Clennell Wilkinson, ed. N.M. Penzer (London: Argonaut Press, 1931), p. 100.

[107] *The First Blast of the Trumpet* was published in 1558. John Knox and Robert M. Healey, "Waiting for Deborah: John Knox and Four Ruling Queens", *Sixteenth Century Journal* 25, 2 (1994): 376.

interpreted Islamic law in line with local adat, which was favourable to women. Thus, the queens did not have to be like a Njinga of Ndongo-Matamba to find acceptance. The first female succession in Aceh neither contradicted adat laws nor Islamic tenets.[108]

Another condition or tradition of succession that can be identified was the preference for a royal native-born rather than a royal foreign-born. The orang kaya of Aceh clearly preferred Safiatuddin Syah, of the Dar al-Kamal and Mahkuta Alam dynasty, to the son of any other foreign royal house. The murder of the foreign-born sultans from Perak and Inderapura attest to this. So does the pact the elites made in Aceh in 1641, never to be ruled by a foreign-born sultan again.[109]

Still, it must be borne in mind that political and religious mind sets do shift, and the formation of new guards among the elites changed the criteria for succession, such as in 1699, as detailed in Chapter 7. Female involvement in politics has been one of the most controversial and highly debated issues in the Muslim world. While in some instances, female participation has been applauded and praised, in other cases it has been condemned as un-Islamic. Historians of different periods look to their own selection of Islamic memory where female participation existed, highlighting either the positive or the negative impacts of female involvement and using this "evidence" as justification for or against female participation in politics.[110] Political conservatism in mainstream Islam, however, does not view women's political participation favourably. Conservatism, usually interpreted only by men, sees a woman's claim to political power as an aggressive violation of the rules of the game. As soon as a woman comes to the throne, a group of men whose power she challenges would oppose her in the name of sharia, thus denying her spiritual validation.

In 1641, the majority of the orang kaya accepted Sultanah Safiatuddin as their rightful ruler. Once on the throne, whether she remained the ruler of Aceh Dar al-Salam depended on her own actions. The qualities

---

[108] This is discussed further in Chapter 5.
[109] However, this pact lasted until 1699: after Sultanah Kamalat Syah was deposed, an Arab succeeded her, probably foreign-born. Even then, this Arab dynasty did not last long with most of the rulers deposed, see Chapter 5.
[110] Hambly, *Women in the Medieval Islamic World*, p. 9.

and attributes of a good ruler, identified in the *Taj*, the *Bustan* and the *Kanun*, are being just, morally upright and possessing the willingness to uphold Islamic law. Was she able to achieve this or would she need to gain acceptance only after demonstrating that she had enough prowess, as most other powerful traditional kings did? Practically, perhaps the most important "condition" that guaranteed a ruler's acceptance and survivability was striking the right balance between meeting the needs and interests of the ruler, the elites and, ultimately, the kingdom. Were Sultanah Safiatuddin Syah and her successors able to achieve this equilibrium? How these women ruled, the factors that facilitated their rule and the obstacles they faced will be the focus of the following chapters.

chapter

2   Sultanah Safiatuddin's Early Years: Keeping Afloat

The analysis of the succession in Aceh Dar al-Salam in Chapter 1 shows that the majority of the orang kaya's consent was needed to install the first female ruler on the throne. That she remained on the throne for the length of time very much depended on the personality and style of leadership of the ruler herself.

    A good start was crucial. It enabled her to tackle the vital matter of securing her position on the throne and getting the support—if not the compliance—of her orang kaya, especially those who initially opposed the accession if, indeed, the alleged debate among the orang kaya did take place. Little is known about who these orang kaya were, the functions they undertook and the power they wielded at the Acehnese court, especially in the sixteenth century. There is more information about these elites in the seventeenth century, when VOC officials wrote about them, especially when these court officials had a hand in the company's affairs. The source material for the events narrated in this chapter comes from the VOC envoys' descriptions of court politics, each of whom resided in Aceh for months on company business. Contrary to popular belief, the narrative in this chapter, dubbed the "jewel affair", shows that the orang kaya were not a homogeneous group. While fractious nobility could work in the sultanah's favour, she had the daunting task of managing and balancing the various factions to keep on top. The jewel affair also illustrates how she dealt with the VOC envoys and provides insights into the workings of the Acehnese court and the sultanah's leadership style. The next section deals with the queen's early days, and how she announced her accession to the throne.

Dealing with Sultan Iskandar Thani's Legacy

Iskandar Thani's sudden death on 15 February 1641 brought confusion to the court. Iskandar Thani ruled for fewer than five years, and historians saw this short interlude in Aceh's history as uneventful.[1] Others viewed him as a pious and mild ruler; however, contemporary records suggest otherwise. Although Iskandar Thani's succession was never contested, as Iskandar Muda chose him as his heir before his death and the orang kaya seemed to have consented to this appointment, his short reign had many opponents. Sultanah Safiatuddin inherited a more precarious legacy than is commonly supposed.

In August 1637, eight months after Iskandar Thani's succession to the throne, there was an attempt to remove him by poisoning. The *Bustan* relates that several people conspired with the official food-taster to poison his food, but, owing to the will of Allah, when his food did not taste as it usually did, he immediately stopped eating.[2] The *Bustan* does not reveal more about this plot or the conspirators, merely stating that Iskandar Thani investigated and duly punished the guilty. The *Bustan* does mention, however, that the *Kadhi Maliku'l Adil* (religious judge) and the prime minister agreed with this punishment.

Another contemporary record written by Peter Mundy, an English traveller who arrived in Aceh in February 1638, mentions an act of treason against the king of Aceh, in all probability referring to the same event. He related that about three to four months prior to his visit:

> [W]ee understood of about four hundred persons putt to death by this king some three or four monthes since with sundry sorts off exquisite torments, *viz.* divers cutt in peeces, others sawne in two ... some hung on iron hookes by the heeles, stretched wide abroad and molten lead powred into the fundaments of the men and privities of the weomen to cause them to conffesse.[3]

Mundy revealed that this plot was hatched by "his wives sister (the old King's daughters both) in beehalffe of her sonne, intending by poison to

---

[1] Andaya, "A Very-Good Natured but Awe-Inspiring Government", p. 65.
[2] Iskandar, ed., *Bustan us-Salatin*, p. 46.
[3] Mundy, *The Travels of Peter Mundy*, p. 330.

take this King away, thatt her said sonne mightt reigne".[4] Her plot was discovered and she was the first to taste his fury, though others who had conspired or were suspected of this treason were also punished.

Iskandar Thani had other enemies, namely the followers of the previous Sheikh al-Islam, Shamsuddin al-Sumatrani. Iskandar Muda had appointed Shamsuddin al-Sumatrani as the leading religious scholar of the kingdom, thereby promoting the teachings of a more mystical, Sufistic brand of Islam, the *Wujudiyyah wihdatul wujud*.[5] Iskandar Thani, in contrast, supported the more orthodox ulama Nuruddin al-Raniri from Gujarat. He appointed him as the Sheikh al-Islam in 1637.[6] These two groups violently clashed during Iskandar Thani's reign. Upon the death of al-Sumatrani in 1630 and with Iskandar Thani's blessings, al-Raniri led a hunt against the *wihdatul wujud* faction and issued a fatwa denouncing them as heretics. This enabled al-Raniri to kill those who refused to renounce their teachings and burn their writings. According to Ahmad Daudy, the *wihdatul wujud* group, followers of Hamzah Fansuri and Shams al-Din, were also involved in a plot to seize power from Iskandar Thani. Thus, the sultan allowed the most brutal killings of those in the *Wujudiyyah* faction to take place and at the same time eliminated this political opposition.[7]

It appears that at the time of Sultanah Safiatuddin's accession, al-Sumatrani's group had been seriously weakened by the executions. It also appears that those who might oppose her succession, or a rival claimant in the person of her nephew (if Mundy's account is accurate), would not be strong enough, as Iskandar Thani had thinned their ranks. Thus, at the beginning of her reign it is safe to venture that this majority group of the important elites in power, both from the orang kaya, that is

---

[4] Ibid.
[5] The brand of *wujuddiyyah* embraced by Shams al-Din and Hamzah Fansuri was *wihdatul wujud*, that is, the belief that the universe is part of God, like foam on the waves. This is in opposition to the brand of *wujuddiyah* al-Raniri followed, that is, *wihdatusshuhud*, the belief that the universe is not part of God but exists as a reflection or witness to the existence of God. Zainuddin, *Tarich Atjeh*, p. 105.
[6] Lombard in Arifin, *Kerajaan Aceh*, pp. 218-9. This rise of orthodoxy was also prevalent in India at that time under Sultan Aurangzeb.
[7] Ahmad Daudy, *Allah dan Manusia dalam Konsepsi Syeikh Nurudin al-Raniri* [God and Man in Sheikh Nurudin al-Raniri's Conception] (Jakarta: C.V. Rajawali, 1983), pp. 41-2.

the prime minister and the ulama, and al-Raniri supported her candidacy. How her late husband's other opponents viewed her accession is not clear. As noted in the previous chapter, it is likely they supported her simply because there was no suitable male heir. However, she had to contend with fractious elites.

Thus, it is fitting that one of Sultanah Safiatuddin's first accomplishments was to secure the support of the dominant orang kaya. Her first responsibility was to ensure the previous ruler had a proper burial, and she organised one of the grandest funerals the kingdom had ever witnessed. The successful execution of this responsibility was significant too, in the sense that it announced to her subjects her inauguration as the first female ruler of Aceh.

Fig. 1 A Dutch engraver's image of Iskandar Thani's funeral in 1641 (used with permission from Anthony Reid).

A Truly Royal and Magnificent Funeral Procession[8]

Sultanah Safiatuddin performed her first responsibility with aplomb. Nicolaus de Graaff wrote:

> [T]he funeral procession was executed in such royal magnificence; with a huge following of princes, the elites, about two hundred and sixty elephants, some were bedecked with expensive golden silk cloth whose tusks were suffused with gold and silver, others with palanquin decorated with costly draperies and multi-coloured flags embroidered in gold and silver threads. Rhinoceros and Persian horses, expensively clothed, strutted proudly with gold and silver bridles. Also, a retinue of the king's women formed part of the funeral procession. The king's coffin was made of *suassa* [a gold-copper alloy] finely draped with gold cloth. At the end of the procession, the king's body was laid to rest beside his predecessors in a royal mausoleum behind the palace. For a hundred days more his women brought tobacco, food and drinks here as if he was still alive. As soon as the king's body was buried, two silver canons were fired, its sound reverberating the whole night long interspersed with shouts of "God Save the new Queen" (*God Bewaar de nieuwe Koningin*). Thereafter, all was calm and in peace.[9]

The *Bustan us-Salatin* goes into greater detail about this magnificent funeral. It vividly describes the grandeur of the ceremony and the richness of the bejewelled tomb the sultanah ordered to be specially made in memory of her husband, who loved jewels. She instructed her stone craftsman to make a headstone, the like of which had never been made for previous kings.[10] The funeral procession started from the palace, reached the main mosque, Masjid Baitu'r-Rahman, and on the orders of the sultanah, camped round its precincts. That night, all the princes, court officials and palace guards kept a vigil over the tombstone. Tents were erected and the entourage occupied themselves with mock fights, games and plays. Interestingly, the *Bustan* relates that many communities took part in these activities. The

---

[8] Warnsinck, ed., *Reisen van Nicolaus de Graaff*, pp. 13-4.
[9] Warnsinck, ed., *Reisen van Nicolaus de Graaff*, pp. 13-4; Lombard in Arifin, *Kerajaan Aceh*, pp. 203-4.
[10] The description of the funeral ceremony is summarised and translated from Iskandar, ed., *Bustan us-Salatin*, pp. 60-73.

Javanese had spear fights and held *wayang* (masked plays). The Chinese also staged their own *wayang* using masks and a man-made dragon. Even the Indian Klings held their own theatre. Much to the delight of the people, these festivities went on all night. The next day Sultanah Safiatuddin mounted an elephant and ordered the procession to continue to the royal gravesite, Kandang Daru'd-Dunia. As this was the last leg of the ceremony, all along the way, the sultanah's officials distributed and scattered on the ground generous alms of gold, silver and gems. The *Bustan* relates that all those who obtained her alms became rich.

Of the 16 pages devoted to her reign, the *Bustan* has about 13 on this ceremony alone.[11] This ceremony was so well executed, so beautifully done and well planned that never before had such a ceremony been witnessed at other courts and other lands, above or below the winds.[12] The *Bustan* asserts that under the sultanah, Aceh truly lived by its name of *Serambi Mekah* (Veranda of Mecca), and her subjects confirmed this testimony.[13]

Not even Iskandar Muda's funeral, which was described by European travellers and in indigenous chronicles alike, was as grand as that staged by the sultanah. The ceremony had the dual purpose of informing the kingdom's subjects of the death of their king and announcing the accession of a new ruler—the sultanah. Safiatuddin proclaimed her inauguration with great effect and style, one that would remain etched in her subjects' memory. They would have certainly appreciated her generosity on this occasion, amply demonstrated by the scale of alms distribution for her people.

The Sultanah and Her Orang Kaya—First Dealings

Besides dealing with her own elites and her subjects, the young sultanah had to manage foreign ambassadors who arrived in her court. VOC officials were among these and she had to treat them with care, especially as the company had just conquered Melaka and was becoming a power to be reckoned with in the Straits. Her relations with company officials

---

[11] Iskandar, ed., *Bustan us-Salatin*, pp. 58–74, where the *Bustan* describes the start and end of her reign, but the funeral ceremony takes centre-stage from pp. 60–73.
[12] Ibid., p. 68.
[13] Ibid.

started on a good footing. Writing on the state of affairs after the first few months of the sultanah's rule, Jacob Compostel, the company's resident in Aceh, wrote that the kingdom continued in peace and prosperity under her temperate rule. Compostel reported on the favourable state of the company's fortune, as its profit of 13 months amounted to f.49445.1.6. Compostel also reported that the sultanah treated him well. Her problem, however, was that in pleasing this foreign elite, she incurred the displeasure of some of her own.

The Dutch reported that there were four principal orang kaya who formed the main council (referred to as the *rijxraaden* [state council members]) who advised the sultanah, and they had considerable influence at court. The Dutch described them as the *Lebai Kita Kali* (kali being the Acehnese variant of the Arabic *qadhi* or religious judge), the Maharaja Sri Maharaja, the laksamana and the Paduka Tuan. Compostel noted that the orang kaya Maharaja Sri Maharaja "had conceived a great distrust against the rising state of the Company" and suspected that the Lebai Kita Kali had conspired with Commissar Schouten and Compostel against the Acehnese crown.[14] According to Compostel, these rumours had been spread by a Portuguese renegade named Manuel Mangbangh. Nevertheless, suspicion had also arisen from the orchestration and promptings of the Maharaja himself. This caused the sultanah great consternation, and she ordered an enquiry. This investigation (not elaborated on by Compostel) found these rumours were unfounded. She took swift action against the alleged rumour-monger, Manuel Mangbangh, who was executed by having molten lead poured down his throat, despite the protests of the Maharaja. The Maharaja, although not punished, fell out of favour with the sultanah who, Compostel was happy to report, continued to favour the Dutch.[15]

The orang kaya were divided not only between the pro- and anti-Iskandar Thani factions mentioned above, but also between the pro- and anti-Dutch factions. Compostel wrote that the sultanah, the Lebai Kita Kali, the Maharaja Adonna Lilla and her eunuchs continued to favour the Dutch, especially the Kali, who showed them "exceptional affection".[16] The anti-Dutch faction consisted of the council member Maharaja Sri

---

[14] Chijs, *Dagh-Register*, 1641–42, p. 96.
[15] Ibid.
[16] Ibid., p. 123.

Maharaja and his follower the Panglima Dalam (in charge of palace security). The Manuel Mangbangh episode, however, illustrates that the sultanah took swift action to secure her rule by quelling rumours and then punishing anyone who might cause instability. The harsh punishment meted out to Manuel Mangbangh served as an example. Interestingly, the sultanah treated opposition from her orang kaya more circumspectly and certainly without the taint of harshness or cruelty that characterised earlier kings. When the Maharaja was disgraced, he was absent from court for a few months, but he was rehabilitated and returned to her favour, and he soon made peace with the Kali. This tactic of the young sultanah apparently worked as Compostel noted that thereafter, the Maharaja was "very friendly" towards him and "publicly showed" that he did not like people who wanted to disadvantage the Dutch![17]

Two months after the Mangbangh episode, Compostel reported that the situation in Aceh was still peaceful, but he noted that there were some hidden jealousies among the four rijxraaden. Compostel made an interesting observation that the sultanah, through her eunuchs, was secretly "feeding these jealousies".[18] He did not elaborate on what this meant but, as will be seen in later sections, her eunuchs became the sultanah's eyes and ears, and helped her manage her fractious elites. Her chief eunuch, Maharaja Adonna Lilla, acted as the sultanah's extended arm in places beyond the formal setting of the *balai* (audience hall) and confines of the court and palace, such as the orang kaya's homes and the merchants' and foreign company lodges. Maharaja Adonna Lilla was the queen's voice where she needed to get her message across directly to the party concerned. Another way she kept her orang kaya in balance was by her prudent dispensation of reward and punishment, as illustrated above, which would characterise her rule and was a key to her success as Aceh's first female ruler. In summarising the sultanah's rule as of November 1641, Compostel noted that her position was well established and that she ruled absolutely and with great authority.[19] Compostel wrote that this princess was worthier of her throne than earlier kings had been.[20]

---

[17] Ibid.
[18] Ibid.
[19] Ibid., p. 163.
[20] Ibid., p. 123.

The sultanah started her reign on a good footing. To a certain extent, her initial actions were a measure of her personal political sagacity and alluded to a shift in leadership style that contrasted with her male predecessors. It is important to note, however, that the peaceful conditions Compostel described were also a result of the orang kaya's willingness to maintain this status quo. This was especially so, considering the kingdom's vulnerability at that time owing to the recent violent internal divisions and the tilt in the regional balance of power in the VOC's favour.

Despite his praise for the sultanah, Compostel warned that there were many factions at the Acehnese court, and many orang kaya mistrusted the Dutch. He recommended to the governors in Melaka and Batavia that the continued residence of a distinguished person was necessary to preserve the company's alliance and prominence.[21] Indeed, the alliance between the VOC and the Acehnese was sorely tested in the jewel affair.

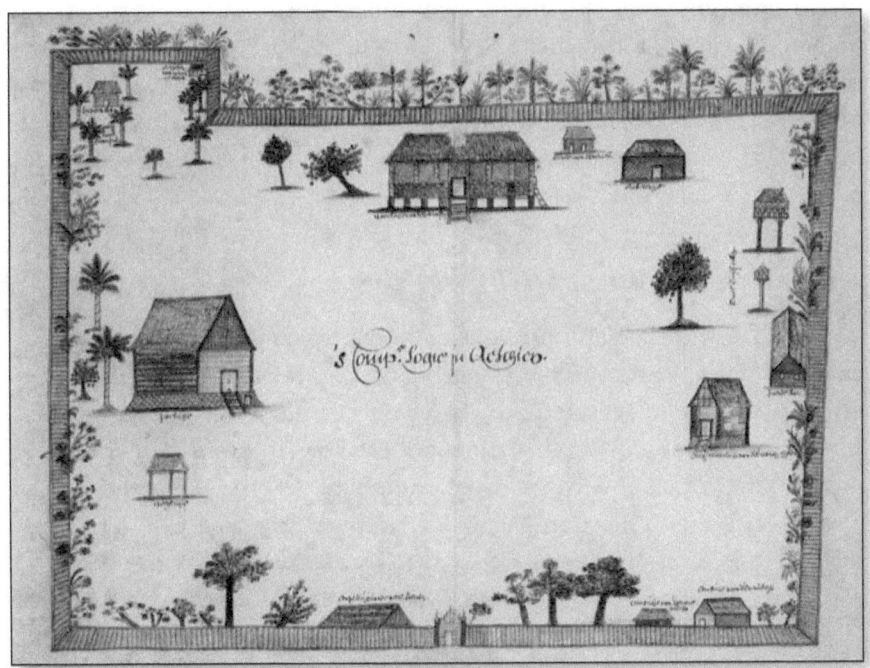

Fig. 2 Seventeenth-century drawing of the VOC factory at Aceh (used with permission from the Nationaal Archief).

---

[21] Ibid., p. 163.

The Jewel Affair: The Sultanah, Her Orang Kaya and the Dutch Foreign Envoys

The jewel affair refers to the VOC officials' attempt to pressure Sultanah Safiatuddin and her orang kaya to accept and pay for some very expensive jewels ordered by her predecessor. At first glance, this episode appears to be just one of the many commercial transactions engaged in by both parties. However, on closer examination it is significant because it helps to illuminate the nature of early Dutch-Aceh relations and the subtle and overt workings of the Acehnese court under the sultanah's reign. As it dragged on for almost four years, this affair tested the will and diplomacy of both parties. It shows that east-west encounters were still in a trial phase during which both powers needed to learn about each other to know when to compete and when to compromise. It shows that east-west encounters were not only about commercial and military contests at the macro level but were also about compromises between personalities and human relations at the micro level. Internally, this episode reveals the shaping of a leadership style that was hinted at in the first few months of her reign. In particular, the jewel affair shows how the sultanah used jewels in political culture and, thereby, highlights the contrasting leadership styles of the late sultan and the new sultanah.

Jewels and the Aura of Kingship

Associations with rare and precious materials, some in the form of regalia, are as important an aspect of kingship in Southeast Asia as they are in other parts of the world. "Crown Jewels" of gold, silver and precious stones are commonly used as symbols of royal magnificence meant to increase the status and charisma of the wearers.[22] The dress and regalia of kings could also have propagandistic significance, such as the *diadema* band of Alexander the Great, believed to be associated with the hero-god and conqueror of the East, Dionysus. This badge became a symbol of his victory and power at Gaugamela and his proclamation as "King of Asia"

---

[22] Bruce Lenman, "The Exiled Stuarts and the Precious Symbols of Sovereignty", *Eighteenth-Century Life* 25, 2 (2001): 185.

at Arbela.²³ During the reign of Suleyman the Magnificent (1520–66), his grand vizier, Ibrahim Pasha, ordered a spectacular golden helmet for the sultan, which Venetian goldsmiths produced in 1532. Although this helmet was foreign to the Ottoman imperial regalia and considered a non-Islamic royal status symbol, it was displayed as part of the parade accessories in ostentatious ceremonies with the aim of communicating Ottoman imperial claims to a European audience.²⁴

Besides being symbols of sovereignty and power, in Southeast Asia such jewels could take on *sakti* (magical) and divine powers.²⁵ Siamese kings regarded the magical *permata sembilan jenis* (nine-stone jewel) as part of their regalia.²⁶ The *Sejarah Melayu*, or *Sulalat us-Salatin*, mentions the importance of precious stones in legitimising the predecessors of all Malay rajas. Chapter Two of the *Sejarah Melayu* brings its readers to a hill named Si-Guntang Mahamiru in the land of Andalas, Palembang, where the first mythical Malay rajas appeared. On this hill lived two widows, Wan Empuk and Wan Malini, who worked on a vast and fertile rice field.²⁷ As the paddies were ripening, one night Wan Empuk and Wan Malini saw what looked like fire on a distant horizon. The next morning, they decided to investigate the source of the light, and, to their amazement, they saw their paddies turning into gold, the leaves turning into silver and the stems into copper. There they found three young and good-looking princes who had ascended from the universe below the sea. Clothed in royal dress and wearing crowns studded with gems, they were riding on white cows.²⁸ The awestruck widows deduced that they were the cause of their paddies turning into gold. When queried on their origin,

---

[23] E.A. Fredricksmeyer, "The Origins of Alexander's Royal Insignia", *Transactions and Proceedings of the American Philological Association* 127 (1997): 97, 107.

[24] Gulru Necipoglu, "Suleyman the Magnificent and the Representation of Power in the Context of Ottoman-Hapsburg-Papal Rivalry", *The Art Bulletin* 71, 3 (1989): 401.

[25] A *chakravartin* is considered to possess seven treasures, one of which is a magic jewel or *cintamani*. J. Gonda, *Ancient Indian Kingship from the Religious Point of View* (Leiden: E.J. Brill, 1969), p. 38.

[26] Annabel Teh Gallop, "Musings on a Piece of 'Wallpaper': Some Thoughts on Early Royal Letters from Aceh", paper presented at the International Workshop on Malay Manuscripts, Leiden University Library, 16-18 March 1988, pp. 12-3.

[27] Abdul Samad Ahmad, ed., *Sulalatus Salatin: Sejarah Melayu* (Kuala Lumpur: Dewan Bahasa dan Pustaka, 1984), p. 19.

[28] Ibid., p. 21.

the three princes related their story and introduced themselves as the great-great-grandsons of Iskandar Dzulkarnain. As proof, they pointed to their gem-studded crowns and clothing, and the magical transformation of the paddy fields.

In Aceh, gold, *suassa* (alloy of copper and gold), precious stones, horses and elephants are symbols of royal wealth and status. Sultan Iskandar Muda was an example of a king whose love for ornate and expensive jewels was not limited to the accoutrements of state power and authority. According to Annabel Teh Gallop, the sultan's immense wealth was strikingly conveyed not so much by his precious regalia—including the nine-stone jewel mentioned above[29]—but by everyday objects fashioned out of solid gold, suassa and silver encrusted with precious stones, such as water pipes, saddles and even his bathing scoop.[30] Iskandar Thani, his successor, inherited not only all the treasures and jewels but also his father-in-law's appreciation of their intrinsic beauty and their reflection of wealth and royal status.

The *Hikayat Aceh* depicts Iskandar Muda as the "King of Kings" in the Malay world.[31] He was seen as the representative of the caliph in the Malay world, the Eastern counterpart of the sultan of Rum (Turkey), the caliph in the Islamic West. In his letter to England's James I, Iskandar Muda presented himself as the "subduer" and "conqueror" of several "kingdoms, territories and sovereignties" of Tiku, Pariaman, Deli, among others, and Johor, with all the territories subjected to it.[32] Iskandar Muda and Iskandar Thani adopted many high-sounding titles, such as *Makhota Alam* (crown of the universe), *Perkasa Alam* (courage or warrior of the universe), *Khalifah Allah* and *Sajjidina as-Sultan* to reflect their universal kingly status.[33]

It is not in the least surprising that these men wishing to project charisma and prowess—kings who claimed the title of king of kings—displayed symbols of magnificence befitting their status to impress other lesser kings. Audience days and royal processions on festival days provided

---

[29] Teh Gallop, "Musings on a Piece of Wallpaper", pp. 12-3.
[30] Ibid., p. 12.
[31] Iskandar, ed., *De Hikajat Atjeh*, pp. 153, 167.
[32] Teh Gallop, "Musings on a Piece of Wallpaper", p. 13.
[33] These are local versions of the Persian title, *Shah-i-Alam* (Ruler of the World).

the perfect opportunity to display these magnificent precious and rare jewels to inspire awe in foreigners and subjects alike. On these important days, the sultans, bedecked with dazzling jewellery, truly resembled the glittering sun and moon with which they were so fond of associating themselves. Iskandar Thani described himself as "King of the whole world who, like God, is glittering like the sun at midday, whose attributes are like the full moon".[34]

For other monarchs who could not admire this visual display of power firsthand, especially European kings whom they sought to impress, they would apportion a substantial part of their letters to describing and enumerating their kingly possessions and treasures ranging from the palace, to gold mines, elephants and horses. Iskandar Muda and Iskandar Thani's letters to foreign potentates best illustrate how they represented themselves, and how they wished to be perceived by other powers.[35] Iskandar Thani drew attention to the gold deposits with which Aceh was blessed, the numerous mosques made of suassa, his throne made of fine gold encrusted with costly precious stones, and his numerous elephants and horses with their golden coverings set with precious stones.[36]

The Sultan Who Loved Jewels

The Dutch officials in Aceh reported that Iskandar Thani had a lust for jewels.[37] Peter Mundy, who had an audience with Iskandar Thani, observed that the sultan's clothes were something ordinary, following the fashion of the country, "but [he] was adorned with many jewells

---

[34] "Coninngh vande gantsche werrelt, die gelyck een Godt daerover is, glinsterende als the son op den middach, een Coningh, die zyn schynsel gelyck de volle maen geeft.", see Iskandar Thani's letter to Antonio van Diemen in Chijs, *Dagh-Register*, 1640-41, pp. 6-7.

[35] Letter from Sultan Iskandar Muda of Aceh to King James I, 1615; Teh Gallop, "Musings on a Piece of Wallpaper", pp. 12-3; Iskandar Thani's letter to Antonio van Diemen in Chijs, *Dagh-Register*, 1640-41, pp. 6-7. In contrast, Sultanah Safiatuddin's letters emphasised her moral attributes to increase her aura as ruler rather than her material treasures. See Chapter 5 of this book.

[36] NA, VOC 1131, Copie missive des Conincks van Atchin aen den Gouverneur General [Letter from Iskandar Thani to the Governor General], 1640, f. 1433.

[37] Chijs, *Dagh-Register*, 1640-41, p. 4.

off diamonds, etts. [and other] pretious stones".[38] Paulus Croocq was certainly impressed with Iskandar Thani's crown and clothing, which he described as dazzlingly encrusted with diamonds and some rare stones. Iskandar Thani's throne, he reported, was newly made and he estimated it to be worth 40 *bahar* (a Malay measurement of approximately 210–30 kg) of heavy gold, or 100,000 guilders![39] So, it is not surprising that the Dutch seized upon Iskandar Thani's fascination with precious stones and often brought all kinds of jewellery to entice him. They learnt that Iskandar Thani was even prepared to accept jewels instead of *reals* (Spanish silver coin) or cash from the Dutch in exchange for pepper and payment of tolls.[40] Interestingly, this sultan had a special fascination for diamonds, in particular very prominent (*aensienelijcke*) diamonds with all the faces cut. Furthermore, Iskandar Thani was not keen on the ready-made ones the Dutch brought, such as the table and pointed diamonds of which other kings were so fond: he preferred to order special designs, and he wanted them crafted in the Netherlands. Commissar Deutecom reported that the sultan was particularly pleased with a sketch of a belt designed in the Persian manner that was woven from silk, set with diamonds and wished to possess this rare and extremely expensive treasure estimated to cost about a few thousand taels.[41] He was very specific in his instructions in that only beautiful pure cut diamonds were to be used and that it must be crafted in the Netherlands.[42] To this order, he added a request for two to three emerald pendants and more beautiful diamond pendants, each of which he wanted with a hole, presumably to be threaded later on chains.[43]

---

[38] Mundy, *The Travels of Peter Mundy*, Vol. 3, pp. 335–6.
[39] NA, VOC 1131, Copie missive van den commissaris Paulus Croocq aen den Gouverneur Generael [Letter from Commissaris Paulus Croocq to the Governor General], 1639, f. 1196.
[40] Chijs, *Dagh-Register*, 1640–41, p. 4. See also NA, VOC 1131, Copie missive van den commissaris Paulus Croocq aen den Gouverneur Generael, 1639, f. 1162.
[41] Coolhaas, *Generale Missiven*, Vol. 2, 1639–55, p. 57. Please see the glossary for details regarding the tael as currency and a measurement of weight: W.F. Stapel, *Pieter van Dam's Beschrijvinge van de Oostindische Compagnie* [Pieter van Dam's Description of the East Indies Company] ('s-Gravenhage: Martinus Nijhoff, 1931), pp. 834–5.
[42] NA, VOC 1131, Copie missive van den commissaris Paulus Croocq, 1639, f. 1165.
[43] Coolhaas, *Generale Missiven*, Vol. 2, 1639–55, p. 109.

The sultan's fondness for rare and costly diamonds was well known not only to the Dutch. Iskandar Thani forgave Radja Tancas of Minangkabau, who had fallen out of favour, after he presented the sultan with a beautiful diamond ring.[44] The English, too, brought jewels to Aceh when they found out that the sultan had purchased some small but costly rare pieces of jewellery from a Mrs Courten, an English merchant's wife, in London.[45] He bought a very expensive *kris* (dagger) with a gold, diamond-studded handle from the Portuguese, which the company officials estimated to be worth about 30,000 reals of eight.[46] Besides being an avid buyer and collector of jewels, Iskandar Thani had a penchant for showing them off to the visiting foreign envoys.[47] Once, when he was showing off some of his jewellery to a company official, he turned to ask him whether Batavia had such big diamonds. The Dutch official diplomatically answered that no king in the whole of the Indies possessed such rich treasures.[48]

This preference for diamonds and the habit of ordering jewels made in Europe were not customary in Aceh. Although it could be argued that this showed nothing more than Iskandar Thani's personal absorption with diamonds, and his narcissistic and spendthrift nature, this practice acquires a greater significance when one considers how this could enhance the status and prestige of his kingship. Wearing glittering cut diamonds made in Europe would certainly add to the status of a sultan who wished to claim that he was the "King of Kings", who was both concerned about his status compared to other neighbouring kings and what other kings might think about him. Iskandar Thani would be the first monarch in maritime Southeast Asia to wear such copious and glamorous accessories during audience days and ceremonial processions. More importantly, the jewels were made in Europe, a fact that would certainly impress and

---

[44] Ibid., p. 4.
[45] Chijs, *Dagh-Register*, 1640, p. 3.
[46] NA, VOC 1131, Copie missive van den commissaris Paulus Croocq, 1639, f. 1167.
[47] Coolhaas, *Generale Missiven*, Vol. 2, 1639-55, p. 57. The Dutch reported that Iskandar Thani had shown his costly jewels at different times to Commissaris Deutecom who was in Aceh in 1639.
[48] NA, VOC 1119, Origineel daghregister van de voijage handel en resconter met't schip d'Revengie near Atchin [Original daily register from the voyage and trade of the ship *Revengie* to Aceh], 1636, f. 1214.

dazzle not only his subjects but also representatives from the surrounding polities and foreigners from afar, especially the numerous Europeans who had begun to frequent Malay courts. It is likely that this focus on diamonds was Iskandar Thani's way of reinventing himself and setting him apart from his predecessors. Similarly, his keenness to possess a Persian-style belt may reflect his intention to present himself on par with other great Muslim kings in the Persian and Mughal courts.

Unfortunately, it is difficult to ascertain exactly what and how much jewellery he had ordered before his death. According to VOC employee and historian, Francois Valentijn, "the Company suffered a heavy loss through the sale of the deceased King of Atsjien jewellery, since but 5,025 taels[49] of the said jewellery were taken over by the Queen".[50] Leonard Andaya stated that the jewels were worth 6,000 taels.[51] A further search of company sources, however, revealed a significantly higher figure. In a letter to Jacob Compostel, Antonio van Diemen mentioned that the total cost of the jewels Schouten brought was f.82018.6.8.[52] More detailed information can be gleaned regarding the jewellery from the queen's letter to Van Diemen. Sultanah Safiatuddin wrote that she acknowledged the receipt of a gold chain with 1,064 diamond stones, 2 arm rings with 306 diamond stones, a golden kris with 211 diamond stones, 2 pendants with 58 diamond stones, 4 hoop rings beset with table diamonds, 4 ruby rings with set diamonds, 4 diamond rings, a hoop ring beset with 16 table diamonds and 4 earrings in gold.[53] This was worth 10,000 taels out of the 15,000 Commissar Sourji brought. The third part of the jewels amounted to about 8,500 taels, making the total sum about 29,500 taels.

---

[49] Stapel, *Pieter van Dam's Beschrijvinge*, pp. 834–5.
[50] Francois Valentyn, "Valentyn's Account of Malacca (Cont.)", trans. D.F.A. Hervey, *Journal of the Straits Branch of the Royal Asiatic Society* 22 (1890): 236–7. Valentijn did not mention the total sum the Dutch brought.
[51] Andaya, "A Very Good-Natured but Awe-Inspiring Government", p. 77.
[52] Batavia's Uitgaande Briefboeken, R0010227, 1634–49: Letter from Antonio van Diemen, Governor General in Batavia, to Jacob Compostel, Resident in Aceh, 1642, f. 225.
[53] NA, VOC 1141, Copie translate missive der Coninginne van Attchin aen den Gouverneur Generael in Batavia [Letter from Queen of Aceh to Governor General in Batavia], 1642, f. 146R.

The Conflict over Paying for the Jewels

The first signs of trouble over the jewel payment appeared in Antonio van Diemen's letter to Iskandar Thani, in which he drew attention to the fact that Iskandar Thani had declined to accept and pay for the jewels he had ordered, brought by a delegation led by Commissar Jan de Meere in 1640.[54] Although Jan de Meere advised to return the jewels and not force Iskandar Thani to accept them to maintain good relations with Aceh as the Dutch needed his help to attack Portuguese Melaka, Van Diemen firmly urged the king "to unburden us [the Dutch] with these and accept them in a pleasant way".[55] The Dutch, he argued, would not make it difficult for the king if the diamonds could be returned to the Netherlands. However, that was impossible because Iskandar Thani had ordered these diamonds to be specially crafted in the Acehnese style.[56] For example, the eight crafted jewels were especially made to decorate the king's shirt which, according to Van Diemen, was very costly. This specific order fashioned in the Acehnese style made it impossible for the Dutch to sell them to other kings. He stressed that if the jewels were not accepted and paid for, they would cause the Dutch great loss.

When the next envoy—Commissar Justus Schouten—arrived in Aceh with the jewels, he found that Iskandar Thani had passed away, and in his place was his young widow, Sultanah Safiatuddin Syah. The Dutch had no idea how this would affect their jewel trade. Indeed, the situation was rather critical as the Dutch officials were also uncertain of how the successor would respond to the company. Dutch-Aceh relations soured under Iskandar Thani when he had reneged on his promise to help the company conquer Melaka in 1640. The Dutch saw this sudden reversal of intent as a reflection of the sultan's ambitious designs in the Straits.[57] So, after taking Melaka from the Portuguese, the company officials were unsure of Aceh's next move.

---

[54] NA, VOC 1136, Copie missive van den Gouverneur van Diemen aen den Coninck van Attchin [Letter from the Governor van Diemen to the King of Aceh], 1640, f. 951V.
[55] Ibid.
[56] Ibid. For instance, the King of Mataram preferred table-shaped diamonds, while the King of Siam liked pointed ones.
[57] For a fuller account of the reasons behind Iskandar Thani's refusal to help the company and the company's perceptions of him, see Sher Banu, "Ties That Unbind", pp. 303–21.

One of the first things Schouten wrote in his report to Van Diemen, informing the governor of the new sultanah's accession, was that she had refused to accept and pay for the very expensive jewels. This, he noted, was very damaging to the company and did not augur well for relations between the company and the new ruler. Schouten reported later that despite his great insistence, only a part of the jewels was accepted, 5,025 taels at f.16 1/5 per tael.[58] The sultanah refused to accept the rest even when Schouten offered to sell them at cost. As far as the Acehnese were concerned, her reasons were impeccable—her extravagant husband had depleted the treasury. Furthermore, these jewels and accessories were specially designed and made for the male king's clothes and certainly could not be worn by a woman![59]

The Sultanah, Her Orang Kaya and Commissar Pieter Sourij

Schouten's successor as commissar was Pieter Sourij, whose task was to get Sultanah Safiatuddin to accept and pay for the remainder of the jewels.[60] Governor General van Diemen had specifically instructed him not to bring them back to Batavia.[61]

Sourij's detailed report is extremely useful, because it gives a rare glimpse of how affairs were conducted under the sultanah's reign. From it we gather that matters of business had to be first discussed with her rijxraaden before they could be forwarded to the queen on audience day. The company officials had to learn quickly whom they needed to petition

---

[58] Batavia's Uitgaande Briefboeken, R0010236, 1634–49, NA, f. 339V. Justus Schouten and Johan van Twist in Malacca, July 1641. This presumably would be the 5,025 taels of jewellery the queen accepted as Valentyn mentioned.
[59] Ibid.
[60] Pieter Sourij stayed in Aceh from 15 May to 18 August 1642.
[61] NA, VOC 1143, Dagh-Register off Journael gehouden bij den Pieter Sourij, 1642, f. 556R. In his letter to Jacob Compostel, Antonio van Diemen mentioned that the total cost of the jewels Sourij brought was f. 82018.6.8. See Batavia's Uitgaande Briefboeken, R0010227, 1634–49 Letter from Antonio van Diemen to Jacob Compostel, 1642, f. 225. Sourij wrote that the jewels' cost of production was 12,000 taels. However, the Dutch asked for 15,000 taels, taking into consideration the danger of transportation at sea.

first and who the company's friends were. In the first year of her reign, the most important council member was the Lebai Kita Kali.[62] Being a friend of the company, he gave Compostel two important pieces of advice: Sourij should visit the other orang kaya to discuss the sale of the jewels, and keep the Kali informed of their answers.[63] He also cautioned Compostel that the Dutch might face problems with the rest of the orang kaya as the kingdom did not need any more jewels. Aceh was already well known for them; there was no need to look any further than Iskandar Thani's jewel-studded grave to prove this.[64] More importantly, the Kali said that as a queen ruled Aceh, it was in the nature of a woman to be unwilling to see her treasury depleted.[65]

On 12 July, Sourij had his first audience with the queen. Much to Sourij's surprise, the sultanah decided to accept the jewels with the consensus of her orang kaya. Happy at this good turn of events, Sourij decided not to be impolite by discussing questions of payment: Sourij did not want to prejudice the good standing the company had at that moment. The first shock Sourij faced was one week later when the queen ordered the orang kaya and her jewellers to gather at the balai to value the price of the jewels. All the orang kaya were present except, interestingly, the Kali. Maharaja Adonna Lilla, the queen's eunuch, with the *shahbandars* (port officials) and two other orang kaya came with the jewel box and opened it for the others and the queen's jewellers to value. After the jewels were carefully examined, the price determined was totally unacceptable to the company delegates—an outrageously low 5,900 taels.[66] The queen herself was not present, being in the inner precinct of her palace. Sourij protested, claiming that either the Acehnese diamond jewellers did not know their stones, or they simply refused to declare the real amount. The Dutch delegates threatened a walk out.

---

[62] The Kali was said to be the illegitimate son of Iskandar Muda, thus the sultanah's half-brother: Ito, "The World of Adat Aceh", p. 71.
[63] NA, VOC 1143, Dagh-Register off Journael gehouden bij den Pieter Sourij, 1642, f. 557R.
[64] Iskandar, ed., *Bustan us-Salatin*, pp. 60–73.
[65] NA, VOC 1143, Dagh-Register off Journael gehouden bij den Pieter Sourij, 1642, f. 560V.
[66] NA, VOC 1143, Dagh-Register off Journael gehouden bij den Pieter Sourij, 1642, ff. 571R–571V.

Maharaja Adonna Lilla then wrote the price down and took it to the queen. This did not help to calm Sourij at all as the queen agreed with the price her jewellers determined. Sourij warned that this had better not be a trick or mere excuses devised by the Acehnese not to take the jewels: they remained obliged to take them and he was not allowed to take them back to Batavia. Sourij stressed that the governor general himself had requested that the Acehnese relieve the Dutch of these expensive jewels because Iskandar Thani had ordered them. The Acehnese retorted that though their king had ordered them, he was now dead, and all that he had done had died with him. They explained to Sourij that Acehnese had no love for the Pahang-born Iskandar Thani, and his name was remembered and honoured less than that of Iskandar Muda. Sourij replied that regardless of the fact Iskandar Thani was a foreigner and was unloved by the Acehnese, the governor general, out of affection for the Acehnese kingdom had obliged him, and their reasons for refusing the jewels were inadequate.[67] From the Dutch point of view, the Acehnese, as the king's subjects—be he dead or not—were obliged to carry out his orders. The Acehnese argued otherwise, stating that according to the law of the land, the queen was not liable to execute her late husband's orders.[68] After Sourij's soft welcome, the situation had indeed turned problematic.

Back at the balai where the Dutch and Acehnese elites were eyeing each other warily, after much whispering and discussion, the shahbandars offered 2,000 taels more. Sourij angrily declared that he would no longer accept such "frivolous talk" and would not accept anything less than the 15,000 taels owing. Sourij warned the Acehnese that their refusal to pay for the jewels would lead to the governor general's displeasure. Maharaja Adonna Lilla then asked whether this meant that the queen would be forced to accept them. This was too much for the company officials to

---

[67] NA, VOC 1143, Dagh-Register off Journael gehouden bij den Pieter Sourij, 1642, f. 572R.

[68] The rights and obligations of successor kings in Aceh (and, it seems, in the Malay world during the pre-modern period) do not appear to be written and codified in any form, thus this law was most probably one belonging to the oral tradition. Snouck Hurgronje, in his epic study of the Acehnese, stated that no Acehnese king felt obliged to fulfil the promises or concessions granted by his predecessor: Snouck Hurgronje, *The Acehnese*, p. 126.

tolerate, and Sourij and his companions started to leave the balai. It was at this tense juncture that the queen decided to intervene and smooth matters over. When the company officials reached the palace compound's third gate, she ordered that Sourij and the others be called back to the balai and treated them to a banquet. It was an offer they accepted with courtesy, after which Sourij complained that from four hours of fruitless discussion they had made no progress, and they subsequently returned to their lodge.[69] The queen's timely intervention left him disappointed, but no longer angry.

In the meantime, Sourij and other Dutch officials had to engage and lobby all the other important orang kaya. To do this, they arranged appropriate gifts to accompany their requests for help. Such gifts were carefully calculated so that their value commensurated with the rank and importance of the orang kaya. Sourij learnt soon enough that though these gifts usually ensured a fair reception, they did not always result in cooperation. The orang kaya at that time were divided into two factions—one comprising those who were against accepting the jewels and the others who were willing to accept them, but at a reduced price. The Maharaja Sri Maharaja and the panglima dalam belonged to the former camp. The panglima dalam was friendly in manner but gave his opinion about buying the jewels. He diplomatically told Sourij that some jewellery might be bought, such as the four golden earrings and some rings, as the queen usually wore some jewellery on important occasions. However, he made it clear to Sourij that the rest of the jewellery was useless: the jewels served no other purpose other than to be admired, so paying for them would be like throwing money away.[70]

Since Sourij's arrival in Aceh, he had been unsuccessful in meeting with the next most important *rijxraad*—the second in rank in the council—the Maharaja Sri Maharaja. Sourij complained that the latter had been avoiding him, saying that he was sick. When Sourij was finally

---

[69] NA, VOC 1143, Dagh-Register off Journael gehouden bij den Pieter Sourij, 1642, ff. 572R–572V.
[70] NA, VOC 1143, Dagh-Register off Journael gehouden bij den Pieter Sourij, 1642, ff. 573R–574R. This is a translation of a Malay proverb, which means that if one throws money like one throws water, then one does not value the money; water, in this context, is seen as abundant, and thus of little value.

able to make an appointment to see the Maharaja at his house, he found him with some other orang kaya. Despite the Maharaja's reluctance to see him, he treated Sourij well and presented him with an Acehnese dress. Sourij remarked that the Maharaja was a man of few words and, as usual, he pretended to be sick. On this occasion though, despite being ill, the Maharaja managed more than a few words. He told the Dutch officials that if it was a matter of 200 to 300 taels, it would not be a problem, especially as the Acehnese had been friends with the Dutch for so long. "Although both parties were so different and their lands were so far apart, in their hearts they were affectionate with each other." He promised that he would prove himself a good friend of the Dutch; nevertheless, he made it clear that as far as it was in his power to do so, he would ensure that the kingdom's interest would not be jeopardised.[71]

The leading orang kaya who supported paying for the jewels were the Lebai Kita Kali and his follower, Maharaja Sestia.[72] They were both secretly trying to work out a compromise price that would be acceptable to the company, the queen and the other orang kaya. Maharaja Sestia's uppermost concern was to maintain good relations with the company. Thus, he wanted this jewel affair settled in a way that was the least damaging to the Aceh-Dutch friendship, especially as the governor general had been friends with Aceh since the queen's father's time. He suggested that the company must continue to show the same friendship to Aceh, even though a woman now ruled. He advised Sourij that this relationship should be strengthened, not diminished, saying that though a radical change had taken place in the Acehnese court with a woman on the throne, this would not affect the friendship previous Acehnese kings had shown the Dutch. Being the daughter of Iskandar Muda, the sultanah would continue in the tradition of her illustrious father, and indeed, he pointed out she had shown herself to be more accommodating towards the Dutch than her male predecessors. As far as Maharaja Sestia and the Kali's arguments were concerned, their decision to accept the jewels not

---

[71] NA, VOC 1143, Dagh-Register off Journael gehouden bij den Pieter Sourij, 1642, f. 576R.

[72] Sourij was convinced that Maharaja Sestia and the Kali had been discussing this matter between themselves as they both spoke "the same words". NA, VOC 1143, Dagh-Register off Journael gehouden bij den Pieter Sourij, 1642, f. 575V.

so much demonstrated their pro-Dutch attitude as the need to maintain strong ties with the Dutch: going to war would certainly damage the kingdom's interests. The Kali and Sestia's private efforts to keep relations with the Dutch cordial seem to have worked. In response to a private offer to pay 10,000 taels, Sourij told them that the company would be willing to lower the price to 12,000–13,000 taels. In the meantime, Possie Melor, their translator, informed Sourij that as so much money was at stake, all the orang kaya, except for Maharaja Sri Maharaja, were gathered at court engaged in an intense discussion about the jewels. Sourij learnt that many of the orang kaya opposed the purchase on similar grounds to the panglima dalam: the jewels served no purpose, and it would be tantamount to throwing good money away. To the orang kaya, keeping the treasury healthy was essential to the kingdom's power.

The tussle for an acceptable jewel price continued at the next audience day in the big balai. Although the sultanah was supposed to be there, she had sent her seal indicating that she would not be present. The sultanah left the preliminary bargaining and haggling to her eunuch, so all attention was on the orang kaya Maharaja Adonna Lilla, the queen's *liefste* (favourite). He raised the Acehnese offer from 5,900 to 9,000 taels, though he claimed that he was not happy with this price: upon closer inspection some of the big stones were worth "no more than pebbles", suggesting that he was suspicious of the company's true intentions.[73] If the Dutch were not satisfied, they should speak to her majesty directly as he dared not tell her himself.

This ploy seemed to work, as Sourij finally relented and asked for 10,000 taels. Maharaja Adonna Lilla promised he would try helping the Dutch fetch that price. He indicated that the sultanah was ready to pay part of the amount in cash while the remainder would have to be in trade goods, and some in the form of discounts on the tolls the company had to pay. Despite this positive change in the Acehnese position, Sourij remained frustrated, and it was only a few days before his departure to Batavia that there were signs the jewel business would eventually be settled. During the audience day on Saturday, 3 August 1642, the sultanah

---

[73] NA, VOC 1143, Dagh-Register off Journael gehouden bij den Pieter Sourij, 1642, f. 577V.

offered 9,000 taels for the jewels. Sourij pointedly but politely said if he accepted this amount he would not dare return to Batavia to face the governor general. In a not-too-subtle threat he told the sultanah that the honour and respect the Dutch had for her would hinge on the reasonable settlement of this dispute, one with serious diplomatic repercussions for Aceh-VOC relations. Over much protest from some orang kaya, the sultanah agreed to pay the 10,000 taels.[74] She promised to make the payment by reducing the tolls that Dutch ships paid by 4,000 taels, and she would pay the balance of 6,000 taels in two *mousum*s (seasons).[75]

The Sultanah, Her Orang Kaya and Commissar Arnold Vlamingh

Unfortunately, this episode with Commissar Sourij was not the end of the jewel affair. It continued to test the tenacity and diplomacy of both parties, because Sourij had managed to sell only a part of the total amount of jewellery. On his return to Batavia, fearing the governor general's wrath, he left the unsold jewels in Aceh with Binthara Can Canan asking the Acehnese envoy to Batavia, Sri Bidia Indra, to bear witness.

The governor general, clearly unhappy with the turn of events, was further incensed that he had had to pay the previous three years' interest on the jewels. He appointed the more formidable Commissar Arnold de Vlamingh van Oudtshoorn as the next envoy to Aceh, where he remained from July to October 1644. His unenviable task was to sell five great diamond pieces for 8,500 taels, preferably to be paid as 7,000 taels in cash and gold, 500 in merchandise and 1,000 in tolls.[76] There were also some other rings the late king had ordered, but the company had given up all hope of ever selling these. Vlamingh boastfully vowed that he would not return to Batavia with the jewels and incur the governor general's

---

[74] NA, VOC 1143, Dagh-Register off Journael gehouden bij den Pieter Sourij, 1642, ff. 581R–581V.
[75] NA, VOC 1141, Copie translate missive der Coninginne van Attchin, 1642, f. 146V.
[76] NA, VOC 1157, Dagh-Register gehouden bij den Commissaris Arnold de Vlamingh, 1644, f. 591V, f. 599R.

indignation, but would rather wear himself out and be miserable and die in Aceh.[77]

When Vlamingh arrived in Aceh on 13 July, he was welcomed with the customary ceremony that greeted all foreign ships in the Acehnese harbour. Vlamingh's first disappointment on landing came when he was told that the queen was away with English and other foreigners on a hunting trip, which the Acehnese court was fond of organising since the time of previous kings. The queen's party was expected to return to court about a week later. However, Vlamingh was forced to wait longer still, and the governor general's letter and gifts were only brought to court in a magnificent procession on 31 July. Vlamingh was not granted his first audience with the queen until 6 August; however, the issue of the jewels was not discussed because it was considered improper to conduct business on one's first visit to court. Vlamingh's patience was severely tested by the Acehnese delaying tactics even before he saw the sultanah.

In the meantime, Vlamingh tried to keep himself useful and busy. He had to lobby and prepare gifts for the orang kaya as follows: Lebai Kita Kali (first in rank and the company's patron), f.176.18.4; Maharaja Sri Maharaja (second), f.131.1.8; laksamana (third), f.123.7.5; Sri Paduka Tuan (fourth in rank and a friend of the company), f.174.17.4; Maharaja Adonna Lilla (the queen's favourite eunuch), f.159.2.4; Maharaja Sestia (another eunuch and company friend), f.123.7.4; and the Lebai Kita Kali's brother-in-law, f.113.3.4.[78]

After learning that the Lebai Kita Kali was away on an elephant hunt, Vlamingh decided to concentrate on lobbying the hardliners, the Maharaja Sri Maharaja and the laksamana or panglima dalam. Vlamingh was well received at the Maharaja's house, but when he brought up the matter of the jewels his host did not bother to mollify the Dutch. He directly reiterated his objections to purchasing the jewels and declined to accept the rest from Vlamingh. He noted that the king who had ordered the jewels was now dead and, according to the Acehnese, the present queen was not obliged to carry out his orders. Furthermore, the sultanah,

---

[77] NA, VOC 1157, Dagh-Register gehouden bij den Commissaris Arnold de Vlamingh, 1644, f. 575V.

[78] NA, VOC 1157, Dagh-Register gehouden bij den Commissaris Arnold de Vlamingh, 1644, ff. 579V–580V.

being a woman, found cash more useful than jewels, which would serve the kingdom better.[79]

Vlamingh next visited the laksamana who, unlike the merely "inconsiderate" Maharaja, was downright contemptuous. After the customary greetings and gifts, Vlamingh told the laksamana that the Acehnese should accept the jewels because of their friendship with the Dutch. The laksamana retorted by questioning the Dutch's sincerity in wanting to preserve friendship with the Acehnese, pointing out that all these professions of friendship ran counter to their attempts to force the queen to accept the jewels. He added that the number of jewels the Dutch put to sale was not worth all the time and effort they had spent trying to get the Acehnese to change their minds. Indeed, if the company was simply interested in selling jewels, the governor general could have sent a mere trader rather than a high-ranking person, who should only concern himself with courtly matters.[80] He reminded Vlamingh of how Sourij had left the jewels behind, hoping the queen would accept them when it was clear that she was not in the least inclined to do so. The laksamana found it strange that the governor general, being aware that the Acehnese were totally averse to accepting the jewels, was still insistent on making matters difficult for the queen. He accused the Dutch of "making her ears warm" with this talk about the jewels, especially after she had given the Dutch exclusive nation treatment on the SWC. The disagreeable posture the Dutch had taken was damaging the old alliance between the two nations, and their insistence on the amount to be paid for the jewels would only lead to Acehnese alienation or, at least, displeasure.[81]

After two months of lobbying and presenting gifts to the orang kaya, Vlamingh wrote that all hope of the queen accepting the jewels was destroyed. His desperation became more apparent when he heard that

---

[79] NA, VOC 1157, Dagh-Register gehouden bij den Commissaris Arnold de Vlamingh, 1644, f. 581R.

[80] NA, VOC 1157, Dagh-Register gehouden bij den Commissaris Arnold de Vlamingh, 1644, f. 582R. This crisis of identity was a perennial problem the VOC faced in the East Indies.

[81] NA, VOC 1157, Dagh-Register gehouden bij den Commissaris Arnold de Vlamingh, 1644, f. 582V.

despite the orang kaya's violent disputes over the jewels,[82] the laksamana still "sang his old tune".[83] He lamented that he had gone so far as to give his gun—which hung in his room—as a gift to the "rude" laksamana as the laksamana's servant had claimed that his master wished to have it.[84] Vlamingh confessed that he had done all that he could and, despite throwing away so many gifts, had not obtained results. He complained that these "hungry vultures remained insatiable".[85]

After exhausting the commissar's spirits for almost one and a half months, Sultanah Safiatuddin instructed the Dutch to bring the jewels to court the following Saturday where they would be valued by her diamond experts, her *naeleer*s (captains) and the shahbandars. A decision would then be made regarding the purchase of the jewels. Like Sourij, Vlamingh became furious when the queen's diamond experts valued the jewels at 3,000 taels, which to him was a disgraceful price for five large diamonds. Vlamingh's ill fortune seemed endless. He reported how the queen's jewellers ridiculed him by asking whether the Dutch had been mistaken and placed the cost in taels when it should have been only in reals.[86] The jewellers asked whether the company officials had ever seen diamonds as they had seen better ones, and alluded to the company having obtained these through dishonourable means.[87] The Acehnese again accused the Dutch of aggressively pushing the jewels on them, and Vlamingh reported on the "extraordinary manner in which he was spoken to" considering he was a commissar and the head of a diplomatic delegation to Aceh appointed by the governor general in Batavia. He expressed shock at how poorly the Dutch were treated considering the

---

[82] NA, VOC 1157, Dagh-Register gehouden bij den Commissaris Arnold de Vlamingh, 1644, f. 591R.
[83] NA, VOC 1157, Dagh-Register gehouden bij den Commissaris Arnold de Vlamingh, 1644, f. 589V.
[84] NA, VOC 1157, Dagh-Register gehouden bij den Commissaris Arnold de Vlamingh, 1644, f. 595R.
[85] NA, VOC 1157, Dagh-Register gehouden bij den Commissaris Arnold de Vlamingh, 1644, f. 589V.
[86] NA, VOC 1157, Dagh-Register gehouden bij den Commissaris Arnold de Vlamingh, 1644, ff. 593V–594R.
[87] NA, VOC 1157, Dagh-Register gehouden bij den Commissaris Arnold de Vlamingh, 1644, f. 594R.

friendship and courtesy they had shown the Acehnese envoys when they were in Batavia.

Vlamingh's fortunes finally turned when he visited Sri Paduka Tuan, the fourth-ranking member of the sultanah's council. Vlamingh did not make much headway with him, but he did give the commissar useful advice on the one advisor who had the most influence of all the orang kaya, "the one who could be where the other orangkaya cannot"—the queen's favourite eunuch, Maharaja Adonna Lilla. Sri Paduka Tuan advised Vlamingh to seek his help and keep him in the company's faction, but warned that the other orang kaya must also be treated just as well and be given presents so as not to stir up jealousies at court.[88]

Realising they were getting nowhere with the orang kaya, Vlamingh and the senior trader in Aceh, Jan Harmanszoon, decided to follow Paduka Tuan's advice. They resolved to approach the queen's favourite to promote the sale of the jewels. When Harmanszoon was finally able to meet Maharaja Adonna Lilla, the eunuch assured him that he was the company's friend, and the Dutch should have no reservations about the queen's goodwill towards the Dutch commissars in Aceh. He told Harmanszoon that the queen had not yet fixed the jewels' price, and the Dutch should not be troubled by the orang kaya offering to pay less than half their desired cost. According to Maharaja Adonna Lilla, this was the Acehnese way of doing things.[89]

This new approach proved invaluable. The queen's favourite eunuch provided the Dutch with much better advice than the orang kaya regarding the sultanah's stand on the matter. Vlamingh's description of the next audience day amply demonstrated this. His detailed report clearly illuminated how the sultanah managed both her orang kaya and the foreign envoys.

On Sunday, 11 September, Sultanah Safiatuddin demonstrated that her foremost concern was still to maintain good relations with the Dutch, which confirmed Maharaja Adonna Lilla's counsel. The young sultanah dealt with the Dutch in a skilled and astute manner. She first put the

---

[88] NA, VOC 1157, Dagh-Register gehouden bij den Commissaris Arnold de Vlamingh, 1644, f. 585R.
[89] NA, VOC 1157, Dagh-Register gehouden bij den Commissaris Arnold de Vlamingh, 1644, f. 596R.

officials in a good temper by generously honouring the *oppercoopman* (senior trader), Harmanszoon, with two titles, orang kaya *poeti* (white orang kaya) and *capitain radja* (prince of captains), which he was at liberty to use in all the lands under her jurisdiction. When it came to the business of the jewels, the sultanah was rather coy. When Vlamingh requested that she settle the price, she declared that it would be 3,000 taels. One can imagine how Vlamingh would have struggled to keep his anger in check standing before this young sultanah. Again he tried to persuade her by appealing to the fact that these had been especially ordered by her late husband and they were very expensive jewels, crafted and brought all the way from the Netherlands. The sultanah replied that the price offered was based on what these jewels were worth, and it was because of her friendship with the Dutch and the governor general that she had agreed to accept the jewels in the first place, though she had no desire for them. But, she said, as a sign of goodwill she would raise the offer to 3,500 taels, which Vlamingh promptly replied was too little. She finally declared that she would offer 4,000 taels and then, as customary, she retired to the inner palace and let the Maharaja Sri Maharaja lead the orang kaya to gather in the balai to discuss the matter. The general feeling among the orang kaya was that they doubted the sincerity of the Dutch, and they were particularly suspicious as to whether the governor general had seriously ordered this course of action, given Vlamingh refused to deviate even a *penning* (a Dutch penny) from the original price. The orang kaya complained that this was making it more difficult for them to persuade the queen. They told Vlamingh that the matter of the jewels depended on them as the queen, being a woman, did not have the greatest knowledge regarding these things and had to be taught.[90] While the orang kaya were still deliberating the price, Maharaja Adonna Lilla appeared at the balai and, after a short discussion with the orang kaya in Malay, the Maharaja Sri Maharaja informed Vlamingh that the orang kaya had agreed to raise the offer to 4,500 taels, but subject to the queen's concurrence. Vlamingh, as expected, disagreed with this slightly higher offer and he showed no sign of relenting. Maharaja Adonna Lilla

---

[90] NA, VOC 1157, Dagh-Register gehouden bij den Commissaris Arnold de Vlamingh, 1644, f. 597R.

went back to the inner balai to talk to the queen but she, unlike her male elites, would not offer more than 4,000 taels. By this time Vlamingh was in despair and he pithily described how sad and hopeless he felt about the whole affair, wishing that he understood the Malay language! Maharaja Adonna Lilla was sent a second time to the queen. When he reappeared, he brought with him a silver dish with all the jewels the Acehnese had bought from the Dutch previously. The Acehnese claimed that the total price of all these jewels was below the price the Dutch demanded for the five big pieces. Realising he was caught in a spot, Vlamingh confessed that he was ignorant of the previous jewel transactions but explained that these other jewels were uncut: the five big pieces were expensive because they were made from cut table diamonds (*tafels diamenten*), which had to be specially ordered and cut in the Netherlands. As they were discussing this, another eunuch appeared from the inner balai, announcing that the sultanah had increased the offer to 5,000 taels.[91]

Feeling desperate and worn down after two months of fruitless negotiations, Vlamingh wanted the affair to be settled before he returned to Batavia. He continued to negotiate with the sultanah's eunuch. Although he was concerned that the eunuch was not one of the four rijxraaden, it appeared that he might have the queen's ear or rather the unique privilege of listening to the queen's whispers. Vlamingh had consistently complained about the "obscure and slow negotiations" he experienced in Aceh: he was not allowed to speak with the queen except through intermediaries which was, he understood, the custom of the land. According to Paduka Tuan, the only man (*man-persoon*) who could speak to the queen was the eunuch Maharaja Adonna Lilla, and the queen's business had to be executed through him. It slowly dawned on the Dutch that they had to treat this particular eunuch well and keep themselves in his favour.[92] True enough, it was Maharaja Adonna Lilla's dealings with the Dutch that finally broke the deadlock. During the discussion with Maharaja Adonna Lilla, Vlamingh finally agreed to reduce the jewels' price to

---

[91] NA, VOC 1157, Dagh-Register gehouden bij den Commissaris Arnold de Vlamingh, 1644, f. 598R.
[92] NA, VOC 1157, Dagh-Register gehouden bij den Commissaris Arnold de Vlamingh, 1644, f. 599R.

6,000 taels, 2,000 in cash, and the rest to be paid in tin and discounts on tolls. To sweeten the deal, the Dutch presented Maharaja Adonna Lilla with a table emerald ring worth f.268 (one of the many rings ordered by the late king that could not be sold), as a token of their hope and appreciation of his willingness to bring the matter to the sultanah. The eunuch ordered Vlamingh to keep this gift a secret from the rest of the orang kaya so as not to arouse any suspicion. He told Vlamingh to make another round of visits to the orang kaya to request their help in bringing the matter of the jewels to court the next audience day on Saturday, 17 September. The eunuch even taught Vlamingh the correct manner to adopt while speaking to the queen and the orang kaya: they should address the sultanah in a submissive manner and use beautiful words for the orang kaya![93]

The next audience day, the sultanah summoned all the orang kaya to court and declared that she had agreed to accept the jewels at 6,000 taels, 1,000 in cash, and the rest to be paid within three years.[94] This amount had to be agreed upon by all the orang kaya, including the laksamana and the Lebai Kita Kali, who had just returned from his elephant hunt. Despite some misgivings from the laksamana and even from the company's friend, Lebai Kita Kali, they agreed on the price by uttering of the word "daulat" at the balai. Finally, both parties had agreed upon a negotiated price. The final outcome of this jewel affair was that the queen accepted a total of just 21,000 taels, which meant that the Dutch lost 8,500 taels. The company was still left with one emerald and five diamond rings.

On Tuesday, 20 September, Sultanah Safiatuddin fulfilled her promise to pay the 1,000 cash. In an unprecedented move, both at court and for a Dutch envoy, she also made the Dutch "pay" for their part of the bargain. Partly owing to her youth and partly feminine mischief, she playfully asked Vlamingh and others to "honour" her by dancing for her and her other women councillors (*state-juffrouwen*). Doubtless mortified, nonetheless, Vlamingh and other company officials indulged the sultanah

---

[93] NA, VOC 1157, Dagh-Register gehouden bij den Commissaris Arnold de Vlamingh, 1644, f. 599V.

[94] NA, VOC 1157, Dagh-Register gehouden bij den Commissaris Arnold de Vlamingh, 1644, f. 600V.

who, he reported was exceptionally amused by their hops, and the court was filled with loud laughter and shouts.[95]

Conclusion

The jewel affair was significant because it tested the young sultanah's mettle in the early years of her reign, not only in her dealings with a foreign merchant power, but in her fledgling relations with the orang kaya. It was also a test of wills and the diplomatic skills of both the orang kaya and the Dutch commissars, who had no idea how the change in Aceh's political leadership would impact their fortunes. The affair demonstrated that despite a difficult situation, Safiatuddin's actions and timely interventions helped to avert a potentially destabilising and threatening hostility. Perhaps Aceh-VOC relations would have unfolded dramatically differently if Iskandar Thani had remained at the helm. In this instance, both the Acehnese and the Dutch had to compromise to reach a mutually acceptable price. On the Dutch's part, there was also the paramount need to maintain the company's good relations with Aceh, if the Dutch were to enjoy trade privileges in pepper and tin, toll-free trade and exclusive nation treatment on the SWC.

The episode also suggests that at the micro level, personalities played an important role in determining the outcome of interstate relations in the early modern era. It reveals the personal rather than the legal nature of diplomatic dealings in the early period of East-West interactions, that is, the ad hoc character of diplomatic dealings and the absence of a systemic set of laws and regulations that dictated rule of conduct in diplomatic relations. While Arnold Vlamingh saw the jewel affair as official company business, the laksamana saw it as outside the official concern of a diplomat and rebuked him for acting as a petty trader.

Another aspect revealed in the jewel affair is the question of how legally binding the words or orders of a king were if they were not in writing, and whether these orders had to be followed by his successor. As far as the Dutch were concerned, Iskandar Thani's orders were legally

---

[95] NA, VOC 1157, Dagh-Register gehouden bij den Commissaris Arnold de Vlamingh, 1644, f. 601R.

binding, while to the Acehnese, his words died with him. Indeed, Iskandar Thani rescinded his own verbal promise to the governor general when he refused to accept and pay for the jewels he had ordered because the Dutch had angered and insulted him by inviting Johor, which he considered a vassal state, to help them conquer Melaka in 1641. The Dutch viewed Iskandar Muda as unpredictable and capricious, and his failure to treat his verbal promises as legally binding had already soured relations with Aceh. The sultanah, in contrast, not only had to take damage control measures in the first year of her reign but had to tackle a problem she had inherited from her husband.

As we will see, another major cause of misunderstanding between Aceh and the Dutch was the nature of treatises signed between European and indigenous powers. While the Dutch saw the numerous treatises as legal documents that were forever binding, Acehnese rulers did not see the need to recognise treatises signed by their predecessors. Despite serious Dutch efforts to implement what they deemed as legal provisions, the actual state of their relationships largely depended on the rapport between them and the local elites in the context of the time.

In the precinct of the balai, the jewel affair revealed the presence of constantly shifting and contested foci of power and influence in the Acehnese court. While the orang kaya thought the resolution of this affair depended on them and the young sovereign, being a woman, needed to be instructed in such matters, it appears that she, too, had her own ideas. The orang kaya were adamant about not paying a higher price for the jewels, but she had the final say in the matter. Compromises, therefore, had to be made by everyone to preserve the Dutch-Acehnese friendship. Even though the orang kaya played an important role in the decision making and were lobbied with gifts and "beautiful words", ultimate authority lay with the sultanah. In the end, her policy of accommodating the Dutch prevailed. As the following chapters show, she consistently pursued this policy throughout her reign.

However, the very fact that the sultanah obtained the concurrence of the orang kaya shows that they remained involved in the decision-making process. Indeed, the sultanah was not directly involved in the preliminary negotiations, but she lent her stature to resolve conflicts when the discussions seemed to be getting out of hand between her orang kaya and the Dutch. Under her reign, the decision-making process was collaborative, reciprocal through consensus-making *muafakat,* quite unlike the authoritarianism practised by her father, Iskandar Muda. In this episode, the orang kaya made important contributions to the decision-making process and were able to give a macro perspective on how the jewels affected the kingdom's finances. The young queen had her jewel experts, her naeleers and the shahbandars to give independent advice about the value of the jewels.

The sultanah was careful to keep relations cordial and on an even keel, as when she affected a rapprochement with Sourij by inviting him to dinner when he threatened to walk out of negotiations in the balai. At opportune times, her views were conveyed through her eunuchs to the orang kaya. She apparently knew when to send her eunuchs to the balai to soothe the tensions on both sides.

The course of the jewel affair also shows that the orang kaya were not a homogenous group, as scholars commonly asserted, and relations between royalty and the elites were not a simple zero-sum game.[96] There were, in fact, pro- and anti-Dutch factions divided in the ways they perceived Dutch intentions and how they should respond to and deal with Dutch officials. The faction led by the Kali supported the queen's undeclared plan of adopting a soft approach. Accommodating the Dutch was important to maintaining good relations, particularly when the company was increasing in strength after conquering Melaka. The other faction, led by the maharaja and the laksamana, took a hard-line approach and would have rejected the jewels rather than be cowed by the Dutch. The laksamana was strident and firm in disagreeing with the price the Dutch demanded for the jewels. And yet, despite these differences, at another level the orang kaya were actually unanimous and united in their objective of protecting the kingdom's interest. To them, purchasing the jewels was an extravagance that the kingdom could ill afford as they served no useful purpose. Even the Kali was unhappy that the Acehnese had to pay so much for unwanted items. In the end, it is clear that despite all the disagreements, all factions and the sultanah were able to come to a compromise in the best interests of the kingdom. Despite the disagreement about the jewels' final price, the orang kaya ultimately rallied

---

[96] See Amirul Hadi and Auni Luthfi.

behind the sultanah and declared their support for her at the balai. Having identified the different factions into which the orang kaya divided, it is clear relations between the orang kaya and the sultanah were complex and contested, and that political dynamics in Aceh were not characterised by an overbearing orang kaya dominating a weak sultanah. More importantly, it shows how relations were successfully managed despite disagreements.

Unlike her predecessor, Iskandar Thani, the sultanah was more concerned for the health of her kingdom's treasury.[97] She stopped her husband's dangerous precedent of accepting payment for pepper in jewels instead of reals. Conspicuous consumption and extravagant displays of wealth to gain charisma, prowess and status worked against an economical use of the kingdom's resources. In contrast to the notion that material wealth enhanced one's charisma and garnered the allegiance of subjects and foreigners alike, extravagant rulers were not popular with the orang kaya. Sultan Sri Alam had been killed and Iskandar Thani was possibly poisoned owing to extravagantly wasting the kingdom's wealth on expensive frivolities, such as diamond jewellery, to boost ego and status.[98] In contrast to her male predecessors' emphasis on material wealth to enhance their stature, Sultanah Safiatuddin's practical and pragmatic style shaped her reign. Chapter 5 further examines Sultanah Safiatuddin's bases of power and legitimacy and illustrates the main differences between her and her male predecessors' leadership style by comparing both their letters and other evidence of how they governed.

The jewel affair illustrates how the sultanah was able to turn gendered perceptions of her behaviour—being inaccessible and apparently inconsistent—to an advantage. The "inaccessibility problem" Vlamingh described during the negotiations proved valuable as her actions, unfathomable to others, gave her more room for manoeuvre. Her "inconsistencies", taken as a characteristic of a woman making decisions,

---

[97] This may attest to Reid's claim that in Southeast Asian societies, women were entrusted with handling money, buying and selling goods, promoting family business and making deals. Anthony Reid, "Charismatic Queens of Southern Asia", *History Today* 53, 6 (2003): 35.
[98] Iskandar, ed., *De Hikajat Atjeh*, p. 96; the *Bustan us-Salatin* said he was killed, Iskandar, ed., *Bustan us-Salatin*, p. 32.

enabled her to buy time for the Acehnese during periods of difficult negotiations.

As a woman ruler in a largely patriarchal court, the sultanah had to devise means to stay abreast of court happenings and rumours. The jewel affair reveals that her sex did impose some limitations on her style of governing: a woman had fewer informal opportunities to be in contact and discuss matters of state with her male elites than her male predecessors. It is in this context that Maharaja Adonna Lilla, the sultanah's favourite but seemingly unimportant eunuch, assumed a crucial role in this affair when he acted as the intermediary between the sultanah, her orang kaya and the company officials. Indeed, Maharaja Adonna Lilla was the perfect conduit for the sultanah to engage with the male sex and to serve as her eyes and ears in a largely male-dominated balai.

Sultanah Safiatuddin managed to keep herself afloat during the early years of her reign by devising a consensual and a pragmatic relationship with her elites. Nevertheless, this was a fledgling relationship, and one that was to be sorely tested in the decades to come.

chapter 3

Sultanah Safiatuddin's Maturing Years: Politics of Consolidation

The male elites surrounding Sultanah Safiatuddin comprised many factions and, in the 1650s, the kingdom experienced coups and counter-coups that sorely tested her ability as a ruler. Indeed, Sultanah Safiatuddin's position and even her life were threatened in the first two decades of her rule. One reason for the unrest was the VOC became increasingly strident in its demands for commercial concessions and did not hesitate to back these demands with force, including a blockade of the Perak River. Growing Dutch demand for tin from Perak and pepper from the SWC caused them to make incursions into these states, which were, at that time, vassals of Aceh, and affected Aceh's traditional overlord-vassal relations. The sultanah was placed in the unenviable situation of not only having to balance her fractious elite but also to balance the VOC's demands, all the while maintaining her sovereignty, Aceh's independence and suzerainty over her vassals. In this chapter, I explore the dynamics between the sultanah, her orang kaya and the VOC officials relating to Perak. I will illustrate how the VOC's incursions into Aceh's political and commercial spheres of influence affected Aceh's traditional relations with her vassals. More importantly, I will illuminate how the contests between the VOC and Aceh over Perak's tin trade had tremendous repercussions on Aceh's court politics. Like the jewel affair, this episode in Aceh's history—which I call the Perak affair—covering Sultanah Safiatuddin's maturing years, is an important case study that reveals the sultanah's leadership style, and the means by which she not only survived on the throne but also consolidated her position.

The Perak Affair

Aceh conquered Perak twice—once in 1575, triumphantly, and again in 1620, traumatically. In 1575, when Ali Riayat Syah attacked Perak, he took the Perak sultan's widow and her children, among others, to Aceh. Her eldest son married an Acehnese princess and later became the sultan of Aceh, taking the title Sultan Alauddin Mansur Shah (r. 1577–86). From 1620, however, Perak's fortunes turned and she instead became a vassal of Aceh. In 1620, the warrior sultan, Iskandar Muda, invaded and devastated Perak, and placed on the throne his chosen ruler, a captive Perak prince, who became Sultan Mahmud Shah.[1] From then on Perak was a vassal state of Aceh.

Three years into her reign, Sultanah Safiatuddin Syah faced serious challenges from the VOC regarding not only her suzerainty over Perak but, more importantly, her control of Perak's tin trade. After conquering Melaka, the VOC was determined to make the port a commercial success, or at least make it pay for its own upkeep.[2] Company officials wanted to ensure that they inherited what they believed were Portuguese rights—one of which was the surrender of half of Perak's tin to Melaka at a fixed price. The problem was that these so-called rights existed merely in theory. After the Dutch conquest of Melaka, they realised that Perak was channelling tin to Aceh, and that the kingdom was reaping the profits of the lucrative tin trade by selling it to English, Indian and other Asian traders.

The VOC's main means of controlling the tin trade on the peninsula were to pressure the tin-producing areas to sign contracts with the company and, when necessary, blockade them. On 11 July 1642, the company signed a contract with Kedah stipulating that Kedah deliver half of its tin to company traders at a fixed price, forbidding all other foreign traders from trading in its port without a company pass. Similar contracts were signed with Ujong Salang on 20 October 1643 and with Bangeri on 1 January 1645. Only Perak refused to sign a contract on the grounds that

---

[1] Andaya, *Perak, the Abode of Grace*, p. 43.
[2] Sinnappah Arasaratnam, "Some Notes on the Dutch in Malacca and the Indo-Malayan Trade 1641–1670", *Journal of Southeast Asian History* 10, 3 (1969): 481.

it had no right to do so, as Perak was a dependency of Aceh.³ Frustrated with the failure to obtain enough tin, Antonio van Diemen, the governor general, blockaded the Perak River in 1644 and 1645, allowing only Acehnese and Perak vessels to pass. The company stated that it blockaded Perak to enforce its right to half the tin of Perak, a right it believed it had inherited from the Portuguese.⁴

The blockade was ineffective as Perak and Acehnese vessels continued transporting tin from Perak to Aceh where it was sold to Indian traders, who were always willing to pay higher prices. These Indian traders established themselves on Sumatra's north coast and transported tin as the sultanah's subjects under the very eyes of Dutch ship captains.

On 24 March 1645 the company sent an envoy, Arnold Vlamingh, to Perak to negotiate a contract, but the sultan again refused to conclude a contract on his own authority and referred Vlamingh to the queen of Aceh.⁵ From Melaka, Governor van Vliet wrote to the High Council in Batavia maintaining that the blockade of Perak was important because the port was the source of Aceh's prosperity. As long as Perak flourished, Aceh was Melaka's ruin. He complained that thanks to the supply of cloth Indian merchants sold in Aceh, from where it was distributed to Perak and other areas on the Peninsula, nobody wanted to come to Melaka. He feared that because of this, Kedah too, wanted to break its contract. On 25 February 1645, Jan Harmanszoon wrote to the governor general that Kedah and Perak had decided to supply each other with cloth.⁶ The following year the company received 300 bahar of tin, half of what it had received in 1645; furthermore, the authorities in Kedah had allowed foreign merchants to trade there once more.⁷

Antonio van Diemen realised that in order to get to Perak's tin he had first to negotiate with Aceh, its overlord. He appointed Arnold Vlamingh

---

³ J.E. Heeres and P.A. Tiele, eds., *Bouwstoffen voor de Geschiedenis der Nederlanders in den Maleischen Archipel* [Information for the History of the Dutch in the Malay Archipelago] Vol. 2 ('s-Gravenhage: Martinus Nijhoff, 1890–95), p. xi; Andaya, *Perak, the Abode of Grace*, pp. 44–5.
⁴ Heeres and Tiele, *Bouwstoffen*, p. xi; Irwin, "The Dutch and the Tin Trade of Malaya", p. 268.
⁵ Heeres and Tiele, *Bouwstoffen*, p. xlv.
⁶ Ibid., p. xlvi.
⁷ Ibid., p. xlviii.

to head this mission. When Vlamingh arrived in Aceh on 23 June 1645 he was well received, but he discovered that the Acehnese were not happy with the Dutch because of the Perak blockade. Despite his perseverance, Vlamingh failed to achieve anything except the sultanah's vague promise that she would order the sultan of Perak to deliver a good quantity of tin to the company.

By 1647 Vlamingh had become governor of Melaka, and he wrote to Jan Thijssen—the man who succeeded him as envoy to Aceh—that he had not received a *kati* (a measure of weight) of tin from Kedah and no more than 10 bahar from Perak, while the Indian traders transported 48,800 pounds of tin to Surat, including 1,500 bahar from Perak alone.[8] Vlamingh proposed a radical measure to force Indian traders to pay tolls in Melaka before they could go to the tin quarters. Vlamingh wanted a new Mataram-Melaka-Batavia trade network to rival that between Surat, Aceh and the SWC. The Dutch in Melaka would obtain rice from Makassar and pepper from the east coast of Sumatra to be exchanged for cloth obtained from Palembang and Inderagiri. Other foreigners were forbidden to trade.[9]

In December 1647, Jochum Roelofszoon van Deutecom was sent to Aceh to address what the Dutch considered an alarming situation whereby the Acehnese were making extraordinary profits and appeared uninterested in maintaining their friendship and alliance with the Dutch.[10] Twenty-four soldiers accompanied Van Deutecom to demonstrate that the Dutch would not discount the use of force if necessary. To appease Van Deutecom, the sultanah sent two Acehnese envoys to Batavia to negotiate about Perak's tin trade. Even after intense negotiations, the Acehnese envoys refused to promise the delivery of a yearly fixed quantity to the company, certainly not the 600 bahar that Van Deutecom demanded. The Acehnese also refused to grant the Dutch the exclusive-nation treatment in Perak. In response, Governor General Cornelis van

---

[8] Ibid., p. i.
[9] Ibid., p. xlix.
[10] NA, VOC 1166, Memorije voor den E. Jochum Roeloffs van Deutecum Raat van Indie gaende de legatie aende Coninghinne van Atchin [Memoir of the E. Jochum Roeloffs van Deutecum delegation from the Council of the Indies to the Queen of Aceh], 1647, f. 733R.

der Lijn warned captains of Muslim ships not to land in Aceh, Perak, Kedah or Ujong Salangh and the surrounding areas.[11] In May 1648, the oppercoopman Huibrecht van den Broek was sent to Aceh to empty the factory and sent a strong message to the sultanah and the Acehnese that they would not benefit from severing their alliance and cooperation with the company.

Truijtman's Missions to Aceh and Perak, 1649–52

Governor General van der Lijn appointed the oppercoopman Johan Truijtman as the commissar to Aceh to carry out the company's plans. On his arrival on 13 September 1649, Truijtman reported that the Acehnese were not in a happy mood at all. One thousand armed men guarded the Aceh River and the Acehnese appeared hostile, as if they were preparing for war. This distrust of the Dutch was apparent when the Acehnese even stationed a number of guards at the company's lodge to monitor its servants.[12] Their suspicion and displeasure were owing to several reasons: the Dutch blockade of the river at Aceh; the continued blockade of the Perak River, which prevented the sultanah's own ships from entering or leaving; the long delay in the return of the sultanah's envoys from Batavia to discuss the Perak issue; and the hostile actions committed against a Malabar ship in Aceh by Dutch patrol vessels.[13]

The Acehnese also intercepted letters sent from Melaka to the Dutch resident in Aceh, Philip de Salengre, who was called to court and interrogated. Although Truijtman did not elaborate on the contents of the letters, they most likely contained instructions to Salengre about the need to maximise the VOC's profits and to minimise those of other traders. The anti-Dutch laksamana chided him, explaining that more people in Aceh were able to read Dutch, and the letters were proof of the company's

---

[11] Cornelis van der Lijn was governor general in Batavia from 1645 to 1650.
[12] Heeres and Tiele, *Bouwstoffen*, p. 483.
[13] NA, VOC 1171, Rapport substanteel aen d' Ed Heer Cornelis van der Lijn Gouverneur Generael ende Heeren Raden van India, over d'expeditien in Aetchijn bij de Coninglijcke Maijt aldaar [Report to Governor General Cornelis van der Lijn about the expedition to Aceh], 1649, ff. 182V–183R.

unfair trading practices, such as forbidding traders from trading and not wanting to pay tolls.[14]

In contrast to the laksamana's rude treatment of Truijtman, Sultanah Safiatuddin granted the oppercoopman an audience on 19 September, a mere six days after his arrival, much sooner than the usual two weeks. This attested to her concern about recent events, but it was also characteristic of her style of accommodating the Dutch. She received Truijtman with her customary hospitality, in sharp contrast to, for instance, Iskandar Thani's very hostile reception of Jan de Meere in 1640 after learning about the Dutch alliance with his vassal, Johor.[15]

Truijtman reported that the Dutch were accompanied to court by Binthara Blangh, Baljouw Shabandar, the naeleer, and the two recently returned envoys from Batavia, Sri Bidia Indra and Tonadja Radja, as well as the Dutch skipper, Resident Salengre, and the bookkeeper, Brittsen. Fifty-two servants carried the governor general's letter, placed on a gold plate and carried by elephant with a palanquin and gifts to court. The sultanah welcomed Truijtman's delegation and treated them to elephant fights and stage plays, but as it was the fasting month of Ramadan, no food or drinks were served during the day. The queen apologised for this and hoped the Dutch would not think ill of her for not treating them with food. However, later in the evening when the fast ended, and after she provided the company officials with more singing performances at the candlelit court, she treated them to sumptuous food served on gold plates and honoured them with betel-box.[16] Later that night, Truijtman and company were sent back to their lodge on elephants and horses, and the sultanah even presented them with a few horses for their own use. Although no official discussions took place, the sultanah, as customary, had laid the groundwork for an easing of tensions with the company officials.

As in the jewel affair, Safiatuddin's treatment of the Dutch should not be interpreted as weakness on her part. At the 2 October audience

---

[14] NA, VOC 1171, Dagh-Register gehouden bij den Oppercoopman Johan Truijtman 1649, f. 200V.
[15] NA, VOC 1171, Rapport substanteel aen d' Ed Heer Cornelis van der Lijn, 1649, f. 184V.
[16] NA, VOC 1171, Dagh-Register gehouden bij Johan Truijtman, 1649, ff. 205R–205V.

with Sultanah Safiatuddin, Truijtman noted how annoyed she was about the affair in Perak and the blockade of the Perak River, "even though I have not mentioned them yet, this was asked repeatedly by the queen. Her majesty had taken the blockade of Perak to heart and showed public displeasure and addressed the court in an angry and harsh manner".[17] She asked, "How come the governor general has now besieged my land so much so that my own vessels could not be allowed to enter and exit the Perak River?"[18] She also questioned Truijtman about the arrival of two Dutch ships—the *Delfshaven* and the *Macareel*—in Aceh's harbour, where they were patrolling without Acehnese consent.[19] Truijtman related that the sultanah took the patrol and blockade of the Aceh River with utmost seriousness, and she would go to war if the blockades of Aceh and Perak continued.[20] Furthermore, she was displeased with the company's actions against foreign ships trading in Aceh. The sultanah complained that "in front of our own eyes the Dutch had fired at a certain Malabar vessel that was anchored in our harbour".

Despite her displeasure, to help resolve these tensions she commissioned a notable named Sri Maharaja Lella to go to Perak. He was to travel with Truijtman, the Perak envoys, and her *boedjangh*s (royal messengers) armed with her *estemie* (the ruler's order bearing the royal seal) to the sultan of Perak, Sultan Muzaffar Shah, within five days to redress the problem. She requested that Truijtman provide a pass for her ministers and three of her vessels that would depart for Perak. She also promised to provide an estemie allowing only ships from Aceh carrying her passes the right to trade in Perak.[21]

On 12 October 1649, the sultanah replied to Truijtman's various requests, and made her own demands clear. She wanted Dutch ships patrolling against Gujarati Muslim traders at Aceh to be taken farther

---

[17] NA, VOC 1171, Rapport substanteel aen d' Ed Heer Cornelis van der Lijn, 1649, f. 186R.

[18] NA, VOC 1171, Dagh-Register gehouden bij den Oppercoopman Johan Truijtman, 1649, f. 186V.

[19] Heeres and Tiele, *Bouwstoffen*, pp. 489–90.

[20] NA, VOC 1171, Rapport substanteel aen d' Ed Heer Cornelis van der Lijn, 1649, f. 187V.

[21] NA, VOC 1171, Rapport substanteel aen d' Ed Heer Cornelis van der Lijn, 1649, f. 187R.

away. For her part the sultanah promised to help and continue to favour the company resident and other officials who would remain in Aceh. The sultanah also registered her displeasure with the company's blockades of Perak and Aceh and said she would write a letter to the governor general to complain and demand restitution. In addition, she commissioned the envoy Sri Bidia Indra to go to Batavia to negotiate about and resolve the grievances.

Despite Safiatuddin's compromises, the Dutch were intransigent. Truijtman insisted that it was the governor general's wish that passes be granted for three vessels to sail to Perak, but that only one vessel would be allowed to return.[22] In addition, they refused to pull their patrol ships out of Aceh. During their last meeting before Truijtman's departure, the sultanah asked why the ships remained, especially when she no longer monitored company officials at their lodge. Truijtman replied that they were keeping watch on the Gujarati Muslims who were their enemies. The sultanah asked, "if the Gujaratis were the enemies of the Dutch, why must you monitor our harbour? Should you not blockade and patrol outside Surat's harbour instead, where your enemies are, not here to the aversion and terror of my people?" Truijtman did not seem to sense the resentment this action caused or the seriousness and urgency of the sultanah's request. He merely replied that if her majesty was displeased, she should write to the governor general!

The Perak affair, Dutch harassment of Indian traders in Aceh's harbour and their high-handed attitude not only brought tensions to the brink of war, but they hardened the divisions between the company's friends and enemies at court. As was customary, Dutch envoys visited the orang kaya with gifts to facilitate the discussion of important matters. On one such visit, the company's friend, the Lebai Kita Kali, appointed by the sultanah in 1644 as the Maharaja Sri Maharaja, advised Truijtman to visit his closest follower, Maharaja Binthara, in secret to clear up some major misunderstandings and to dispel suspicions that the company was about to wage war against the kingdom.[23] Truijtman explained to

---

[22] NA, VOC 1171, Dagh-Register gehouden bij den Oppercoopman Johan Truijtman, 1649, f. 237V.

[23] The Kali's son took over his position. It is not known what happened to the earlier anti-Dutch Maharaja.

the Maharaja that the company was patrolling Aceh's harbour because the Muslims in Surat had attacked and murdered Dutch traders and destroyed the company's lodge.[24] The Dutch ships were merely keeping a close watch on their Surat enemies. Truijtman claimed that the Dutch blockade of the Perak River had no other aim than to execute the queen's order to the sultan of Perak that the Dutch be allowed to procure tin which, Truijtman claimed, had not been properly obeyed. Maharaja Binthara assured Truijtman that he would keep the sultanah informed of the Dutch's intentions. In return he asked Truijtman to grant the sultanah's request for passes for her and the orang kaya's ships. Despite the pro-Dutch faction's efforts to ease tensions on the last audience day, when the sultanah requested passes for three vessels to sail to Perak, Truijtman adamantly refused.

This merely served to increase the ire of the anti-Dutch faction—especially the laksamana and his supporter, Paduka Tuan. Throughout Truijtman's stay in Aceh they had both refused to see him on the excuse that they were ill, and they had been absent at court when the company officials were there. They even boycotted the sultanah's fishing trip, organised before Truijtman and his delegates departed.[25] However, they had to attend Truijtman's last audience if they wished to make their displeasure known. Upon hearing Truijtman's excuses regarding the Dutch patrol ships in Aceh's harbour and the Perak blockade, the laksamana and Sri Paduka Tuan responded by saying "there is no sincere friendship when men seek strange ways to become enemies". They continued, "you should ask yourself why you need to blockade a friend's harbour and why we should continue to maintain that friendship, it is better to just say what your real intentions are".

Despite the pro-Dutch faction's last-ditch effort to warn Truijtman about the importance of acceding to the sultanah's request, nothing was done. The final exchange between Truijtman and the company's friends revealed the high tensions at court and the great suspicion with which the Acehnese viewed the company.[26] A day before Truijtman's departure he

---

[24] Heeres and Tiele, *Bouwstoffen*, p. 484.
[25] NA, VOC 1171, Dagh-Register gehouden bij den Oppercoopman Johan Truijtman, 1649, f. 236V.
[26] Heeres and Tiele, *Bouwstoffen*, p. 496.

and Salengre went to court to fetch the queen's letter. At the orang kaya's balai they met with the company's friends, the Maharaja Sri Maharaja, his good friend, Maharaja Binthara, and his son-in-law, the Maharaja de Radia, together with two or three *binthara*s (royal court officials) and the envoys, Sri Bidia Indra and Radia Moedeliar. While they were eating the Maharaja requested that the governor general facilitate the speedy return of her majesty's envoys once the business between the company and the Acehnese had been settled. He signalled to Truijtman that this mission was critical as it could result in the alliance continuing or going to war. He said:

> [N]ow or never you must succeed, considering the friendship between us and the knowledge that her majesty more than ever, henceforth, had allowed no other foreigners to trade in Perak and that the tin remained only for her majesty and the company.

The Maharaja Binthara added "the affair and the outcome of this embassy now remain in God's hands, whether it ends in the maintenance of friendship or in war, because we have contributed in all ways towards the preservation of this friendship".[27] The Maharaja concluded by reassuring the company officials that they had the sultanah's favour and thus should not worry she would change the exclusive trade privileges granted to them.

Despite Truijtman's insensitivities and intransigence, he reported that the sultanah treated him well right up to his departure. However, she made her displeasure known by presenting him with a mere copper dagger, rather than the typically sumptuous gifts of tin, pepper and luxuries such as Acehnese dress. She apologised for the small value of the dagger saying that it was owing to Truijtman's hasty departure.[28]

Truijtman left without reassuring the Acehnese of the company's good intentions towards them and did not alleviate the suspicions of the anti-Dutch faction. He had managed to secure some verbal promises regarding the company's new prerogatives for the tin trade in Perak. The sultanah agreed that only the company and Aceh could trade in Perak and

---

[27] Ibid., p. 497.
[28] NA, VOC 1171, Dagh-Register gehouden bij den Oppercoopman Johan Truijtman, 1649, f. 248V.

no European or Indian traders were allowed there, a provision included in her written mandate to the sultan of Perak. She then sent her own envoys to accompany Truijtman to Perak to negotiate the contract with the sultan, after which her envoys were to return to Aceh, before proceeding to Batavia to conclude and ratify the contract. On 11 August 1650, Truijtman arrived in Perak and reported that the sultan had accepted the sultanah's order. A contract was then signed between the sultan and the company representatives on 15 August 1650. Governor General van der Lijn wrote to the *Heren Zeventien* that the sultan of Perak had readily submitted to the disposition of her Acehnese majesty. He added that the exclusion of all other foreigners from Perak and the SWC granted by the queen of Aceh was extremely favourable to the company.[29] In his *Dagh-Register* Truijtman noted that although the sultan of Perak generally agreed with most of the points, he was not happy with the company's request to pay a fixed price for tin and receive toll-free privileges.[30] The sultan stressed that this old custom must be respected and, more importantly, this was a source of his livelihood.

Trouble in the Acehnese Court

After the seemingly smooth reception in Perak, Truijtman brought the sultan's letter to the sultanah. When he arrived he once again found the Acehnese in a state of agitation and confusion: the *Delfshaven* and *Macareel* were still blockading Aceh's harbour and keeping watch over what the company claimed were Surat ships. This action had an adverse effect on Aceh's trade for that year, and Truijtman reported that the suspension of the Muslim traders' activities resulted in a scarcity of cloth and an increase in prices.[31] The Acehnese were also angry because Dutch officials had mistreated their envoys to Perak—whom the Dutch accused

---

[29] *Generale Missiven*, Vol. 2, 1639 to 1655, p. 457.
[30] NA, VOC 1175, Origineel rapport aen d'Ed. Hr Gouverneur Generael ende heren Raad van Indie door den Oppercoopman Johan Truijtman [Original report to the Governor General and the Council of the Indies from senior trader Johan Truijtman], 1651, f. 307R.
[31] NA, VOC 1175, Origineel rapport aen d'Ed. Hr Gouverneur Generael ende heren Raad van Indie door den Oppercoopman Johan Truijtman, 1651, ff. 307R–307V.

of not having proper passes—and the company continued to blockade the Perak River.

A few days before Truijtman's arrival, the laksamana and the Paduka Tuan decided to move against the company and the orang kaya faction keen to uphold the company's interest in Aceh. Truijtman reported that they publicly reproached the Maharaja Sri Maharaja and accused him of seeking to usurp the throne with Dutch help.[32] He also related that the laksamana and his followers were trying to strip the Maharaja Sri Maharaja of his position as the first in the council by spreading lies about him that aroused fear and suspicion with the sultanah and the rest of the orang kaya.[33] Truijtman wrote that the laksamana libelled his enemy in the queen's presence. Nevertheless, the Maharaja remained calm and patient, stoically enduring this incident. The Acehnese court was waiting for the governor general's letter and his response regarding the problem in Perak. Truijtman believed that with this letter all the accusations and lies concocted against the Maharaja would be proven wrong, and he could once again be elevated at court. For the time being he continued to be suspected. Indeed, Truijtman reported that just before his arrival the Maharaja had gone on an elephant hunt. It was highly likely that the sultanah had provided this opportunity for the Maharaja so he did not have to face the Dutch delegation and be put in a difficult position.[34]

However, the sultanah herself was in a difficult situation: she had to accommodate an increasingly uncompromising and insensitive envoy in Truijtman on the one hand and an increasingly hostile anti-Dutch faction on the other. A few days after Truijtman's arrival, the governor general's letter and gifts were brought to court on audience day. The envoy found a very hostile court, and the Maharaja's followers were very silent.[35] Where a little diplomacy and sensitivity could have helped ease tensions, Truijtman was instead arrogant and defensive. Acting more

---

[32] NA, VOC 1175, Origineel rapport aen d'Ed. Hr Gouverneur Generael ende heren Raad van Indie door den Oppercoopman Johan Truijtman, 1651, f. 308R.
[33] Ibid.
[34] NA, VOC 1175, Origineel rapport aen d'Ed. Hr Gouverneur Generael ende heren Raad van Indie door den Oppercoopman Johan Truijtman, 1651, f. 308V.
[35] Ibid.

like a merchant than the diplomat he was, he immediately proceeded to demand new commercial privileges! He wanted the sultanah's permission to purchase some elephants and requested the customary visits to the orang kaya, so he could discuss the company's business. Entries in his *Dagh-Register* demonstrate his total lack of diplomatic finesse and sensitivity. "Wholly unexpectedly," he wrote, "her majesty promptly denied this request and with such violent demeanour". Sultanah Safiatuddin explained that since the time of her father, al-Marhom Makota Alam, the company had neither bought nor exported any elephants, and she insisted this would continue. Furthermore, she argued that she had given the company enough privileges on the SWC and Perak to the exclusion of all other foreign traders, European and Indian. The sultanah concluded that the company officials should be contented and should not make further annual demands. The sultanah also postponed Truijtman's visits to the orang kaya, both as a sign of displeasure and to delay the execution of the company's business.[36] Truijtman concluded that all the Acehnese resistance and hostility were owing to the "malicious party" at court. He saw the sultanah's explanations of her total rejection to grant permission to purchase some elephants as "frivolous" reasons, "futile objections" and mere excuses. The real reason, Truijtman suspected, was the Muslim trade from Masulipatnam and Bengal—whose traders since time immemorial had annually bought a great number of elephants—brought great profits to the Acehnese queen and her orang kaya. In addition, they received a lot of profit from the tolls and other heavy duties imposed on this trade.[37] In this assessment Truijtman was correct—the elephant trade was too lucrative for Safiatuddin to bow to Dutch pressure. She managed to maintain the profitable Aceh-India elephant trade unmolested by the Dutch. The sultanah's outright rejection of Truijtman's new requests and the absence of the pro-Dutch Maharaja emboldened the anti-Dutch faction. Truijtman complained that the "malicious faction" led by the laksamana, seeing her majesty take their arguments into consideration, spoke out against the company's position.

---

[36] NA, VOC 1175, Origineel rapport aen d'Ed. Hr Gouverneur Generael ende heren Raad van Indie door den Oppercoopman Johan Truijtman, 1651, f. 309R.
[37] NA, VOC 1175, Origineel rapport aen d'Ed. Hr Gouverneur Generael ende heren Raad van Indie door den Oppercoopman Johan Truijtman, 1651, ff. 323V–324R.

They urged the sultanah and the rest of the orang kaya to annul the company's existing prerogatives on the grounds that the whole court had never consented to the privileges. The laksamana added that the Dutch had proven themselves unworthy of such privileges and that it was time for them to leave.[38]

By this time Truijtman's patience with the anti-Dutch faction had run out, as the notations in his *Dagh-Register* make clear. He calls the laksamana "base and vile" and describes his followers as "crazy-headed and spiteful" (*dol-koppigen wrevel moedigen*). As for the sultanah, Truijtman wrote that she was to be pitied and deplored because she appeared to have given the laksamana's faction so much of a hearing that she was unduly influenced by them.[39] He also recorded that he had twice warned the sultanah of his intention to absent himself from court as a sign of his displeasure, a threat he believed would give her majesty time to reconsider her actions.

Truijtman could not have been more wrong in his assessment of the sultanah and his ability to threaten the Acehnese. While the sultanah had remained firm in her refusal to grant Truijtman's new requests, it did not mean she was under the control of the anti-Dutch faction. She continued to keep in touch with the pro-Dutch Maharaja and together they managed to restrain the anti-Dutch faction at court. Every single day, Truijtman wrote, the Maharaja and his followers continued to pursue their course of action. He noted that although the Maharaja was absent from court, secret messengers kept him informed. This explains why the Maharaja was not only able to make a timely return to court but that he did so in grand style, accompanied by a large number of captured elephants for the sultanah. The sultanah honoured him and, according to Truijtman, the threats spun by the malicious party ended, and the Maharaja was no longer regarded with suspicion. It is important to note, however, that even in his absence—when the laksamana and his followers dominated the court—the sultanah maintained her favour for the Dutch, proving Truijtman wrong.

---

[38] NA, VOC 1175, Origineel rapport aen d'Ed. Hr Gouverneur Generael ende heren Raad van Indie door den Oppercoopman Johan Truijtman, 1651, ff. 310R–310V.

[39] NA, VOC 1175, Origineel rapport aen d'Ed. Hr Gouverneur Generael ende heren Raad van Indie door den Oppercoopman Johan Truijtman, 1651, ff. 310V–311R.

Sultanah Safiatuddin's Maturing Years: Politics of Consolidation 107

True, the sultanah had rejected the company's demands for new privileges, but she remained firm in accommodating the Dutch regarding the tin trade in Perak. She rejected the laksamana's demands to arbitrarily annul all Dutch privileges. Instead she confirmed the earlier treaty provision of excluding all other traders in Perak, except for the Acehnese and the Dutch. The queen specified that no vessels could go to Perak apart from her own, the company's and two each from her orang kaya. The sultanah ratified the contract of 15 August 1650 and allowed new concessions regarding the tin trade. She even agreed to fix the price of tin at 31¼ in *spetie* (cash) per bahar (the market price fluctuated between 31 and 43 per bahar) over the sultan of Perak's objection.[40] However, she protected her vassal's interests by not allowing toll-free privileges for the company, a privilege that the sultan of Perak himself was unwilling to give as this was his and his orang kaya's main source of revenue. The sultanah was "completely horrified" by this request and argued that this would greatly prejudice her sovereignty and lessen her authority in the eyes of her Perak subjects. She told Truijtman that the Dutch should not complain about this as now they could obtain most of the tin.[41] She also refused to fix the amount of tin the company could obtain. With the wise counsel of the Maharaja, Truijtman decided not to press this demand. The Maharaja explained that the sultanah did not want to taint her credibility/authority by promising something she could not deliver: no one could ensure the amount of tin in the mountains as it was God-given and did not depend on the weather.[42]

With the conclusion of this episode, Truijtman's criticisms of the sultanah vanished. He reported that the company not only had the queen's goodwill and generosity but also enjoyed her favour.[43] He added "although the orangkaya could sustain their influence, she still had enough authority to decide over our affairs, although her authority over Perak and the

---

[40] NA, VOC 1175, Origineel rapport aen d'Ed. Hr Gouverneur Generael ende heren Raad van Indie door den Oppercoopman Johan Truijtman, 1651, f. 315R.
[41] *Generale Missiven*, Vol. 2, p. 463.
[42] NA, VOC 1175, Origineel rapport aen d'Ed. Hr Gouverneur Generael ende heren Raad van Indie door den Oppercoopman Johan Truijtman, 1651, f. 313R.
[43] NA, VOC 1175, Origineel rapport aen d'Ed. Hr Gouverneur Generael ende heren Raad van Indie door den Oppercoopman Johan Truijtman, 1651, f. 313V.

Malay people may have declined". He quoted her as saying: "Commander, we shall give the order to Sultan Muzaffar Shah that only the Dutch and Acehnese could trade and export tin from Perak, as much as they can obtain". However, she emphasised Aceh's independence and, despite Dutch pressure, she was not keen to exclude non-Dutch traders from Aceh's trade. She pointed out that Aceh was peaceful, and she was able to provide protection to all merchants trading there. Truijtman reported that she said "since you came here with your family last year to stay, you could see for yourself our good intentions".[44]

> We shall write to the governor general so that the Muslims could come here to trade and would not be expelled. If there were new troubles, then we would take care of it. I can reassure the governor general that I could rule my land in peace as my predecessors had done.[45]

By this she promised that the Dutch could trade in peace.

Truijtman reported that from that point on war was averted and the old friendship between Aceh and the Dutch was renewed. In particular, the Dutch were allowed to use the old English quarters for their new lodge, an arrangement the sultanah guaranteed with the blessed words *Zalla Talla* (Insha Allah/God Willing), which was confirmed by all the orang kaya and their followers with the word "daulat".[46] Truijtman concluded his report of this episode by noting that his respect at court had been restored, and her majesty had addressed his just complaints over things of importance so their reciprocal and trustworthy old alliance was not subverted by the evil intention of a few opponents.[47] Truijtman boasted that his actions and threats had resulted in the sultanah's rejection of the "audacious (*stouten*) laksamana who had come to the extreme".

To demonstrate that all was well, the sultanah presented Truijtman with three bahar of pepper and two of tin, and she instructed the four

---

[44] NA, VOC 1175, Origineel rapport aen d'Ed. Hr Gouverneur Generael ende heren Raad van Indie door den Oppercoopman Johan Truijtman, 1651, f. 314R.

[45] NA, VOC 1175, Origineel rapport aen d'Ed. Hr Gouverneur Generael ende heren Raad van Indie door den Oppercoopman Johan Truijtman, 1651, f. 314V.

[46] NA, VOC 1175, Origineel rapport aen d'Ed. Hr Gouverneur Generael ende heren Raad van Indie door den Oppercoopman Johan Truijtman, 1651, f. 312R.

[47] NA, VOC 1175, Origineel rapport aen d'Ed. Hr Gouverneur Generael ende heren Raad van Indie door den Oppercoopman Johan Truijtman, 1651, f. 311V.

members of the rijxraad, the governor of elephants and other officials at court to extend an exceptional welcome to Truijtman which, according to his account, they did. Sultanah Safiatuddin herself concluded the affair by inviting him for the second time to the innermost court and seating him in front of the throne. Before a sumptuous meal was laid out, he was treated to a very beautiful Javanese dance performed by 26 girls and 28 boys expensively dressed and made up. When he was about to depart, her majesty's letter and gifts were presented to him with great reverence.

Truijtman sailed to Perak on 9 November 1650 and arrived in Perak on 6 December. Notwithstanding the sultan's ill health, the Acehnese boedjangh lost no time in bringing the queen's estemie to the balai. Despite this immediate reception, the Perak orang kaya refused to agree to fix the price of tin at 31¼ per bahar and instead wanted it increased to 40 per bahar. They were also not inclined to expel the Muslim traders who were residing in Perak. Truijtman reported that at this point the Acehnese boedjangh returned to Aceh to ask for advice. After this second consultation with Aceh, the Perak court elites finally agreed that the Muslims traders and residents in Perak would depart and the price of tin was to be fixed at 31¼ per bahar.[48] This shows that the sultan of Perak still deferred to Aceh for instructions, accepting the sultanah's commands. After striking this agreement, Truijtman departed from Perak to Melaka and then to Batavia. Despite these concessions, however, the three-year siege of Perak continued.

In his report to the *Heren Zeventien* about Truijtman's mission, the governor general wrote that it was only thanks to the pleasure and affection of the queen herself that Commissioner Truijtman had ultimately won respect and good treatment from the whole court.[49] Despite the initial hostilities Truijtman faced from the laksamana and his followers, an envoy of the company had never been so well received in Aceh. The court was pleasant and charming, and the sultanah was honourable and generous, presenting a gift of 46 bahar of tin for the governor general, and for

---

[48] NA, VOC 1175, Origineel rapport aen d'Ed. Hr Gouverneur Generael ende heren Raad van Indie door den Oppercoopman Johan Truijtman, 1651, f. 317R.
[49] *Generale Missiven*, Vol. 2, 1639 to 1655, p. 463.

Truijtman three bahar of pepper, two bahar of tin, a dress, a sword and a kris.[50] Her majesty continued to govern a calm government, she was well disposed to the company and she had effectively shown her interest in the company's welfare regarding the trade in Perak. In addition, she was keen to continue the friendship and alliance—so long maintained—and there remained no differences between the company and her majesty.[51] The queen had even proposed that Truijtman take up residence in Aceh with his family. More importantly, the governor general continued, the sultan and the orang kaya of Perak accepted the queen's estemie and confirmed the previous articles of the 15 August 1650 contract regarding Perak's tin trade.

Truijtman's assessment of the sultanah reflected his own bias which was, in turn, shaped by the course of his negotiations. Her majesty, he noted, was as variable as the wind which often gave rise to problems with business that otherwise could be easily executed. When she had denied his request, he judged her to be weak and under the influence of the "malicious faction", and he described her as strong when she continued to accommodate the company's interests. Despite the intense resentment against the Dutch at court and the absence of the Maharaja, she remained mindful of the dangers of escalating tensions with the Dutch and the importance of maintaining good relations with the company, and she was able to stick to her position. She did not annul any of the privileges granted to the company as the laksamana requested, but neither did she grant all of the company's demands after the Maharaja returned. Despite all the challenges facing her, and Truijtman's boastful comments about his influence over the sultanah, the governor general's report recognises the queen's role in supporting Truijtman and maintaining good relations with the VOC, as well as her ability to bring the orang kaya to ratify the contract.

Sultanah Safiatuddin had survived the challenges by balancing the pro- and anti-Dutch factions and was largely successful in maintaining the alliance with the VOC by accommodating some, but not all, of the Dutch demands. She was also able to restrain the laksamana and his followers

---

[50] Ibid.
[51] Ibid., p. 519.

from challenging her authority to accommodate the Dutch. However, this was just a temporary respite before the sultanah faced even greater threats from her male elites. In Truijtman's report to the *opperhooft* (head resident) in Bengal, he confided that "the Acehnese friendship remained as treacherous and unstable as their character. We can justly perceive that no matter how much courtesy and humility we show from our honest alliance, this arrogant people appear to become more bold and spiteful." He warned that it was important to ameliorate the great anger, envy and discord of the rijxraaden and the orang kaya: such discord was not to the company's advantage.[52]

More Trouble at Aceh's Court[53]

Truijtman's warnings proved prescient, and the VOC officials in Batavia soon received news from a *burgher* (free Dutch citizen) vessel that the whole Acehnese court was in an uproar. Governor General Joan Maetsuyker, in his report to the *Heren Zeventien* found in the *Generale Missiven* of 1651, reported the coup as such:

> ... from a free burgher vessel came the following rumour that the whole court there [Aceh] was in an uproar. The *grooten laximana* [great Laksamana], with two or three of his accomplices together with some members of the council who did not favour the Company had rebelled against the *oppersten rijxraet Maradja Siri Maradja* [first Councillor, Maharaja Sri Maharaja], a loyal and exceptional friend of the Dutch nation, and publicly accused him of wanting to seize the throne with the help of the Dutch. This caused such a great revolt at court under the orangkaya and their followers that for a long time no audience or access to the court was given and it was uncertain whether the Queen was sick, dead or alive, so that finally the mentioned Laksamana with his followers, through sly practices, had gained sufficient control of the court, that in the mentioned confusion, Maradja de Radja

---

[52] NA, VOC 1175, Origineel rapport aen d'Ed. Hr Gouverneur Generael ende heren Raad van Indie door den Oppercoopman Johan Truijtman, 1651, ff. 326R–326V.
[53] I believe this revolt took place between the end of 1650 and early 1651, as it was shortly after Truijtman's departure from Aceh on 9 November 1650 and before the Perak massacre of April 1651.

[Maharaja de Raja], son-in-law of Maharaja Sri Maharaja, who was riding an elephant to court was shot to the head and died. Maharaja Sri Maharaja, with the help of some people remained alive but he was stripped of his weapons, elephants, his charges and authority and was emplaced to live as a private person. Sibi d'Indra and Radja Modliaer who were in Batavia during the previous year [1650], were accused by the Laksamana of conspiring with the Dutch to sell Aceh to the Company. He accused them of trying to bring soldiers and ships to Aceh to install Maharaja Sri Maharaja as King. The Laksamana and his followers cruelly tormented the envoys. Finally, they were set free but all their followers, women, children and slaves were confiscated and like Maharaja Sri Maharaja, were stripped of all authority. There was still no news about whether the Queen was alive or not.[54]

The Massacre of VOC Officials in Perak

Shortly after this revolt in Aceh, officials in Batavia received news from Melaka about the massacre of company officials and servants in Perak.[55] Trouble over the contract with Perak began shortly after Commissioner Truijtman's departure in 1650, as some foreigners who had lived there for a long time proved unwilling to leave. It also appears that the company obtained little tin, the sultan and orang kaya were unwilling to execute the terms of the contract because of problems with some of the provisions. They were especially unhappy about the clause requiring them to expel Muslim traders who had resided there for a long time. Furthermore, the Acehnese officials in Perak were also anti-Dutch. It seems likely that the successful revolt led by the anti-Dutch faction at the Acehnese court had emboldened anti-Dutch elements in Perak as well.

Hostilities seem to have erupted spontaneously. An ailing company soldier was attacked by an Acehnese *boedjangh* while walking on the street. The *boedjangh* threw the soldier to the ground and threatened him while holding him down with his foot on the Dutchman's chest. He subsequently threatened another *ondercoopman* (junior merchant),

---

[54] This news was received on 13 and 25 August 1651: *Generale Missiven*, Vol. 2, 1639 to 1655, pp. 519-20.
[55] Ibid., p. 519.

Nicolas Mombers, whom he later murdered, reportedly because a Kling from the Coromandel Coast had told the boedjangh that Mombers had a lustful or carnal (*vleeselijk*) conversation with his concubine. The Acehnese boedjangh escaped these crimes without punishment. These incidents made the Dutch, especially the governor of Melaka, uncertain about the company's situation in Perak.[56]

In April 1651, the governor of Melaka commissioned the *coopman* (trader) Michiel Curre, who had resided for some years in Perak, to submit the governor's letter to the sultan and set about the task of building the company lodge. On 6 May 1651, the yacht, *Grijpskerken*, which was involved in the blockade of Perak, reported that the crews of the *Velsen* and *Waterhont*—a total of 30 Dutch men, together with Curre and his wife—had been massacred and the goods from the company's warehouse looted. It was later discovered that Curre and his wife had been protected by a few of the Perak orang kaya. The governor in Melaka could not ascertain the truth of these reports, as no one from Perak wanted to speak to them, even though the company emissaries flew a white flag at the Perak River. The governor then decided to send a certain Muslim envoy to Perak to confirm what had happened, and enquire what the sultan planned to do next. In the meantime, on 2 July, another Muslim trader arrived in Melaka bringing a letter from Curre, dated 16 June 1651, which reported how the massacre had begun.

Curre wrote that for some time the sultan had been hearing malicious rumours that the company's building—made of stone—looked more like a fortress than a lodge, and the company's men had secretly brought canons on land. In April 1651, when Curre was bringing the governor's letter to court, some Malays from the court attacked him, and eight soldiers who were guarding Curre were attacked by a mob. The soldiers, together with other people from the *Velsen*, the *Waterhont* and another small vessel, were all killed. The only Dutch survivors were Curre, his wife, an assistant, two sailors, four hired help from Melaka, and one carpenter with his wife and their three children. Altogether, 27 men died; the survivors were all placed under house arrest—Curre in the Orangkaya Besar's house, his wife and

---

[56] Ibid., pp. 511–2.

assistant at the shahbandar's, and the rest in other places.[57] Curre reported that he did not know whether it was the sultan who did not want to cooperate with the company, or whether the order for the murders was obtained from Aceh. He also did not know whether the king had begun to regret this act after discovering that there were no canons. Curre called for an investigation of the attacks and demanded that the murderers be brought to justice.[58]

Commissioner Truijtman was dispatched to Aceh for the third time to discover who was the real mastermind of the Perak murders and had orders to defer to the high court in Aceh in seeking justice. He was to prove that the company officials were innocent, and they were victims of malicious rumours; but at the same time, he was to assert that the company was unwilling to break its alliance and friendship with the crown of Aceh. Truijtman was also tasked to investigate the state of affairs in the kingdom, and in particular, to ascertain whether the sultanah was still alive with her earlier authority still intact or whether her throne—as rumoured—had been usurped by the laksamana.[59] The governor general also wanted to know if she had anything to do with the Perak murders. If she were responsible, this would be tantamount to a declaration of war, and the company would retaliate by blocking Aceh's harbour, expelling all foreigners and nobody would be allowed to enter the kingdom until the company was satisfied.[60] Furthermore, those in Perak who committed the murders could also expect the company's punishment, depending on whether they had committed the acts based on orders from Aceh or had simply taken matters into their own hands. If the Acehnese court was innocent, then it was those in Perak which had not only made themselves the formal enemies of the Dutch nation but had also rebelled against their Acehnese overlord. As overlords, the Acehnese would have to give the company assurances that the imprisoned company officials were released; compensate the company for its losses; punish the murderers and their accomplices, whether these included the orang kaya or the sultan himself; and re-establish trade with the Dutch. As far as the

---

[57] Ibid.
[58] Ibid., p. 513.
[59] Ibid., p. 514.
[60] Ibid., p. 515.

company was concerned, all these conditions had to be met in order for the company to get the deserved justice and respect.[61] However, the governor general was not sure of the Acehnese response or the outcome of these measures against Aceh, or especially how these might affect the company's privileges on the SWC.[62] Because of the need to preserve the company's interests on the SWC, he recommended a more conciliatory stance when dealing with the Acehnese. Truijtman was to be responsible for the success of this mission.

Truijtman's Mission to Perak and Aceh for the Perak Murders

Truijtman departed from Melaka on 4 September 1651 with four companies of soldiers and seven armed vessels. He arrived in Perak at the end of the month and asked for the release of the Dutch prisoners, and that the sultan and the *temenggong* (chief of public security) go to Melaka.[63] Again, the company had failed to follow Malay diplomatic protocol and, predictably, the people in Perak explained that this could not be done without the explicit permission or orders from Aceh. Truijtman thus departed from Perak on 11 October and arrived in Aceh on the 28th. The Acehnese had anticipated the arrival of the Dutch delegation which was met by joyous crowds. Within four days—which was deemed extraordinary by the Dutch, being accustomed to lengthy delays—Truijtman was summoned to court for an audience with the sultanah. The company officials, who had been uncertain whether the queen was dead or alive, found her in good health. Truijtman reported to the governor general that the whole court was either ignorant of or pretended not to know about the affair in Perak. However, Truijtman confirmed the earlier news about the dissent in the Acehnese court and reported that he found a newly formed court that had been assembled after the laksamana's attempted coup against the Maharaja. Maharaja Sri Maharaja remained in disgrace. Maharaja Binthara, the Maharaja's

---

[61] NA, VOC 1188, Generale Missiven Manuscript, 1651, f. 94V.
[62] NA, VOC 1188, Generale Missiven Manuscript, 1651, f. 95R.
[63] *Generale Missiven*, Vol. 2, 1639 to 1655, pp. 568-9.

right-hand man, had died, and the company's friends the envoys that had recently gone to Batavia, Sri Bidia Indra and Raja Modlier—also remained in disgrace, with their possessions confiscated on the accusation that they and their accomplices had sold Aceh to the Dutch.[64]

Although most of the more influential orang kaya were now anti-Dutch, Truijtman reported that he was well treated.[65] This was in stark contrast to his earlier treatment where the laksamana roundly told him that the company should be shown the door. In part, the court may have been concerned about Truijtman's armed guards and that the smallest trigger could lead to an outbreak of war between the two nations. No matter how resentful some of the orang kaya were of the company officials, an outright war with the company was critically detrimental to the kingdom's interests. Although the now anti-Dutch council disagreed with the sultanah's accommodative stance towards the company, it appears that the sultanah was once again in charge and, despite the rising tensions over Dutch demands for a redress of their grievances, the sultanah was needed to ease relations. After the usual greetings and ceremonies, Truijtman wrote that he sought a prompt resolution of the dispute: he insisted that those who were responsible for the murder of the Dutch servants in Perak be punished to the company's satisfaction in order to preserve the company's alliance with the Acehnese kingdom. Within a mere two days, Truijtman received the resolution at court and on 11 November had another audience with the sultanah during which she declared publicly that she gave her permission to seek justice for the Dutch: "*Mahamulia* (Her Highness) gives *kurnia* (grant from above/gift) and grace, upon the request of the governor general, to punish the murderers in Perak."[66] An estemie was prepared and handed to two boedjanghs who would accompany Truijtman to Perak to deliver it personally to the sultan of Perak, Muzaffar Shah. Sultanah Safiatuddin summoned him, upon the receipt of her order, to release all Dutch prisoners and hand them over to Commander Truijtman. The Dato' Temenggong and the shahbandar were to be stripped of

---

[64] Ibid., p. 569.
[65] NA, VOC 1191, Rapport bij den Oppercoopman Johan Truijtman, 1652, f. 750R.
[66] NA, VOC 1191, Rapport bij den Oppercoopman Johan Truijtman, 1652, f. 750V.

their offices, and their followers who had murdered the Dutch officials were to be put to death with another Kling who murdered a Dutch ondercoopman. The Orangkaya Besar would succeed the temenggong and another capable person would replace the shahbandar. In addition, the Acehnese boedjangh who had mistreated the sick Dutch soldier was to be punished by having his hands and feet amputated. The sultanah, however, requested that the sultan of Perak be excused of wrong doing and took him under her protection: he was related by blood to her dead husband.[67] If he was found to be the instigator of the murder, however, the sultanah commanded that he would be removed from his position and replaced.[68] The costs of punishment and building a new company lodge to replace the one that was destroyed would be borne by the people of Perak.[69]

Truijtman reported that his mission in Aceh was a success, as he had managed to obtain a resolution that conformed closely to the governor general's request.[70] In a later report sent to the *Heren Zeventien*, the governor general wrote that the sultanah's orders showed her diligence and determination to punish criminals.[71] Truijtman noted that besides her two boedjanghs instructed to deliver her estemie to Perak, the sultanah appointed two other Acehnese notables to travel separately and ensure that her orders would be promptly obeyed to the company's satisfaction. Contrary to Truijtman's assumption, the point of sending her own representatives was not to follow the company's orders, but to ensure that the settlement of the Perak problem remained in the hands of her representatives. The sultanah said:

> Commander, you should not wage war against those in Perak because it is my land. I myself will punish those who have caused trouble and no other. That is a promise, because I am powerful enough to do that.

---

[67] According to B. Andaya, this sultan was from Siak by birth but was brought up at the Acehnese court. He then married a Perak princess and was installed as the sultan of Perak (1636–d.1654) with the title Sultan Muzaffar Shah. Andaya, *Perak, the Abode of Grace*, p. 20.
[68] *Generale Missiven*, Vol. 2, 1639 to 1655, p. 571.
[69] NA, VOC 1191, Rapport bij den Oppercoopman Johan Truijtman, 1652, f. 751R.
[70] Ibid.
[71] *Generale Missiven*, Vol. 2, 1639 to 1655, p. 570.

> You should not do anything against my consent in my land and you should not incite anything against me that might bring about a war with the Dutch.[72]

On 18 November, Truijtman, Salengre and provisional lieutenant Paulus Ketesar received the queen's estemie at the balai in the presence of the newly formed *raadraden* (council). The estemie was read aloud and sufficiently translated, and Truijtman wrote that it appeared that the affair had been resolved. The sultanah treated him honourably and presented him with a gold kris and five bahar of pepper, and recommended that Truijtman visit her rijxraaden and her court often. She also wanted Truijtman to return to Aceh to report on the events in Perak before he went back to Batavia.[73]

Truijtman also received the queen's letter in reply to the governor general. Before Truijtman departed for Perak, the sultanah stressed her orders again:

> Commander, you should listen to what I have to say, the land of Perak is my own land but the tin that is found in Perak is in part for the Dutch and the people that live there. It is a rough and proud people full of spite, who well deserve the punishment. Especially since these past few years they have not properly paid their homage and come to court here as they would usually do, or had been done. Although the Dutch have blockaded their river, notwithstanding this, I request that you do not spoil this land where the Dutch could harvest the most fruit.[74]

Sultanah Safiatuddin reiterated the point that no war was to be waged in Perak, the land was not to be ruined and only she could mete out the punishments due. The sultanah was determined that the problem in Perak would not result in the rupture of the alliance she had carefully cultivated with the Dutch, much less lead to an outbreak of war between the two nations. In this instance, Truijtman had no doubt of the sultanah's sincerity: he noted that in her affection and her arguments for peace there

---

[72] NA, VOC 1191, Rapport bij den Oppercoopman Johan Truijtman, 1652, ff. 751R–751V.
[73] NA, VOC 1191, Rapport bij den Oppercoopman Johan Truijtman, 1652, f. 751V.
[74] NA, VOC 1191, Rapport bij den Oppercoopman Johan Truijtman, 1652, f. 752R.

appeared to be no difference between her heart and her countenance, notwithstanding the cunning and hypocrisy that the Acehnese sowed, which generated falsehood and deceit. But, he concluded, everyone had to be patient to discover the true outcome of this affair.[75]

According to Barbara Andaya, the sultanah's declaration to the company officials that the people of Perak were proud and rebellious showed the sultanah's weakness and proved that it was impossible for the Acehnese court to force Sultan Muzaffar Shah to surrender the guilty Orang Besar to the Dutch.[76] On the contrary, the report from the company's resident in Aceh—Salengre—that five Perak vessels were in Aceh to ask for help and advice shows that Aceh still controlled Perak. In short, the two states were still bound by overlord-vassal ties, and the sultan of Perak would not enter into any negotiations with the company without prior permission from the sultanah. It was not a case of the sultanah's weakness and her inability to surrender the guilty party in Perak to the Dutch; rather it was her attempt to ensure that the guilty were punished by the Acehnese themselves. She commanded that only the Dutch prisoners were to be released and surrendered to the company, and she repeatedly stressed the fact that Perak was her land and the Dutch should not interfere in her authority. She even took Sultan Muzaffar under her protection, but promised that he would be replaced if found guilty.

It is interesting, though, why she mentioned that the Perak people had been disobedient and had not sent their envoys when Salengre had reported that five Perak vessels were in Aceh asking for help and advice. In all probability, the sultanah was referring to an official trip where Perak, as a vassal state, should have sent its envoys to Aceh to report the Perak rebellion against the Dutch. These ought to be separate missions compared to the trips taken by Perak envoys to Aceh who travelled with Truijtman to address the company demands in Perak. The sultanah was most probably unaware of the five Perak vessels that reportedly had landed in Aceh.

---

[75] NA, VOC 1191, Rapport bij den Oppercoopman Johan Truijtman, 1652, f. 752V.
[76] Andaya, *Perak, the Abode of Grace*, p. 46.

So, who were these people from Perak and whom did they contact in Aceh? Recall that the most recent coup had elevated more anti-Dutch orang kaya to positions of influence at court, and they had demanded action against the Dutch. Also, the Dutch had reported attacks on company officials in Perak by anti-Dutch Acehnese before the murder of the ships' crews took place. In all probability, it was the laksamana faction from the Aceh rijxraad that had instigated these murders in Perak as a lesson to the company for its arrogance and incessant, unreasonable demands. The murders in Perak closely followed the defeat of the Maharaja's pro-Dutch faction, when the sultanah's life was apparently in danger. The laksamana group would have worked with the anti-Dutch faction in Perak and capitalised on the dissatisfactions there regarding the company's demands.

Nevertheless, even though the laksamana faction had the upper hand in this struggle, it was either not strong enough to get rid of the sultanah altogether, or she had entrenched herself well enough to survive the orang kaya's factional struggles. After the Perak massacre, when the possibility of war between the company and Aceh was highly likely, the laksamana and his followers certainly needed her as an authority once again to soothe matters when the company representatives came to seek redress and compensation.

More Troubled Currents in the Perak River

Truijtman departed Aceh on 22 November and arrived in Perak on 6 December accompanied by two Acehnese boedjangh bearing the queen's estemie. After six days in Perak, Truijtman tried to secure the release of the prisoners: Coopman Michiel Curre and his wife, their three Melakan hired helpers and some of their slaves. As for the two young sailors who worked in the tin mines, one was dead and the other had been sent to Melaka.[77] This first point of the estemie was promptly obeyed. The second, and more important, point to deport the temenggong and shahbandar believed to be party to the murders was not so easily executed.

---

[77] NA, VOC 1191, Rapport bij den Oppercoopman Johan Truijtman, 1652, f. 752V.

Truijtman reported that the two Acehnese orang kaya, delegated by the sultanah to investigate the affair, had arrived before him.[78] These Acehnese orang kaya and the sultan invited Truijtman to witness the capital punishment of the aforementioned officials and their helpers. Truijtman then advanced along the Perak River with seven Dutch vessels and on 20 December met with the Acehnese orang kaya at the first fort. After a long meeting, it was agreed that the sultan's final decision regarding the punishment of the murderers would be made known to Truijtman within three days.

The next day, "these murderous Perak people", with the knowledge or even on the direction of the "hypocritical" Acehnese mediators, broke off the talks and attacked the Dutch at the fort where several officials lost their lives.[79] Truijtman summoned the rest of the Dutch soldiers stationed down the Perak River, but because the water level was high at that time, the vessels could not sail upriver, much less have soldiers disembark in Perak. No other help was in sight: provisions and soldiers took 29 days to come from Melaka. Luckily for Truijtman and company it was the rainy season which made it difficult for the Perak people to attack them, though many of the Dutch developed beriberi and other fatal diseases.[80] The Dutch were held at the Perak River for 15 days. The company put up a white flag and an agreement was reached whereby the company continued the siege and the Perak people retained their possession of the three forts. Judging from the number of guns and amount of ammunition used, as well as reports from Kedah, Truijtman suspected that people from Aceh had contributed more than a little to the effort.[81] By this time the exhausted Truijtman wrote that even though he had been tasked to investigate the Perak murders and did not intend to let this unfortunate turn of events thwart him, he confessed that he could do no more, and after receiving orders from the governor in Melaka, he returned to Aceh.

Truijtman arrived in Aceh on 8 March and four days later had an audience with the sultanah. He bitterly complained about how those

---

[78] NA, VOC 1191, Rapport bij den Oppercoopman Johan Truijtman, 1652, f. 753R.
[79] NA, VOC 1191, Rapport bij den Oppercoopman Johan Truijtman, 1652, f. 753V.
[80] NA, VOC 1191, Rapport bij den Oppercoopman Johan Truijtman, 1652, f. 754R.
[81] NA, VOC 1191, Rapport bij den Oppercoopman Johan Truijtman, 1652, f. 754V.

from Perak had not only neglected to do what her majesty promised and the mission had failed, but they actually committed new acts of hostility against company officials.[82] The sultanah then ordered one of her notables tasked with investigating the murders and some other Acehnese to relate their version of events. Curre was also called to testify before her majesty, but the anti-Dutch orang kaya prevented him from doing so. Truijtman concluded that the attacks on the Dutch were set in train by the newly formed anti-Dutch faction at court in Aceh who induced those from Perak to commit these murderous deeds against the Dutch.[83] It appeared that the anti-Dutch at the Acehnese court had not only advised those from Perak but had actually assisted them. Truijtman noted that the massacre of the Dutch in Perak followed shortly after the Acehnese revolt. Three hundred Acehnese soldiers armed with four canons and other weapons reached Perak via Deli. Truijtman was informed by a certain Kling named Maracq Yunos, who appears to have been sent from Perak and Kedah. Truijtman believed that one of the more important reasons for the murders was to frighten off the company, which some Acehnese feared was becoming too powerful.[84]

Given the strong anti-Dutch sentiment at court it is not surprising that after the sultanah's earlier estemie to Perak and the recommended measures addressing the Perak murders, no compensation was made to the company. The final resolution concluded at the Acehnese court did not satisfy the Dutch one bit: the council decided "to let the dead remain dead" (let bygones be bygones) so that they could henceforth live with each other in peace, and the Dutch could continue trading as before. The Acehnese justified their stand by arguing that the company officials had abused the Perak people long enough and given them enough cause to take matters into their own hands. The Dutch had not only blockaded the Perak River without reason, but in doing so had also belittled and disrespected the Acehnese crown. Besides these complaints, the company had proceeded to build not a lodge as promised, but had instead constructed a stone

---

[82] NA, VOC 1191, Rapport bij den Oppercoopman Johan Truijtman, 1652, ff. 754V–755R.
[83] NA, VOC 1191, Rapport bij den Oppercoopman Johan Truijtman, 1652, ff. 756R–756V.
[84] NA, VOC 1191, Rapport bij den Oppercoopman Johan Truijtman, 1652, f. 755R.

house higher and more prominent than the sultan's palace, which "had pierced the eyes of his subjects". Indeed, they had actually built a castle or a strong fort rather than a house and had also smuggled cannons on land. All these odious practices had provoked the embittered elites and commoners in Perak to murder.[85]

Truijtman was convinced that these recent events proved his suspicions about Acehnese deceit and hypocrisy. Utterly dejected, he claimed that the recently despatched estemie to the sultan of Perak was a ploy. He concluded that the company would get no satisfaction in this affair owing to Acehnese lies.[86] In despair, he requested that the governor general allow him to leave Aceh.[87] After much delay, though notably laden with the sultanah's gifts including 36 bahar of pepper and her majesty's letter to the governor general, Truijtman was finally allowed to depart on the yacht *Saphier*. So, he wrote, the conclusion of this affair was his discovery of Acehnese falsehood and the failed Perak exploit.

What was the sultanah's role in all this? Truijtman's report mentions nothing about the sultanah's complicity, nor does he reveal any suspicions about her role in the Perak murders. However, in his dejected state, he questioned the sultanah's sincerity, even though she kept her promise and sentenced the Perak temenggong and the shahbandar and their helpers, and the Kling murderer to capital punishment. She also demoted some of her own officials; and yet Truijtman believed that these were not sincere and true punishments.[88] This may have been owing to the delay in carrying out the sentences. According to Governor General Carel Reniers's report, Sultanah Safiatuddin herself had not respected her words and had not brought the temenggong and shahbandar to justice.[89] She had punished only the other lower-ranking persons involved in the murder, such as the Kling.

The anti-Dutch faction had the upper hand at court and appeared to have got away with murder, as the company did not retaliate or declare war

---

[85] *Generale Missiven*, Vol. 2, 1639 to 1655, p. 643.
[86] NA, VOC 1191, Rapport bij den Oppercoopman Johan Truijtman, 1652, f. 756R.
[87] Joan Maetsuycker was the governor general in Batavia from 1653 to 1678.
[88] NA, VOC 1191, Rapport bij den Oppercoopman Johan Truijtman, 1652, f. 755V.
[89] Carel Reniers was the governor general in Batavia from 1650 to 1653.

on Aceh. Why this was so, despite the company's power, will be explained in the next chapter. In the meantime, the sultanah was restrained by the strong anti-Dutch faction at court. However, the sultanah maintained her position on the throne because she was the only one who could deal with the Dutch and maintain the friendship she had established with the company. Despite her precarious situation, she was keen to accommodate the Dutch and keep relations on an even keel, and she remained generous to Truijtman to the very end. She was not safe for long though: new troubles at court would soon threaten not only her position but also her honour and even her life.

More Crises at Aceh's Court: Coup and Counter-Coup[90]

Governor General Joan Maetsuyker reported that there was a great calm among the rijxraaden after the laksamana's coup and the death of Maharaja di Raja, the son-in-law of Maharaja Sri Maharaja. He confirmed Truijtman's report that the sultanah survived this ordeal and appeared on the throne as usual. Maetsuyker further reported that after this coup, one audience day the laksamana and a great number of armed men had come to court to kill the "highest pontiff" (*oppersten paep*), one of her majesty's great officers. This individual most probably was Sheikh Syaiful Rijal, the Sheikh al-Islam—that is, the highest religious authority in Aceh, whom the sultanah had appointed when al-Raniri left Aceh in 1644.[91] It so happened on that day the sheikh was absent when the laksamana arrived, though whether he had prior knowledge of the laksamana's intention was not clear. The laksamana's attempt on the sheikh's life caused great alarm at court. He openly defended his action on the grounds that the sheikh had committed adultery (*boelerende*) with the sultanah and that he was seizing after the throne.[92] Adultery, the most fatal charge that could be made against a high religious figure, such as the

---

[90] This crisis happened in 1652 as reported in *Generale Missiven*, 1653, p. 647.
[91] If it was indeed Syaiful Rijal who was murdered in 1652, this explains why there were no kitabs in his name and why his writings did not survive.
[92] *Generale Missiven*, Vol. 2, 1639 to 1655, p. 647. This highest priest was referred to as the queen's *mingon* (sweetheart).

Sheikh al-Islam, and usurpation of the throne, if proven, would have been tantamount to *derhaka* (treason), the highest crime a subject could commit against his ruler. The orang kaya council concurred with the decision that the sheikh had to be executed.[93] The allegation of sexual liaison was fatal to the widowed sultanah, so at this critical juncture, she swore an oath in public that she never had sexual intercourse with the sheikh and threatened to set fire to the palace and burn herself alive. This must have proved her innocence in the eyes of her subjects. Sultanah Safiatuddin's intervention saved not only the sheikh but also herself.

The laksamana's failed power bid did not bring about an end to the troubles at court. According to the account from the *Dagh-Register*, a letter from the junior trader and resident, Philips Carel de Salengre from Aceh, dated 30 January 1653, mentioned a new revolt led by another orang kaya faction.[94] His report is translated below:

> ... in the meantime there was a new revolt under the orangkaya and it was the work of Paducca Mamentry [Paduka Maha Menteri], royal in command, together with the deposed men namely Maradja Sire Maradja [Maharaja Sri Maharaja], the Company's friend, Laxamana Radja Odane Lella [Maharaja Adona Lella] and Sire Paducca Tuwan [Sri Paduka Tuan]. Paduka Tuan and all his relatives were sacked and removed from court. Maharaja Lella replaced Paduka Tuan as the Governor of Elephants. Seven days after that, an unusually well manned and [well] armed [band], broke into the Queen's court and forced her to remove the aforementioned Maharaja Lella, and to replace him with a certain Intchi Rembau, who at one time served as the Panglima of Deli, [the above mentioned armed band] massacred, beyond the instruction, nay even against the express prohibition of Her Majesty, together with ten to eleven [other] persons, the *"grooten priester"* [high priest] who before he was deposed, through the help from Maharaja Lella would be made king, following a secret oath made to Her Majesty. They [the coup-leaders] had forced the governing officials to this massacre. Also Her Majesty had to distribute the *"priester's"* belongings especially the king's daggers, kris etc. to her ladies-in-waiting (*bysittende*). She then

---

[93] Maetsuyker did not detail who in this orang kaya council agreed to this execution and whether they formed the majority in the council.

[94] *Dagh-Register*, 1653, pp. 39–40.

also had to grant the aforementioned coup leaders renewed access to court, honouring them with elephants, people and what belongs to that.[95]

From the *Dagh-Register*'s report, it cannot be clearly ascertained in what manner the sultanah was forced to appoint Intchi Rembau, how she tried to forbid the murders and how she distributed the sheikh and his followers' belongings to whom. It is not too surprising that the sultanah honoured the group who executed this counter-coup as this group supported her policy of accommodating the Dutch. Nevertheless, she clearly opposed their murder of the sheikh. It appears from this incident that the Acehnese elites were more fractious than originally appeared as, besides the pro- and anti-Dutch factions, there was a third led by the sheikh who had tried to appoint his supporter as the governor of elephants and remove Paduka Tuan, belonging to the Maharaja's faction.[96]

There are no other references to these internal disturbances in the Aceh court as the Dutch in Aceh were more focused on salvaging the company's reputation from the humiliations it had endured in Aceh and Perak. It is safe to conclude, however, that from 1653, though there was a power struggle between different factions of the orang kaya, the faction led by the sheikh was disposed of. It is not clear how far the allegations against the sheikh were true, but he paid for this with his life. The sultanah's position was seriously threatened during these tumultuous times when the laksamana accused her of sexual dalliance. However, neither the laksamana nor the Maharaja faction claimed the throne nor deposed the sultanah. It appears that by this time the sultanah's position on the throne was accepted by all factions, and no orang kaya faction was strong enough to put up one of its own without causing a crisis of legitimacy. Sultanah Safiatuddin not only had royal authority but she proved to be a useful balance to the different factions, stabilising the kingdom. After 1653, it became clear that she had consolidated her position as the ruler of Aceh.

---

[95] *Dagh-Register*, 1653, p. 40.
[96] For a fuller analysis, please refer to Sher Banu A.L. Khan, "What Happened to Sayf al-Rijal?", *Bijdragen tot de Taal-, Land- en Volkenkunde* (*BKI*) 168, 1 (2012): 100–11.

Conclusion

Sultanah Safiatuddin experienced many crises in the 1640s and 1650s. Nevertheless, by the middle of the latter decade, she emerged unscathed and managed to consolidate her position on the throne. She did this through a mixture of measures and by distancing herself from the in-fighting among her orang kaya. To "bend with the wind", as Truijtman described it, was not, I suggest, a sign of weakness, rather it was a means of flexibility and trying to work with whichever faction that emerged as the winner at the time. She continued, however, to work with those who supported her policies. Although at times she appeared to be submerged, she was able to weather the storm and prevailed in the end.

By this time it was clear she was accepted as the ruling sovereign, though the different orang kaya and ulama factions continued to jostle for power. She was recognised as a source of stability: no orang kaya would accept one of their own as sultan, and no faction was strong enough to place one of its own candidates on the throne and support him by force. She was seen as the legitimate arbiter, a sovereign who was above the constant power struggles. The fact that she was a woman was important because it kept her out of the royal-elite jealousies that typically characterised male relations. Her flexible and "soft" rule by accommodation rather than confrontation helped her soothe ruffled feathers and reduce the many tensions with the Dutch which could have resulted in a war. She drew prestige from her father's stature, al-Marhom Sultan Iskandar Muda, instead of her unpopular husband, Iskandar Thani, and emphasised that she continued her father's policies, such as preserving the royal monopoly for the elephant trade. However, as will be detailed in Chapters 5 and 6, she developed a personal style which her female successors followed.

Besides the sultanah's political sagacity and sex, another factor that helps explain why the kingdom did not degenerate into chaos was the role of orang kaya, such as the laksamana, who realised the need to maintain order for the sake of the kingdom. Just as in the case of the jewel affair, when the orang kaya finally acceded to the sultanah's policy of accommodating the Dutch during the jewel purchase, the laksamana had to agree with the treaty provisions granting the VOC trading privileges to avoid a potential conflict.

The next chapter continues the story of the struggle between Aceh and the VOC over Perak and her vassals in the SWC and shows how traditional overlord-vassal relations were played out when they faced increased political and commercial incursions from the European companies. This story illustrates not one of decline and the replacement of indigenous powers but, surprisingly, a narrative of response and resilience in the face of increased European intervention in Acehnese affairs.

chapter

4 Ties That Bind? Aceh's Overlord-Vassal Relations

The Struggle between Aceh and VOC over Perak

The last chapter showed how the contests between the VOC and Aceh over Perak's tin trade had tremendous repercussions on Aceh's court politics. Although the factional struggles between the Acehnese orang kaya resulted

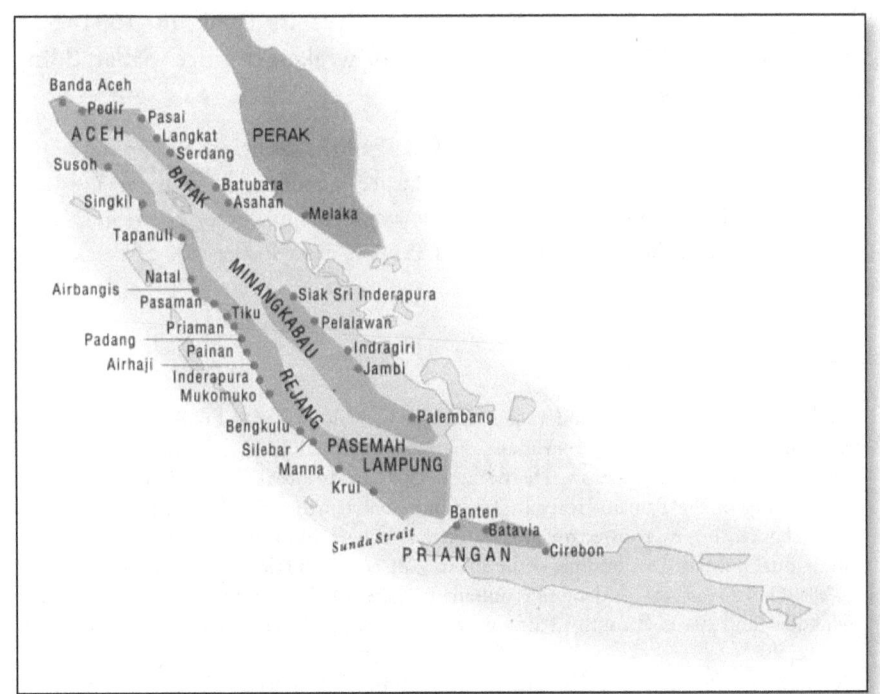

Fig. 3   Map of Sumatra, West Java and the Malay Peninsula, c. 1700.

in disturbances at court and a serious challenge to defame the sultanah threatened her position on the throne, by 1653 Safiatuddin had survived and managed to gain acceptance for her rule. VOC officials, however, continued to demand concessions, and the company's armed commercial incursions into Perak and her vassal states on the SWC threatened Safiatuddin's suzerainty there.

The first half of this chapter examines Aceh-Perak relations while the second relates to Aceh's relations with her vassals on the SWC with an emphasis on how increasing VOC incursions affected traditional overlord-vassal relations.[1] The central questions are whether Aceh declined under the rule of Sultanah Safiatuddin, and whether Aceh lost her vassal states and her overlord status owing to this weakened position, as commonly claimed. In the case of Perak, there is some support for this point of view, both in the sources of the time and in current historical orthodoxy. Balthasar Bort—governor of Melaka—reported in 1678, "Aceh is impotent and has no appearance of once more attaining considerable power."[2] Barbara Andaya claimed that the murder of the VOC representatives in Perak in 1651 bare the extent to which Aceh's control had weakened since Safiatuddin's succession. She asserted that:

> The Queen had for some time been aware of the decline in her prestige and had earlier refused the Dutch inspection of Aceh ships leaving Perak with tin on the grounds that it would prejudice her sovereignty and diminish her absolute power in Perak at least in the eyes of Perak subjects.[3]

---

[1] No such analysis has been undertaken, though E. Francis (1856) provided a descriptive account of the Dutch's establishment on the SWC, and J.C.M. Radermacher (1824) gave descriptions of Sumatra. De Leeuw's 1926 study on these relations ended with the signing of the Painan Treaty in 1663 and some further developments up to 1665. This chapter, however, owes much to studies that have been undertaken by scholars on individual polities. For example, F. de Haan (1897) on Middle Sumatra, Kathirithamby-Wells (1976) on the Inderapura Sultanate, Jane Drakard (1990) on Minangkabau kingdom and Barus, Timothy Barnard (2003) on Siak, and Barbara W. Andaya (1979) on Perak.

[2] Richard O. Winstedt (and Richard J. Wilkinson), "A History of Perak", *Journal of the Malayan Branch of the Royal Asiatic Society* 12, 1 (1934): 23.

[3] Andaya, *Perak, the Abode of Grace*, p. 46.

She argued that Safiatuddin was weak because she was unable to force Perak's Muzaffar Shah to surrender the guilty parties (recall the Perak massacre) to the Dutch. R.O. Winstedt, however, suggested that even though she lost all her other vassals, she was able to hold on to Perak. Winstedt claimed "partly female rule, partly the growing power of the Dutch and their protection of Johor and her allies led to the surrender by Aceh of all her conquests in the Malay Peninsula except Perak".[4]

A closer examination of the events that unfolded between Aceh, Perak and the VOC, as revealed in company reports, discloses a story of resilience and shows a more powerful Aceh with stronger and more binding overlord-vassal ties than is commonly believed. They were ties that continued to bind despite the challenges that tend to sever. It was these very ties that helped Perak continue as a major tin producer and reap profits for many more years.[5]

The previous chapter illustrates that Perak saw itself as Aceh's vassal as it took no action without prior approval from Sultanah Safiatuddin. Despite unhappiness over some of her resolutions, they generally followed her instructions. The sultanah also took Perak and Sultan Muzaffar under her protection and ensured that not all Dutch demands were met, especially those, such as abolishing tolls, that might injure her subjects' livelihoods. Despite the anti-Dutch faction's attempts to thwart Safiatuddin's efforts to accommodate Dutch demands, the sultanah was able to maintain cordial relations with them. The Perak murders served the interests of the anti-Dutch faction by disrupting relations between the company and the sultanah and pro-Dutch orang kaya; however, the interruption proved short-lived. The VOC was unable to punish Perak and receive satisfactory reparations: even the relentless Truijtman had to concede defeat. Safiatuddin's efforts at balancing the pro- and anti-Dutch factions were successful to the extent that their disagreements did not degenerate into war. However, given Dutch military power, their anger at the numerous provocations and insults, and their determination to seek justice, one has to wonder why the VOC did not punish Perak or declare war on Aceh?

---

[4] Winstedt, "A History of Perak", p. 23.
[5] Andaya, *Perak, the Abode of Grace*, p. 48.

To Go or Not to Go to War?

While the sentiment in the Acehnese court after the Perak murders was to favour peace and accommodation, and Safiatuddin advised the Dutch to let bygone be bygones, this feeling was not reciprocated in the VOC camp. One issue stands out in the *Generale Missiven* of 1653 and 1654: how best to respond to the humiliations and losses the company had suffered, specifically, whether to go to war with Aceh? Given the murders of company officials in Perak and Kedah, and the indignities suffered by Truijtman and his delegates in Perak and Aceh, the desire for revenge was understandable. However, there were two points of view put forward by the Dutch officials. The pro-war faction wanted war because after the Dutch conquest of Melaka, the port's trade moved to Aceh.[6] Indian merchants brought cloth to Aceh, and this attracted other traders there to exchange their wares for this cloth which was much cheaper than that which the company sold in Melaka. In 1660, Aceh had so much cloth that one bale of Guinea cloth as good as a bale sold by the company fetched only between 48 and 50 reals, while the usual price was 80 reals.[7] Furthermore, war was justifiable because of the "inhuman acts" committed against company officers by people from Perak, who were then under Aceh's protection. Without war with Aceh, the company could not forbid the Gujaratis, Klings, Bengalis and others from sailing to Aceh; nor could they claim the previous Portuguese rights in Melaka, which they believed they had inherited.

The anti-war faction argued that war with Aceh would bring more trouble because it would further alienate Indian traders, whose supplies of cloth were still needed to generate trade. Furthermore, the blockade of Aceh's harbour might not bring a corresponding benefit to Melaka, as Aceh's trade could instead be diverted to Tennasserij, situated between Pegu and Aceh around 60 miles from the former. This was an area of great traffic, where Indian traders supplied the whole area and its hinterland

---

[6] *Generale Missiven*, Vol. 2, 1639 to 1655, p. 687.
[7] "Report of Governor Balthasar Bort on Malacca 1678", trans. M.J. Bremner with Introduction and Notes by C.O. Blagden, *Journal of the Malayan Branch of the Royal Asiatic Society* 5, 1 (1927): 132.

with cloth and other merchandise in exchange for tin and elephants brought overland from Siam.[8] In addition, the company had only enough ships to blockade Aceh's harbour and not the surrounding areas; if this blockade was weak, the company would be unable to monopolise and centralise trade in Melaka. Governor General Joan Maetsuyker confessed that a monopoly would be ineffective if foreign traders knew that the Dutch could not enforce it, and they did not see that the company had any right to wage war on Aceh.[9]

The governor was also afraid that war with Aceh would benefit the English. For example, an English yacht, belonging to a Mr Winter from Masulipatnam, returned from Aceh with 16 elephants, benzoin resin, camphor, tin and gold.[10] He had been well received in Aceh, and though he was denied permission to trade on the SWC, Maetsuyker reasoned that the English might return there if the Dutch waged war on Aceh. "Now that we are at peace with the English nation, we fear that they would go to Aceh, and if troubles between us and Aceh remain, then it would be to our disadvantage."[11] The Dutch feared that the English would fish in their troubled waters, and they had no legal justification to prevent English traders from trading in any port that had not signed the exclusive nation treatment agreement with the company—Aceh was one such kingdom. In addition, the Anglo-Dutch peace had given Indian traders an ingenious way to circumvent the company's blockade. They simply loaded their cargo onto English ships or they employed Englishmen to sail their ships and flew the English flag. The English freely issued passes to these Indian traders to frequent ports in Aceh and other parts of Southeast Asia, and the company faced the dilemma of whether to honour these or not.[12] Thus, the company concluded that war with Aceh was not advisable.

Maetsuyker also reported that despite the company's threats, many more English yachts and Muslim ships from different places

---

[8] *Generale Missiven*, Vol. 2, 1639 to 1655, p. 688.
[9] Ibid.
[10] Ibid.
[11] Ibid., p. 752.
[12] Arasaratnam, "Some Notes on the Dutch in Malacca", p. 488.

were frequenting Aceh in 1653 than had been the previous year.[13] Even as he wrote, there were already eight Muslim ships in Aceh, one belonging to the governor of Masulipatnam.[14] The company remained gravely concerned about Muslim traders. More and more were arriving to supply the surrounding area with cloth and other merchandise, to the detriment of Melaka, where there was no cloth for sale.[15] Bengal ships brought nine elephants from Kedah in return for cloth. Twenty-six vessels from Perak were said to have sailed to Aceh loaded with tin. The governor began to wonder whether "our siege of Perak is in vain; that this could be stopped and more money ... spent on more advantageous things".[16] Even with the blockade, a great many vessels with tin had gone to Aceh.[17] It appeared that those in Perak had enough opportunities to take care of their necessities without any need to break the blockade, as they had found a new way to transport these supplies into Perak from Kedah. Three Muslim ships in Kedah—two from Masulipatnam and one from Bengal—had passes from respective countries, and they easily obtained tin from Perak overland.[18] The company faced a similar situation in Aceh where, despite the blockade, 36 tin-laden ships arrived from Perak. In Aceh's harbour, the company found three ships from Surat, four from the Coromandel Coast, one from the Maldives, one belonging to the sultanah of Aceh, two from Macassar and one free burgher ship from Cambodia.[19]

In his report to the *Heren Zeventien*, Maetsuyker wrote that he had already made his objections known regarding the English ships and the

---

[13] Arasaratnam and Raychaudhuri stated that Indian trade with Aceh increased in the 1660s. Indian traders, selling cloth and buying tin and spices, continued to frequent Aceh, using it as their centre for the Southeast Asian trade. However, evidence discussed here shows that trade between these traders and Aceh had increased a decade earlier— in the 1650s. Arasaratnam, "Some Notes on the Dutch in Malacca", pp. 488–9; Tapan Kumar Raychaudhuri, *Jan Company in Coromandel, 1605–1690: A Study in the Interrelations of European Commerce and Traditional Economies* ('s-Gravenhage: Martinus Nijhoff, 1962), pp. 123–4.
[14] *Generale Missiven*, Vol. 2, 1639 to 1655, p. 752.
[15] Ibid.
[16] *Generale Missiven*, Vol. 2, 1639 to 1655, p. 775.
[17] NA, VOC 1202, Generale Missiven Manuscript, 1655, f. 47V.
[18] *Generale Missiven*, Vol. 2, 1639 to 1655, p. 752.
[19] Ibid., p. 819.

great Muslim traffic to Aceh, which had caused the trade in Melaka to stagnate. He stated that war against Aceh would be justified; however, he stressed that he would leave this decision to the *Heren Zeventien* as this was an affair of profound importance that needed great consideration. In the meantime, the Dutch would continue to deal with Aceh using diplomatic means and to respond to the sultanah's peace-making gestures and her efforts to build more trust.[20] The governor general wrote that the sultanah and the orang kaya had shown an inclination towards peace and accommodation, and had sent letters and gifts to both Batavia and Melaka.[21] Sultanah Safiatuddin had specially sent Abdul Latiff, their best interpreter, and other representatives of quality, so there would be no occasion for the Dutch to take revenge for the recent disrespect to Truijtman.[22] Although the murderers in Perak had not been surrendered, peace was more achievable thanks to the deaths of the alleged instigators, Sultan Muda, *Dato' Bendahara* (first ranking member of court) and the temenggong of Perak in 1653, and the fact that the shahbandar was now provisionally the head of state.[23] The governor general reasoned that even if the Dutch opted to besiege Aceh to stop the Muslim trade, it would still be difficult to keep the English out because this action would cause displeasure and trouble. "If we go to war with Aceh a great door would be opened for the English nation so that they would undercut our privileges in Sumatra West Coast and in Aceh, which could not be easily repaired."[24]

Maetsuyker then decided to send Dirk Schouten—the company bookkeeper general, an experienced hand who spoke the Malay language well—to Aceh via Melaka.[25] His tasks were to get the sultanah to punish the guilty in Perak and pay reparation costs for the damages incurred in Perak as promised; renew and grant privileges on a permanent basis regarding the tin trade in Perak; and request that the sultanah not allow the English and the Portuguese to trade in Aceh and other places under her control.

---

[20] Ibid., p. 775.
[21] Ibid., p. 818.
[22] Ibid., p. 819.
[23] Ibid., pp. 751–2.
[24] Ibid., p. 821.
[25] Ibid., p. 822.

Dirk Schouten's Mission to Aceh

As all parties sought peace, Aceh, Perak and the company signed another treaty in 1655. Among the provisions were the cessation of all hostilities and Perak's payment of an indemnity of 50,000 reals for damages caused to the company's lodge in 1651. No one had been punished for the Perak murders the same year, so this provision was included in this treaty. Sultan Muzaffar Shah had died of smallpox in 1654 and was replaced by his young son, Sultan Mahmud,[26] whose elderly aunt—Sultanah Amina Todijn—was appointed as regent.[27] The shahbandar was to be executed for murder, however the former temenggong (another alleged accomplice) who had replaced the Dato' Bendahara after the latter's death, was to remain in the post. One reason he not only escaped punishment but was even promoted to the position of bendahara was because his uncle was a leading member of the Aceh Council. Safiatuddin Syah also refused to take any action against the new bendahara on the grounds that he could not be deposed, as the new ruler was too young and the regent too old.[28] He was allowed to remain in this post despite the company's protests. The Perak council gave the company land to build a new lodge; other clauses of the 1650 treaty, by which the company would obtain half of Perak's tin at a fixed price, remained in place, as did the Dutch blockades of Aceh and Perak.

The Continuing Tussle for Tin

Four years later the treaties remained in force. The bendahara dominated the Perak assembly and his hostility to the VOC made it impossible for the Dutch to get their quota of tin. The company pressed for another

---

[26] His mother had died shortly before Sultan Muzaffar Shah, according to the indigenous source, *Silsilah Melaka Kerajaan Negeri Perak* [Genealogy of Melaka and the Government of Perak]; the sultanah of Aceh adopted this boy-king. Andaya, *Perak, the Abode of Grace*, p. 47.

[27] Unfortunately, no more information is available regarding this elderly aunt.

[28] Andaya, *Perak, the Abode of Grace*, p. 47.

treaty with Aceh, and this was duly signed in 1659.[29] Again, the company demanded compensation for the loss of lives and goods in 1651, half of the tin produce to be shared with Aceh, and exclusive nation treatment; however, the new provisions were actually more disadvantageous to the company. Sultanah Safiatuddin now forgave the anti-Dutch bendahara and allowed him to remain in his position. The shahbandar, however, was not so lucky: the sultanah summoned him to Aceh for a trial.[30] The sultanah generously granted 50 bahar of tin—to be obtained from Perak—in compensation for the company's goods stolen in 1651. The price of tin had earlier been fixed at 31¼ reals for the company, but as the indemnity payment had a balance of 44,000 reals, the price the company paid for the tin would be only 30 reals until the debt was paid. Under this contract the company failed once again to obtain toll-free privilege; the Acehnese argued that this customary right could not be violated.[31]

The company officials persevered in what they thought was a "legal" option of signing treatises with Aceh and optimistically declared that these provisions were permanent: "herewith all the above articles are settled irrevocably and shall endure as long as the world . . . amen".[32] The Acehnese saw these unequal treaties imposed on them as unfair and high-handed Dutch trade practices. One year later, this treaty was again broken. In 1660, 122 bahar of tin reached Melaka, but Aceh obtained 585 bahar, much of it thanks to smuggling via the profitable markets of Aceh and Kedah.[33] The English envoy, Henry Gary, came to Aceh from Surat bringing presents for the sultanah, and he departed with 200 bahar of tin.[34] Joannes Massys, bringing only 51 bahar of tin for the Dutch, bitterly complained that Aceh still got all the tin. The

---

[29] J.E. Heeres and F.W. Stapel, eds., *Corpus Diplomaticum Neerlando-Indicum*, 6 Vols. ('s-Gravenhage: Martinus Nijhoff, 1907–55), pp. 151–5.
[30] "Report of Governor Balthasar Bort on Malacca 1678", p. 139.
[31] Ibid.
[32] Ibid., pp. 140, 147. While the Dutch wanted to be granted privileges on a permanent basis, the Dutch revoked privileges given after death. For example, the Dutch had granted the right to export 30 bahar of tin from Perak to Paduka Tuan, Governor of Foreigners in Aceh, and this right ceased to exist after his death.
[33] Winstedt, "A History of Perak", p. 31.
[34] Ibid.

Dutch sailed to Perak to enforce the terms of the treaty, but as soon as they left Perak broke them again. Aceh's agents took away *all* of Perak's tin on the pretext that the tin belonged to their queen. When the Dutch tried to stop three Perak vessels carrying 180 bahar of tin going to Aceh, the sultan declared that they were his own emissaries. On 30 October 1662, the Dutch resident, Gabriel Bruyl, reported that the English had persuaded the queen to order the sultan of Perak to help them export 60 bahar of tin. In 1663, the company had to abandon enforcing Perak's indemnity payment and paid about 34 to 36 reals per bahar against the 30 reals fixed, because the Acehnese were paying as much as 42 reals.[35]

The company's relations with Perak, however, took a turn for the better over the decade between 1664 and 1675. In July 1663, the company resolved to close its factories in Aceh, Perak and Ligor.[36] Lucaszoon—the resident at Perak—reported that the queen of Aceh, dismayed at the company closing its lodge in her capital, had written to Perak to allow the Dutch to trade as friends. She added that although they had quit Aceh, she knew of no reason for hostilities. Perak, too, began to make its own overtures to the company. When the anti-Dutch bendahara died in 1663, his successor decided to adopt a more independent policy for Perak by playing the Dutch off against the Acehnese.[37] The Perak people had grown tired and bitter because of the continuous blockade and incessant interference by outside powers. The now mature Sultan Mahmud started to favour the company, and he sent a delegation to Melaka to invite the company to reopen its lodge. He told the Dutch that he would sell all the tin to them and sever ties with Aceh if the company could protect him.[38] That March, when Aceh demanded the customary annual tribute accompanying their homage (40 bahar of tin), Perak envoys replied that because of the perpetual VOC blockade—which remained thanks to the treaty Aceh had with the Dutch—they could not afford it. If Aceh resorted to force, they would ask Johor to be their suzerain.[39] Perak also made

---

[35] Ibid., p. 34.
[36] Ibid.
[37] Andaya, *Perak, the Abode of Grace*, p. 48.
[38] Ibid.
[39] Winstedt, "A History of Perak", p. 31.

overtures to the anti-Dutch sultan of Kedah to seek an alliance. Sultan Mahmud also began to sell tin to the sultan of Bantam and the Johorese.

This change of favour, however, brought no significant improvements to the company's tin trade. In 1667, opponents of the pro-Dutch bendahara rebelled on the grounds that he had sold too much tin to Melaka. Although this rebellion was quelled, this bendahara died in 1674, and the Dutch governor in Melaka started complaining once more that the company was receiving a mere 200 bahar of tin when Perak produced 700 to 800 bahar a year.[40] The anti-Dutch faction still wielded formidable influence and, in 1674 a new bendahara was appointed who soon emerged as leader of the anti-Dutch faction.

In 1678, Balthasar Bort—the governor of Melaka—in his assessment of the relative strengths of the Malay powers reported that the power of Johor was much reduced, the kings of Perak and Kedah were of little account, and Aceh was impotent and seemed in no danger of attaining any considerable power. Only European foes were to be feared here. Perak was still Aceh's vassal, but her suzerain demanded little tin.[41] Bort, however, had underestimated these Malay polities' ability to thwart and cause damage to the company. In 1685, the Dutch resident and 11 other officials were killed in Perak in an act the company officials accused the bendahara of engineering. According to Andaya, the sultan opposed this attack, and yet the company received no redress. This was because the bendahara—married to Sultan Mahmud's sister—was too powerful. His position was rivalled by the *saudagar raja* (the king's merchant), an Indian named Sedelebe. By 1686, he was in charge of virtually all the tin trade in Perak.[42]

By the turn of the century, the VOC had to admit defeat in its efforts to monopolise Perak's tin. In 1681 the *Dagh-Register* recorded that trade had dwindled. After the end of the third Anglo-Dutch war in 1674, the Dutch not only again faced competition from the English, but also the perennial problem of rivalry from the local, Indian and Portuguese traders. By this time these traders were undercutting the Dutch at will.[43]

---

[40] Irwin, "The Dutch and Tin Trade in Malaya", p. 286.
[41] Winstedt, "A History of Perak", p. 38.
[42] Andaya, *Perak, the Abode of Grace*, p. 50.
[43] Irwin, "The Dutch and Tin Trade in Malaya", p. 286.

"Smuggling" was rampant in Aceh and Kedah.[44] The scourge of piracy in the 1690s compounded the problems the company faced. In 1689, a Panglima Kulup, deemed to be a pirate, burnt the Dutch redoubt in Dinding Island.[45] The company withdrew the blockade at the mouth of the Perak River in 1689, because it served no useful purpose.[46] After the Dutch departure in 1690, Perak was free from trade restrictions and outside threats.[47] In September 1694, the Council of Batavia wrote off the outstanding f. 130,885 due from the sultan and nobles of Perak as a bad debt.[48]

Perak, the Vassal That Lasted

According to Andaya, the history of Perak in the seventeenth century was one dominated by its failed search for a new powerful friend to replace Aceh. Vassalage had brought no benefits, and with Aceh's decline, it could no longer enforce its former control over Perak.[49] However, evidence showed a different picture. Before 1670, Aceh had important leverage over the company for the trade in Perak on the basis of its overlordship. The VOC's unwillingness to go to war with Aceh meant that it had to continue to negotiate for concessions and accept compromises. Perak benefitted from this situation as it did not have to fend for itself. Under the reign of Safiatuddin, Perak was able to use Aceh as an ally and a protector, evoking the traditional overlord-vassal relationship not because Perak was forced to submit to Aceh, but because Aceh was useful to protect the tin trade. By and large, the relationship was mutually beneficial.

The Perak affair discloses a story of resilience in which traditional power relations survived for decades, despite the continuous pressure of circumstances that might have been expected to change the political and commercial rules of the game. The outcome of the Perak affair supports John Wills' view that Aceh did a far better job than its neighbours in

---

[44] Winstedt, "A History of Perak", p. 52.
[45] Andaya, *Perak, the Abode of Grace*, p. 50.
[46] Irwin, "The Dutch and Tin Trade in Malaya", p. 287.
[47] Andaya, *Perak, the Abode of Grace*, p. 52.
[48] Irwin, "The Dutch and Tin Trade in Malaya", p. 285.
[49] Andaya, *Perak, the Abode of Grace*, p. 48.

maintaining independence and a trading network, and in engaging and countering the Europeans in the seventeenth century.⁵⁰ It also supports Van Leur's argument that western dominance was not yet in place. Van Leur stressed the ability of indigenous institutions to absorb and adapt to new influences. In contrast to Eurocentric historians who viewed indigenous people as passive, he saw the importance of local agents and internal forces in stimulating change.⁵¹ In its early encounters in Southeast Asia, the VOC was still learning the ways and structures of indigenous polities without necessarily being able to manipulate them for the company's benefit.⁵² The sultanah and the Aceh elites, on the other hand, could work the traditional system of patron-client relationships to maintain hold of Perak.

Ties That Unbind? Aceh and Her Vassals on the Sumatra West Coast

A different story seems to arise in connection with the pepper trade and the company's relations with Aceh and its vassal states, such as Tiku, Pariaman, Barus, among others on the SWC. The Treaty of Painan of March 1663 and another treaty signed in April 1668 placed a number of these states under Dutch protection.⁵³ According to Kathirithamby-Wells, the decline of Aceh made the VOC protectorate possible. She argued that the Dutch capture of Melaka in 1641 severely eroded Aceh's commercial supremacy and political importance, boosted Dutch prestige and damaged Aceh's bargaining power to such an extent that Sultanah Safiatuddin Syah was obliged to adopt a conciliatory policy. Kathirithamby-Wells claimed that Safiatuddin's reign saw the steady

---

⁵⁰ Wills, "Maritime Asia", p. 98. Although Wills makes this claim, he did not elaborate on his argument.
⁵¹ Jacob Cornelius van Leur, *Indonesian Trade and Society: Essays in Asian Social and Economic History* ('s-Gravenhage: W. van Hoeve, 1955).
⁵² In Newbury's view, the imperialists benefited when they clearly understood and took advantage of these very same local and regional political structures. Colin Newbury, *Patrons, Clients and Empire: Chieftaincy, and Over-rule in Asia, Africa, and the Pacific* (Oxford: Oxford University Press, 2003), p. 70.
⁵³ Kathirithamby-Wells, "Acehnese Control over West Sumatra", pp. 473, 478.

decline of Acehnese power overseas and the increasing powers of the orang kaya at home.[54] The sultanate's territorial reach diminished or became less effective as a result of internal weakness and external commercial pressure from the Dutch. The improved conditions for the Dutch were largely owing to the decline of Acehnese trade, including with foreign Muslims as a result of Dutch attacks on their shipping.[55] Kathirithamby-Wells pointed out that the sultanah's *firman* (ruler's order) of 1641 gave the Dutch a nominally free hand on the west coast and allowed Dutch officials to transact directly with the rajas—a course of action she viewed as a departure from established procedure. In her view, although it was difficult to judge the sincerity of the queen's motives in conceding to Dutch demands, the sultanah found it difficult to force the local chiefs to comply.[56] She concluded that in the second half of the seventeenth century, the rajas of the SWC, with Dutch assistance, forcibly cast off their Acehnese overlord and voluntarily refurbished their ties with Pagarruyong, capital of the Minangkabau kingdom. The inhabitants took advantage of an opportunity to rid themselves of the Acehnese whom they saw as a foreign authority which, despite its long-established connections with the area, had remained indifferent to the populace.[57]

To what extent did these treaties really change the distribution of power in North Sumatra? Did Dutch "ascendance" in the straits bring about such a decline in Aceh's trade resulting in a loss of authority that Sultanah Safiatuddin was obliged to adopt a conciliatory policy on the SWC? Did events in the SWC result in European commercial, political and military power displacing indigenous institutions, which brought about European ascendance and local decline? Or could Wills' paradigm of interactive emergence be applied here as well as in Perak, where both local and European powers were still relatively comparable, where both had to adapt and compromise in order to protect their own interests? According to Jurrien van Goor, in highly personalised small states, such as those in the Malay world, intergenerational rivalry and unstable power sharing were the norm. It was common for one rival or the other to call

---

[54] Ibid., p. 465.
[55] No evidence is given for this assertion.
[56] Kathirithamby-Wells, "Acehnese Control over West Sumatra", pp. 466–7.
[57] Ibid., p. 479.

for Dutch assistance, just as they had previously called on other local maritime overlords.[58] These alliances tended to be as transient and fluid as the politics surrounding them. In Colin Newbury's view, the most effective impositions of authority developed not when Europeans imposed alien forms, but when they understood and took advantage of local and regional political structures.[59]

However, both Newbury and Kathirithamby-Wells tended to view the European companies as the active agents leading these encounters while reducing local polities to the status of mere pawns. Newbury showed Europeans exploiting local institutions. Kathirithamby-Wells saw local disintegration and Western triumph, claiming that the VOC was successful in controlling local leaders, shipping and trade by the mid-seventeenth century. Judging from the evidence, however, I believe that inhabitants of the SWC, rather than merely being sandwiched between the Acehnese and the VOC, created their own opportunities to obtain better political and commercial deals. Indeed, VOC involvement in west coast politics, marked by signing the Painan Treaty in 1663, did not signify the end of Acehnese control and the beginning of VOC domination. On the contrary, it launched a contest for influence and power among a growing number of elites and stakeholders, while power became even more diffused. Aceh's so-called decline did not make the SWC polities surrender to the VOC for protection. Rather, the company's keenness to get involved in local politics in order to protect its commercial interests made the VOC just another alternative power in regional politics. Local elites resentful of the *panglima*s (governors) appointed by Aceh's rulers— who were at times not local-born—used the VOC to support their efforts to oust these panglimas. A few of the most ambitious even used the VOC to regain lost status and inheritance. The willingness of the elites to acquire new patrons and the VOC's desire to obtain new clients explains Aceh's loss of control over some of these west coast states. The Painan Treaty was perhaps the first step on the road to Dutch dominance but hardly a definitive one. The treaty did not end Aceh's control over the SWC area,

---

[58] Jurrien van Goor, "Seapower, Trade and State-Formation: Pontianak and the Dutch, 1780–1840", in *Trading Companies in Asia, 1600–1830*, ed. Jurrien van Goor (Utrecht: HES Utigevers, 1986), p. 84.

[59] Newbury, "Patrons, Clients and Empire", pp. 12, 70.

but it signalled the beginning of a long, drawn-out struggle for power between Aceh, the VOC and local elites.[60]

Early Relations between Aceh and the Sumatra West Coast

Before examining the contest for power between Aceh and the VOC over the SWC polities during Safiatuddin's reign, it is necessary to sketch the situation she inherited. By 1621, Sultan Iskandar Muda controlled many peripheral areas of the northern half of coastal Sumatra, including Pidir, Pasai, Deli, Aru, Daya, Labu, Singkel, Barus, Batahan, Pasaman, Priaman, Tiku and Padang through patrimonial relations by appointing Acehnese panglimas.[61] The incentive for Acehnese control over the west coast during Iskandar Muda's period was, as in earlier times, to gain pepper and gold. Iskandar Muda stationed panglimas of Acehnese origin at the main centres of production and export: Tiku, Pariaman, Salida and Inderapura. Under a system whereby Iskandar Muda claimed 15 per cent of the gold and pepper produced and fixed the price of the rest, the success of this monopoly depended on the panglimas who were harshly punished for disobeying Iskandar Muda's orders.

Europeans, meanwhile, traded at Kota Raja (Banda Aceh) under royal licence, and permission to trade elsewhere were extremely difficult to secure. According to Kathirithamby-Wells, Iskandar Muda resisted European pressure for commercial concessions, and thus preserved his empire from the inroads of colonial exploitation. However, she also observed that his 1629 defeat at the hands of the Portuguese during the siege of Melaka tragically dealt so severe a blow to his confidence that, in return for an alliance against the Portuguese, in 1632 he signed away to the Dutch some of the very concessions that he had prudently withheld for so long. By this agreement, Iskandar Muda allowed the Dutch toll-free trade for several years in the whole kingdom, including the SWC, as well as the freedom to participate in the Perak tin trade.

---

[60] Willem Johan Adriaan de Leeuw, *Het Painansch Contract* [The Painan Contract] (Amsterdam: H.J. Paris, 1926), p. 82.
[61] Lombard, *Le Sultanat d'Atjeh au Temps d'Iskandar Muda, 1607–1636*, p. 132.

Kathirithamby-Wells claimed that the privileges granted in 1638 on the same grounds—to secure an alliance with the Dutch against Portuguese Melaka—by his successor, Iskandar Thani, proved to be a worthless sacrifice as in the end he abstained from attacking Melaka.[62] In addition to exclusive trade for an indefinite period, he granted other privileges that constituted a surrender of royal prerogatives. The west coast pepper—formerly collected by the sultan only as tribute and traded under royal licence—could henceforth be directly obtained by the Dutch and paid for at the capital. The panglimas did not welcome the change: those at Tiku, Priaman and Inderapura withheld the delivery of pepper unless the king's tolls and duties were paid locally on the pretext that the Dutch traders could not produce a written document from Iskandar Thani authorising them to do so.

It is important to note that the sultanah's predecessors opened the door to the SWC, thus paving the way for a deeper penetration of Dutch influence and control. The concessions here were granted not because Aceh was weak, but to incentivise the Dutch against the Portuguese. Meanwhile, the VOC's willingness to interfere in local politics made the company attractive to local elites with ambitions of their own. As early as 1619, some local elites on the SWC offered to transfer their allegiance to the VOC in return for protection and freedom from Acehnese domination: the futile attempt by the ruler of Inderapura to seek Dutch protection is an example. At other times, anti-Aceh sentiment took the form of monopoly evasions whenever Acehnese vigilance was relaxed. The predatory and exploitative attitude of Iskandar Muda and Iskandar Thani drove local elites to search for other patrons.

Aceh's Relations with the Sumatra West Coast under Sultanah Safiatuddin Syah

When Safiatuddin came to power she had to deal with the VOC's increasing interest in obtaining pepper, with its attendant pressures on the SWC. To show that she welcomed company officers, she issued a firman

---

[62] Kathirithamby-Wells, "Acehnese Control over West Sumatra", p. 465.

in 1641 concerning privileges her predecessors had verbally promised.[63] However, she awarded exemption from toll for only *one* ship, the *Groll*, trading annually in Tiku, Priaman, Inderapura and Padang; other ships still had to pay in *rijksdaalder*s (Dutch silver coins).[64] This grant actually *limited* the blanket grant Iskandar Muda promised to the Dutch under which the company could trade toll-free for several years in all his dominions. She conceded, however, her late husband's promise of exclusive trade in the specified places. This was one of the company's top demands which, by then, had learnt that verbal promises could be changed or conveniently forgotten.

For instance, when the company tried to pin Iskandar Thani down to enforce his promise of exclusivity, he sidestepped with the explanation that it had been a custom in these places to trade with merchants from all nations and that this practice would continue. He assured the Dutch that there would be no problems if they joined the queue together with the other traders![65]

Pieter Sourij—visiting Aceh from May to August 1642—complained that traders from Bengal, Dabul, Masulipatnam and Arakan were still "infecting" the SWC, even with the existence of the 1641 contract. In 1641, when Sultanah Safiatuddin ascended the throne, Gujarati merchants were the most powerful traders in Aceh. Company officials complained that Indian traders evaded tolls by shipping goods in small quantities. The Dutch were unhappy that the sultanah had granted exemption for only the *Groll*. They also wanted the Indian traders expelled so that they could take over cloth deliveries to exchange for pepper instead of having to pay in gold.[66] In addition to the Indians, both the Dutch and English

---

[63] "CXXXVI. Atjeh-Sumatra Westkust. Februari-Maart 1641", in *Corpus Diplomaticum*, ed. J.E. Heeres, Vol. 1, pp. 345–6. This same act was originally written in Malay and a Dutch translation can also be found in Chijs, *Dagh-Register*, 1640–41, pp. 423–5. The queen's act of goodwill was reinforced in her first letter to Governor General Antonio van Diemen in Batavia. This letter was translated from Malay into Dutch and the main contents could be found in Chijs, *Dagh-Register*, 1640–41, pp. 428–30.

[64] Ibid., p. 346.

[65] NA, VOC 1136, Copie missive van den Gouverneur van Diemen aen den Coninck van Attchin, 1640, f. 1209R.

[66] NA, VOC 1143, Dagh-Register off Journael gehouden bij den Pieter Sourij, 1642, f. 579R.

East India companies faced other local rivals, such as those from Johor and Macassar.[67]

Seven years later, on 2 October 1649, Johan Truijtman visited Aceh and made complaints similar to those voiced by Sourij. In an audience with the sultanah, he asked for her written estemie to be given to her panglima on the SWC to confirm the company's earlier privileges there. He complained that the Dutch had received no pepper from Sillida and Inderapura, and very little pepper from Tiku and Priaman.[68] He demanded a fixed price for the company's cloth in exchange for pepper. Next, Truijtman requested the execution of a promise, made in the previous treaty, to exempt one ship from tolls to the amount of 1,070 bahar of pepper in Tiku. This request raised the ire of some of the orang kaya, though the Maharaja Sri Maharaja and the sultanah promised they would accommodate these requests.

Encouraged, perhaps, Truijtman requested exemption from tolls for the pepper trade along the whole of the SWC. This time the sultanah not only refused the request but reacted harshly. Truijtman reported that she said, "How could I accept a condition never before applied that could take the bread out of the mouths of my people? I will follow the old customs."[69] Hereupon the orang kaya rose together as a sign of concurrence, and gravely called out "daulat". The toll would amount to some 8,000 reals; however, she emphasised that, regardless of the amount, her people should enjoy their rights to collect tolls and this custom should remain indefinitely. This was consistent with her policy of denying the Dutch toll-free privileges in Perak. She did, however, reassure the Dutch that in case they feared that the panglima on the SWC would not acknowledge the company's privilege for the *Groll*, she would annually reissue the written order.[70] Members of the anti-Dutch faction protested over the sultanah's

---

[67] William Foster, *The English Factories in India 1668–1669: A Calendar of Documents in the India Office, British Museum and Public Record Office* (Oxford: The Clarendon Press, 1927), p. 169.

[68] Heeres, *Bouwstoffen*, p. 487.

[69] NA, VOC 1171, Rapport substanteel aen d' Ed Heer Cornelis van der Lijn, 1649, f. 185R.

[70] NA, VOC 1171, Rapport substanteel aen d' Ed Heer Cornelis van der Lijn, 1649, f. 185V.

offer to renew existing Dutch privileges, and even Maharaja Sri Maharaja was silent this time. However, Maharaja Binthara, the Maharaja's follower, interjected that it was the sultanah's right to determine the matter as she wished.

On 12 October 1649, the sultanah made a contract with the company fixing the price of cloth in exchange for pepper on the SWC. As in the Perak case, she not only gave a written firman to her panglima, but she also commissioned two qualified people to go to Tiku with Truijtman to execute the contract. This firman to the panglima of Tiku confirmed her *kurnia* (permission to grant) for the company to receive the rest of the 1,070 bahar of pepper toll-free. However, she also wrote to the governor general explaining her refusal to offer a permanent exemption from tolls for the whole of the SWC. Her resolution in these matters shows that the sultanah was keen to maintain friendly relations with the company. She did accommodate the Dutch on several demands, despite protests from the laksamana and his followers, but she was adamant on key points. Toll exacted on the pepper trade on the SWC was the main revenue for the sultanah and her orang kaya, and this right had to be protected.

True to her word, the sultanah sent a firman reiterating the promises made to the company. After initial resistance from the panglimas of Tiku and Priaman, the envoys of the Acehnese crown—Sribidia Indra and Radia Moedeliar—signed a contract in Tiku on 6 November 1649 with oppercoopmans Joan Truijtman, Henrick Creijerszoon and Joannes Waghter. Another contract was confirmed in Priaman three days later. In substance, the contracts stated that as long as there was trade between the two parties, the price of cloth supplied by the company in exchange for pepper on the SWC would remain fixed. All foreign nations were to be excluded from the SWC except for the company.[71]

Six years later, in 1655, despite the Dutch company officials' trading privileges, they were still not able to monopolise trade in Sumatra, and they continued to complain bitterly about the damage Muslim trade did to the VOC.[72] The Dutch reported that the Muslim merchants from

---

[71] Heeres, *Bouwstoffen*, pp. 501–3; Heeres, *Corpus Diplomaticum*, pp. 528–9.
[72] Coolhaas, *Generale Missiven*, Vol. 3, 1655 to 1674, pp. 19, 23.

Surat, Masulipatnam and Pegu were able to sell their cloth at very low prices in Aceh, which Asian local traders bought in exchange for their own products, such as cloves. A great quantity of Chinese wares brought from Johor, Patani and Melaka were also traded in Aceh. The Dutch also faced competition from the English on the SWC from 1658, as the English decided to reverse their policy of withdrawal made a decade earlier.[73] However, the Dutch were not ready to tolerate this competition, thus three of their ships forcibly attempted to stop the English *Mayflower* from being loaded with pepper. When they failed to do so, the Dutch then seized 50 bahars of pepper from the ship. The Dutch adopted similar coercive measures against other rivals by patrolling the coasts, emptying foreign vessels of pepper on the justification that the sultanah had promised them exclusive trade.[74] Their incessant demands and high-handed acts inspired local anger that culminated in the imprisonment of Coopman Van Voorst and other company officials in Priaman, Tiku and Sillida. The Dutch believed this was instigated by the Acehnese, as some of the Dutch prisoners were taken to Aceh.[75] In 1657, the Dutch fortified their factory at Sillida and then went to Priaman, where negotiations for an exchange of prisoners proved fruitless. They decided to patrol off Priaman instead.[76]

Balthasar Bort led a delegation to Aceh in 1659 to settle these differences and reconfirm company privileges on the SWC. Another agreement between the company and the sultanah promised that the panglima responsible would pay the company 49,518¼ reals for damages incurred in 1657. The agreement also reconfirmed the company's exclusive privileges on the SWC, and the yearly toll-free grant of now 1,200 bahar of pepper to be obtained from Priaman in the first year, Tiku in the second and Sillida in the third.[77] After departing Aceh, Bort went to the

---

[73] Foster, *English Factories*, pp. 181, 207, 255.
[74] The Dutch went to Inderapura to collect pepper, but they found an English ship there and unloaded their pepper. J.L. van Basel, "Begin en Voortgang van onzen Handel en Bezittingen op Sumatra's Westkust" [Start and Progress of Our Trade and Properties on the West Coast of Sumatra], *Tijdschrift voor Neerland's Indie* 9, 2 (1847): 17.
[75] Heeres, *Corpus Diplomaticum*, p. 152.
[76] Basel, "Begin en Voortgang", p. 16.
[77] Heeres, *Corpus Diplomaticum*, p. 154.

SWC and concluded a treaty with Sillida in 1660. Bort then went to Inderapura, Padang and Tiku where he concluded similar treaties and placed a resident in each place to oversee trade. He reported that he found the panglimas willing to trade with the VOC, but they could not afford to pay debts.[78]

From 1655 to 1659 the VOC's intensified blockades of the Aceh and Perak harbours in retaliation for the company officials' murders in Perak in 1651 temporarily dampened Aceh's trade with the Gujaratis. However, after Aceh and the VOC signed the 1659 peace treaty, the merchants who had been forced to go to Melaka returned to Aceh to trade. The VOC's trade in Melaka was again badly affected,[79] with company officials complaining that, as a result of the great Muslim traffic in textiles, the company's own textile trade had suffered.[80]

So, far from giving the Dutch a free hand on the west coast, the sultanah actually limited the VOC's privileges. Her resistance to blanket privileges indicated her desire to protect the subjects of states subordinate to Aceh. By allowing her vassals on the SWC to trade directly with the VOC, she dismantled the policies of Iskandar Muda which had caused so much local resentment. Although she gave her panglimas a freer hand to trade with the VOC, she did not tolerate those who contravened her commands, especially when this might hurt Aceh's strategic interests. When Bort went to Aceh in 1659, the sultanah allowed the Dutch to build a temporary lodge in Padang. The Dutch, however, schemed to build a permanent lodge. Two local village heads supported the VOC plan, however the panglima vetoed a lodge of any sort for fear that the company might fortify their factory.[81] With this attempt prevented, company representatives raised a temporary wooden lodge further south at Sillida. When the sultanah learnt about this she became very angry. Gabriel Bruyl, then the resident in Aceh, wrote to Jan Groenewegen—the company coopman-resident on the SWC—that the sultanah had summoned those from Padang to Aceh to register her anger at having her orders disobeyed. She also sent an estemie to Sillida to punish the

---

[78] Basel, "Begin en Voortgang", pp. 17–9.
[79] Coolhaas, *Generale Missiven*, Vol. 3, 1655 to 1674, p. 324.
[80] Ibid., p. 337.
[81] Chijs, *Dagh-Register*, 1663, p. 85.

panglima for allowing the company to build a house for year-long use, when she only gave license for the company to build a temporary factory in Sillida to be used for a month or two a year. The panglima was replaced, and the sultanah ordered Groenewegen to move from Sillida. She would only allow the Dutch to build a more permanent lodge at Tiku or Priaman. These were Acehnese strongholds and closer to Aceh's capital, thus the Dutch could be closely monitored.[82] The company finally decided to establish a lodge at Pulau Chinco, an island off Padang, which was not only a healthier site but was well away from the Acehnese. It later became the company's headquarters for the SWC, and the Dutch closed their factory in Aceh in 1663. Thus, even after her male predecessors had fully swung wide the doors to the SWC, 22 years into her reign, Sultanah Safiatuddin was able to keep the Dutch at bay.

VOC and the SWC Polities: From Traders to Protectors?

The ship *De Remedie* sailed into Batavia in 1663 with a letter—dated 24 February—from Groenewegen to the governor general reporting on his secret meetings with the rajas of the SWC in 1662 who offered to put themselves under VOC protection.[83] Three orang kaya from formerly Minangkabau-ruled Bajang—Raja Poety, Sultan Mamoulia and Maharaja Lella—appeared with Dato Pekepia in Sillida in January 1663 and promised the Dutch, in unbreakable friendship, to deliver their pepper to no one else but the company.[84] Their unhappiness with what they claimed was Acehnese domination—considered foreign—was compounded by the heavy taxes and oppressive behaviour of the Acehnese panglima.[85] A provisional agreement was concluded with Groenewegen to be later ratified in Batavia.

This "secret" negotiation was well known to other local elites. When Groenewegen visited Tiku a few weeks later, the *penghulu* (village head)

---

[82] Ibid., pp. 83–4.
[83] Ibid., p. 81.
[84] Ibid., p. 82.
[85] Those on the SWC paid homage to Aceh—one *peteh* (two *stuivers*) per house yearly. Chijs, *Dagh-Register*, 1663, p. 88.

orang kaya Suri Radja, representing Duabelas Kota (a federation of 12 cities on the SWC) declared that he, too, wanted to sign an everlasting contract with the company to throw off the Acehnese yoke. Similarly, when Groenewegen visited Padang, the penghulu, orang kaya Ketjil welcomed Groenewegen to stay at his house and discuss the possibility of putting Padang under the company's protection and chase away the Acehnese panglima. Sultan Muzaffar Syah, his son, Muhammad Syah, and son-in-law, Raja Sulaiman, met Groenewegen in Sillida offering to sign a similar agreement.[86]

In July 1663, the provisional contract became the Painan Treaty, formally ratified between representatives from Bandar Sepuloh, Inderapura, Tiku and Padang, and the Dutch Governor General Joan Maetsuyker and the Council of the Indies in Batavia. The main provisions were for exclusive trade—banning the English under threat of Dutch fines or chastisement; exemption from tolls except for the usual *ruba* (customary dues) and other anchorage fees to local rulers; non-interference in religion; and the company's right to build lodges in the signatory polities. The locals were to expel all Acehnese. They would be under company protection against all enemies from the sea but not from land. The company would try its own officers and determine the price of gold.[87]

Why did the VOC shift its focus from Aceh to the SWC in 1663? According to Kathirithamby-Wells, the shift in Dutch policy was conducted, initially at least, in strict secrecy in response to Aceh's alleged duplicity over the Perak tin trade. The cordial relations which then existed between Aceh and Perak and Aceh's friendly reception of foreign Muslim traders at Perak generated well-founded suspicions of collusion.[88] Another reason was Aceh's steady decline under Dutch pressure, which contributed to increased Dutch encroachment on the SWC. Kathirithamby-Wells argued that the sultanah was anxious to save the remnants of a once flourishing trade from total destruction by the Dutch. Furthermore, she argued that as Aceh's internal administration was weak and Safiatuddin Syah was getting

---

[86] Mohammad Dahlan Mansoer et al., *Sedjarah Minangkabau* (Djakarta: Bhratara, 1970), pp. 93–4.
[87] Chijs, *Dagh-Register, 1663*, pp. 88, 349–50.
[88] Kathirithamby-Wells, "Acehnese Control over West Sumatra", p. 470.

on in years, and helpless in the face of dissension among court officials and unreasonable Dutch demands, she was no longer in a position to reject Dutch demands. Through a conciliatory policy, she tried placating the Dutch officials with gifts, royal honours and unusual friendliness.[89] The final reason was the progressive strengthening of the VOC's position after 1650, when officials became obsessed with the idea of cornering the bulk of the westward flow of pepper and gold, which hitherto had been a closely held Acehnese monopoly. With the intention of being close to the main sources of both products, the company proposed to establish its main factory at Padang.[90]

And yet there is little evidence to show that Aceh was in decline. Aceh's tin trade continued to thrive, her elephant trade actually increased, Melaka was not able to subsume Aceh and, internally, Safiatuddin's position was consolidated by the mid-1650s. Perhaps by 1660, the company was tired of dealing with Aceh in order to gain concessions on the SWC, as shown in successive failures to enforce their privileges. The company officials were unable to procure even the 1,200 bahar of toll-free pepper promised to them in any of the places stipulated. They complained that they could not get even half the amount in Sillida and had to try to procure the rest from Tiku.[91] The Acehnese panglima on the SWC also prevented the company from trading gold on the grounds that the sultanah had not granted the company access to gold in her dominions. The Dutch countered this by citing the 1659 agreement, which they interpreted as covering not only pepper but gold and other goods. In the last two years the company officials reported that the Acehnese had engrossed about 400 kati of gold (about 720 Dutch pounds). The Dutch were eager to get their hands on this gold, deemed as a "remarkable trade": for about one tael of heavy inland gold, they could get much more cloth than for one bahar of pepper.[92]

With frequent setbacks, local company officials, especially under Groenwegen, had begun to sidestep Aceh. For example, after some Dutch officials were taken prisoner in Sillida, Tiku and Priaman in 1657, the

---

[89] Ibid., p. 472.
[90] Ibid., p. 473.
[91] Chijs, *Dagh-Register*, 1663, p. 83.
[92] Ibid., p. 82. One *kati*—a Malay measure of weight, about 625 g, or 20 taels.

company tried unsuccessfully to take matters into its own hands and retaliate in Tiku and Priaman, and tried to strengthen the factory in Sillida. The VOC was also encouraged by some local elites' initiatives to make deals independent of Acehnese authority. It is important to note that local elites took this initiative, contrary to the common belief that the VOC and the Acehnese deprived them of agency. Collusion worked better both for the VOC and the SWC elites eager to be independent from Aceh to pursue their own interests: outright war with Aceh was against the company's policy, and for locals an attempt to overthrow Aceh's overlordship was risky. These are among the reasons for the company's initial covert actions in dealing with Aceh's SWC vassals, which paved the way for the VOC's increasing involvement in the area. Involvement was not because of the VOC's ascendance and the decline of Aceh after 1650.

The Painan Treaty signified the beginning of the contest between the Acehnese, the VOC and the local elites for political and economic control. Affairs on the SWC, where local elites were vying for power and wealth, were conducive for the company to shift policy from depending on the Acehnese to patronage in its own right and the cultivation of clients to protect Dutch interests. In common with the traditions of a region where stranger-kings were rife, and with the practical advantages of favouring distant, possibly easily manipulated rulers, the SWC elites increasingly preferred the Dutch to the Acehnese.[93] The VOC wrested vassals from Aceh and worked towards controlling the SWC's trade. However, as with other contracts, the company needed a few more decades to begin to translate the terms of the Painan Treaty from paper to reality.

Sultanah Safiatuddin's Response

Safiatuddin and her orang kaya were naturally suspicious of Dutch actions on the SWC. Even before the Painan Treaty, the sultanah had courted the English and Siamese to counter-balance Dutch incursions in Perak

---

[93] David Henley, "Conflict, Justice, and the Stranger-King Indigenous Roots of Colonial Rule in Indonesia and Elsewhere", *Modern Asian Studies* 38, 1 (2004): 87.

and the SWC. Although the English presence in Sumatra was negligible and intermittent, the sultanah wrote to Charles II on 12 October 1661[94] to renew what she deemed ties of friendship from the time of her father.[95] She urged the English to continue sending their ships to Aceh, as they had in the past, for the sake of lasting friendship. As proof of her good intentions, she mentioned the privileges she had granted Henry Gary, the EIC officer who had resided in her kingdom for the previous 18 months. She had allowed him to construct a warehouse at the port and granted permission to English merchants to trade in Aceh. Furthermore, she allowed three English ships a year to trade in Aceh and its dominions. She informed Charles II that she had done all she could to facilitate trade for the English, but they were forcibly stopped and pepper removed from their ships by the "accursed" (*celaka*) Dutch. She besought Charles to safeguard English traders from harm.

Safiatuddin clearly wanted to use the English as a bulwark against a possible VOC attack and invited them to establish their presence in Aceh. This plea did not appeal, however, because English trade in Aceh was already dwindling, and they were not willing to be drawn into a brawl between the Acehnese and the Dutch. The sultanah attempted to renew her alliance with Siam in 1662,[96] and even sent envoys to Aceh's old arch-enemy, Johor, but neither effort yielded positive results.[97]

The signing of the Painan Treaty initially made little difference. In July 1663, Groenewegen and the SWC representatives returned to the SWC from Batavia to find more troubles erupting in their territories. Having discovered its vassals' "betrayal", Aceh was extremely suspicious of the VOC's next moves. Earlier news from Perak that the VOC intended to

---

[94] Translation of letter from Queen of Aceh to Charles II in C.O. 77, Vol. VIII, pp. 192, 194, 196, Public Records Office (now The National Archives): William Foster, *The English Factories in India 1661–1664* (Oxford: The Clarendon Press, 1923), p. 83. For the letter in Malay, see Annabel Teh Gallop, "Gold, Silver and Lapis Lazuli: Royal letters from Aceh in the 17th Century", in *Mapping the Acehnese Past*, ed. R. Michael Feener, Patrick Daly and Anthony Reid (Leiden: KITLV Press, 2011), pp. 124–5.
[95] English trading relations with Aceh first began when James Lancaster brought a letter from Queen Elizabeth to the sultan and landed in Aceh in 1602. Dasgupta, "Aceh in Indonesian Trade and Politics, 1600–1641", p. 54.
[96] Chijs, *Dagh-Register*, 1663, p. 208. No more details were provided regarding the mission.
[97] Ibid., p. 433. No more details were given here either.

close its factories in Aceh and Perak prompted the Acehnese to believe that the VOC might wage war on them this time. A letter from Groenewegen in Pulau Chinco to the governor general mentioned how in December 1663 the sultanah sent an estemie to her panglimas in Tiku and all other lands to inform them that the Dutch had broken away from Aceh and Perak. Therefore, they must be vigilant against Dutch activities in Bajang, and the queen's lands must be maintained and kept in submission. This news alarmed the pro-Dutch faction in Sungei Pagou, and they pleaded with Groenewegen not to let them down. They informed him that their panglima and the Acehnese representative had asked them to go to Aceh to explain.[98]

While attempting to stem Dutch encroachments on the SWC, the sultanah simultaneously tried to improve relations with the company. On 26 August 1664, two of the sultanah's boedjanghs arrived in Melaka carrying her letter and gifts. The sultanah wrote that she was very surprised at the company's decision to empty the factory in Aceh and Perak and, for two years now, no Dutch envoys or ships had been to Aceh. She informed the governor of Melaka that company officials still in Aceh were in such a state that Resident Bruyl had to borrow 450 taels from her! The Dutch did not respond. The Acehnese boedjanghs were treated well, but evidence that the company was sidestepping Aceh to concentrate on the SWC without Aceh's mediation now seemed irrefutable.[99]

Nevertheless, the Dutch were to discover that even though the local elites invited their protection in return for trade, the company could not easily reap the benefits. By sidestepping the Acehnese, the VOC lost the advantage of a single authority, albeit a troublesome one, in dealing with the SWC polities, and instead encountered a much more fluid environment, difficult to understand and harder still to master. Power on the SWC had multiple centres.[100] Local rivalries added to the complexity and fragility of the political situation, and the VOC's attempts to promote local rulers encouraged more jostling for power. The absence

---

[98] Chijs, *Dagh-Register*, 1664, p. 45.
[99] Ibid., p. 443.
[100] For a detailed study on nature of Minangkabau authority, see Timothy Barnard, *Multiple Centres of Authority: Society and Environment in Siak and Eastern Sumatra, 1674–1827* (Leiden: KITLV Press, 2003).

of a dominant foreign presence facilitated internecine wars which the Dutch were unable to suppress until the end of the century. Instability intermittently stopped trade, while different factions used the Acehnese and the VOC as supporting powers in their conflicts.

It is beyond the scope of this chapter to detail the political developments and the changing fortunes of the VOC in the SWC's small polities, such as Inderapura,[101] Kota Tengah and Barus.[102] Nevertheless, a brief case study of Padang is illustrative of the political situation's fluidity in the absence of a strong hegemony.

Troubles in Padang

The VOC faced obstacles even in areas that were distant from Aceh and inclined to ally with the company. In most of these locales, politics was characterised by the competition for power and wealth between leaders who were pro-company, and those who remained loyal to Aceh. The company's fortunes ebbed and flowed depending on who had the upper hand. In Padang, the company officials found the orang kaya very divided, the more powerful group being pro-Aceh. The deaths of two leaders who had signed a contract with the company brought about a grave deterioration of the VOC's affairs. Groenewegen sent a small force but failed to chase the Acehnese away. The Dutch reported that the pro-Aceh faction was promising money to those who could help expel the company from Padang.[103] Company officials were in a dilemma because they were not inclined to force the Padang inhabitants to adhere to the contract, and they were not willing to leave Padang as it was an important place whose example other polities followed. It was only a year later that the pro-company faction managed to gain power there and even brought another troubled area—Kota Tengah—to their side. The Dutch reported that the leaders of Padang even pawned their wives' jewellery to lure Kota

---

[101] For a detailed account of the history of Inderapura see Kathirithamby-Wells, "The Inderapura Sultanate", pp. 65–84.
[102] Jane Drakard, "An Indian Ocean Port: Sources for the Earlier History of Barus", *Archipel* 37 (1989): 73.
[103] Letter from Jacob Cauw from Padang to Governor General, dated 9 November 1664. Chijs, *Dagh-Register*, 1664, p. 550.

Tengah with gifts.[104] Padang became the company's main administrative centre on the SWC in 1666, though it failed to extend its influence into Acehnese strongholds, such as Tiku and Priaman. Groenewegen reported in 1665 that Jacob Corneliszoon, who was in charge in Tiku, was murdered with two other soldiers.[105] The company retaliated by burning houses and vessels, and stationed two yachts near Tiku and Priaman. The Dutch in Batavia gave no passes to those who wished to visit these places.[106] Groenewegen's death in December 1665 was another setback for the company and its allies.[107]

Groenewegen was ultimately succeeded by Abraham Verspreet, who landed in Padang with ships and soldiers to wage a war on all the places which were anti-Dutch, including Pauw, Priaman, Tiku, Kota Tengah and Oelakkan. Besides the leaders from Padang and Ambon, Raja Bugis joined Verspreet. A letter from Padang to Governor Maetsuyker reported that the Acehnese from Priaman and Tiku had been removed, and that orang kaya Kecil had become governor of Padang, Raja Bugis king of Oelakkan, and Raja Ambon panglima of Priaman, while the company subdued Pauw and Kota Tengah.[108]

However, not all was as reported. A letter from Jacob Pits mentioned that no matter how they dissembled, the hearts of Tiku and Priaman were with Aceh.[109] As long as the Acehnese remained in these areas, they swore with their mouths but never with their hearts.[110] Troubles for the company recurred in Kota Tengah and Priaman. The promotion of Padang under the VOC interfered with trade in these areas, and by the late 1660s they had become centres of fierce opposition to the company. The company's SWC allies wrote to the governor general appealing for soldiers. One other reason for these renewed troubles was the arrival of Raja Palawan from Aceh—not from the sea but from the eastern, landward side of the SWC, presumably to avoid clashes with Dutch naval patrols. Raja Palawan

---

[104] Chijs, *Dagh-Register*, 1665, p. 238.
[105] Ibid., p. 48.
[106] Ibid., p. 312.
[107] Chijs, *Dagh-Register*, 1666–67, p. 8.
[108] Ibid., p. 175.
[109] Ibid., p. 404.
[110] Chijs, *Dagh-Register*, 1668–69, p. 278.

spread the news that the sultanah intended to send forces within three months to bring all her former vassals under her control.[111] He declared that the ulama in these areas had now allied with him against the enemies of religion.[112]

Religion was important. Aceh had played a big part in the dissemination and development of Islam in western Sumatra. Barus was an important religious centre with close connections to Aceh from as early as the second half of the sixteenth century. In the first half of the seventeenth century, Barus—where the famous ulama, Hamzah Fansuri, was said to have originated—was home to many religious exiles who had escaped the persecutions of Nuruddin al-Raniri in Aceh.[113] Indeed, one of the obstacles encountered during the initial treaty negotiations with Barus in 1668 was local opposition to the VOC's demand that all Acehnese be expelled. There were many Acehnese residents in Barus, some of whom married members of the local nobility.[114] Another important religious centre, Oelakkan, had numerous Acehnese residents whose expulsion, on the company's demand, also provoked outrage. Verspreet described Oelakkan as fanatically Muslim and very inclined towards the Acehnese.[115]

This arrival of Raja Palawan caused disturbances in Kota Tengah, where about half the council members—led by Bendahara Raja Macatta (Mahkota), Raja Setia Wangsa and Maharaja Adonna Lilla—rebelled against the company. Jacob Pits went to Kota Tengah with Sultan Muhammad Syah of Inderapura and Panglima Raja of Padang to investigate and faced demands that the company expel its Panglima Orang Kaya Putih and have the rebels' houses and property burnt. In the end, the company closed its lodge and brought all its goods to Padang.[116] Padang and the company soldiers only subdued Kota Tengah in 1680.[117]

---

[111] See Chijs, *Dagh-Register*, 1665, p. 239.
[112] Chijs, *Dagh-Register*, 1670–71, p. 69.
[113] Drakard, "An Indian Ocean Port", p. 73.
[114] Hendrick Kroeskamp, *De Westkust en Minangkabau 1665–1668* [The West Coast and Minangkabau] (Utrecht: Drukkerij Fa. Schotanus and Jens, 1931), p. 138.
[115] Ibid., p. 88.
[116] Chijs, *Dagh-Register*, 1670–71, p. 71.
[117] Chijs, *Dagh-Register*, 1680, p. 712.

VOC as the New Overlord?

The company did not attempt to replace Aceh as the overlord and protector of its former vassals on the SWC. This was partly because of the existence of pro-Aceh factions, but also because of the ulama's religious opposition to the company, which appeared to have some clout. After 1666, opposition to the VOC grew and anti-Dutch protests on the west coast were frequently described in the VOC records as having a "Muslim" character; this religious sentiment strengthened the Acehnese link in anti-company activities.[118] VOC strategy was to revive the old kingdom of Minangkabau and to emplace Minangkabau as the new Muslim overlord but loyal to the Dutch. In 1665, the VOC made the first contact with the Minangkabau ruler, Sultan Ahmad Syah, whose claim to overlordship, unless neutralised, might prove dangerous to the VOC's prospects of subjugating the west coast to control the pepper and gold trade.

Despite the Painan Treaty's contractual language, the VOC essentially regarded the SWC as conquered territory.[119] Verspreet, however, recognised that religious opposition to the company was invariably linked to local support for Aceh. In a letter to his superiors in Batavia dated 23 May 1667, he considered the desirability of finding a way to soften Muslim resentment of subservience to the Hollander.[120] He proposed recognising the Minangkabau king as a sovereign in exchange for his renunciation of any intention to tax the people of the west coast or to act independently of the Dutch. According to Drakard, implicit in Verspreet's plan was the idea of placing a Muslim overlord between the company and the people of the SWC.[121]

This plan was accepted and Verspreet and his successor, Jacob Pits, were each recognised as the Minangkabau king's representative, *stadthouder*, or *wakil raja* (deputy raja).[122] Verspreet reported that the mere mention

---

[118] Jane Drakard, *A Kingdom of Words: Language and Power in Sumatra* (London: Oxford University Press, 1999), p. 55.
[119] Kroeskamp, *De Westkust*, p. 110; Drakard, *A Kingdom of Words*, p. 69.
[120] Kroeskamp, *De Westkust*, p. 97.
[121] Drakard, *A Kingdom of Words*, p. 69.
[122] Ibid., p. 70. According to Drakard, Verspreet's correspondence with the Minangkabau court has not survived, but Verspreet's account described his new position and authority.

of the king's name immediately eased the flow of trade. The company faced no more difficulties, and it obtained 400 taels of pure gold from the inhabitants.[123] According to Drakard, Verspreet distinguished formal authority from actual power: real Dutch power must back nominal Minangkabau sovereignty.[124]

The Dutch appeared to have hit upon a remarkable and unique solution by reviving this old shadowy kingdom in the clouds, using its former relations with the west coast polities as a source of legitimacy while executing its own policies.[125] However, the company officials later learnt that other parties could play a similar game. Local protagonists also used the king's name to dignify themselves. For example, in June 1667 Verspreet travelled to Batavia with two Minangkabau envoys carrying a letter ostensibly from the king. The envoys returned with letters and gifts from the governor general for the king. They went instead to Bendahara Putih, a leading chief of one of the highland communities who, it turned out, was the real author of the purportedly royal letter to Batavia.[126] According to Drakard, in selecting the Minangkabau court to act as a local intermediary, the VOC had entered into a perplexing and often frustrating alliance.[127]

By the 1690s no place on the SWC was really calm. On Batoe, Raja Ibrahim, head of Tiku, son of the former Padang Panglima, murdered Johannis Sas and three soldiers before taking refuge in Aceh. In Barus, the son of the pro-Aceh Raja Di Hulu murdered a Dutch surgeon, and problems between Di Hulu and his co-ruler, Di Hilir, continued.[128] Although the English could not make much headway in Priaman and had to establish their base further south in Bencoolen, the orang kaya of Manjutta welcomed them with open arms. Although the sultan of Inderapura had been the company's ally for a long time, the Dutch

---

[123] Ibid., p. 72.
[124] Ibid., p. 73.
[125] Ibid., p. 70. A survey of published VOC letters in the seventeenth century suggests that the SWC was the only region where VOC representatives used this term to designate their own role.
[126] Ibid., p. 74.
[127] Ibid., p. 64.
[128] Basel, "Begin en Voortgang", p. 51.

had little trust in those from Inderapura. Pau remained at war with Padang.[129] In the words of the editors of the *Corpus Diplomaticum*—the collected contracts and treaties signed between the VOC and local rulers—"in no other region of the Company's operations were so many sacred agreements sworn, violated and re-sworn as on the west coast of Sumatra".[130]

Did Sultanah Safiatuddin Lose Aceh's Sumatra West Coast Vassal States?

The VOC closed its factory in Aceh in 1663, and official records subsequently provide little information on Acehnese activities. Instead, evidence had to be gathered from various places outside Aceh giving an external vantage point. Given the fluidity and complex contestations of power among the political players, the extent to which Sultanah Safiatuddin was responsible for the loss of Aceh's vassal states on the SWC is difficult to determine. Unlike in Perak, the VOC made some significant gains in some of the SWC polities, and managed to establish bases in Padang and Pulau Chinco, while Aceh lost the dominant position it had enjoyed since Iskandar Muda's time.

While many scholars have taken these changes as evidence of Aceh's decline and of the failures of female rule in particular, there is enough evidence to reconsider this assumption. I believe that Aceh's control over her vassals on the SWC had begun to weaken even before Safiatuddin's accession. Her male predecessors had opened the way for the Dutch with blanket concessions and by allowing the Dutch toll-free privileges, much to the unhappiness of the local elites. The capricious behaviour of Iskandar Muda and Iskandar Thani, and how they used their vassals as pawns to serve their interest of courting the Dutch, drove local elites to search for other patrons. Iskandar Muda's recourse to violence as a means of control was a sign of weakness rather than strength. Where politics and alliances were fluid and loyalties shifting, territorial domination through coercion was illusory.

---

[129] Ibid., p. 53.
[130] Heeres and Stapel, *Corpus Diplomaticum, BKI* 91 (1934): 423.

The symbiotic and mutually beneficial patron-client relationship nurtured under Sultanah Safiatuddin appeared to be more effective in maintaining overlord-vassal relations. Although she signed numerous treatises accommodating Dutch demands, she was careful to limit the concessions and to protect her subjects' livelihoods. Personal bonds based on reciprocal emotional, kinship and religious ties tended to engender more lasting loyalties than force. Aceh, for instance, was more successful in Perak because the sultanah supported Perak's own royal family and did not attempt to place Aceh's representatives on the throne. Of course, the Aceh royal family had kinship ties with the Perak royal family, but Aceh under the sultanah ensured that her candidate for the Perak throne was not a puppet, and had support from Perak's own people.

The narrative of east-west interactions on the SWC is not a simple one of western ascendency and indigenous decline. Power was contested and shifting. The VOC's increased influence and intervention in the SWC polities were the result of initiatives and negotiations to advance mutual interests on the part of both the Dutch and local elites. The VOC's efforts to use the indigenous system on the SWC for its own ends achieved limited results. While obtaining sufficient local brokers and allies to procure pepper, the VOC also alienated groups whose interests it jeopardised. While some saw the VOC as a useful ally because of its power, the VOC could not create a sense of spiritual loyalty or bonds as sovereign lords. Steenbrink argued that "some contracts safeguarded the privileges of pagans or Muslims reveals a lenient (and therefore possibly weak) position of the Company". The company's influence on the local population was strongest in Sri Lanka, Malabar and the Moluccas where a paragraph on religion was always included in the contracts. Relations with the rulers of Sumatra were still superficial in the seventeenth and eighteenth centuries, which was why religion was not discussed. The Painan Treaty, which explicitly called for non-interference in religion, showed that the VOC's influence was still very much restricted to commerce.[131] In its attempt to revive the old Minangkabau kingdom, the VOC entered into a shadowy

---

[131] Karel A. Steenbrink, *Dutch Colonialism and Indonesian Islam: Contacts and Conflicts, 1596–1950*, trans. Jan Steenbrink and Henry Jansen (Amsterdam: Rodopi, 2nd ed., 2006), pp. 66–9.

and confusing world it found hard to fathom. Indeed, the Dutch's political dependency could be said to have increased when they tried to reinterpret and abuse the reciprocal rules of overlord-vassal relations.

By the end of Safiatuddin's reign, one could conclude that Aceh's political and commercial control of the SWC had weakened vis-à-vis the VOC, however, Aceh's spiritual and cultural ties to her SWC vassals endured. By the 1670s, Aceh's independence was assured and there were no more challenges as serious as those posed by the VOC in the 1650s and 1660s. Sultanah Safiatuddin did not make deals with the VOC that jeopardised the kingdom's independence, as happened in other areas in the archipelago. Internal disputes, succession troubles, and the need to control their territories and vassals were reasons for other local monarchs to bargain away their sovereignty. For example, Mataram's Amangkurat I (1646-77) appealed to the VOC to suppress rebels and regents, and gave the company great privileges in return for its military support.[132]

Although Aceh's continued independence was assured by the time of Sultanah Safiatuddin's death in 1675, her successors still had to face challenges from another emerging European power—the English—who came to threaten their control of Aceh's SWC vassals. As will be shown below, the third queen to come to power, Sultanah Zakiatuddin Syah (r. 1678–88) largely continued Safiatuddin's policy of accommodation with an external power while at the same time fiercely guarding Aceh's sovereignty.

Sultanah Zakiatuddin Syah and the EIC on the Sumatra West Coast

Despite the combination of diplomatic and military tactics employed by the VOC, the company was still unable to exclude the English and Asian traders from the SWC. Before 1680, the Dutch had made more inroads into local commercial and political affairs in the Indies than the English, but this situation changed when the EIC began to think in terms of

---

[132] Luc W. Nagtegaal, "The Dutch East India Company and the Relations between Kartasura and the Javanese North Coast c. 1680 to c. 1740", in *Trading Companies*, ed. Van Goor, p. 66.

fortifying its factories or settlements in Asian ports and using force.[133] In 1682, after 80 years of having a settlement in Bantam, the English lost to the Dutch not only their largest single source of pepper, but their last toehold in the region.[134] Pepper was not only important as an article of trade. It was also a vital element in resisting Dutch monopolistic ambitions, as well as a matter of national pride.[135] With Bantam closed to the English company, the English began to cast their eyes on the only other free port in the region where they could obtain pepper without Dutch restrictions—Aceh.

In a letter to the president and council at Fort St. George, the EIC directors in London stated that for the purpose of having a "settled head factory" for the South Sea and pepper trade, they knew no better place than Aceh or the Princess Island.[136] They were uncertain about Princess Island as there the Dutch had challenged the EIC official, Thomas Grantham, and he had been instructed not to open hostilities. As for Aceh, though it had long been a port where the English obtained pepper, relations had at best been lukewarm. The English, despite the offers from Sultanah Safiatuddin in 1661, had not seized the opportunity to build a factory, partly owing to their inability to compete with the Surat merchants—who sold cloth and bought pepper in Aceh—and partly to Dutch restrictions and the primacy of the factory in Bantam.

After 20 years, the English finally decided to take up Sultanah Safiatuddin's offer. Given the changed circumstances, this time the English wanted more than just a factory—they sought a fortified settlement. On 1 October 1684, the EIC directors wrote to Sultanah Zakiatuddin Syah requesting permission to trade.[137] The directors argued that it was in the interests of both the English and the Acehnese for the English "to settle a standing factory" at or near Aceh where they could defend themselves

---

[133] I.B. Watson discussed this policy of fortification and the idea of force in the EIC relations with India in the introduction of *The East India Company, 1600–1858*, Vol. 4, ed. Patrick J.N. Tuck (New York: Routledge, 1998), p. viii.
[134] Anthony Farrington, "Negotiations at Aceh in 1684: An Unpublished English Document", *Indonesia and the Malay World* 27, 77 (1999): 19.
[135] Ibid., p. 19.
[136] BL, IOR: E/3/90 fol. 445. Letter dated 16 March 1684 from London to President and Council at Fort St. George.
[137] BL, IOR: E/3/90 fol. 376.

against the designs of the Dutch and preserve their trade in case the Dutch attempted to blockade Aceh's harbour. With the English proposed "fortified settlement", the directors pointed out, the Dutch could not blockade Aceh: this act would be tantamount to declaring war on the EIC and the English king.

The London directors, however, left the EIC's Madras Council to take charge of this matter,[138] with instructions to strike an agreement with the queen of Aceh in the name of the EIC, not the English nation.[139] The council sent Ralph Ord and William Cawley to Aceh, where they stayed from October to December 1684.[140] They found a thriving Aceh that in the previous decade had become a popular port for emerging country trade partnerships between Indian merchants, free residents in Madras, private merchants, adventurers and entrepreneurs. Richard Mohun, a former member of the Madras Council on private trade in Aceh in 1684, reported to London that the English could procure good ladings of pepper from Sumatra.[141]

The report from Ord and Cawley reveals that the practices Sultanah Safiatuddin initiated had been institutionalised by her successors. The Acehnese elite welcomed the English representatives with the usual hospitality.[142] The representatives described the procedure for landing, the procession to court with presents for the queen, attending audience day with the queen on Saturdays, and the discussions and lobbying of the Aceh orang kaya. The main difference described here was the number of orang kaya who appeared to form the council. Instead of four, there

---

[138] BL, IOR: E/3/90 fol. 445. Another letter was sent on the ship *Dragon* dated 24 September 1684 to the Captain at Aceh, fol. 346.

[139] Letter to the Agent and Council at Fort St. George, dated 19 October 1683, in East India Company, *Despatches from England* [to fort St. George. V.] 1681–1686 (Madras: Government Press), p. 58.

[140] The diary of Ord and Cawley is found in the Original Correspondence of the EIC archives. BL, IOR: E/3/44, fol. 171–81. This whole diary was reproduced in Farrington's article. Citations from the diary are taken from this published version.

[141] BL, IOR: E/3/44 no. 5612, Mohun to Sir Josiah Child, dated 24 June 1684: Farrington, "Negotiations at Aceh in 1684", p. 32.

[142] Ord and Cawleys's account gives a detailed narrative of court procedures in the 1680s. This serves as a useful comparison to the time under Sultanah Safiatuddin, as after the Dutch closed its factory in 1663, there were no envoys exchanged between the Dutch and Aceh. This diary is also the most detailed—the only comprehensive—account of the English encounter with the Acehnese court.

were 12.¹⁴³ The most senior was the orang kaya Maharaja. At his house, Ord and Cawley explained that after the king of Bantam had given the port to the Dutch, the English decided to bring their profitable trade to Aceh. The Maharaja replied that the Acehnese had always regarded the English as friends, notwithstanding their absence for many years. He welcomed their return. It was here that the envoys broached the subject of a fort: the Madras president no longer wished to have an English settlement without building a fort for protection. They gave the examples of Macassar and Bantam where the English factory and goods were damaged when the rulers deferred to the Dutch. The only free port left was Aceh, and Ord and Cawley did not hesitate to point out to the Maharaja that, in all probability, the Dutch would try to ruin Aceh, too. Thus, Ord reasoned, a fort would not only protect the English but also deter the Dutch. Just as in Safiatuddin's reign, the Maharaja replied that he had to report this request to the sultanah and the rest of the orang kaya first. Next in importance to the Maharaja were the shahbandar and the *panglima bandar* (governor of the port/city), who was in charge of foreigners. Judging from the important ranking of the orang kaya in charge of foreigners, this meant that trade with foreigners was still a high priority for the kingdom as it was during the reign of Safiatuddin.

Two months later, the English became impatient with the delays and met the orang kaya to enquire about the sultanah's reply. The reason given for the delay was that the letter from the Madras Council included nothing about building a fort in Aceh, and they questioned why it was necessary for the English to request a fort now when they had never wanted one before. Ord reassured the orang kaya that the English—unlike the Dutch—were not interested in conquest but wanted to avoid what happened at Bantam. The orang kaya replied that in Aceh, unlike Bantam, the Dutch were mortal enemies, and every Acehnese would rather die than allow the Dutch a footing in the kingdom. He declared that even though the Dutch had the greatest force, they had not yet been able to inflict anything on the Acehnese. Ord replied that it was true in the past, but now they could lay siege and, as Aceh was dependent on imported rice, they could starve the port city. The orang kaya repeated

---

¹⁴³ Farrington, "Negotiations at Aceh in 1684", p. 25.

that they would rather die than surrender. This exchange should have given the English a clear indication of how much the Acehnese cherished their independence. Sultanah Zakiatuddin's final answer, given through the shahbandar, was that the English had asked for too much, which was against the indispensable rules of the kingdom. She added that even if the president of Madras had filled her kingdom with gold she could not grant him permission to build a fort or house with stone and bricks. The English, however, were welcome to build a factory with planks.

Ord and Cawley's mission was not entirely fruitless though. Although building a fort in Aceh was out of the question, Zakiatuddin gave the English permission to fortify her dominions on the SWC, either at Priaman or Tiku, though she would not place this permission in writing in a firman. This shows that as late as the 1680s Aceh still had influence over Priaman and Tiku. The reason given for why a firman was not to be issued was the Acehnese did not want to be held responsible for any injuries or loss of goods the English may sustain.

In the meantime, owing to the delays in Aceh, the English were already exploring other areas for a possible settlement, especially as the chiefs in Bencoolen had invited the English to establish a settlement there. The English knew that quite a large supply of pepper from Bantam could be collected near Bencoolen at a place called Silebar.[144] After receiving the invitation, Ord arrived in Bencoolen and, after signing an agreement to establish an English fort, left a Mr Benjamin Bloome in charge. The settlement, however, was not approved by the directors in London who wrote that a "fatal error" was made in breaking their orders regarding Priaman. They were angry that ships, money and men were spent to found a settlement at such "an unhealthful" place as Bencoolen.[145] They also objected because it was too near Batavia, and therefore indefensible if war broke out. Furthermore, there was no trade in Bencoolen for European goods and, whether for fear of the Dutch or otherwise, there was little pepper for the English. The directors reiterated that they had always wanted the seat of the pepper trade to be in Priaman or Aceh: for

---

[144] Marsden, *The History of Sumatra*, p. 451.
[145] BL, IOR E/3/91. Letter sent on the ships *Loyall Merchant* and *Pink James* to Our Chief and Council at Bencoolen, dated 3 August 1687, fol. 351–6, fol. 352.

among other reasons these places were farthest from Batavia.[146] However, precisely because Bencoolen was so disadvantageous, the Dutch saw no reason to spend money to wrest it from the English. So the sickly crew called the Pryaman Company was left in peace to build the first fortified English settlement in Sumatra, York Fort.[147]

In the 1690s the EIC gradually consolidated its position in southwestern Sumatra from its base in Bencoolen. In 1691, the Dutch failed to exert influence at Silebar and other southern areas in the name of the sultan of Bantam. The English factory in Silebar and the region of Bencoolen were strengthened. Two more English settlements appeared: in 1695 in Triamang and in 1697 at Kattaun and Sablat.

It is safe to conclude that by the end of the 1690s, both the VOC and EIC had failed to establish themselves in Aceh. It is important to note, however, that Aceh was by no means cut off from trade or a backwater. Although the EIC factors had made no headway in Aceh, the Madras Council received a letter from Mr Mohun, and another letter from Mr Pitt and Mr Constable in 1685, stating that though market was bad for the English company, there was "a great fleet of ships that lay in the road", not less than 30 sails in Aceh's harbour, "with bales of cloth and laden with rice".[148] In contrast to the EIC factors, private English merchants had a lucrative stay from the late 1680s to the end of the century. When the Mergui massacre occurred in July 1687, English traders expelled from Siam, such as Francis Delton and Tyler, escaped to Aceh.[149] William Dampier and Charles Lockyer observed that there was a semi-autonomous English community in Aceh and a William Soames became the semi-official EIC correspondent and resident. Captain Thomas Oyles and Mr Walsh, besides trading were

---

[146] BL, IOR E/3/91. Letter sent on the *Loyall Merchant and Pink James* to Our Chief and Council at Bencoolen, fol. 356.

[147] For a detailed description of how York Fort was constructed and the deplorable conditions the soldiers faced, see Alan G. Harfield, *Bencoolen: A History of the Honourable East India Company's Garrison on the West Coast of Sumatra 1685–1825* (Barton-on-Sea, Hampshire: A and J Partnership, 1995), pp. 1–15.

[148] East India Company, *Records of Fort St. George: Diary and Consultation Book of 1686*, Vol. 11 (Madras: Printed by the Superintendent Government Press, 1913), p. 10.

[149] D.K. Bassett, "British 'Country' Trade and Local Trade Networks in the Thai and Malay States, c. 1680–1770", *Modern Asian Studies* 23, 4 (1989): 629.

intermediaries between the EIC and the English community. Mr Walsh even made presentations to the sultanah and received gifts in return.

Conclusion

The ties that bound Aceh and its vassals were certainly threatened by increased European incursions but, unlike their male predecessors, the women sovereigns did not treat their vassals as pawns serving Aceh's interests, binding them tightly through coercive means. Indeed, a looser—but not necessarily weaker—more elastic bond based on spiritual and personal loyalties proved to be more resilient. Aceh lost some vassals and both the Dutch and the English gained footholds in Sumatra, but Aceh's independence was preserved.

Sultanah Zakiatuddin continued Safiatuddin's policy of accommodating European powers but granted them only limited concessions. She was careful to maintain Aceh's independence and was uncompromising in not allowing the English to build any sort of fort in Aceh, even if the "English poured gold into Aceh". Although the number of orang kaya on the council had grown to 12, they still had to defer to the sultanah for the final decision, much like the practice instituted by Safiatuddin. Ord and Cawley's exchange with the orang kaya Maharaja reveals an individual who was loyal to the kingdom and its ruler, not only proud to be Acehnese but willing to defend independence until death. The description of Aceh by the likes of Richard Mohun, a private English trader, in the 1670s and 1680s does not paint a picture of a kingdom in decline and succumbing to European incursions, but one that was remarkably resilient.

chapter

5 Female Rulers Negotiating Islam and Patriarchy

In Chapter 3, I showed how Sultanah Safiatuddin Syah dealt with her male elites and managed to consolidate her position by the mid-1650s. Chapter 4 showed how she negotiated with VOC envoys, managing their increasing demands for commercial concessions, which threatened the kingdom's independence and her suzerainty over the vassal states of Perak and the SWC. By the 1670s—three decades into her rule—Sultanah Safiatuddin was not only secure on her throne but under her reign, Aceh was a peaceful, stable and thriving kingdom.

Here I examine other features of her reign, namely how Islam was practised under female rule, and her relations with the male elites and ulama. I will illustrate how her leadership style was adopted and continued by her three women successors—Sultanah Naqiatuddin, Sultanah Zakiatuddin and Sultanah Kamalat Syah. I will explain the ways in which and the extent her leadership style differed from that of her male predecessors, and why she was able to maintain power for 34 years, even longer than her famous father, Iskandar Muda. This chapter primarily focuses on Safiatuddin's reign, not only because she ruled the longest but also because little information is available on the last three queens. It is not possible to use the detailed daily registers of the Dutch envoys and residents as the Dutch closed their Aceh factory in 1663. Other sources for their reigns include the English East India Company records, and reports by European merchants and travellers who resided in Aceh in the last three decades of the seventeenth century.

Female Rulers and the Practice of Islam in Aceh

The very name of the kingdom—Aceh Dar al-Salam, Aceh the Abode of Peace—shows that Islam played an important if not integral role in the kingdom from its inception. The sultans of Melaka had used Islam to develop concepts of monarchical government and embark on a process of institutionalising law codes and governance. Aceh's sultans further strengthened the monarchy by adopting local and global Islamic Ottoman and Persian notions of universal kingship and correspondingly grandiose titles. Iskandar Muda was known as *Mahkota Alam* (Crown of the Universe), *Johan Berdaulat* (Champion Sovereign), *Perkasa Alam* (Might of the Universe), *Khalifah Allah* (the Representative of God on Earth) and *Sayyiduna wa mawlana paduka seri Sultan* (Our Lord and Master, His Majesty the Auspicious Sultan).[1] When the Malay maritime polities of Southeast Asia embraced Islam, the concept of *chakravartin* (an ideal universal ruler) was replaced by the khalifah, ruling the Muslim *ummah* (community of believers).[2] The khalifah, however, could be only a shadow of the divine—as opposed to the Hindu concept of *dewa-raja*, or the ruler possessing divine powers: in Islam, divine power belongs to God alone. It is important to note that the Acehnese sultans saw themselves as caliphs and as the representative of the ummah in their part of the world. This is partly to illustrate that Acehnese rulers were not mere kings, but that Aceh was extending its powers globally and was thus on par with other great Muslim empires, such as the Mughals and Ottomans. Both the *Hikayat Aceh* and the *Bustan us-Salatin* were at pains to show Aceh's close relations with the Ottoman Empire. In the *Hikayat Aceh*, the sultan of Rum (Turkey) is credited with having declared that "at the present time" and by divine decree there were two great kings who shared the world: the king of Rum in the West and the

---

[1] Hadi, *Islam and State in Sumatra*, p. 60.
[2] Michael Laffan, "Dispersing God's Shadows—Reflections on the Translation of Arabic Political Concepts into Malay and Indonesian", paper written for the project, "History of Translations into Indonesian and Malaysian Languages", p. 3. Ian Proudfoot, *Malay Concordance Project*. Available at http://mcp.anu.edu.au/papers/laffan_apc.html [accessed 10 Oct. 2015]; Marshall G.S. Hodgson, *The Venture of Islam: Conscience and History in a World Civilisation*, trans. Mastuti Haji Isa and Rosiah Abdul Latiff as *Kebangkitan Islam*, Vol. 1 (Kuala Lumpur: Dewan Bahasa dan Pustaka, 2004), p. 326.

king of Aceh in the East. They were then compared to the two great kings of yore: Solomon and Alexander the Great.³

According to Anthony Reid, Aceh's self-image in the sixteenth century was bound up with two issues—its Islamic struggle against the Portuguese and its pivotal role in the revived Islamic trading system supplying pepper to the Mediterranean. Aceh viewed itself as a vassal of the Ottomans and as the "Veranda of Mecca" for Southeast Asia.⁴ Under Iskandar Muda and Iskandar Thani diplomatic missions and alliances with Turkey were no longer realities, and only the idea that Aceh had a privileged position as *the* representative of the local Islamic ummah remained. Interestingly, the justification for this superior position in the seventeenth century did not merely rest on the Islamic notion of the caliphate. It was also supported by older, pre-Islamic indigenous notions of supernatural power and universal kinghood. According to Reid, Iskandar Thani introduced what may reasonably be seen as a more Malay style of kingship. His emphasis on sacral kingship and the weakened link with the Red Sea suggests a shift towards a more Nusantaran pattern.⁵

Iskandar Muda and Iskandar Thani's relations with their vassal states were also shaped by Indianised concepts of *chakravartin,* or universal monarchs, "kings of kings", and *dewa-raja,* to whom lesser kings ruling weaker states had to pay tribute and homage. According to Pierre Manguin, for the centre to achieve the status of *primus inter pares* (first among equals) the universal ruler must possess some measure of legitimacy, charisma derived from prowess, divine radiance, soul-stuff or *sakti*. Only then could he lure, retain and regulate overseas exchanges at his ports to provide foreign income and mobilise, manipulate and redistribute the resulting wealth as a political weapon to extend his authority and attract a still larger clientele.⁶ Both sultans controlled their vassals through a

---

³ Iskandar, ed., *De Hikajat Atjeh,* pp. 161–7.
⁴ Anthony Reid, "The Pre-Modern Sultanate's View of its Place in the World", in *Verandah of Violence: The Historical Background of the Aceh Problem,* ed. Anthony Reid (Singapore: Singapore University Press, 2006), p. 55.
⁵ Ibid., p. 60.
⁶ Pierre-Yves Manguin, "The Amorphous Nature of Coastal Polities in Insular Southeast Asia: Restricted Centres, Extended Peripheries", *Moussons* 5 (2002): 77–8. Available at https://moussons.revues.org/2699 [accessed 20 Oct. 2015].

measure of charisma and prowess based on coercion and hierarchical relations.

Successful kingship in Southeast Asia has generally been understood as necessarily male (masculine) and royal power is based on his charisma, prowess and wealth. According to Wolters, "men of prowess" endowed with an abnormal amount of personal and innate soul-stuff enabled them to distinguish their performance from their kinsmen and contemporaries. However, in his revised edition to *History, Culture and Region in Southeast Asian Perspectives*, Wolters considered the roles and positions of women and questions whether women too should be attributed with this "vastly energetic role of women of prowess", wondering what their relationship would have been with men of prowess.[7]

So what did female leadership or *queenship* look like? Under Aceh's women sovereigns, the basis of power and authority relied less on notions of sacral and charismatic power from prowess but instead shifted to Muslim notions of piety and the just ruler. In her conduct during the jewel affair, Sultanah Safiatuddin was pragmatic and prudent, more concerned with preserving her kingdom's wealth than with basing her power on ostentatious displays of personal wealth to awe subjects and foreigners. Similarly, in the Perak affair she relied less on charismatic and coercive powers to control her vassals but instead shifted to win loyalty by protecting her vassals' rights to collect tolls and enjoy a share of the economic wealth.

As mentioned in Chapter 1, while Islam spread to other regions from its heartland in the Middle East, the process of religious localisation brought about a plurality of beliefs and Islamic practices.[8] For example, one of the problems Mongol princes faced after converting to Islam was how to reconcile the very public status of women in their culture with the very private status of women in Arabic mainland Islam. Judging from the numerous *khatun* (women who held political authority) in the Mongol and Turkish dynasties, it is clear that Islam was interpreted through the lens of local culture and traditions. The great Moroccan traveller Ibn Battuta was struck by women's constant involvement in politics when he

---

[7] Wolters, *History, Culture and Region*, p. 169.
[8] Mernissi, *The Forgotten Queens of Islam*, p. 21.

crossed the Mongol Empire. He noted that the wives of Turks and Tartars enjoyed a very high position; when they issued an order, they decreed it in the name of the sultan and the khatuns. Similarly, as a result of a long tradition of female autonomy in this region and of accepting females in positions of high authority, even to the highest political position of a ruler, the ulama accepted Sultanah Safiatuddin's adoption of the title khalifah (detailed below). Female rule was not seen as anathema to Islam; indeed, according to the *Taj us-Salatin*, in the absence of a male heir female rule was legal to prevent chaos. A ruler was considered exemplary if she (or he) possessed good moral values and ruled according to God's laws.

A comparison of her letters with those of Iskandar Muda and Iskandar Thani illustrates how she represented herself as the ruler of Aceh, and her version of what an Islamic and pious ruler should be. In this regard, I argue that rather than employing religion to enhance her power, Sultanah Safiatuddin used power tempered by religion. She used moral force (piety) as the basis of politics and executed *piety politics* instead of the *politics of piety*, or politicisation of religion favoured by her male predecessors.

Piety versus Pageantry: Comparing the Royal Letters

According to Annabel Teh Gallop, the single most striking feature of the compliments in Iskandar Muda's letter of 1615 to England's James I was the absence of any specifically Islamic formulae or references.[9] Instead there were recognisable Indic vestiges. His titles appeared to have more in common with those of his contemporaries in Ayutthaya and Rakhine than those found in later Malay correspondence. What particularly sets these compliments apart from those in subsequent royal Malay letters is the emphasis on the possession of material goods (even when these might have symbolic or ritual value) and worldly success, rather than moral attributes. Teh Gallop argued that:

---

[9] Teh Gallop, "Gold, Silver and Lapis Lazuli", p. 111.

> [T]he lack of overtly Islamic or otherwise spiritual or moral elements should be seen as a deliberate omission; the focus on material goods and worldly success reflecting both a relationship which was fundamentally materialistic in nature, and the subject matter of the letter, namely a request for trading rights.[10]

Nonetheless, she concluded "the religious allegiance of the sovereign was unmistakable in the heading situated at the very top of the letter, in tiny letters but indubitably there".[11]

It is unfortunate that none of Iskandar Muda's original Malay letters to other Malay Muslim powers survive to allow a comparison between his letters to Muslim and non-Muslim powers. Perhaps the reason why Iskandar Muda used fewer Islamic references was because the idea of holy war that characterised relations between the sultans of Aceh in the sixteenth century with the Portuguese had taken a more commercial turn in the seventeenth. Unlike the Portuguese, the English and the Dutch sailed to the East in search of commerce not converts. The other reason for the lack of Islamic references, I believe, is the more mystical and syncretic brand of Islam favoured in Aceh during Iskandar Muda's reign. According to Teh Gallop, Iskandar Thani retained the emphasis on self-description in the compliments Iskandar Muda initiated, but that a completely different flavour prevailed; the emphasis was on virtues appropriate for a king who was the shadow of God on earth.

Teh Gallop did not suggest why more Islamic imagery was projected. I venture that Iskandar Thani's style was similar to his father-in-law's and they both adopted a more Indianised, Nusantaran conception of kingship. Iskandar Thani used the title caliph to present himself as a Muslim monarch, while at the same time claiming the right to be *the* representative of the Muslim polities (the ummah) in the region, but retaining Iskandar Muda's idea of a universal king, chakravartin, as will be shown below.

The women sovereigns of Aceh adopted their predecessors' titles with no gendered changes. The indubitably male sovereign epithets *sultan al-muazzam wa-al-khaqan al-mukarram*, "the Great Sultan and

---

[10] Ibid., p. 113.
[11] Ibid.

Illustrious King", applied to them as well.[12] The *Bustan us-Salatin* and the *Adat Aceh* addressed Safiatuddin and her successors as *Paduka Sri Sultan* (His Majesty, the Auspicious Sultan). Indeed, the only gendered epithet was the uniquely Acehnese *Berdaulat* (the Sovereign One), accorded to all queens of Aceh, while all the kings of Aceh, from the time of Iskandar Muda, bore the title *Johan Berdaulat*, "the Sovereign Champion".[13]

In Iskandar Thani's letter he is heralded as the *sultan al-muazzam wa-al-khaqan al-mukarram,* and his proper name and title are followed by Muslim epithets of kingship, *zill Allah fi al-'alam* (Shadow of Allah on Earth) and *khalifat Allah*. It is noteworthy that the sultanah also took the full Muslim epithets, *zill Allah fi al-'alam* and *khalifat Allah*, that is, she was the *khalifat* or caliph, to illustrate that her role and duties as the shadow of Allah or representative of Allah on earth were similar to those of her male predecessors. However, by the very title she chose, *Taj al-Alam Safiatuddin Syah* or *Safiyyat al-Din Syah*[14] (*Taj al-Alam* meaning "Crown of the World" and *al-Din* in reference to being subject to Allah's laws) to set herself apart from her male predecessors.[15] While basing her rule on her status as crown or sovereign of the world, she placed her rule firmly on the foundation that she was chosen by Allah to be His representative to rule according to His laws.

The foundation of her rule and her emphasis on her roles and duties as a Muslim ruler are major differences between Sultanah Safiatuddin's and her predecessors' letters, reflecting the different bases of legitimacy and power. There are 26 distinct sets of attributes in Iskandar Thani's letter. All but five are repeated in Safiatuddin's letter, which includes several new formulations, giving a total of 32 sets of attributes. The five that are not repeated pertain to descriptions of the king's material wealth, such as how shiny (*cemerlang cahayanya*) his gold (*mas kudrati*) is and

---

[12] Ibid., p. 127.
[13] Ibid.
[14] This refers to the Arabic spelling of Safiatuddin, Safiyat al-Din.
[15] The word *al-Din* also refers to the establishment of a way of life in which obedience is only to Allah. It can also mean "a way of dispensing judgement and rewards following Allah's laws". Available at http://onlinequranteaching.co.uk [accessed 10 Oct. 2015].

how bright (*gilang gemilang*) his copper (*suassa*). The other omission is the description of the ruler as studded and decorated with gems and precious stones. In contrast to her husband's emphasis on the material, almost all of the sultanah's new formulations were of a religious or moral nature. The interesting difference is though Safiatuddin adopted the title of khalifah, it was not the more egoistic and narcissistic concept of God's shadow on earth following the pre-Islamic conception of the king as semi-divine, but khalifah as God's vicegerent/deputy on earth to execute God's laws. In this letter, she wrote that she was one:

> [W]ho manifests Allah's wisdom and blessings, who upholds Allah's laws, who clarifies those that are in doubt, whose shine brings forth Allah's light and goodness, who exhorts people to Allah's path, who treats Allah's creations with mercy, who dispenses Allah's justice with utmost care, who hides that which is ugly and forgives those who have sinned, and whose words are gracious.[16]

In contrast, Iskandar Thani attributed no such roles to himself. By describing herself as dispensing Allah's laws, the sultanah's modesty and humility contrasted with Iskandar Thani's depiction of his own powers. For example, the clause found in Iskandar Thani's letter, but not in Safiatuddin's, is "*lagi raja yang ngurniai kesukaan akan yang dikasihinya dan kedukaan akan yang dimarahinya*" (a king who dispenses good fortune to those he favours and misfortune to those who have incurred his wrath).[17] Gallop pointed out that Iskandar Thani likened his sense of justice to that of Nusyirwan Adil and compared his liberality to Hatim Tai.[18] The names of these pre-Islamic figures are omitted from Taj al-Alam's letter. Instead, she equated her sense of justice to that of "Sultan" Ibn Abd al-Aziz, referring to Umar ibn Abd al-Aziz, the fifth

---

[16] This is the author's translation.
[17] Teh Gallop's translation in "Gold, Silver and Lapis Lazuli", p. 126.
[18] Hatim Al-Taeei, also Hatemtai (that is, Hatim of the Tayy tribe), was a famous (pre-Islamic *Jahiliyyah*) Arabian poet whose extreme generosity made him an icon to Arabs to the present day. Rozat-ul-Sufa mentioned that "in the eighth year after the birth of his eminence the Prophet, around 579 CE, died Noushirwan the Just, and Hatem Tai the generous, both famous for their virtues". *The Adventures of Hatim Tai: A Romance*, trans. from Persian by Duncan Forbes, A.M. (London: Printed for the Oriental Translation Fund, 1830), p. x.

Umayyad caliph (r. 717–20) and "an exemplar of the Muslim virtues of piety, equity and humility" to later generations.[19]

It is unfortunate that this is the sultanah's only surviving original Malay letter. The rest of her correspondences with the Dutch in Batavia and Melaka and other polities are Dutch translations, with all the attendant problems of omissions, additions and genuine misinterpretations. Nevertheless, they are very useful and the fact most of her letters to the Dutch survive makes it possible to gain some insights and offer some generalisations on the way the sultanah represented herself and her legitimacy and authority. In other letters to various Dutch governors in Batavia she usually described herself as one who was chosen by God to succeed and sit on the throne of Aceh Dar al-Salam. One letter in particular stands out not only for the compliments attached to the beginning of the letter but for its main content. Indeed, the quote below is the letter's main message, the other being her request to the governor general to send a capable and powerful envoy to Aceh to carry out his assignment according to the governor's intention. To Governor General Joan Maetsuyker in 1659, she wrote:

> God says that since antiquity there are no better things than these two things; namely, think always about God above all and always do good to other people. That the Governor-General on his part I trust shall do. Over such actions work, one is more and more blessed and is honoured and praised by all other men in this world. The Acehnese and the Dutch have for many years continued in peace and friendship, but now as it has pleased God, we have come to war, but these differences are small, and with the help from God Almighty and the good resolve of a good outcome from the Governor-General, once again the Acehnese and the Dutch are one. Therefore, the Governor-General, herein, would do no other but to settle [the differences]. The wise people in earlier times say to warn [us] that always remember two things, namely always think foremost of God and of death and forget two things, all the virtues that we do to other men and all the bad things that are done to us, so that our conscience will remain pure and calm.[20]

---

[19] Teh Gallop, "Gold, Silver and Lapis Lazuli", p. 126.
[20] Chijs, *Dagh-Register*, 1659, pp. 103–4.

In this letter, Sultanah Safiatuddin was almost preaching to the governor general, using religion to exhort the Dutch to undertake good deeds. Unlike in the past, when her male predecessors—especially Sultan Al-Kahar—used religion to wage jihad against the Portuguese, Islam was used not as a means to show the difference between the *kafir* (infidels) and Muslims but as a common denominator, a universal call to do good and bring peace to all mankind. This letter was carefully composed to persuade the Dutch not to wage war against Aceh, an appeal to peace by diplomacy, as tensions between the VOC and Aceh were high after the murders of Dutch officials in Perak and the SWC. This sermon, in all probability, would not have swayed the governor general. Nonetheless, this letter offers an interesting insight into how the sultanah used diplomacy tempered by religion.

Her religious tolerance was also manifested in her allowing Franciscan priests to minister to the Catholic community in Aceh, a practice continued under Sultanah Naqiatuddin and Sultanah Zakiatuddin. With the death of the third queen, some orang kaya and conservative ulama, opposed to the appointment of another female ruler, captured Father Bento de Christo and took away his possessions. It was only after Kamalat Syah was appointed as the fourth queen that Father Bento was released and returned to his duties.[21] This freedom for foreigners to practise their religion was denied when male rule was restored in 1699.

To what extent was this more Islamic orientation initiated by the sultanah herself, or was she influenced by the ulama, especially the Sheikh al-Islam? In 1642, Pieter Sourij mentioned that the Lebai Kita Kali, the sultanah's half brother and the high religious judge of the kingdom, was responsible for drafting the sultanah's letters and firman.[22] By 1649, however, the position of the Lebai Kita Kali was held by a young and inexperienced man, most probably his son.[23] The Dutch sources do not mention the role of Nuruddin al-Raniri, the Sheikh al-Islam, in letter writing. Furthermore,

---

[21] Account by Jeronymo dos Reis, 24 October 1688 in Achilles Meersman, *The Franciscans in the Indonesian Archipelago, 1300–1775* (Nauwelaerts: Lovain, 1967), pp. 129–30. Quoted in Anthony Reid, ed., *Witnesses to Sumatra, A Travellers' Anthology* (Singapore: Oxford University Press, 1995), p. 52.

[22] NA, VOC 1143, Dagh-Register gehouden bij Pieter Sourij, 1642, f. 586R.

[23] NA, VOC 1171, Dagh-Register gehouden bij den Oppercoopman Johan Truijtman, 1649, ff. 207V–208R.

he left Aceh in 1644 and Syaiful Rijal replaced him. The most senior role in the council at that time was the Maharaja Sri Maharaja. Furthermore, if as stated in the *Dagh-Register*, the *grooten priester* (high priest) murdered in 1653 was Syaiful Rijal, then in 1659 Aceh was without any known prominent religious scholar and leader. The other known prominent ulama, Abdul Rauf al-Singkel, returned to Aceh from Mecca only in 1661. Therefore, it is most likely that the 1659 "letter of sermon" sent to Governor General Maetsuyker reflects the sultanah's own personal leanings.

Another interesting feature that distinguishes her letter, and perhaps reflects a more feminine orientation, is the mention of *lagi yang mengitarkan segala bau-bauwan kemurahannya pada segala tepi langit takhta kerajaan* (one who spreads her fragrance of generosity to all areas under her rule).[24] Sultanah Safiatuddin used the same imagery in her letter to the Viceroy of the *Estado da* India.[25]

Fig. 4 The seal of the Sultanah of Aceh Dar al-Salam with her name and title, Paduka Sri Sultanah Taj al-Alam Safiatuddin Syah berdaulat Zilallah fil alam abnat—at the centre of the seal (showing the reigning sovereign), and the names of her eight predecessors inscribed in each of the circles surrounding the centre.

---

[24] Letter from Sultanah Tajul Alam to Charles II in 1661. Quoted in Teh Gallop, "Gold, Silver and Lapis Lazuli", p. 252.

[25] Letter from Sultanah Safiatuddin Tajul Alam to the Viceroy of the Estado da India, 1668. Portuguese copy, Arquivos Nacionais, Ministerio dos Negocios Estrangeiros [National Archives, Portuguese Foreign Ministry], Portugal 558, n. 119.

Other Symbols of Sovereignty—Seals and Coins

According to Fatima Mernissi, the few Muslim queens who actually ruled in their own right had two mandatory symbols that recognised their sovereignty; coins bearing their names, and the *khutbah* (Friday sermon), in which the imam mentioned their names as sovereigns. In Aceh, the coins and the royal *chap sikureueng* (seal) bore the names of the female rulers; and as the Sheikh al-Islam supported the queens, it is likely that their names were included in the Friday sermon with the salutations that would have followed.

As mentioned earlier, there was no difference in titles between the kings and queens in Aceh's royal letters. However, on the royal seals and coins Safiatuddin and her female successors chose to employ the title "sultanah".[26] During her reign, her name and title—*Paduka Sri Sultanah Taj al-Alam Safiatuddin Syah berdaulat Zilallah fil alam abnat*—is at the centre of the seal (showing the reigning sovereign), and the names of her eight predecessors are inscribed in each of the circles surrounding the centre.[27] Safiatuddin also used the title "sultanah" on coins minted during her reign: the obverse sides stated her title *Paduka Sri Sultanah Taj al-Alam* and reverse sides simply her name Safiat al-Din Syah Berdaulat (Safiat al-Din Syah, the Sovereign). Unlike her father's coins, she did not use *Sri Sultan Perkasa Alam* (Lord of the Universe) or *Johan Berdaulat* (Champion Sovereign). The same format was used by her female successors: the title *Paduka Sri Sultanah Nur al-Alam* and her name Naqiat al-Din Syah Berdaulat for the second queen, *Paduka Sri Sultanah Inayat Syah* and Zakiat al-Din Syah Berdaulat for the third, and *Paduka Sri Sultanah Kamalat Syah* and Zinat al-Din Syah Berdaulat for the fourth.[28]

---

[26] Teh Gallop, "Malay Seal Inscription", p. 112.
[27] Sufi, "Sultanah Safiatuddin Syah", p. 54.
[28] Van Langen, *De Inrichting van het Atjehsche*, p. 66; T. Ibrahim Alfian, *Mata Uang Emas Kerajaan-Kerajaan di Aceh* [Gold Coins of the Aceh Kingdom] (Banda Aceh: Projek Rehabilitasi dan Perluasan Museum Daerah Istimewa Aceh, 1979), p. 45; Nicholas Rhodes, Goh Han Peng and V. Mihailovs, "The Gold Coinages of Samudra Pasai and Aceh Dar as-Salam, c. 1280–1760", unpublished manuscript, Singapore, 2007, pp. 56–60.

Islam and State in Seventeenth-century Aceh

Christiaan Snouck Hurgronje and more recently Takeshi Ito and Amirul Hadi examined the historical role of Islam in seventeenth-century Aceh. The first scholar who attempted to study Islam in Aceh, Snouck Hurgronje, wrote that though there was no reason to doubt the good intentions of Acehnese rulers in their edicts relating to the purely religious sphere, they wrote in a purely formal manner out of respect due to the institution ordained by Allah, but they were less keenly observant of religious practice.[29] Ito stated that the sultans of Aceh "were heads of the Islamic community or state and were the central figures in purely Islamic rituals and that these religious rituals were very much syncretic in nature".[30] Hadi concluded that as Aceh was neither the heir to any ancient higher culture nor an inland state, it showed itself to be more prone to Islamic influences. These in turn played a significant role in shaping the strong Islamic elements in the polity. Hadi believed that Snouck Hurgronje underestimated the role the Islamic faith had in Acehnese political life.[31]

Very little is known about how Islam was practised at court and in the kingdom, or of the role of religious officials and scholars in the sixteenth century. The *Bustan* mentions a few famous foreign scholars who came to Aceh from Mecca, such as Sheikh Abu al-Khair and Sheikh Muhammad Yamani, and Sheikh Muhammad Jailani from Gujarat. The *Bustan* suggests that these ulama had a tremendous influence on the sultans of Aceh, such as Sultan Alauddin (1579–86), described as being very pious, who exhorted his subjects to pray, fast and even sport beards.[32]

According to Ito, by the end of the sixteenth century, Islamic law had become an integral part of the sultanate's law.[33] The ruler was represented by a group of religious judges headed by the Kadhi Malik al-Adil, and administered law and order in the realm. A more detailed

---

[29] Snouck Hurgronje, *The Acehnese*, Vol. 1, pp. 6–7.
[30] Ito, "The World of the Adat Aceh", p. 248.
[31] Hadi, *Islam and State in Sumatra*, p. 247.
[32] Iskandar, ed., *Bustan us-Salatin*, p. 33.
[33] Ito, "The World of the Adat Aceh", p. 155.

picture of the law and courts system in Aceh emerged in the reign of Iskandar Muda based on European observations, such as those of Beaulieu and Peter Mundy.[34] According to these sources and information from the *Adat Aceh*, the kingdom had four courts of law: one pertaining to ritual, family and inheritance; a second dealing with criminal cases; a third concerning commercial law; and the last pertaining to the purely religious requirements and observances, such as praying, fasting and so on. As Muslim jurists did not recognise any distinction between civil, criminal and other branches of law, the first three courts were also based on Islamic law. However, it appears that cases were generally judged according to adat and the law of the land. Ito inferred that the former referred to indigenous legal practice, while the latter referred to Islamic law.[35] This practice was very much in line with the famous Acehnese motto "*Adat bersendikan syarak*" (Customs supported by Islamic law).

It is, however, important to note that though Islamic law was already integral to the kingdom's governance and an Islamic bureaucracy was in place, the administration and execution of Islam largely depended on the rulers. Iskandar Muda and Iskandar Thani often modified the sultanate's sharia law. In many cases the penalties inflicted were harsher than the provisions of the sharia. Penalties were meted out based on traditional judicial practices, which Ito described as trial by ordeal, and at the discretion (more often whim) of the sovereign.[36] Examples of trials by ordeal include plunging one's hand into boiling oil and licking heated iron. These were cruel enough by normal standards, but the punishments meted out by these two male rulers went far beyond these. European observers reported on the harsh punishments, especially during the reign of Iskandar Muda, where it appears punishments were meted out based on caprice, jealousy or just plain bad temper. Verhoeff, Broecke, Best and Beaulieu mentioned that delays in attending to his needs, defeating him in cockfights or wearing too costly ornaments

---

[34] For a description of Aceh's law and court administration, see Ito, "The World of the Adat Aceh", pp. 156–61.
[35] Ibid., p. 174.
[36] Ibid., p. 178.

could lead to a loss of limbs and life. An orang kaya's wealth and popularity could cost him his life or his property.[37] For actual crimes, real or imagined, such as military indiscipline, breach of court etiquette and treason, his cruelty had no limits. An orang kaya who asked Iskandar Muda for a deferment in preparing for war was killed, together with his whole family. As if death was not punishment enough, they all had their noses, lips, ears, genitals and bellies cut off. Iskandar Muda forced his son to eat both his own faeces and his mother's fingers for failing to make his obeisance. The mother's punishment was for neglecting her responsibility to teach her son. For those suspected of attempting to assassinate him, Iskandar Thani meted the same tortures and death by execution as Iskandar Muda.[38] In 1636, Iskandar Thani punished four of his concubines, whom he suspected of trying to poison him, by amputating their hands, feet and noses. Their bellies were then opened and the flesh excised from the bones, after which their bodies were burnt.[39] Iskandar Thani imprisoned Francisco de Souza de Castro, the Portuguese envoy, for failing to mount the elephant sent to convey him to the palace. Other orang kaya were castrated, flogged or had limbs amputated owing to delays in offering their services.

Administration of Law and Justice under the Sultanahs

Such caprice and cruelty were not reported during the reigns of the female rulers. Ironically, their penalties, checked by moral and religious values, were deemed as soft or weak. When Maharaja Sri Maharaja was accused of taking Safiatuddin's royal lands, the sultanah admonished him at court, where he had to sit with his hands folded on top of his head and beg for forgiveness for hours. This humiliation was as effective a deterrent as any as he refrained from troubling the sultanah any further. After attending an audience day on 12 July 1642, Pieter Sourij described her as merciful. He related that on that day, many criminal and civil cases

---

[37] Ibid., p. 180.
[38] Ibid., p. 181.
[39] Ibid., p. 172.

were discussed; one delinquent was brought before the sultanah but someone pleaded for him to be spared. Pieter Sourij believed this was owing to her nature as a woman, and the delinquent was pardoned.[40] In another case, a member of the congregation at a mosque opposed the *penghulu kawal*, an official at court in charge of policing. He was supposed to receive a death sentence, but thanks to appeals from many Indian Muslim traders requesting his pardon, the perpetrator's life was spared. However, as he had committed the grave crime of beating the penghulu kawal in a mosque, his left hand was amputated.[41]

Another characteristic feature of justice under Sultanah Safiatuddin was the greater institutionalisation of Islamic practice. She called upon the relevant courts to administer cases rather than to mete out punishment based on the ruler's personal whim and caprice. For example, a Muslim captain from Bengal by the name of Mirs Mamoet was accused of having sexual intercourse with the daughter of a certain Sayyid Sierip. While the case was still being investigated, Sayyid Sierip killed Mirs Mamoet because he had refused to marry his daughter. A fellow Bengali merchant requested that the sultanah execute Sierip and his daughter. The sultanah instead referred this to the relevant courts and adjudicators. The laksamana and the Lebai Kita Kali eventually settled the case as it involved a murder (to be tried at the criminal court) and a sexual liaison (under the jurisdiction of the religious court). The verdict was death for both father and daughter; however, the sultanah had the right to hear the final appeal. She saved the father from the death sentence, but the daughter was sentenced to strangling for fornication.[42]

Under the sultanah, the punishment for adultery was consistent—either flogging or strangling, which was in accordance with the law of the land. In one case, Sultanah Safiatuddin ordered the Lebai Kita Kali to investigate and try the case of a man who wanted her to punish his wife for committing adultery while he was working on a fort. The

---

[40] NA, VOC 1143, Dagh-Register gehouden bij Pieter Sourij, 1642, f. 565V.
[41] NA, VOC 1143, Dagh-Register gehouden bij Pieter Sourij, 1642, ff. 567V–568R.
[42] NA, VOC 1143, Dagh-Register gehouden bij den Oppercoopman Pieter Willemsz, 1642, ff. 503R–503V.

punishment meted out in this case was similar to another case where both the adulterer and adulteress were punished by flogging. Thomas Best reported that during Iskandar Muda's reign, a man who committed adultery was put to death (he does not mention how) and his corpse was left lying near the gate of the palace to be eaten by dogs.[43] This was unnecessarily cruel, even to the dead, and ran counter to both custom and Islam.

Little detailed information is available about how Safiatuddin's successors approached and executed justice. Observations from European travellers residing in Aceh, such as Thomas Bowrey and William Dampier (who collectively spent 20 years there, from 1669 to 1689), do not reveal or describe any unnecessarily harsh punishments capriciously meted out. The most severe penalties were the customary amputation of hands and feet for theft, and banishment to a nearby island, Pulo Wei, for incorrigibles. Dampier wrote that he had never heard of anyone who suffered death for theft.[44] Bowrey, however, observed that for the theft of things of considerable value, such as cow or buffalo, a death sentence would be more welcome to thieves than the amputations and banishment, and this would be meted out as an example to others.[45] Although it is not clear whether the death sentence in this case was carried out, it is clear from both Dampier's and Bowrey's reports that Aceh was a place where punishment was swift, and foreigners had legal recourse to protect their lives and property. As Dampier wrote:

> The laws of this country are very strict, and offenders are punished with great severity. Neither are there any delays of justice here; for as soon as the offender is taken, he is immediately brought before the magistrate, who presently hears the matter, and according as he finds it, so he either acquits, or orders punishment to be inflicted on the party immediately.[46]

---

[43] Thomas Best, *The Voyage of Thomas Best to the East Indies, 1612–14*, ed. Sir William Foster (London: The Hakluyt Society, 1934), p. 164.
[44] Dampier, *Voyages and Discoveries*, pp. 96–7.
[45] Bowrey, *A Geographical Account*, p. 315.
[46] Dampier, *Voyages and Discoveries*, p. 138.

The Sultanahs and the Ulama

Sultanah Safiatuddin's ascension to the throne as the first female ruler of Aceh Dar al-Salam in 1641 was not opposed by the ulama. More significantly, her position as both the political and religious authority was recognised. In her letters, as her male predecessors had done, she took the full title of *Khalifah zill Allah fi al-alam*, though she emphasised her role as the deputy of Allah chosen to execute God's laws. According to Hadi, in his *Mir'at al-Tullab* the ulama Abdul Rauf al-Singkel recognised Sultanah Safiatuddin as a khalifah, serving as "the deputy of God in executing our Lord's orders in the blessed country of Aceh Dar al-Salam".[47] As stated in the *Bustan* and *Adat Aceh*, Iskandar Muda and Iskandar Thani bore a second title suggesting a claim to religious authority: *sayyiduna wa mawlana paduka seri sultan Iskandar Muda johan berdaulat zil Allah fi al-alam* (Our Lord and Master, His Majesty the Auspicious Sultan Iskandar Muda, the Sovereign of the World, the Shadow of God on Earth) as did all four sultanahs.[48] Similarly in his *Mir'at al-Tullab*, al-Singkel accorded Safiatuddin the title *Sayyidatuna wa mawlatuna* (Our Lady Lord and Master). The fact she bore the title meant supreme religious authority lay in the ruler's hands, which actually allowed the ruler's will to be imposed on the law of the land and Islamic law. This does not mean the ruler needed to possess religious knowledge on par with the ulama's; indeed, nowhere in the Islamic theory of state is it claimed that a ruler should possess profound religious knowledge. However, executing the ruler's religious laws does require the ruler to possess divinely sanctioned authority.[49]

In return for the ulama's support to Safiatuddin, she treated them well. As discussed earlier, Sultan Iskandar Muda's and Iskandar Thani's execution of justice was at times harsher than the sharia, and their decision-making style was more despotic, while Safiatuddin tended to defer to the ulama and the Islamic courts for arbitration. Although the final decision remained hers—as Sourij reported—she tended to mete out justice with a softer hand. She also welcomed religious scholars to Aceh, and Ito pointed

---

[47] Hadi, *Islam and State in Sumatra*, p. 60.
[48] Ibid., pp. 59–60.
[49] Ibid., p. 64.

out that the *Adat Aceh* mentions the existence of a number of religious scholars from Pidie during her reign. The Kadhi Malik al-Adil, referred to by the Dutch as Lebai Kita Kali (kali, the Acehnese of the Arabic, qadhi) was given first place in the order of rank during Saturday audiences.

Hadi stated that besides Islamic laws, the rulers also determined Islamic orientations. Al-Mukammil and Iskandar Muda favoured the Wujudiyyah teachings of Hamzah Fansuri and Shams al-Din, while Iskandar Thani acted as a patron of the more legal-orthodox teachings of al-Raniri. And yet another major difference between Safiatuddin's rule and her male predecessors is that she neither favoured nor supported any particular theosophical leanings nor any particular ulama faction. She kept herself as far as possible above the politico-religious debates and struggles that gripped the kingdom at the time.

Iskandar Muda had embraced a monistic brand of Sufism under his protégé the Sheikh al-Islam, Shams al-Din, while Iskandar Thani preferred a more orthodox approach and supported another faction by appointing al-Raniri as the Sheikh al-Islam in Aceh in 1637.[50] The direct involvement of the rulers in supporting the Sheikhs of the different *tariqat* (schools of Sufism) caused a major rift in the ulama that resulted in a bloody struggle for power. When Sheikh Shams al-Din died in 1630, al-Raniri carried out a bloody purge of his followers, with Iskandar Thani's blessing. Many were executed and their books burnt, and some fled the kingdom. This bitter struggle between these two groups resumed in 1643, following the return from Mecca of Syaiful Rijal, a native of Minangkabau who had been a student of Jamal al-Din and follower of Sheikh Shams al-Din. Pieter Sourij described the chaotic conditions at court when the sultanah was called upon to settle this dispute. Instead of taking sides, the sultanah declared that she knew little about these religious debates and asked her elites to solve this conflict themselves.[51] The sultanah then waited until the struggle had played itself out. Only after Syaiful Rijal had emerged as a clear winner did the sultanah decide to call him to court

---

[50] Riddell, *Islam and the Malay-Indonesian World*, pp. 110–21.
[51] NA, VOC 1143, Dagh-Register gehouden bij Pieter Sourij, 1642, ff. 671V–672R; Takeshi Ito, "Why did Nuruddin al-Raniri leave Aceh in 1054 A.H.?", in *Bijdragen tot de Taal-, Land- en Volkenkunde* 134, 4 (1978): 489–91.

to honour him and appoint him as the Sheikh al-Islam.[52] It is especially important to note that despite the parallels to the earlier struggle, this time there were no mass executions or bloodshed. Al-Raniri was allowed to return to Gujarat in 1644 where he died in 1658. It is also important to note that even if Safiatuddin had preferred one tariqat over the other, she did not publicise or politicise her theosophical leanings. She adopted a more balanced approach and allowed the majority view to stand, but did not allow the minority group to be persecuted.

As mentioned in Chapter 3, after the 1651 coup and the murder of the *opperste bischop* (high bishop), whom I suggest was Syaiful Rijal, Safiatuddin worked with the Lebai Kita Kali and other judges to administer sharia law, using the law courts that were established under Iskandar Muda. No more religious feuds akin to that which took place in 1643 happened under her reign. This shows that Sultanah Safiatuddin refrained from actively supporting or giving political patronage to any particular ulama and their followers. Nor was there any evidence of her embracing a particular Islamic order, be it orthodox or mystical. One thing was clear though; she was a patron of religion.

In 1661, the Acehnese ulama Abdul Rauf al-Singkel, returned to Aceh from Mecca. He had left Aceh 19 years previously when he was 26, and he must have witnessed the killings and bloodshed between al-Raniri's and Jamal al-Din's groups. It is not known whether he played any role in supporting Safiatuddin when she ascended the throne in 1641, but on his return it is clear he fully supported her. He was appointed as the Sheikh al-Islam and it appears that his appointment was well-received. Unlike Syaiful Rijal, who seems to have had close relations with Safiatuddin and political ambitions that aroused the suspicion of the laksamana, al-Singkel was more focused on matters of religion. He was particularly devoted to writing *kitab*s (religious texts) and was very moderate in his views.[53] He had no objections to a woman ascending the throne and, as mentioned earlier, he also recognised her religious authority to rule as khalifah. Al-Singkel's return and the sultanah's continued royal patronage

---

[52] NA, VOC 1143, Dagh-Register gehouden bij Pieter Sourij, 1642, ff. 671V–673R.
[53] Hadi, *Islam and State in Sumatra*, pp. 158–9.

of Islam further stimulated and encouraged the orientation to Islamic law in the sultanate's judicial administration.[54]

The proliferation of Islamic learning and literature, leading to an Islamic and Malay golden age in Aceh unrivalled until today, testifies to the effective collaboration between the sultanah and the ulama. Al-Raniri wrote at least seven well-known books not only on religion but also history, literature and law, including *Shiratul Mustaqim* (The Straight Path), *Syaiful-Qutub* (Medicine for the Heart), and *Bustanul Salathin fi Dzikril-awwalin wal-Akhirin* (The Garden of Sultans Concerning Biographies of People in the Past and Future). Safiatuddin also commissioned Abdul Rauf al-Singkel to write a book on *fiqh* (laws pertaining to ritual obligations), the result of which is the *Mir'at al Tullab*, the first book on canon law written in Malay, completed in 1663.[55]

The third sultanah, Inayat Zakiatuddin Syah, also collaborated closely with the ulama and continued Safiatuddin's style of piety politics. She commissioned Abdul Rauf to write a kitab, which became his *Commentary on Forty Hadiths* (sayings of the Prophet).[56] Although there is no mention of mosques being built on the instruction or sponsorship of these female sovereigns, Dampier noted in 1689 that the kingdom had a great number of them.[57]

The Ruler's Attributes

I have shown that neither religious knowledge nor sex was among the prerequisites in the selection of a ruler, nor was either used as a yardstick by which to judge the quality of the sultan or sultanah. The main tasks of an exemplary ruler—the defender of the faith—were laid out in the *Kanun Syarak Kerajaan Aceh*, *Taj us-Salatin*, *Bustan us-Salatin* and the *Adat Aceh*. The main responsibilities were to uphold Allah's laws, pursue prosperity for the subjects and ensure public welfare: success or failure in

---

[54] Ito, "The World of the Adat Aceh", p. 164.
[55] Rusdi, "Sultanah Safiatuddin Syah", pp. 47–9.
[56] Hadi, *Islam and State in Sumatra*, p. 74.
[57] Dampier, *Voyages and Discoveries*, p. 90.

these depended on his or her moral attributes. The ruler must be just, merciful, generous, prudent, knowledgeable, pleasant/good looking and possess good conduct.[58]

To a large extent, the Acehnese queens possessed many of these qualities. In her piety, especially, Sultanah Safiatuddin was exemplary. The *Bustan us-Salatin* states:

> Her royal highness, our lord Seri Sultan Tajul Alam Safiyyat al-Din Shah Berdaulat, the shadow of Allah on earth, possessed many praiseworthy and virtuous traits, as well as being fearful of Allah and always praying five times a day and reading the Quran aloud, repeating the name of Allah and always reading the book of Allah, and commanding people to perform good deeds and forbidding them to commit bad deeds, as was sent down by Allah to our Prophet Muhammad, and was extremely just in the matter of examining and sentencing all the servants of Allah. On account of the blessing of the royal power and good fortune of *Yang Maha Mulia*, there were many of the servants of Allah who were faithful believers and prayed five times a day and pursued knowledge.[59]

It is important to note that apart from the indigenous court chronicles, which may be biased towards royalty, other reports written by Muslim and non-Muslim foreigners who went to Aceh corroborate the evidence found in local records. A Muslim traveller named Al-Mutawakkil, who arrived in Aceh during Safiatuddin's reign, gave this interesting description of the sultanah:

> A very gracious, perfect Muslim woman, generous with money, rules them. She can read and knows science, beneficence and agreement on the Quran. She is called Safiyati 'l-Din Shah Bardawla [*Berdaulat*, meaning sovereign]. Her name is written on the coins, on one side Safiyati 'l-Din and on the other side Shah Berdawla.[60]

---

[58] Hussain, *Taj us-Salatin*, p. 59.
[59] Salleh, ed., *Bustan al-Salatin*, p. 62.
[60] *The Hollanders in the Sirrah of Al-Mutawakkil*, from the papers of R.B. Serjeant found in Edinburgh University Library, p. 124. I am indebted to Michael Laffan for this source.

Her piety was also attested to by VOC officials in Aceh, who mentioned that the sultanah observed fasting in Ramadan, the third pillar of Islam. Truijtman described one audience day:

> It was fasting month, thus one could not eat or drink. The Sultanah asked to be excused for this and hope that we would not blame her for not treating us with food.... Later in the evening, we were entertained with more singing performances at court where the whole court was alight with lighted candles. We were treated with food served in gold plates and honoured with betel-box.[61]

Vlamingh noted that during Ramadan, foreigners and guests at court were not served any food or drinks. However, in the evenings after sunset, when Muslims broke their fast, the palace halls were filled with banquets once again. Also, if audience days fell during the time when the Acehnese celebrated the two Muslim canonical festivals, these days were cancelled. Of course, no mention was made about the sultanah's observances of daily prayers and reciting the Qu'ran: these were private rituals performed in the inner sanctum of the palace.

The *Bustan* also depicts Sultanah Safiatuddin as a great and generous queen. It states that she never failed to reward her nobles, captains and soldiers handsomely. She also accorded missions from abroad with great hospitality. The *Bustan* cites the example of Sultanah Safiatuddin presenting one mission from Gujarat with 28 elephants unparalleled in their size and courage—one of which had four tusks instead of the usual two.[62] The *Bustan* concludes that no ruler could give a more generous reward.

Sultanah Safiatuddin's generosity was reported in VOC records, evident from the many observations of various company delegates who resided in Aceh. Pieter Willemszoon reported in 1642 that the sultanah granted an English surgeon, by the name of Mr Thomas, the title of "orang kaya" and gave him four slaves as a gift.[63] Besides the customary

---

[61] NA, VOC 1171, Dagh-Register gehouden bij Johan Truijtman, 1649, ff. 205R–205V.
[62] Salleh, ed., *Bustan al-Salatin*, pp. 43–4.
[63] NA, VOC 1143, Dagh-Register gehouden bij den Oppercoopman Pieter Willemsz, 1642, f. 508R.

offerings of clothes and daggers to the Dutch envoys attending her court, and her generous presents of large amounts of pepper and tin to the governors in Melaka and Batavia, company officials in Aceh mentioned the thoughtful and frequent gifts of baked foods and fruits that the sultanah ordered to be taken to the company's lodge.[64]

Sultanah Safiatuddin dispensed generous rewards to her own orang kaya too. When Maharaja Adonna Lilla returned from an elephant hunt with 11 huge elephants for the queen, she proclaimed that the elephants be presented to her orang kaya instead: the biggest one and two others for Maharaja Adonna Lilla himself, one for the laksamana, one for the son of Maharaja Lilla, one for Maharaja di Raja, one for Raja Lila Wangsa and the remaining four to be given to the children at court.[65] On another occasion, the sultanah was presented with 30 young Acehnese who had been taken as slaves. She instead ordered these slaves to be distributed as gifts among her orang kaya. Another example was when the *Paduka Mamentri* offered her 20 young slaves, but she answered that those slaves under him should be kept by him.[66]

The third sultanah, Inayat Zakiatuddin Syah was another example of a generous queen. In 1683, she welcomed the delegation from the *sharif* (governor) of Mecca, headed with great ceremony by the representative of Sharif Barakat, El Hajj Yusuf E. Qodri. When the envoys returned to Mecca, they were laden with gifts of gold, five golden lamps for the Ka'aba, sandalwood, camphor and money to be donated to the poor people in Mecca.[67]

---

[64] Several European visitors reported that upon arrival in Patani, Raja Ijau also sent fruits and other food as gifts in her name to their ships. Amirell, "The Blessings and Perils of Female Rule", p. 311.

[65] NA, VOC 1143, Dagh-Register gehouden bij den Oppercoopman Pieter Willemsz, 1642, f. 523R.

[66] NA, VOC 1143, Dagh-Register gehouden bij den Oppercoopman Pieter Willemsz, 1642, f. 523V.

[67] Christiaan Snouck Hurgronje, "Een Mekkaansch Gezantschap naar Atjeh in 1683" [A Meccan Delegation to Aceh in 1683], *Bijdragen tot de Taal-, Land-en-Volkenkunde* 5, 3 (1888): 553–4 and n. 246.

Islamic Rituals and Festivities

There were several pillars among the indices for assessing commitment to Islam in seventeenth-century Aceh. These were attending Friday prayers and celebrating the two canonical festivals of the Muslim year—*Eid al-Fitr*, celebrated after the Ramadan month of fasting, and *Eid al-Adha*, the festival of sacrifice celebrated on the tenth of the month of Dhu al-Hijjah.[68] The third part of the *Adat Aceh* provides a detailed description of these feasts, including the sovereign's role, which can be briefly summarised.[69] Seated on an elephant, the sultan led a procession from the palace to the main mosque, Bait al-Rahman, accompanied by state officials, courtiers and servants. He then entered the mosque and proceeded to a private alcove where the curtains were drawn.[70] After he had performed the obligatory imam-led prayers, all the officials and nobility pledged allegiance to the sultan. The procession then reformed and made its way back to the palace with the sultan riding an elephant. Upon his arrival, the sultan was welcomed by old womenfolk at the palace with sprinkles of yellow-toasted rice mixed with gold foil. An additional ritual took place during the celebration of *Eid al-Adha*, the feast of sacrifice. After the prayers at the mosque the sultan, led by religious officials, would begin the sacrifice by putting his knife to the jugular vein of the animal specially prepared for this occasion. After the first cut, as soon as blood began to flow, the Sheikh al-Islam took over this ceremony.

No Islamic doctrine based on the Qu'ran and Hadith forbids a woman from appearing in public processions. Nor is there one that forbids a woman from going to the mosque to pray, though this is generally not encouraged in orthodoxy. And yet, no evidence has been found in either indigenous records or in European accounts or observations regarding the participation of female rulers in the above religious rituals and festivals. Does this silence mean that these rituals

---

[68] Ito, "The World of the Adat Aceh", p. 206.
[69] For a detailed description of how these rituals were performed and festivals celebrated, see Ito's study on the *Adat Aceh*, in Ito, "The World of the Adat Aceh", pp. 209–48.
[70] According to the *Adat Aceh*, this curtained alcove is called *mesjid kelambu*. Ito, "The World of the Adat Aceh", p. 216.

did not take place under female rulers? This is difficult to believe as these rituals are mandatory for all adult male Muslims. Thus, the question is how or on what scale were these ceremonies and processions undertaken? As no evidence mentions the participation of the various sultanahs in these mosque processions or in congregational prayers and the ritual sacrifice, it is difficult to conclude that they did. The responsibility of attending congregational prayer—Friday prayers in particular—in mosques falls only on adult male Muslims: the imam must necessarily be male, and the prayer hall in the mosque is strictly regarded as a male domain. The *Taj us-Salatin* differentiates a male from a female ruler by stating that a male ruler—mandatory for all adult male Muslims—ought (*harus*) to go to the mosque for Friday and Eid prayers. The *Taj* goes on to say that the male ruler ought to go to the mosque adorned and accompanied by his ministers and soldiers. A female ruler could not do this (*raja perempuan itu tiada dapat berbuat demikian*).[71] A female ruler could only pray in a place that was quiet so as not to be seen by males (*sembahyang pada suatu tempat yang sunyi supaya jangan dilihat orang laki-laki adanya*). Given these injunctions, which are followed strictly in almost all Muslim communities worldwide, the silence in the sources and unless new evidence is found, it appears the sultanahs did not lead the processions to the mosques during these religious rituals. Nor would they perform any prayers in the curtained alcove in the main prayer hall of the mosque. *Eid al-Fitr* and *Eid al Adha*, however, were celebrated with much pomp and fanfare. Truijtman recounted one such celebration for *Eid al-Fitr* at the end of fasting during the reign of Safiatuddin. He mentioned that, as customary, 400 buffaloes were slaughtered and the meat eaten to mark the ceremony.[72]

The previous paragraph seems to suggest that the female ruler's capacity to manifest Allah's laws was limited. Furthermore, in a "theatre state",[73] the construction of these ceremonies and public rituals was an important means of enhancing the sovereign's charisma and status—in

---

[71] Hussain, *Taj us-Salatin*, p. 61.
[72] NA, VOC 1171, Dagh-Register gehouden bij Johan Truijtman, 1649, f. 224R.
[73] Clifford Geertz, *Negara: The Theatre State in Nineteenth-Century Bali* (Princeton: Princeton University Press, 1980), p. 103.

this instance his religious authority.[74] Upon closer examination, however, it is important to note that the above religious rituals were mandatory for all adult male believers but not for rulers. The ruler's roles in these processions were merely ceremonial, based on the culture and politics of power, but not on religion.[75] The authority of the ruler was religiously sanctioned, but the ruler himself was not a religious leader. The need for rulers to take part in these ceremonies was invented, designed to balance the authority of religious leaders or show that the ruler held supreme or ultimate authority. These ceremonies and processions were designed to enhance the ruler's power and his religiously sanctioned authority, but were in no way obligated by religious doctrines. Indeed the palace, not the mosque, was used as the starting and end points of these ceremonies. The palace, as the ruler's abode, was where the royal insignia and regalia were kept. During such processions, these were carried to the mosque and returned to the palace in a way that created a new pivot of authority and power that balanced the mosque complex. The main task of the ruler of a Muslim community was to uphold religious laws and ensure that the people could practise the religion freely and in peace. The ruler was never expected to be an imam leading congregational prayers or initiate the sacrifice during the feast of *Eid al-Adha*. These were court traditions given the veneer of religion.

I believe that the female ruler's absence from rituals returned religious duty to its proper sphere. This was in line with other features of female rule: where governance and the execution of laws justice were left to authorised persons but the monarch was the ultimate arbiter. This might

---

[74] According to Anthony Milner, many un-Islamic practices pertaining to kingship and pageantry survived even after the adoption of Islam. For an assessment of Malay political culture, see A.C. Milner, *Kerajaan: Malay Political Culture on the Eve of Colonial Rule* (Tucson: Arizona University Press, 1982).

[75] In her study of the Byzantine *Book of Ceremonies*, Averil Cameron observed that the more centralised the government became, the more the rituals themselves would need to include all officials who mattered. Thus, the ceremonial was both self-generating and self-reinforcing. Ambition engendered ceremony and ceremony made ambition respectable. Averil Cameron, "The Construction of Court Ritual: The Byzantine *Book of Ceremonies*", in *Rituals of Royalty: Power and Ceremonial in Traditional Societies*, ed. David Cannadine and Simon Price (Cambridge: Cambridge University Press, 1987), p. 131.

have created a more limited monarchy, but not one that was necessarily weak, much less in decline, as most writers have claimed. Female rulers might not have taken part in processions that were really a showcase of power rather than faith and, consequently, they might have appeared less charismatic. They might have erased the veneer of religious grandiosity and pageantry, but they upheld the piety, the substance of the faith.

Absence from processions to the mosque during these strictly religious rituals did not mean these female rulers were secluded or did not take part in other public processions. Numerous observations by European travellers, residents and VOC officials in Aceh illustrate that the sultanahs ventured out in public on elephants to perform other rituals that were more adat-based, such as funeral ceremonies, visiting graves of the deceased and taking part in the bathing ceremony during the Islamic month of Safar.

The *Bustan* describes in detail the ceremony to place the headstone at Iskandar Thani's tomb, noting how the sultanah, just a few months after taking power, led the procession mounted on an elephant.[76] Bowrey witnessed the bathing ceremony in the month of Safar during the reign of Sultanah Inayat Zakiatuddin Syah. He described it as a royal procession down the river, "the like I believe was never paralleled in the universe", which took place shortly after Zakiatuddin became queen.[77]

Glimpsing the Invisible

In theory, the *Taj us-Salatin* differentiates between male and female rulers according to their degree of visibility. The *Taj* states that a male raja was seen and not hidden, but a female raja was hidden and should not be seen.[78] The male raja sat in front of those who had an audience with him without any intervening curtain (*tirai*) and had to be clearly in sight. A female raja, on the other hand, ought not to be seen and must view

---

[76] Salleh, ed., *Bustan al-Salatin*, p. 57.
[77] For a fuller description of this procession, see Bowrey, *A Geographical Account*, pp. 325–6.
[78] Hussain, *Taj us-Salatin*, p. 60.

her audience from behind a curtain.[79] Only the wives of ministers, other females and males who had not reached puberty were allowed to face the queen in the audience hall.[80] This restriction was even extended to her voice. The *Taj* states that a female raja's voice could not be heard except from behind the curtain.

Unlike this clear delineation of visibility and space in the *Taj*'s gender-based construct on leadership, readings of the *Bustan us-Salatin* and the *Sejarah Melayu* provide a more ambiguous picture. On the one hand, the *Bustan* describes the sultanah as hidden from public view. It states that the queen received her ministers and subjects in the audience hall (*Peratna Sembah*) from behind a curtain of gold brocade. The ladies of the court, seated outside the curtain, became her voice and acted as intermediaries between her and her audience.[81] And yet on special occasions, such as placing the headstone on Iskandar Thani's tomb, the *Bustan* mentions that the queen ventured out to appear in public.[82] The *Bustan* gives the impression Sultanah Safiatuddin rode on an elephant and instructed on placing the headstone. Unfortunately, the *Bustan* is vague here and does not clearly describe whether the queen was visible to the public or whether she remained hidden in a curtained pavilion on the elephant.[83] The *Sejarah Melayu* describes the mother of Sultan Mahmud I who, from behind a door, eavesdropped on a discussion on choosing a new bendahara. When Sultan Mahmud asked which among them should become bendahara, the chiefs answered that all nine chiefs were eligible—whoever his highness preferred should be made bendahara. At this juncture, the sultan's mother is said to have shouted out, "Let it be Tun Mutahir." The sultan immediately agreed with his mother's choice and announced that Tun Mutahir should be bendahara, and the chiefs all agreed. Even the writer of the *Sejarah Melayu* recognised her choice as excellent, as Tun Mutahir (her younger brother) turned out to be one of the best bendahara Melaka had ever had. The ambiguities of women's

---

[79] Ibid.
[80] Ibid., p. 61.
[81] Salleh, ed., *Bustan al-Salatin*, p. 46.
[82] Ibid., p. 57.
[83] Ibid.

power are starkly presented in this episode: she made one of the best political choices in the kingdom and yet she remained behind the door. This not only presents a complex picture of women's status and roles but also blurs the distinction between private and public. Physical barriers or spaces do not clearly mark the distinction between inside and outside, private and public.

As in the indigenous records, evidence gathered from European records and other travellers' accounts do not paint a clear picture either. A number of company officials, European and other visitors to Aceh left their observations of how the sultanahs behaved in public. In 1642, Pieter Sourij related that upon the arrival of the company's delegates, and despite the rainy weather, Sultanah Safiatuddin appeared outside in the presence of 3,000 to 4,000 men.[84] He also reported that when the business at hand was urgent, the sultanah commanded the Dutch men to sit right in front of the throne (*recht over des Coninckljken troon*).[85] Vlamingh and Truijtman also noted that in some cases when the queen was displeased, she would raise her voice and speak in anger. They did not mention whether the sultanah spoke only through her female attendants or an intervening curtain. According to Balthasar Bort, the VOC envoy to Aceh in 1660, Sultanah Safiatuddin handled business in the same fashion as her male counterparts; the only difference was that she was not visible to the audience. She had to make sure, however, that her voice was recognisable to all. Thus during the entire audience, Bort reported that the sultanah spoke in such a loud voice that her words could be fully heard and understood by all.[86]

A Muslim traveller, al-Mutawakkil, in Aceh during the reign of Sultanah Safiatuddin, made another interesting and rare observation.

---

[84] NA, VOC 1143, Dagh-Register gehouden bij Pieter Sourij, 1642, f. 554R. A Dutch chaplain on board one of Admiral Van Neck's ships, Roelof Roelofszoon, described a similar procession in Patani in 1602, when Raja Ijau was greeted by around 4,000 men. Amirell, "The Blessings and Perils of Female Rule", p. 310.

[85] NA, VOC 1143, Dagh-Register gehouden bij Pieter Sourij, 1642, f. 558V.

[86] NA, VOC 1237, Verbael gehouden bij den Commissaris Balthasar Bort, 1661, f. 354V, f. 356R. Quoted in Andaya, "A Very Good-Natured But Awe-Inspiring Government", p. 71. Andaya mentioned that during audience days, the sultanah was always seated behind a screen or door.

He described her as a good Muslim ruler and noted that "she puts between her and the ministers an overflowing curtain when she gives orders. When she is riding on the hunt or strolling about she is completely veiled."[87]

Thomas Bowrey reported that when he accompanied the English commander to the palace for an audience with Sultanah Zakiatuddin, they sat on fine carpets "with our faces directly towards the queen's lodgings ... making a *sembah* (obeisance) to the queen's windows, she all the while looks upon us although we cannot see her".[88] Bowrey estimated Sultanah Zakiatuddin to be at least 60 years old. William Dampier related that after ascending the throne, Sultanah Zakiatuddin was largely confined to the palace and was rarely able to "go abroad". He also described her as an "old Maid".[89] Neither was she seen by people of inferior quality or rank except for some of her "Domesticks". The exception was that once a year, dressed in white, she would ride an elephant to the river to wash herself.[90] Dampier was unable to affirm whether the common folk could see her in the parade. He observed that it was the custom of Eastern princes to screen themselves from the sight of their subjects. If they did venture out, the people would be ordered to turn their backs or hold their hands before their eyes.[91] When Ralph Ord and William Cawley had an audience with Sultanah Zakiatuddin, the queen sat on a throne of ivory and tortoise shell surrounded by a row of ladies in an upper room adjoining the audience hall. Below the throne sat two more rows of ladies. In front of the room hung a thin gauze that did not interfere with the audience but did prevent any perfect view of the queen. They commented that the sultanah had a strong but not a manly voice: "The queen appears not to be forty years of age, is of a large size and the strongest voice that we have heard," which made them suspicious enough to think that she might have been

---

[87] *The Hollanders in the Sirrah of Al-Mutawakkil*, p. 124.
[88] Bowrey, *A Geographical Account*, p. 307.
[89] Dampier, *Voyages and Discoveries*, p. 99. Dampier was in Aceh from 1688 to 1689.
[90] Bowrey, *A Geographical Account*, pp. 325–6.
[91] Dampier, *Voyages and Discoveries*, p. 99.

a eunuch dressed in woman's apparel.[92] Interestingly, to the best of my knowledge, no other account describes the physical appearance of any of the queens, except for an estimate of their age.[93] For that matter, there are also no descriptions available of the kings, even one as famous as Iskandar Muda, though imaginary depictions in paintings abound!

While Sultanah Safiatuddin reportedly went on frequent outings—fishing, hunting and amusement trips—Sultanah Zakiatuddin did not venture out much. At times the queens were said to have been behind thin gauze, and on other occasions behind a screen, a door or even a window. Interestingly, more references were made to an intervening barrier between the queens and their audience from the 1660s onwards, which suggests that the Acehnese court was becoming more conservative towards the latter part of the seventeenth century. Opposition to female rule increased noticeably in the 1680s when a group of Arab delegates arrived in Aceh, and it was from this group that the fatwa forbidding female rule was procured from Mecca. Alternatively, age may have affected the kinds of activities in which the queens participated. Sultanah Zakiatuddin was certainly old when she ascended the throne. This may be why she appeared in public less often and took part in fewer hunting and fishing expeditions than Sultanah Safiatuddin, who was only 29 years old when she assumed the throne. As mentioned earlier, the evidence is inconclusive.

Were the Acehnese female sovereigns following the tenets of Islam by remaining behind the curtain when they were discoursing in public? To all intents and purposes, these female monarchs appear to have accepted the construction of female leadership articulated in the *Taj us-Salatin*. As mentioned earlier, there is no evidence that they participated in the procession to the mosque, as women were not encouraged to go to the mosque or pray in public, and one could surmise that with the coming of Islam, local females—at least those in the upper class—became more

---

[92] Farrington, "Negotiations at Aceh in 1684", p. 25. This was four years before Dampier's description of the sultanah in 1688.

[93] In contrast, English adventurer, Peter Floris, who visited Patani in 1612–13, described Raja Ijau, who was about 60 years old, as a "comely olde woman" and "tall of person and full of majestie, having in all the Indies not seene many lyke unto hir". Quoted in Amirell, "The Blessings and Perils of Female Rule", p. 310.

secluded. Barbara Andaya asserted that Sultanah Safiatuddin spoke to men from behind a screen because of the strongly Islamic court of Aceh.[94] She also claimed that Qu'ranic teaching differentiated respectable women from their social inferiors by their degree of visibility; the more respectable a woman was, the further she retreated into the confines of domestic space.[95] Contrary to Andaya's assertion, the Qu'ran neither makes a distinction between upper-class and lower-class women, nor does the Qu'ran advocate seclusion of women. The Qu'ran does urge women to dress modestly and to cover their bosoms and jewellery, and it asks the wives of the Prophet Muhammad to cloak their bodies so that they will not be bothered in public, but it does not mention veiling or the seclusion of women from public space. A woman's face is not part of *aurat* (that which is forbidden to be seen by a male who is not kin, or *muhrim*). Indeed, even in prayers, women are not allowed to cover their faces. Women during the Prophet Muhammad's time joined their men in battles, fighting alongside men, nursing the wounded and burying the dead. They too were given a share of the war booty. Thus, the idea of seclusion and veiling did not originate in Islam. It was part of the complexities and pluralities in the practice of Islam that the veiling habit spread so widely, and people assumed it to be sanctioned in the Qu'ran.

If this practice did not originate from Islam then did it come from adat? On the contrary, one of the identifying features of Southeast Asian society was the relative freedom of women to appear in public, though the arrival of Islam encouraged women to cover a larger part of their bodies. The "Islamic" *hijab* and veiling of women never really became established in the region, and certainly not among the common people. And yet the idea of seclusion and exclusion did take root among the ruling class and royalty as a sign of elite status. As Dampier observed, lowly subjects could not look upon eastern monarchs. This was part of the aura of mystery and semi-divinity these rulers wished to project to inspire awe in their subjects.[96] The idea of veiling and seclusion, signifying the sexual

---

[94] Andaya, *The Flaming Womb*, p. 85.
[95] Ibid., p. 86.
[96] Milner, *Kerajaan*, p. 26; John M. Gullick, *Malay Society in the Late Nineteenth Century* (Singapore: Oxford University Press, 1987), p. 282.

unavailability of respectable women, originated from the Eastern Roman Empire and Persia and spread to the pre-Islamic Middle East.[97] Arab Muslims adopted the practice of veiling from the people they conquered, and this became part of the practice in royal households.[98] Al-Jauhari, the author of the *Taj us-Salatin*, adopted the Persian and Sassanid tradition found in the Umayyad and Abbasid courts in which upper-class women were veiled and invisible to the gaze of non-muhrim men. As mentioned earlier, al-Jauhari might not have wanted to veer too far from what was believed to be the established orthodox view of Muslims in the heartland, thus his conditional acceptance of female rule in the region. However, in copying the practice of women's seclusion, he was adopting not Islamic practices but a syncretic version of Islam. In the Umayyad and Abbasid caliphates there were some Arab women who were very politically influential, but they held power from *behind* the throne. In contrast, the ladies who held power in Malay Muslim polities actually held power *on* the throne as reigning monarchs in their own right.

Evidence presented earlier shows that the sultanahs of Aceh were not mere figureheads or shadow queens. One can conclude that even if these female monarchs ruled from behind some sort of barrier, preventing a clear view of them, they were not invisible. How else could Ord and Cawley know that Sultanah Zakiatuddin sat on the throne of ivory and tortoise shell, unless it was something they imagined? Furthermore, though they ruled from behind a curtain, they were neither isolated nor powerless. The idea that women belonged to the *dalam* (inside/private) domain, and men the outside or public domain was blurred here. The physical barrier did not confine or seclude these rulers in any way, nor did it impede their very public roles as reigning monarchs. As was true of Sultan Mahmud's mother, their voices and authority emanated from behind this curtain, and they were obeyed throughout the kingdom. This curtain also did not prevent them from being plugged into the news, rumours and happenings around their sultanate: the network of eunuchs and women was well used by these queens as evidenced in the jewel affair in Chapter 2. Neither

---

[97] Fatima Mernissi, *The Veil and the Male Elite: A Feminist Interpretation of Women's Rights in Islam*, trans. Mary Jo Lakeland (Cambridge, MA: Perseus Books, 1991), pp. 94–5.
[98] Peter N. Stearns, *Gender in World History* (London: Routledge, 2000), p. 40.

did the curtain make the queens more inaccessible, as under these queens any man or woman could appear before them on audience days. Indeed, under female monarchs, the palace became more accessible: the harem—the private chambers of the sultan's numerous wives and concubines—no longer had to be protected or was out of bounds to others. Other court ladies were not secluded from the male gaze. Iskandar Muda and Iskandar Thani were always described as surrounded by hundreds of women guards and eunuchs. Beaulieu mentioned that Iskandar Muda had 3,000 women in his palace.[99] Peter Mundy described an elephant fight in Aceh in 1637 where Iskandar Thani was seated on an elevated stone platform, under a pavilion and surrounded by his guards of women.[100] In a letter from Iskandar Muda to King James I of England, he described himself as "he who is not seen by the seers, who is not heard by the hearers".[101] Thus, one may conclude that though female sovereigns ruled from behind a curtain, this was not so much a function of their sex, religion or owing to the need to protect female modesty. It was more a function of a governing style that emphasised the exclusivity of the ruler, which was influenced by a mixture of a syncretic tradition of Islam originating from the Middle East and the region's own Indic past.

This practice was not unique to the female sex. Indeed, in the Middle East—the heartland of Islam—male monarchs followed the tradition of creating an aura of inaccessibility that frequently proved advantageous.[102] Indeed, the hijab not only refers to female dress or coverings, but also to a curtain. The curtain or hijab is a three dimensional concept—visual, spatial and ethical. Understood in its visual dimension, it means to hide; spatially it means to separate, mark a border or threshold; ethically, it refers to something that belongs to the realm of the forbidden. Used in the political context of governance, it marks a separation between the ruler and the ruled. The *Hijab al-Amir*, hijab of the prince or the caliph—the

---

[99] Van Goens noted that Sultan Agung of Mataram had ten thousand. From Reid, *Southeast Asia*, Vol. 1, p. 167.
[100] Mundy, *The Travels of Peter Mundy*, pp. 126–30.
[101] Annabel Teh Gallop and B. Arps, *Golden Letters: Writing Traditions of Indonesia* (London-Jakarta: The British Library-Yayasan Lontar, 1991), p. 128. Quoted in Hijjas, "The Woman Raja", p. 78.
[102] Reid, *Southeast Asia*, Vol. 1, pp. 179–81.

most powerful man in the Muslim community—refers to the curtain behind which the caliph sat to avoid the gaze of his court members. Quoting the *Encyclopaedia of Islam*, Mernissi stated that this custom was unknown to the early inhabitants of the Hidjaz (the western region of present-day Saudi Arabia), and it seems it was introduced into Islam by the Umayyads under the influence of the Sassanid civilisation. This custom was first practised by the fifth caliph, Mu'awiya, and was adopted by the rulers of Andalusia, North Africa and Egypt. The Fatimid dynasty (909–1171) institutionalised this custom as a veritable ceremony. With the Fatimids, the sacred aspect of the caliph acquired special significance. The caliph, considered the hypostasis of the world's active intelligence, almost became the object of worship. As such, he had to hide himself from the eyes of his faithful followers who were thus protected from the radiance of his countenance.[103]

A Dutch resident in Siam during the reign of Prasat Thong described a procession on the river. The king was seated in the finest boat, under a decorated canopy, hidden among all kinds of costly things so that neither his body nor his face could be seen. He was surrounded by nobles and courtiers who paid reverence at his feet. In seventeenth-century Siam, only Europeans defied the rule that no one should look upon the king as he passed on his elephant or in his galley. The combination of outward displays of wealth and the power of secluding the ruler's person is a characteristic feature of Southeast Asian kingship during the period.[104] Thus, seclusion seems to have been a function of royal status rather than of sex. It is indeed powerful to see and yet not be seen. How else can one reconcile the idea of a female ruler's seclusion owing to her sex with her very public participation in the numerous processions, amusement trips and outings?

Conclusion

How and to what extent Islam was adopted and adapted in Aceh depended on the main power holders at the time. The sultanahs were able to rule

---

[103] Mernissi, *The Veil and the Male Elite*, pp. 94–5.
[104] Reid, *Southeast Asia*, Vol. 1, pp. 179–81.

the kingdom without religious opposition from the ulama, at least until the death of al-Singkel in 1693. He did not view female rule as forbidden in Islam and emphasised the moral attributes of the ruler rather than other features. It is significant that the sultanahs played a major role in negotiating female rule within Islam and managed to get the religious elites' continued support. This they did by basing their authority on God's will and legitimising their rule based on the ways in which they executed God's laws. It is interesting to note that Elizabeth I of England (r. 1533–1603) and Empress Wu Zetian of China (r. 683–708) also used providentialism as the most effective means of legitimating a woman sovereign.[105] Empress Wu Zetian argued, against strict patriarchal custom, that she should be allowed to serve her country on the grounds that she was the reincarnation of a previous female saint whom Buddha had promised spiritual rebirth.[106]

The Acehnese sultanahs' piety, generosity, prudence and patronage of Islam ensured that they were good Muslim rulers. The challenge they faced was to negotiate between exercising their authority in a male-dominated court and assuming public roles as rulers, without transgressing their limits. Although the queens were not secluded or invisible, they did not intrude into areas that would be considered distinctively male, such as the main hall of the mosque; nor did they undertake religious rituals usually reserved for the imam. Spatial and functional bounds were respected. This they did by collaborating with the male ulama and allowing them to exercise their religious authority and jurisdiction without interference, though the final say lay with the ruler.

The very character and emphasis of Islamic teaching in Aceh largely depended on the sovereign's will. The position of Islam and how it was negotiated and reconciled with existing customary laws must be understood in the context of the political situation, and the ruler's own attitude and approach. Unlike their male predecessors, the sultanahs did not support any particular religious faction or orientation so, in this sense, they took the politics out of religion. And yet in the practice of court traditions and

---

[105] Anne Mclaren, "Elizabeth I as Deborah: Biblical Typology, Prophecy and Political Power", in *Gender, Power and Privilege in Early Modern Europe: 1500–1700*, ed. Jessica Munns and Penny Richards (Harlow: Pearson Education, 2003), pp. 99, 105.
[106] Stearns, *Gender in World History*, p. 36.

governance, they were tempered by moral and religious values. Pageantry, theatre-politics and an emphasis on material wealth and prowess were less important to these female rulers than piety and thriftiness. Iskandar Muda and Iskandar Thani were acutely aware of their image and wanted to be perceived as kings of kings by other rulers. A slight to their ego or personal honour would invite their wrath and a violent response, regardless of whether this had the potential to harm the kingdom. On the contrary, Sultanah Safiatuddin Syah emphasised her role to uphold God's laws and wished to be seen as a just, merciful and generous ruler. Execution of the law and justice were both more humane and more Islamic under these female monarchs. Although the sultanahs' own Islamic leanings—whether orthodox or Sufistic/mystical—are unknown, they were dedicated patrons of religion, and their court became the most important centre of Islamic studies and learning in the region. Under female rulers Islam was more publicised but less politicised. A study of Muslim women rulers in Bhopal shows that they too were pious, using Islam as a moral force and social capital as the basis of their rule and legitimacy. Their rule was successful because of their personal integrity, their humane and fair treatment of their subjects, and their dedicated commitment to good governance.[107]

Why, then, did female rule end in 1699 with the deposition of the fourth Sultanah Kamalat Syah, on the basis of an alleged fatwa forbidding female rule? Islam, like other major religions, has complex and sometimes ambiguous ideas regarding women.[108] Furthermore, Islam, born in the Middle East, had picked up some older practices concerning gender—an instance of syncretism within the Middle East—such as the isolation and veiling of women, that were not integral to Islam but came to seem so.[109] Complexities, such as these, affected Islam's impact on gender construction and practices in the more peripheral areas of Islam.[110]

---

[107] Shaharyar M. Khan, *The Begums of Bhopal: A Dynasty of Women Rulers in Raj India* (London: I.B. Tauris, 2000), p. 217. The study by Fleschenberg and Derichs, ed., *Women and Politics in Asia* also demonstrated that women leaders tend to base their authority on moral force and social capital.

[108] Stearns, *Gender in World History*, p. 40.

[109] Ibid., p. 38.

[110] Ibid., p. 39.

"Cultural shopping" inevitably took place, depending on the context and circumstances of the time.[111] The way the gender balance was tilted then became a matter of emphasis, which would also change through time. Hence, the seemingly paradoxical situation where Islam was used to legitimise the accession of the first sultanah, and used again 59 years later to end the reign of the last female ruler. Before discussing this in greater detail, the next chapter examines why the sultanahs were able to remain in power for as long as they did.

---

[111] Ibid., p. 44.

chapter

6 The Practice of Queenship

From *Ira et Malevolentia* to *Pax et Custodia*[1]

Were there unique features that set female monarchs apart from their male counterparts? Women rarely transgressed the political sphere—seen as a prerogative of men—so how did three Acehnese queens survive in power until they died of natural causes, when most of their male predecessors were either assassinated or deposed? How did these female sovereigns deal with their male elites?

Anthony Reid identified three stages of development in his study of royal power in Aceh from 1550 to 1700: the period to 1589 where the orang kaya dominated power; a period of "royal absolutism" from 1589 to 1636 where power was in the hands of the rulers; and a final stage where royal power declined and there was the rise of the three *sagi* (federation of districts), each ruled by a panglima.[2] However, Reid argued that the end of royal absolutism had already set in as early as 1629 with the defeat of Iskandar Muda's forces in Melaka. The reduced skill and authority of the rulers after Iskandar Muda and the growing commercial power of the Dutch speeded up the process. Although there was no immediate change in the system of government, Iskandar Muda's successors, the milder Iskandar Thani and his widow Safiatuddin, quickly transformed

---

[1] These concepts are borrowed from Robert Bartlett, *England under the Norman and Angevin Kings, 1075–1225* (New York: Oxford University Press, 2000), see footnotes 659–61.

[2] Anthony Reid, "Trade and the Problem of Royal Power", in *Pre-Colonial State Systems in Southeast Asia*, ed. Reid and Castles, pp. 47–55.

the style. Royal absolutism[3] continued, Reid argued, but without the royal jealousy that made life hazardous to the wealthy.[4] Reid noted that in the course of Safiatuddin's long reign, fundamental changes were taking place in the balance of power that ultimately produced a radically different state structure.

Reid's analysis raises several questions. What was the context in which these shifts in royal power took place? How was power contested during the reigns of the female rulers? And how did this impact the kingdom's political order, royal power, and the fortunes of both the elites and the kingdom? Aceh, like most other polities in the region, was ruled by a monarch whose legitimacy was derived from age-old customs and tradition, lineage and religion.[5] Temporal and religious powers, in theory, rested in the ruler's hands. His royal prerogatives included political appointments and ownership of land and resources. Other political institutions were in place to assist the ruler in his task of governing. It is not known with certainty when these institutions were created, but Aceh did have executive and legislative councils and a judiciary.[6] Customs and religious traditions determined the norms and values of ideal leadership and exemplary subjects, in addition to laying out their codes of conduct, rights and responsibilities. The ancient Malay oath of allegiance or social contract was based on the ruler's task of manifesting his *daulat* (sovereignty), and his subjects' obligation to obey him and never commit *derhaka* (treason). The prescribed style of governance was one in which the ruler and elites were engaged in mutual respect and provided advice.

In reality, royal power was never absolute. The ruler was checked by the merchants and landed nobility, whose main objectives were to promote their own interests and protect their descendants. This often brought about clashes of interests, and struggles for power and wealth

---

[3] Reid, "Charismatic Queens of Southern Asia", p. 35.
[4] Reid, "Trade and the Problem of Royal Power in Aceh", p. 52.
[5] For a general discussion on the features of monarchy: W.M. Spellman, *Monarchies 1000–2000* (London: Reaktion Books, 2001), p. 17.
[6] Van Langen, *De Inrichting van het Atjehshe Staatsbestuur*, p. iv; Ali Hasjmy, *Iskandar Muda Meukuta Alam* (Jakarta: Bulan Bintang, 1975), pp. 70–3. These institutions are dealt with in greater detail in the following sections.

between royalty and nobility, as described by Reid in his first two stages (1550–1636). The tension between monarchical prerogative and noble power, however, was not necessarily a zero-sum game. The nature of royal-elite relations depended largely on the rulers' personalities and indeed, as will be shown below, royal-elite relations could be mutually beneficial, characterised by interdependence and patronage.

The nature of power and how it was wielded in Aceh depended to a considerable extent on the personalities and leadership styles of the rulers concerned and the kingdom's circumstances. The personal nature of the monarchical system made it fluid and dynamic, where powers contracted and expanded, and institutional lines blurred. A reduction in royal power did not necessarily signify its decline. Similarly, though royal absolutism might exist in theory, in reality absolutism was limited by circumstances, such as the nobility, the rulers' personalities and provincial or local conditions.[7] Provincial leaders could temper a strong ruler, such as Iskandar Muda, as the control of outlying territories and levying soldiers for war came under their purview.[8] For example, local elites on the SWC, unhappy with the trade conditions Iskandar Muda imposed, requested a change of allegiance from Aceh to the VOC in Batavia, even when they were supposedly still under the yoke of this mighty king. "Absolutist states" could be fragile as they depended on force of personality, wealth and coercion, and no permanent institutions or rule of law supported them. Iskandar Muda's "absolutism" was a function of his personality and a reaction to the powers previously wielded by the orang kaya. Sensitive to the elites' potential to dethrone or even assassinate him—as had happened to his predecessors—Iskandar Muda resorted to force to strike fear and obedience into the hearts of his elites. His insecure yet

---

[7] Reid, "Trade and the Problem of Royal Power in Aceh", pp. 45–55; J. Kathirithamby-Wells, "Restraints on the Development of Merchant Capitalism in Southeast Asia before c. 1800", in *Southeast Asia in the Early Modern Era: Trade, Power and Belief*, ed. Anthony Reid (Ithaca: Cornell University Press, 1993), p. 125.

[8] Ito, "The World of the Adat Aceh", p. 62; Augustine de Beaulieu, "Memoirs of Admiral Beaulieu's Voyage to the East Indies (1619–1622), drawn up by himself", in *Navgantium atque Itineratium Bibiotheca. Or a Compleat Collection of Voyages and Travels*, Vol. 1, trans. M. Thevenot, ed. John Harris (London: Printed for T. Bennet, 1705), p. 107.

showy disposition further inclined him to resort to terror and violent executions of those who dared to defy him, which made him more of a despot than one upholding an absolute monarchy. According to W.M. Spellman, despotic rule normally begins with military conquest and is marked by the unchecked power and capricious decision making of one individual. Despotism does not allow for political opposition, free expression, transparent rule of law, an impartial judiciary or private property free from the ruler's depredations. Under a despot, a subject has no temporal existence independent of the master and no private sphere where one's autonomy is respected.[9]

Iskandar Muda's overlord-vassal relations were exploitative and destructive. Iskandar Muda even saw Johor as Aceh's vassal after he razed Johor to the ground in 1613 and brought the crown prince to Aceh to marry his sister.[10] An incident related in the *Hikayat Aceh* illustrates how unforgiving Aceh was to vassals that wished to change allegiance or "turn away" (*berpaling*), and how she sought to punish them as traitors.[11] It describes an incident when Ghori (in Sumatra) tried to break away from the Acehnese yoke to be under Johor's protection. Iskandar Muda was furious at Ghori's disloyalty, and was so incensed with Johor's impudence that, according to the *Hikayat Aceh*, when Aceh's warriors attacked Batu Sawar—the Johor capital—the raja of Johor's pleas for mercy were ignored. The warriors were instructed to attack the capital and prevent anyone from escaping, including women and children.[12]

The *Hikayat Aceh* depicts how Iskandar Muda viewed himself and his diplomatic relations with other conquered Malay states around the Melaka Strait. In the *Hikayat Aceh*, Iskandar Muda is introduced at the age of 13 to the other nobles as the:

---

[9] Spellman, *Monarchies*, p. 20.
[10] Peter Borschberg, "Luso-Johor-Dutch Relations in the Straits of Malacca and Singapore c. 1600–1623", *Itinerario* 28, 2 (2004): 28–9; Lombard, *Le Sultanat d'Atjeh au temps d'Iskandar Muda, 1607–1636*, p. 122.
[11] Ibid., pp. 153, 171–5, 182.
[12] Ibid., pp. 175, 182.

Muhammad Hanafiah[13] of his epoch, who defeats Deli and captures Merah Miru and *enslaves* [*berhamba*] the raja of Johor and other Malay rajas, who defeats other Malay raja who does not want to *submit* [*tiada mau ta'luk ke Atjeh*] to Aceh. He has been blessed by Allah to be the caliph of Allah in the land of Atjeh Dar as-Salam and the land of Tiku and Priaman and to be just to all the subjects entrusted to him by Allah and he is the one who subjects [*mengempukan*] and makes all the other Malay rajas to be *slaves* [*hamba*] to him and to his power.[14]

Iskandar Thani was not as mild as he is commonly depicted. Indeed, his style of leadership displayed many similarities to that of his predecessor. His violent executions of those who threatened him were testimony to his cruel streak. Iskandar Thani, however, was unable to protect himself as effectively as his father-in-law, as is proven by his short-lived reign involving a highly suspicious and unexpected death. Opponents may have seen him as being too dangerous and a potential source of instability to the kingdom. Internally he supported al-Raniri's more orthodox religious stance and allowed him to undertake a bloody and divisive purge of Hamzah Fansuri and Sheikh Syamsudin's followers. Externally, despite the VOC's more threatening position towards Aceh after the conquest of Melaka, his refusal to accept and pay for the very expensive jewels he had ordered irritated the Dutch. A despot as unstable as Iskandar Thani could have brought real and lasting harm to the kingdom. Iskandar Muda, though despotic and arbitrary, had not put the kingdom in harm's way. Furthermore, Iskandar Muda was a "son of the soil", whereas Iskandar Thani was a foreigner, as far as the orang kaya were concerned. Iskandar Thani was neither supported nor feared by his orang kaya.

A different style of leadership and royal-elite relations was manifested under Aceh's women sovereigns. Both Iskandar Muda and Iskandar Thani

---

[13] Iskandar Muda was likened to Muhammad Hanafiah, brother of Hasan and Husain, grandsons of the Prophet Muhammad.

[14] Iskandar, ed., *De Hikajat Atjeh*, p. 153. Translation and emphasis are by the author of this publication.

exhibited a style that could be described as characterised by wrath and malevolence (*ira et malevolentia*). This does not signify a subjective mood, but a system by which a king could consciously and explicitly decide to deal with those who offended him by distraint to ensure obedience.[15] Royal anger could effectively, though not technically, put a man outside the law.[16] After 1641, the personalities of subsequent rulers and Aceh's circumstances brought about a different, more benevolent and moral style of leadership. In contrast to their predecessors, who tended to be predatory and punitive, the female sovereigns were more peaceful and protective of their subjects (*pax et custodia*).[17] Whether rule based on coercion and fear was more expensive and difficult to execute or whether it was perhaps offensive to women, Aceh's sultanahs preferred to ensure support based on respect and loyalty to ensure a collective stake in the kingdom's survival. In other words, soft power was preferred to hard power. Indeed, Aceh saw its longest period of peace and prosperity under its female sovereigns as a workable relationship, based on cooperation between royalty and the nobility, replaced the perpetual conflict that characterised royal-elite relations under earlier male kings.

Female rulers do not have a monopoly on pious and benevolent rule; there are pious male rulers, just as there are iron ladies or warrior queens. For example, Raja Ungu of Patani, apparently without consulting her councillors, gave orders for the mobilisation of 3,000 men to undertake a war expedition against Siam.[18] However, Aceh's sultanahs did introduce a different type of leadership and management of the orang kaya. Decision making depended less on the ruler's personality and whim, and became more regular and institutionalised, based on the rule of law as is illustrated in previous chapters. It is also important to note that royal-elite power was generally contested and fluid, but it did not swing from one extreme to another.

---

[15] Bartlett, *England under the Norman and Angevin Kings*, p. 48.
[16] J.E.A. Jolliffe, *Angevin Kingship* (London: Adam and Charles Black, 1955), pp. 96–8.
[17] *Pax et custodia* is the counterpart of *ita et malevolentia*. Ibid., p. 97.
[18] Amirell, "The Blessings and Perils of Female Rule", p. 314.

Decentralisation and Decline or Recentralisation?

According to Reid, after 1636 Aceh witnessed the crown's decline and the rise of the three sagi. The smallest socio-political unit in Aceh was the *gampung* (village), followed by the *mukim* (a district comprising several villages), then the *nanggroe/negeri* (district) headed by an *uleebalang,* a sort of commander-in-chief (holding political and military authority). The highest level was the sagi headed by a panglima.[19] There are a few explanations of the sagi's establishment. One is that it was established long before the female rulers' time, and another that it came about during the time of either the first or the second sultanah.[20] Snouck Hurgronje claimed that the sagi was developed long before the Sultanate of Dar al-Salam. An old manuscript describing the Acehnese court and its institutions, *Peta Acheh dan Susunan Kabinet Pemerintahan Acheh* (Aceh's Map and Aceh's Government Cabinet), shows the sagi already existed during the reign of Iskandar Muda. As the manuscript's copyist mentioned that the work was based on an even earlier kitab, *Tazkirah Tabakah* (Canon Law and Genealogy of Kings) the sagi could even pre-date Iskandar Muda's reign.[21]

Others disagree. It is not clear, however, whether the formation of the three sagi was undertaken during the reign of Sultanah Safiatuddin or her successor, Sultanah Naqiatuddin Syah. The *Adat Aceh*, an indigenous text, mentions the sagi was formed during the reign of Sultanah Naqiatuddin Syah.[22] K.F.H. van Langen also argued that Sultanah Naqiatuddin formed the three sagi, each under a panglima, as an attempt to centralise the administration of eastern, western and southern Aceh. Although no information is available about how these panglima were appointed or

---

[19] For a detailed explanation of the workings of the mukim, nanggroe and sagi, see Ito, "The World of the Adat Aceh", pp. 57–78.
[20] Ito, "The World of the Adat Aceh", pp. 19, 70; Tjut Rahmah M.A. Gani and Ramli Harun, *Adat Aceh* (Jakarta: Departemen Pendidikan dan Kebudayaan, Proyek Penerbitan Buku Sastra Indonesia dan Daerah, 1985), p. 29.
[21] Usman, *Kanun Syarak Kerajaan Aceh*, p.154.
[22] The *Adat Aceh*, believed to have been written in Aceh in the early seventeenth century, states otherwise. The *Adat Aceh* consists of a collection of royal edicts (*sarakata*). The first edicts were compiled in 1607, during the reign of Iskandar Muda, the second during the reign of Safiatuddin Syah in 1645 to 1646, and the third in 1708 to 1709. The *Adat Aceh* was compiled in its present format in the 1810s.

who they were, Van Langen asserted that the panglima's function was to execute royal orders and ensure that these were carried out by the numerous uleebalang in the nanggroe.[23]

Veltman and Ito took slightly different positions. Veltman argued that the sagi probably came into being during the reign of Safiatuddin Syah. They were developed with the aim of forming a counter-federation to the nobility, but assumed their more definitive form during the reign of Naqiatuddin Syah, when each sagi was headed by its own panglima.[24] Ito pointed out that the institution of the three sagi was most probably created during Safiatuddin's reign. In the 1643 *Dagh-Register*, Pieter Sourij mentioned the *drie gemeenten* (three municipalities) of the capital in relation to the disappearance of a ship's crew member. This was in contrast to Beaulieu's description in 1621 where the capital was divided into four districts, each governed by a penghulu kawal, to maintain law and order.[25]

Another intriguing question is whether the sagi was instituted by the ruler or by the powerful district uleebalang. According to Reid, Naqiatuddin Syah's reign brought a shift in the balance of power from the royal capital to the provinces, especially in Aceh's upland region, which saw the creation of the three sagi consisting of mukims (a collection of villages) 22, 25 and 26. Reid suggested that Panglima Polem, the illegitimate son of Iskandar Muda, who headed mukim 22, established the sagi. This in turn brought about the formation of the other two lowland sagi, which tilted the kingdom's economic strength in favour of rural Aceh.[26] Reid claimed that sagi mukim 22 became a source of political opposition to female rule. It also posed an economic challenge to the port capital as its economy was based on rice cultivation which, according to Reid, appeared to have been on the increase in the latter half of the seventeenth century. Reid argued that Panglima Polem's men from mukim 22 succeeded in overthrowing the fourth queen, Kamalat Syah, aided by a letter from Mecca forbidding female rule.[27] Reid concluded

---

[23] Van Langen, *De Inrichting van het Atjehsche*, p. 14.
[24] Veltman, "Nota over de Geschiedenis", pp. 67–8.
[25] Ito, "The World of the Adat Aceh", pp. 70–1.
[26] Reid, "Trade and the Problem of Royal Power", pp. 53–4.
[27] Ibid., p. 54.

that the promising movement towards institutionalised government broke down in the face of this disruptive challenge from the interior and the loss of trade to the Dutch.[28]

How can the different versions be reconciled? *Peta Aceh dan Susunan Kabinet Pemerintahan Aceh* mentions the three sagi consisting of mukims 22, 25 and 26, which indicates that this institution might have pre-dated Iskandar Muda reign.[29] There is no mention, however, in any of the sources thus far identified, that the sagi were active during Iskandar Muda's reign. Given his centralising and despotic style, this is not surprising. If this is indeed the case, in all likelihood Sultanah Safiatuddin did not create the sagi, but was responsible for reviving the institution in her efforts to reorganise administration at the provincial level. This is in line with her leadership style of decentralising power and regulating the kingdom's institutions. Thus, Peter Sourij mentions the *drie gemeenten* in 1643.

In the first few years of her reign, Sultanah Safiatuddin repossessed the land her husband had granted some orang kaya and redistributed it according to earlier grants her father made to other orang kaya, probably as a way of thanking them for supporting her policies. A *sarakata* (a document without the ruler's seal) records that in 1613, Iskandar Muda granted orang kaya Teuku Bahra six mukims in Samalanga, an area on the north coast. Sultanah Safiatuddin confirmed the orang kaya's right over this territory under the title *Seri Paduka Tuan Seberang*. She also appointed him to the position of panglima bandar, executive administrator of foreign traders and the port of Aceh. This was a new position created under Safiatuddin in a move to reduce the responsibilities and powers of the anti-Dutch laksamana.[30] Previously, the laksamana had been in charge of the palace and city security, including the port. This shows that the sultanah was no mere figurehead without the right to make appointments. When orang kaya Teuku Bahra died in 1658, his son Teuku Cik di Blang

---

[28] Ibid., p. 55.
[29] *Peta Acheh dan Susunan Kabinet Pemerintahan Aceh* [Map of Aceh and Aceh Cabinet Line-up] MS 4 (Kuala Lumpur; Bangi: Universiti Kebangsaan Malaysia, Tun Sri Lanang Library).
[30] Recall in previous chapters how the laksamana was anti-Dutch and opposed the sultanah's policy of conciliation with the VOC.

succeeded him.³¹ Another general assertion made against female rule is that the sultanahs made the position of some orang kaya hereditary, thereby surrendering the right to make appointments and diluting royal power. It is not clear in this case whether the sultanah actually appointed Teuku Cik di Blang or if he was exercising his hereditary right. Whatever the case, by keeping this position within Teuku Bahra's family, the sultanah was ensuring their loyalty to her and was in no way undermining royal power.

Another instance of the sultanah redistributing land to new stakeholders occurred in October 1642, when a dispute arose between Sri Bijaya, the eunuch in charge of keeping track of the queen's land revenue, and a *tandil* (bodyguard). A month later the sultanah resolved the issue by reclaiming all the land situated around Pidie ceded by her husband and reconfirming the legality of grants her father made. The sultanah charged the panglima of Pidie to effect this change.³² Another incident illustrates even more clearly how the sultanah authorised appointments and used land grants to reward her supporters. As mentioned in previous chapters, the sultanah adopted a pro-Dutch policy during the early years of her reign. While the Lebai Kita Kali supported her, the laksamana and the Maharaja Sri Maharaja and their followers were anti-Dutch. In November 1642, the laksamana accused the sultanah's eunuchs of dispossessing a certain person of land granted by Iskandar Thani after what he considered only a perfunctory examination. The sultanah disregarded the laksamana's complaint and instead granted this land to an uleebalang. The sultanah thwarted the Maharaja Sri Maharaja's own attempt to take some land for himself at Pidie. He had even built a canal for irrigation through these royal estates without asking the sultanah's permission. The sultanah was furious and reprimanded him

---

[31] Ito, "The World of the Adat Aceh", pp. 60–1. According to Ito, Tichelman first brought attention to the *sarakata* referred to here, and it was probably issued during the reign of Jamal al-Alam Badr al-Munir (1703–26). Quoted in Ito, G. Tichelman, "Een Atjehsche Sarakata (Afschrift van een besluit van Sultan Iskandar Muda)", in *Tijdschrift voor Indische Taal, Land, en Volkenkunde uitgegeven door het Bataviaasch Genootschap van Kunst en Wetenschappen* 73 (1933): 368–73.

[32] NA, VOC 1143, Dagh-Register gehouden bij den Oppercoopman Pieter Willemsz, 1642, f. 520V.

harshly. Unlike her father, however, it was enough that her wrath was assuaged by making him apologise by sitting with his hands on his head for two hours.[33]

Even during Iskandar Muda's "absolute" reign, there was a group of senior orang kaya in the capital and in their nanggroe who had jurisdiction and authority over the inhabitants, even though they paid tribute to the ruler.[34] Therefore, Sultanah Safiatuddin's possession and redistribution of lands was an attempt to reorganise and streamline the administration of the disparate areas under these commanders around the capital. More important, by redistributing land and titles to the orang kaya of her choice, Sultanah Safiatuddin was making sure that she received their necessary support and loyalty.

It is not surprising that her successor, Naqiatuddin Syah, continued and institutionalised the three sagi. As Van Langen argued, three panglimas were appointed during her reign to command the sagis to regulate administration in the provinces, and ensure that the uleebalang in the various nanggroe executed the sultanah's orders. He further added that these panglimas were not elected from their own people, but were appointees chosen from the royal family. Panglima Polem became the panglima sagi of mukim 22.[35] Thus the sagi had been created before the queens' reigns but was revived by Safiatuddin and institutionalised by Naqiatuddin. The ruler appointed the panglima to regulate provincial administration with some local jurisdiction of his own, but he was not elected by local authorities in opposition to the centre. This contrasts with Reid's argument that Panglima Polem created the sagi and led mukim 22, which became a source of opposition to female rule. True, there was some opposition from this mukim regarding the election of Kamalat Syah as the fourth queen in 1688, but this was perhaps owing to her youth rather than in opposition to female rule or an attempt to challenge royal power. In any event, the opposition was short-lived, and Kamalat was accepted for another decade. The opposition that led to her

---

[33] NA, VOC 1143, Dagh-Register gehouden bij den Oppercoopman Pieter Willemsz, 1642, f. 527R.
[34] Quoted in Ito, "The World of the Adat Aceh", p. 62; Beaulieu, "Memoirs of Admiral Beaulieu's Voyage", p. 107.
[35] Van Langen, *De Inrichting van het Atjehsche*, p. 15.

deposition did not originate from this mukim but from the court itself. This will be explained in greater detail in the next chapter.

Little information can be gleaned on the effect this new feature had on the workings of the government. Whether decentralisation helped to increase support for and loyalty to the sultanahs and regulate administration more effectively is unclear, but it did not bring about a decline of royal power. Moreover, the institutionalisation of the three sagi survived the four sultanahs, and the gradual increase in their political strength brought about a shift in power to the provinces, but only in the eighteenth and nineteenth centuries.[36] It appears that these seventeenth-century panglimas supported and accepted the female monarchs as they made no attempt to depose them, except for a few token protests from mukim 22. The same cannot be said of the panglimas after the sultanahs' deaths. In the eighteenth century, the panglimas Muda Setia, Imam Muda and Perbawang Syah—when they were in agreement—could set up and depose kings.[37] To illustrate, Sultan Jamal al-Alam (r. 1703–23) tried to bring Muda Setia of mukim 22 under his control because, according to the sultan, the panglima had given him umbrage. The panglima retaliated: the sultan had to retreat and was finally deposed. The three panglimas set up a panglima maharaja, with the title Johar al-Alam, as his successor. After seven days in power, this king was afflicted with a convulsive neck disorder and died. A nephew of Jamal al-Alam named Undei Tebang, having bribed the three panglimas with 30 kati of gold, was placed on the throne. After allowing him to enjoy his position for a few days, the panglimas deposed him.[38]

From "Absolute" to Limited Monarchy

According to Hamka, an indigenous manuscript entitled *Qanun al-Asji Darussalam* (Canon Law of Aceh Dar al-Salam) laid out several

---

[36] The institution of the panglima sagi played the most significant role in the political life of the sultanate in the eighteenth and nineteenth centuries. Ito, "The World of the Adat Aceh", p. 60.
[37] Marsden, *The History of Sumatra*, p. 457.
[38] Ibid., p. 458.

institutions, the duties of which were to assist the ruler in governing the kingdom. The ruler's closest advisors were the *wazir* (vizier), *perdana menteri* (prime minister) and the *kadhi malikul adil* (religious judge). The executive branch consisted of the *balai laksamana*, a kind of military arm and the *menteri dirham* and *balai furdah*, the commercial arm in charge of taxes and issuing money.[39] The legislative branch, called the *balai musyawarah*, the task of which was to swear on the consensus undertaken (*angkat muafakat*), consisted of three divisions: the *balai rungsari*; *balai gadeng*; and *balai majelis mahkamah rakyat*. The *balai rungsari* consisted of the four senior orang kaya, the *balai gadeng* was made up of 22 prominent religious scholars, and the *balai majelis mahkamah rakyat* had 73 members, each representing a mukim.[40] The *Adat Meukuta Alam* (a code of laws) states that an uleebalang, representing a particular mukim, must be elected by the village head (*keuchik*), the religious head (imam) and the elders (*orang tuha-tuha*), through consensus.[41]

It is not clear how and to what extent these institutions functioned under Iskandar Muda and Iskandar Thani, but the limitation of royal power is one significant feature of female rule in Aceh. This section illustrates that rather than reducing royal power, female rule in Aceh, to a large extent, demonstrated the political ideals laid out in indigenous political treatises, such as the *Taj us-Salatin* and the *Bustan us-Salatin*. The idea that rulers needed to share responsibilities with their ministers and discuss matters of state with them was not merely a customary ideal, but also a religious one. This responsibility stated in the *Taj us-Salatin* was reinforced in the *Bustan us-Salatin*. However, the author of the *Taj* emphasised that women rulers, in particular, were encouraged to

---

[39] (Haji Abdul Malik Karim Amrullah) Hamka, "Dewan Perwakilan Rakjat Atjeh Diabad Ketujuhbelas" [Aceh's House of Representatives in the 17th C], *Gema Islam* No. 36/37 (15 July 1963): 11–2. According to Hamka, this *Qanun al-Asji Darussalam* was written during Iskandar Muda's reign and was copied from generation to generation by the family of Tengku di Abai, Ibnu Ahmad from Habib Abubakar bin Usman bin Hasan bin Wundi Molek Sjarif Abdullah bin Sultan Djamalu'll Alam Badrul Munir Djamalullail Ba'alawi, the Sultan of Aceh of Arab descent. The last copy was rewritten in 1310 AH/1893 AD.
[40] Ibid., p. 11.
[41] Tuanku Abdul Jalil, ed., *Adat Meukuta Alam* (Banda Aceh: Pusat Dokumentasi dan Informasi Aceh, 1991), pp. 1–2.

do this. The jewel affair illustrates the decision-making process at court under the sultanah on audience days, which signalled a distinct departure from the period of her male predecessors. One feature was the orang kaya's involvement in decision making through discussion (muafakat). The custom of muafakat had long been practised in Aceh, and the tradition was ingrained in its people from the simple villager to the nobility at court.[42] It formed the basis of Acehnese decision making from the level of the gampong, to the mukim and the sagi. Snouck Hurgronje wrote that Habib Abdurrahman (one of the leading ulama in the Aceh-Dutch War, 1873–1903) told him the muafakat (Arabic-*muwafakah*) formed the strongest factor in an administrator's statecraft. The administration of the gampong was composed of three elements: the *keuchik* (village head), *teungku* (religious village head) and *ureueng tuha* (man of wisdom). All three components had a role in the discussion and decision-making process. In reviving this age-old decision-making process, the sultanahs similarly obtained advice from both the orang kaya and the ulama.

Sultanah Safiatuddin also regularised the practice of decision making by having regular audience days, and institutionalising the protocol for seating arrangements and passing resolutions. In the early years of her reign, she allowed the orang kaya free access to the inner court, which had been restricted under her male predecessors.[43] According to Ito, it is not clear that the orang kaya had to be present at court regularly during Iskandar Muda's reign. The orang kaya's duty was to guard the *dalam* (palace quarters) every third day and night. Except for a few senior orang kaya summoned to the royal presence on an ad hoc basis, there were no court audiences except on state and religious occasions. There was no need to hold audiences regularly under Iskandar Muda.[44] Jan de Meere first mentioned a Saturday audience in 1640 when he visited Iskandar Thani at court.

---

[42] Snouck Hurgronje, *The Acehnese*, Vol. 1, pp. 64–77.
[43] Ito, "The World of the Adat Aceh", p. 31, quoting Beaulieu, "Memoirs of Admiral Beaulieu's Voyage", pp. 49–50, 102–3. This may be a strange practice under female rulers, but this writer suggests that under male rulers, the harem would be the private quarters, while under a female ruler the harem would not exist.
[44] Ito, "The World of the Adat Aceh", p. 32.

The *Adat Aceh* states that the seating order of state officials based on rank was first regularised and established under Sultanah Safiatuddin Syah.[45] She also institutionalised the practice of regular audiences: Dutch envoys mentioned weekly Saturday audiences during her reign and under her successors.[46] Two English envoys, William Cawley and Ralph Ord, visiting Aceh in 1684 noted that every Saturday the orang kaya met at the palace, where all that had any business appeared before Sultanah Zakiatuddin Syah.[47] Here matters were heard and determined, and the orang kaya were silent unless the queen called upon them.[48] Saturday audiences were held regularly and were cancelled only during heavy rain and flooding, or when they fell during important religious and state festivities; in which case Sunday audiences replaced them. The sultanah and her orang kaya were only absent because of illness.[49] Many important matters were debated and discussed, and decisions were made through consensus and affirmed by all in attendance with the word "daulat".

This regularised decision-making process did not make the Aceh court free from behind-the-scenes power struggles. As we have seen, company officials reported intrigues, rumours, scandals, coups and counter-coups, and assassinations. Likewise, many matters were discussed outside the court's audience hall in the corridors and houses of the different orang kaya, in secret and in the dark of the night, away from the eyes and ears of enemies and their followers. Many power struggles were played out before they were arbitrated during audience days. Company officials also lobbied the different orang kaya with numerous gifts, and always ensured that they knew who the company's friends were before their affairs were brought up at court, manoeuvrings that helped determine when, how and who would bring up company matters on audience days. These occasions were not always peaceful or civil: the orang kaya bickered between themselves

---

[45] Ito, "The World of the Adat Aceh", p. 44; Gani and Harun, *Adat Aceh*, p. 69.
[46] Ito, "The World of the Adat Aceh", pp. 32, 43. This practice was mentioned right up until 1660, the last year when the *Dagh-Register*s of the company commissars are available.
[47] Farrington, "Negotiations at Aceh in 1684", p. 25.
[48] Ibid.
[49] The company officials attending court would faithfully report on who was present during these audiences and who was sick, especially when company affairs were discussed.

and made their protests known. However, decisions were made and the sultanah had the final say, which was still the mark of legitimacy. For example, Pieter Sourij advised the Dutch that they be content with Sultanah Safiatuddin's verbal orders and that a written contract could not always be demanded. He told his superiors that the queen was absolute, whose words and verbal orders were the law.[50] Sourij remarked in 1642 that the Acehnese were subject to a *zeer debonnaire echter ontsaghelijk* (mild but awe-inspiring) government. Each of the kingdom's councillors was respected as a king: without their counsel and advice the queen could not perform.[51] His observations captured the essence of Sultanah Safiatuddin's reign; benevolent but not weak. It also revealed the interdependent and reciprocal relationship between the sultanah and her elites. Thus, although she had absolute authority over the final decision, she adopted a more collaborative style of decision making.

Similar observations were made of Safiatuddin's successors. Thomas Bowrey explained that the men who served under Sultanah Zakiatuddin were deferential to the queen, and dared not do anything until they had thoroughly acquainted her with the matter. If she agreed, she sent her seal to signal her permission to grant their request.[52] There was, however, a conflict of opinion among European observers. William Dampier observed that though her subjects respected and revered her, the queen had little power or authority and was more of a figurehead with power resting in the hands of the orang kaya.[53] This is in contrast with the observations of a Dutch private trader residing in Aceh in the 1690s, Jacob de Roy. He went so far as to describe the kingdom as a "republic". Although the term "republic" is an exaggeration, Sultanah Kamalat, he wrote, "is a queen that presumes an unlimited power and authority and convenes the Assembly but she is obliged to wait for a favourable resolution from the

---

[50] NA, VOC 1144, Gehouden dagh-register van de heer Commissaris Pieter Sourij wegen't verrichten sijnde legatie aen den Jambysen coninck ende majesteit Atchin [Daily Register of Commissioner Pieter Sourij regarding his delegation to the Jambi's king and the majesty of Aceh], 1643, f. 680R.

[51] NA, VOC 1143, Dagh-Register off Journael gehouden bij den Pieter Sourij, 1642, f. 565V.

[52] Bowrey, *A Geographical Account*, pp. 299–300.

[53] Dampier, *Voyages and Discoveries*, p. 100.

majority of her courtiers".⁵⁴ By the last decade of the seventeenth century, the kingdom of Aceh had evolved from a despotic monarchy into one that was more consociational, characterised by a regularised and inclusive decision-making process based on consensus.

To summarise, the female rulers collaborated with the nobility, which became an outstanding feature of the political system. Another example from the region is from 1604, when Dutch Admiral Jacob van Neck described Patani as "governed by a woman who ruled very peacefully together with her councillors".⁵⁵ Decision making was through a process of musyawarah/muafakat. Given the ideal of Malay leadership that kings should discuss and take their ministers' advice, collaboration did not signify the queens' weakness, but rather their exemplary behaviour. Indeed, it made good political sense too. Most if not all local rulers had to rule over or by means of their elites or orang kaya and all had the wealth to support themselves and their armed followers. The elites also had a high sense of dignity and honour concerning their rights as individuals in the kingdom, and their responsibilities towards their ruler and kingdom. It is not surprising that they displayed resentment or even violent opposition towards rulers who violated their rights and honour.⁵⁶ A ruler who respected these would be recognised as worthy to remain their sovereign.

The assassinations and frequent toppling of the rulers and the orang kaya, and the perpetual fear and suspicion between royalty and nobility that characterised the period in the sixteenth century were minimised during the reigns of these sultanahs. Indeed, the period of women sovereigns saw the most successful and cooperative relationship between royalty and nobility. All three queens ruled until they peacefully died, except for the fourth. With the ascendance of male rulers from 1699, the aggressive and violent contest for power in the form of frequent depositions and

---

⁵⁴ "Voyage Made by Jacob Janssen de Roy to Borneo and Atcheen, 1691. Completed in 1698 in Batavia at the order of William van Oudtshoorn, Governor General of Netherlands East Indies. Translated from Dutch into English in 1816" (British Library, East India Office Records: MSS Eur/Mack (1822/5) (orig. publ. Holland, ed. Johannes Oosterwijk, 1716), p. 366.

⁵⁵ Amirell, "The Blessings and Perils of Female Rule", p. 311.

⁵⁶ Bartlett discussed different types of noble opposition to threats from the royal government: Bartlett, *England under the Norman and Angevin Kings*, p. 51.

assassinations of unpopular sultans became a feature of the political system once again in eighteenth-century Aceh. Badr al-Alam Sharif Hashim who replaced Kamalat Ayah was himself induced to abdicate after a mere two years in power. Badr al-Alam's successor, Perkasa Alam, was deposed after one year in power. His successor, Jamal al-Alam, though he managed to rule until 1723, was also deposed. Of the eight kings who succeeded him, only one died a natural death.[57] Collaborative rule during the reigns of women rulers brought about a more limited monarchy, but a stronger political system and greater stability and peace for the kingdom.

Trade under Female Rule

John Villiers argued that one important effect of the highly political character of commerce in Southeast Asia, where trade was a royal or oligarchic monopoly, was to impede the development of capitalism.[58] Kathirithamby-Wells argued that in the interests of a ruler-centred state, individual merchant interests became subordinated. Commercial monopolies exercised by rulers through their officials meant that trade procedures were arbitrary, and trade practices did not follow any form.[59] If such were the political economy and commercial ethics of Southeast Asian polities, how does one explain the periods of thriving commerce, whereby the region was a magnet to traders from all over the world? Although one can agree that the political and commercial culture of Southeast Asian polities was ruler-centric, the political and commercial ethics of each ruler differed. Denys Lombard argued that royal-elite relations may be categorised into two models; one for strong rulers and another for weak ones. In the first model, the ruler was powerful and managed his rebellious orang kaya by means of manipulation, and he

---

[57] Thomas Braddell, "On the History of Acheen", p. 20; Marsden, *The History of Sumatra*, pp. 455, 458.
[58] John Villiers, "Doing Business with the Infidel: Merchants, Missionaries, and Monarchs in Sixteenth Century Southeast Asia", in *Maritime Asia: Profit Maximisation, Ethics, and Trade Structure c. 1300–1800*, ed. Karl Anton Sprengard and Roderich Ptak (Wiesbaden: Harrassowitz Verlag, 1994), pp. 153–5.
[59] J. Kathirithamby-Wells, "Ethics and Entrepreneurship in Southeast Asia, c. 1400–1800", in *Maritime Asia*, ed. Sprengard and Ptak, pp. 175, 183.

dealt with foreign merchants via commercial monopolies and tyranny. In the second model, when the ruler was weak the orang kaya may get tired of the ruler, arrange for his assassination/execution and install another.[60] While those two models aptly described royal-elite relations during the periods when male sultans ruled Aceh, I suggest that a third model—collaborative rule—better describes the Acehnese sultanahs' rule.

With collaborative rule, commercial relations were characterised by the elites' freedom to trade and acquire wealth. According to the French Admiral, Augustine de Beaulieu, the surest ways for the orang kaya to court death during Iskandar Muda's reign was to be notable for "the good reputation they have among the people, and secondly their wealth".[61] Such royal predatory behaviour was not attested during the queens' reigns when the orang kaya were free to make profits in peace. VOC officials, such as Pieter Sourij, Pieter Willemszoon and Arnold Vlamingh, reported on the numerous orders from the orang kaya for gold thread and Japanese paper in exchange for the pepper they procured from them. Despite tremendous pressures from the Dutch for a larger share in the Perak tin trade, the sultanah protected her orang kaya's right to procure tin from Perak for their own trade. Jan Harmanszoon, who was left in charge of company affairs after Vlamingh's departure, reported that eight vessels sailed to Perak belonging to the Acehnese orang kaya. The sultanah, for her part, traded Gujarati cloth in exchange for tin in Perak.[62] Harmanszoon also noted the numerous trading ships belonging to the sultanah and her orang kaya, which traded on the SWC. The laksamana's ship, for instance, brought gold, benzoin resin and camphor from the SWC. The sultanah's ship alone brought 100 bahar of pepper from the SWC; the laksamana's had 15 bahar; and the Acehnese panglima's, 20 bahar.[63] In return, the orang kaya presented the customary tribute to the sultanah. Truijtman mentioned that the usual gifts from the shahbandars were ceremoniously

---

[60] Denys Lombard, "The Malay Sultanate as a Socio-Economic Model", in *Asian Merchants and Businessmen in the Indian Ocean and the China Sea*, ed. Denys Lombard and Jean Aubin (Oxford: Oxford University Press, 2000), pp. 116–7.
[61] Beaulieu, "The Expedition of Commodore Beaulieu to the East Indies", p. 257.
[62] NA, VOC 1155, Vervolch van Atchin's Dagh-Register, 1645, f. 460R.
[63] NA, VOC 1155, Vervolch van Atchin's Dagh-Register, 1649, f. 442V.

brought to court for her majesty's satisfaction, as part of their duty in serving her.[64] In Perak and on the SWC, Sultanah Safiatuddin successfully protected her vassals' rights to collect tolls, despite the VOC's incessant demand for toll-free privileges.

Besides protecting royal wealth and her orang kaya's interests on the one hand, Sultanah Safiatuddin had to balance the interests of foreign merchants in her port vis-à-vis the demands made both by the Dutch and English company officials. One commodity the sultanah highly prized and successfully protected from covetous VOC officials was elephants. These were not only sources of great wealth, but also symbols of power and prestige. Truijtman reported that the sultanah so jealously guarded her prized possessions that she would not consent to the VOC buying even one head of an animal. The Acehnese also did not want to jeopardise the age-old commercial links they enjoyed with the Indian traders from Coromandel and Bengal—the main elephant buyers—which they exchanged for cloth.[65] The import of elephants from Pegu, Tenasserim and Aceh had been most profitable to Masulipatnam merchants, and the rulers and generals of Golconda state were the main purchasers. Not only were the Dutch unable to gain a hold in the elephant trade, Aceh's trade in this commodity actually grew from the 1640s to 1660s. Between 1628 and 1635, around 62 elephants were shipped to Bengal and Masulipatnam. However, in 1641 alone the number of elephants exported from Aceh to Masulipatnam, Bengal, Orissa and Coromandel was 32. In 1644, Shah Shuja, the son of the Mughal Emperor Shah Jahan, sent an envoy to Aceh on a three-year appointment to arrange the purchase of 125 elephants on his behalf. Although the number fluctuated from 1641 to 1662, ranging between 2 and 32, in 1663 it reached 43.[66]

Two incidents perhaps explain why Indian—especially Gujarati— merchants continued to trade in Aceh, despite constant Dutch pressure on Sultanah Safiatuddin to expel them. Once a Courteen (EIC's rival company) ship seized two Surat junks in Aceh's harbour and threatened

---

[64] NA, VOC 1171, Dagh-Register gehouden bij den oppercoopman Johan Truijtman, 1649, f. 223V.
[65] NA, VOC 1175, Origineel Rapport aen de'Ed.hr Gouverneur Generael ende heren Raad van Indie, 1651, ff. 323V–324R.
[66] Ito, "The World of the Adat Aceh", pp. 415-6.

to confiscate them unless a ransom was paid. The sultanah reacted swiftly by imprisoning the Courteen factors until they repaid the Surat merchants for their losses. An account in the *Bustan al-Salatin* relates how the Gujarati delegation in Aceh expressed disappointment: they believed that what Iskandar Thani had promised them would not be realised after his unexpected death in 1641. They were proven wrong as not only did Safiatuddin grant exactly what was promised without a single change, she also presented the Gujarati delegates with eight elephants. One of these in particular deserves a special mention because it had four tusks![67]

The policy of welcoming traders from all nations and guaranteeing the security of their life and property was an important feature of female rule in Aceh.[68] The previous chapters have shown that Sultanah Safiatuddin was careful to maintain peaceful relations with the Dutch, keeping them as allies and allowing commerce to prosper. Dutch demands had to be accommodated and balanced, and the sultanah made sure that she took care of complaints regarding trade. In his study of the *Adat Aceh*, Ito concluded that the structure and offices of Aceh's port Dar al-Salam were put in place during Iskandar Muda's reign, and by 1621 "the bureaucratic system of the port administration had reached a level of stability".[69] Prior to that time, the main areas of administration were under a secretariat that looked after the ruler's interests, including taxable goods and the customs house officials, overseen by a *penghulu kerkun* (head scribe). The officials in charge of law and order were under the penghulu kawal. During Iskandar Muda's reign, both functions—protecting the ruler's interests and overall policing of the port—were centralised in the hands of the laksamana, the ruler's most senior representative. It was also the laksamana's duty to provide foreigners trading in Aceh with protection and assistance. According to Ito, one noticeable modification to the port bureaucracy occurred during the reign of Sultanah Safiatuddin, when in 1641 the duties of the laksamana were divided into two and a new position, the

---

[67] Iskandar, ed., *Bustan us-Salatin*, pp. 59–60.
[68] Similarly, Raja Ijau's reign saw increased trade with the outside world, and she granted permission to both the Dutch and English to open factories. Amirell, "The Blessings and Perils of Female Rule", p. 311.
[69] Ito, "The World of the Adat Aceh", pp. 278–9, 284. For a detailed description of the port officials, refer to pp. 276–324.

panglima bandar was created.⁷⁰ This official was tasked with matters related to general trade, foreign merchants and the west coast pepper trade. The sole responsibility of the laksamana (now also known as the panglima dalam) was policing and security. Sultanah Safiatuddin ensured that the orang kaya in charge of foreigners supported her policies towards them, especially the Dutch. Therefore, the post of panglima bandar went first to the previously mentioned orang kaya Seri Paduka Tuan Seberang, who held this post until his death in 1658, and not the laksamana, who at that time belonged to the anti-Dutch faction. This is contrary to Ito's observation that this change was insignificant, "nothing more than a demarcation of the dual function of the laksamana".⁷¹ In a similar move the sultanah appointed her half-brother, the Kadhi Malik al-Adil, another friend of the Dutch, to the position of Maharaja Sri Maharaja in 1645. This was when anti-Dutch sentiments in Aceh were high, owing to the company's blockade of Perak's and Aceh's harbours. It is not known what happened to the Maharaja he replaced, but it appears that the Lebai's son took over his position as the Kadhi.

The kingdom under the sultanahs saw the maintenance of strict laws on theft and murder. To this end, the Acehnese were concerned to facilitate trade and prevent a flight of capital. When the city was besieged by men from the hinterlands who opposed Sultanah Zakiatuddin's accession, Dampier wrote:

> [T]he *Shabander* sent to the Foreigners, and desired them to keep in their own Houses in the night, and told them, that whatever might happen in the City by their own civil Broyls, yet no harm should come to them.⁷²

Between the 1670s and 1690s, when there were more private merchants and free burghers trading in Aceh than the official VOC and EIC traders, Sultanah Kamalat Syah made sure they received the same protection as the employees of the European companies. This protection was not just from the sultanahs' subjects. Once the EIC requested that the queen extradite an English merchant to Madras to be put on trial for misdeeds

---

⁷⁰ Ibid., p. 291.
⁷¹ Ibid., p. 298.
⁷² Dampier, *Voyages and Discoveries*, p. 145.

he had committed. This request was refused. In addition, the sultanah was reported to have generously provided help to a Dutch ship that had caught fire by giving the merchants loans and sending them to Melaka.[73] Under Iskandar Muda and Iskandar Thani, goods and treasures on wrecked ships were confiscated.

The jewel affair illustrates how Sultanah Safiatuddin was unwilling to see her treasury depleted on useless adornments or "dead assets". Pieter Sourij reported that the Lebai Kita Kali told him it was in the nature of woman not willing to see her treasury depleted.[74] Neither did Aceh's female rulers waste the kingdom's resources on weaponry. The import of guns on a large scale had taken place around 1540 with the influx of military assistance from Ottoman Turks in the form of guns and gunners.[75] In the 1560s, during Aceh's holy war against the Portuguese in Melaka, al-Kahar imported more weapons in the form of heavy bronze guns, small guns and ammunition. While Sultanah Safiatuddin used elephants for trade, her father prized and kept them as war-elephants, 900 in number at least, according to Beaulieu. Iskandar Muda demanded such stringent training for these war-elephants that two of his nobles were nearly castrated for failing to get ready the animals at the set time. Apart from slaves and the elephant corps, there is no indication of a standing army: the orang kaya were obliged to raise the army needed for the ruler as part of their tribute to him, but Iskandar Muda had to provide their guns and ammunition. Iskandar Muda's glorious army was nearly wiped out during the 1629 attack on Melaka. In 1633, recovering from this disastrous setback, he began to rebuild his forces by constructing 30 galleys and purchasing artillery from the Dutch. By 1635, there was an adequate naval force, though it was not as strong as the pre-1629 fleet. Iskandar Thani continued his father-in-law's practice of accumulating guns, and he bought iron from the Dutch. Jan de Meere reported that Iskandar Thani queried him about the methods of founding guns and making mortar

---

[73] "Voyage Made by Jacob Janssen de Roy to Borneo and Atcheen, 1691", p. 328.
[74] NA, VOC 1143, Dagh-Register off Journael gehouden bij den Pieter Sourij, 1642, f. 560V.
[75] Anthony Reid, "Sixteenth Century Turkish Influence in Western Indonesia", *Journal of Southeast Asian History* 10, 3 (1969): 402–3, quoted in Ito, "The World of the Adat Aceh", p. 47.

shells, and the destructive power of these weapons.[76] It is not known to what extent the artillery forces were rebuilt, but according to Ito, they did not seem to have been restored to the pre-1629 scale, owing to difficulties in replacing manpower and the decline in royal power after Iskandar Muda's death.[77]

This accumulation of weaponry appears to have stopped during the reigns of the female rulers, as no European sources mentioned the reconstruction of Acehnese forces from 1641. In 1661, Sultanah Safiatuddin bought 60 metal guns (*metale stukies geschut*) from the English, most likely for defensive purposes.[78] This was at a time when tensions were high between the VOC and the sultanate, and when the Acehnese elites were expecting a war with the Dutch. Nevertheless, this was an exception rather than the rule, as the sultanah preferred to tackle problems with diplomacy rather than guns.

In the 1690s, De Roy commented on the lack of fortifications in Aceh, and concluded that the VOC could easily capture and subdue Aceh and with little expense.[79] Although this might well have been the case, European companies saw no reason to take Aceh by force, as the sultanahs provided no reason or pretext for them to do so. Aceh remained politically stable and traders were able to make money and wealth without many problems. The testimony from both local and foreign accounts described the kingdom as economically thriving during the queens' reigns. According to the *Bustan us-Salatin*, Aceh's port was never quiet during Sultanah Safiatuddin's reign, but busy with ships, junks and boats from many foreign lands that came to trade. The author of the *Bustan* elaborated that under her rule, food items were cheap, and the kingdom was prosperous.[80] The *Bustan* mentions the important find of abundant gold deposits during the sultanah's rule and claims that this increased her kingdom's revenue.[81] These deposits were mined with the utmost care, and

---

[76] NA, VOC 1133, Dagh-Register gehouden bij den Commissaris Jan de Meere, 1640, f. 125V.
[77] Ito, "The World of the Adat Aceh", p. 55.
[78] Chijs, *Dagh-Register*, 1661, p. 16; Ito, "The World of the Adat Aceh", p. 126.
[79] "Voyage Made by Jacob Janssen de Roy to Borneo and Atcheen, 1691", p. 369.
[80] Salleh, ed., *Bustan al-Salatin*, p. 43.
[81] Ibid., p. 63.

no foreigners were allowed to know where they were or set foot there. De Roy attested that as late as the 1690s, gold was still exported in very large quantities from three excellent goldmines.[82] Acehnese coins (*mas*) were minted and the sultanah had the right to coin money without any interference from her ministers. The Acehnese were reputed to be richer than most both because of these goldmines, and the frequent visits by traders and merchants. In 1696, the largest ships carrying merchandise to Aceh would be emptied in the course of three months owing to the high level of consumption; every article was sold promptly and paid for in ready money or gold dust.[83]

"Stranger-Queens"[84]

The above sections illustrate that there are distinct differences in leadership styles between the women sovereigns and their male predecessors. This does not mean that these differences were necessarily owing to their sex and a gendered leadership style. Nevertheless, as I shall illustrate below, there are features which could be unique to women sovereigns, which makes "queenship" a useful and distinct concept to be studied as another model of leadership in pre-colonial Southeast Asia. Although more research is needed, this study on the Acehnese queens shows that there are similar features shared by women rulers, such as the case of the Bhopal queens using piety as moral capital as mentioned in the previous chapter. Francis Bradley's study on Raja Ijau of Patani showed that she too actively took part in trade negotiations, protected private property and established opportunities conducive to trade.[85] Just as Safiatuddin

---

[82] Dampier, *Voyages and Discoveries*, pp. 84–9; "Voyage Made by Jacob Janssen de Roy to Borneo and Atcheen, 1691", p. 356.

[83] "Voyage Made by Jacob Janssen de Roy to Borneo and Atcheen, 1691", p. 361.

[84] The concept of "Stranger-Kings" outlined by Marshall Sahlins provides an important model for rethinking the early modern history of insular Southeast Asia. Fernandez-Armesto's version of this concept is where the Stranger-King model is extended to Stranger-hood. Felipe Fernández-Armesto, "The Stranger-Effect in Early Modern Asia", in *Shifting Communities and Identity Formation in Early Modern Asia*, ed. Leonard Blussé and Felipe Fernández-Armesto (Leiden: Leiden University Press, 2003).

[85] Francis Bradley, "Piracy, Smuggling and Trade in the Rise of Patani, 1490–1600", *Journal of the Siam Society* 96 (2008): 45.

had a unique way of dealing with her errant orang kaya, making him apologise with his hands on his head as a punishment, Raja Ijau too dealt with her male elites in a manner in which no king would. The *Hikayat Patani* relates that her orang kaya, Bendahara Kayu Kelat, had gathered about 5,000 men to march to the palace to oppose Raja Ijau's rule. When the bendahara reached the palace steps, Raja Ijau, dressed in a green dress and a golden headscarf, went to greet him at the top of the steps accompanied by her *bentara* (herald) and court ladies. She threw her golden scarf to the bendahara, who immediately caught it and wrapped it round his head. He then placed his kris on the ground and, kneeling, he paid obeisance to the queen by uttering the phrase "*daulat tuanku*", literally "long live the king".[86]

As for the Acehnese sultanahs, the very fact that they were women lent a different dynamic to royal-elite relations from the usual male-male relations. Simply being women set them apart from the male elite, and this gave a distinctively gendered overtone to royal-elite relations. This enabled them to function as something of an outsider/stranger, and provided an excellent platform from which they could act as arbiters in managing the different male elite factions at court. The concept of stranger-hood, formulated by Felipe Fernández-Armesto, offers an important schema to help explain the various numerous cultural encounters in the early modern era and to understand the formation of early colonial societies. His stranger-as-arbitrator or stranger-as-king model helps us understand why strangers were entrusted with power. The female ruler here could be seen as a stranger in two senses. She was differentiated by her sex, which was a novel development in the history of Acehnese sovereigns, and she did not belong to any of the male-dominated political factions, and thus was not bound to any. As a result, she was more likely to be accepted as non-partisan and a mediator.

In his study of the Sultanate of Aceh in the seventeenth century, Takeshi Ito observed that "the Sultanate under Safiyyat al-Din was undermined by the Dutch who pursued an aggressive commercial policy and promoted the disintegration of political unity and royal power by

---

[86] Salleh, ed., *Hikayat Patani*, pp. 29–31.

causing discord and at times power struggles amongst senior orangkaya".[87] Thus far, there is no conclusive evidence pointing to the decline of either royal power or the kingdom under these female sovereigns. The assertion that Aceh declined under female rulers will be explored further in the last section of this book. It suffices to say here that factionalism within the orang kaya's ranks did exist during the period of women rulers, as illustrated in Chapter 3. However, this had been a prominent feature of Aceh's politics even before the sultanahs' reigns and the arrival of the Dutch. Indeed factionalism was more politically destructive during the time of the male rulers as when the sultans took sides, it often resulted in bloodshed and fatalities. For example, the orang kaya were plagued by violent religious debates, and were hopelessly disunited during the reigns of Iskandar Muda and Iskandar Thani. The Dutch exploited these feuding factions to advance their interests at court.

Viewed from another perspective, however, such factions need not always be destructive. They represented the plurality of interests in the kingdom, providing some degree of checks and balances to each other, with the sultanah acting as the final arbiter and balancer. As the jewel and Perak affairs illustrate, the Dutch demands split the elites, who differed in how they should respond to the Dutch pressure. Nevertheless, these differences did not bring about political disintegration as these elites and the sultanah had to compromise for the kingdom's sake. Whether factionalism led to political instability and the kingdom's decline depended on how the ruler managed these divisions. Dutch factors present at the court observed that jealousies were kept in check, and the sultanah was successful in maintaining peace and authority as the final arbiter.[88] More significantly, the male elites accepted the queen's balancing act between the different factions, and the arbiter and mediator role. The coup and counter-coup of the 1650s show that while the orang kaya factions were killing each other, the sultanah was able to intervene at crucial moments to prevent matters from getting more out of hand; her presence was necessary to restore stability and legitimacy. This suggests that the sultanah was not a mere figurehead, restrained by obligations to the nobility. The

---

[87] Ito, "The World of the Adat Aceh", pp. 103–4.
[88] Chijs, *Dagh-Register*, 1641–42, pp. 96, 123.

queen's presence, on the contrary, was crucial to preventing differences in the nobility from degenerating into civil wars that could have consigned Aceh to the same fate as that of so many other polities in the region. In a private confession to a Dutch factor, one of the orang kaya admitted that he would not have been able to last for even an hour without the sultanah as he had so many enemies.[89]

Not all the Dutch officials held a positive view of the sultanah's reign. Pieter Willemszoon noted that the orang kaya were so partisan that they shunned each other, and their followers were likewise mutually suspicious. Willemszoon predicted that the government would not last long in peace under the "soft and gentle" government of the queen because this "bold and strong" nation had to be ruled the hard way. The more fear and awe the elites knew, he commented, the less resistance they would offer.[90] Willemszoon's prediction did not come true, of course, and Sultanah Safiatuddin's role of moderator and arbiter served to enhance her unique position and her ability to survive on the throne for 35 years. Her leadership style was continued by her female successors, and this model of queenship ensured Aceh's stability for almost 60 years.

Network of Women and Eunuchs

Another feature of female rule that may be considered unique to queenship was the availability and utilisation of a supporting network of women. This is somewhat similar to a group of male confidantes that some sultans nurtured to act as their closest trustees in balancing hostile nobles. Eunuchs may not be unique to female rule, but under the queens they appeared to have extensive functions.[91] Sultanah Safiatuddin established a network of these two groups to assist her in her execution of her policies and act as a counter-weight to the male elites. According to Hamka, Sultanah Safiatuddin made a royal decree in 1649 renewing the members

---

[89] NA, VOC 1143, Dagh-Register off Journael gehouden bij den Pieter Sourij, 1642, ff. 559V–560R.
[90] NA, VOC 1143, Dagh-Register gehouden bij den Oppercoopman Hr Pieter Willemsz, 1642, f. 511V.
[91] A eunuch is referred to by the Portuguese term *capado* in Dutch sources.

of the *balai majelis mahkamah rakyat* and added 17 women members. The *Qanun al-Asji Darussalam* lists the names of these women: Si Njak Bunga, Si Halifah, Si Sanah, Hidajat, Munabinah, Siti Tjahaya, Mahkijah, Si Bukih, Si Nyak Ukat, Si Manjak Puan, Nadisah, Si Djibah, Uli Puan Siti Awan, Si Njak Angka, Si Njak Tampli, Si Mawar and Si Manis.[92] It is unclear whether the sultanah appointed these women or they were elected by the people in their own mukim.

Although it is difficult to verify the above source and there is no other mention of these women members at court in indigenous sources, there are two references to women council members in Pieter Willemszoon's and Arnold Vlamingh's *Dagh-Register* (discussed in the next section). Willemszoon was in Aceh as the resident and senior VOC trader after Sourij's mission departed in August 1642, when Dutch-Aceh relations were tense because of the jewel affair. When Sourij left Aceh, the task of persuading the orang kaya to accept the jewels was left to Willemszoon.[93] In early November, Willemszoon got into financial trouble and tried to borrow 2,000 taels from the orang kaya. Given the sour relations at that time, the anti-Dutch Maharaja Sri Maharaja refused to lend him any money and instead told him to request this from the sultanah.[94]

After a month of unsuccessfully lobbying the orang kaya, Willemszoon was desperate and decided to go to court to request the 2,000 taels. He reported that despite making obeisance to the orang kaya four times, he received no hearing. For good measure, the orang kaya told him that her majesty had no money because she had paid 4,000 for the jewels and still owed the Dutch 6,000.[95] However, Maharaja Adonna Lilla, the company's friend and sultanah's favourite eunuch, provided him with a ray of hope. The eunuch told him that one of the principal woman members of the council (*een der principaale Raadt Vrouwen*) had said that her majesty would grant Willemszoon's request on the condition that he gave her and

---

[92] Hamka, "Dewan Perwakilan", p. 11.
[93] NA, VOC 1143, Dagh-Register gehouden bij den Oppercoopman Hr Pieter Willemsz, 1642, ff. 526V–527R.
[94] NA, VOC 1143, Dagh-Register gehouden bij den Oppercoopman Hr Pieter Willemsz, 1642, f. 516V.
[95] NA, VOC 1143, Dagh-Register gehouden bij den Oppercoopman Hr Pieter Willemsz, 1642, f. 526V.

her followers gifts as customary. She and two other women councillors would see to it that the Dutch obtained the 2,000 tael in Acehnese mas.[96] A few days later Willemszoon received word that these ladies wanted him to go to court and make obeisance to the sultanah that Saturday, and without doubt the Dutch would see their request granted. The Dutch were reminded again that they should be mindful of these women councillors.[97] Unfortunately, Willemszoon did not report on the outcome of this affair; however, this significantly illustrates another power base Safiatuddin used to counter the male elites.

A powerful woman at court, related to the royal family and a close confidant of Sultanah Safiatuddin, was Putra Dewa. Under strong pressure from the orang kaya, she was exiled to the Maldives in 1653 after being accused of arranging a sexual dalliance between the sultanah and her Muslim tutor.[98] It is difficult to ascertain whether the reason for her exile was owing to her involvement in this alleged scandal or the orang kaya's fear of her increasing power at court. As Safiatuddin's very throne was in danger in 1653, the sultanah may have relented and allowed her close confidant to be taken from her side.[99] By 1660, Sultanah Safiatuddin was once again secure on the throne. She decided that enough time had lapsed for her to grant a pardon, so Putra Dewa—now an old woman—returned from the Maldives that year in a Surat ship named the *Moessady* belonging to a Mamer Talcki, a resident in Aceh. It appears that during her exile she had gone on *hajj* (Islamic pilgrimage to Mecca), as the Dutch sources mention that she had visited the grave of *Mahomet* (Muhammad). They also report that the sultanah was very happy that she had returned to Aceh, though the orang kaya wished she had not.[100]

It appears that these powerful women who held the purse strings, and who the orang kaya saw as threats, were influential at court as late as the

---

[96] NA, VOC 1143, Dagh-Register gehouden bij den Oppercoopman Hr Pieter Willemsz, 1642, f. 527R.
[97] NA, VOC 1143, Dagh-Register gehouden bij den Oppercoopman Hr Pieter Willemsz, 1642, f. 528R.
[98] Andaya, "A Very Good-Natured but Awe-Inspiring Government", p. 72.
[99] See Chapter 3.
[100] Chijs, *Dagh-Register*, 1661, p. 17.

1690s. De Roy noted that in the council of ministers during Sultanah Kamalat Syah's reign, political power correlated to wealth. Besides the politically powerful and wealthy women, more of the male elites in the council were supported by their wealthy wives and their daughter in-laws when their sons married into rich women's families.[101]

Sultanah Safiatuddin established a women's network of sorts, together with her eunuchs, to assist her in the execution of her policies and to act as a counter-weight to the male elites. Eunuchs were common in most eastern courts, such as the Ottoman's and Mughal's, and their general functions were to serve guests at court, ladies in the harem, bear messages and participate in royal processions. Eunuchs were not prevalent in Malay courts. The term *sida-sida* used in the *Sejarah Melayu* and *Misa Melayu* and translated as "eunuchs" referred to court officials who had access to the inner chambers of the court and whose tasks, among others, were to supervise ceremonies and bear letters. According to Leonard Andaya, however, these *sida-sida* were most probably effeminate men who may have been a residual pre-Islamic priestly class associated with royalty. In Aceh, the eunuchs would have indeed been eunuchs and the kingdom was unique in this region in using eunuchs extensively, drawing inspiration from other great Muslim empires. This practice was continued during the reigns of the sultanahs where the commander of the eunuchs was given the title Maharaja Setia and another eunuch served as the queen's bookkeeper.[102] During Safiatuddin's reign, a few eunuchs rose to positions of political prominence. As a key intermediary between the sultanah and the Dutch envoys in the jewel affair, Maharaja Adonna Lilla was critical to achieving an outcome favourable to the sultanah, at the expense of the hardliners headed by the laksamana. Enjoying free access—from the inner court recesses to the orang kaya's houses, foreign factories and lodges—eunuchs were uniquely positioned to report on the latest rumours and intrigues, and to convey the sultanah's instructions directly, outside the formality of the audience hall. Although there is less information on the eunuchs' roles at court

---

[101] "Voyage Made by Jacob Janssen de Roy to Borneo and Atcheen, 1691", p. 367.
[102] Leonard Andaya, "Aceh's Contribution to Standards of Malayness", *Archipel* 61, 1 (2001): 29–68, esp. 56–8.

during the reigns of Safiatuddin's successors, they continued to serve in varying capacities. Describing the situation in Aceh during the reigns of Sultanah Naqiatuddin and Sultanah Zakiatuddin, Thomas Bowrey related that about 500 women and eunuchs attended to them. He mentioned that Sultanah Zakiatuddin had several eunuchs "of very acute wit about her that advise with her to condescend to what is requisite".[103] Although these eunuchs are mentioned in both European and indigenous sources, unfortunately, none shed light on their origins.[104]

Women's Interests—Mrs Harmanszoon and European Fashion

Typical of a court ruled by a woman, but certainly not of her male predecessors, was the personal interest the sultanah took in the envoys the company appointed to the Acehnese court. Some of Sultanah Safiatuddin's favourites, such as Willem Harmanszoon and Balthasar Bort, were personally invited to stay in Aceh with their families. So fond was she of Bort that there was a rumour she wished to marry him but the company prevented it.[105] When she heard Harmanszoon had brought his wife and 8-year-old son to Aceh with him, the sultanah invited them to her palace even while they were still on board their ship. Indeed, they were taken to the palace for an informal audience with her before even Arnold Vlamingh, the commissar in charge of the Dutch delegation, was summoned to court for a formal audience.

On 29 July 1644, just four days after the company delegation had arrived, a number of female slaves belonging to Sri Bidia Indra—the main Acehnese envoy to Batavia and a good friend of the company—came to the company's lodge to fetch Mrs Harmanszoon to his house. Sri Bidia Indra's wife and daughter accompanied Mrs Harmanszoon, with

---

[103] Bowrey, *A Geographical Account*, p. 299.
[104] In classical Malay literature, the term *sida-sida* sometimes refers to eunuchs. See Leonard Y. Andaya, "The Seventeenth-Century Acehnese Model of Malay Society", in *Reading Asia: New Research in Asian Studies*, ed. Frans Husken and Dick van der Meij (Richmond, Surrey: Curzon Press, 2001), p. 94.
[105] Marsden, *The History of Sumatra*, p. 448.

a stately procession of female slaves, to court. Mrs Harmanszoon, placed in a palanquin, rode an elephant which was expensively dressed in the Acehnese manner. She remained at the palace for four hours. Vlamingh wrote that Mrs Harmanszoon said she was treated with many dishes, in a very friendly manner, and given gifts, and she had a nice discussion with the sultanah and her noble women (*groote vrouwen*). Jan Harmanszoon also reported that when he sent his wife to court there were very powerful women who were with the sultanah day and night, and he had to prepare gifts for them, too.[106] Sultanah Safiatuddin invited Mrs Harmanszoon to the palace again on Sunday and requested that she wear clothes in which Dutch women would attend church. Mrs Harmanszoon was then taken back to the company's lodge.[107]

Mrs Harmanszoon returned once more to the palace, again at the sultanah's request. She was asked to bring her son along, but when he saw the formidable escort of women bearing gold and silver weapons, he was too frightened to go. The sultanah, upon hearing this, sent the boy a special gift of Acehnese clothing. On this occasion, one is reminded of the *Bustan*'s characterisation of her reign: "she loves her subjects as a mother would her children".[108] Mrs Harmanszoon remained at court for the whole day. Vlamingh tried to exploit this women's network or affinity by asking Mrs Harmanszoon to get the sultanah's ear. Vlamingh must have been rather impressed by this women's network as there were discussions regarding the suitable gifts that Mrs Harmanszoon should give to the sultanah, so the company need no longer waste money on gifts for the orang kaya and eunuchs to advance their agenda. The Dutch finally decided to present the sultanah with a beautiful Spanish wine glass and gold and silver cloth, as the Dutch were told that the sultanah already had an over-abundance of gold, silver, gems and cloth. Nothing seems to have come of the relationship between these two women. Nevertheless, these visits happened two to three more times according to Vlamingh, who was

---

[106] NA, VOC 1157, Dagh-Register gehouden bij den Arnold Vlamingh, 1644, ff. 576V–577V. It is unfortunate that there is no account of this event, or the Acehnese court written by Mrs Harmanszoon.
[107] Ibid.
[108] Salleh, ed., *Bustan al-Salatin*, pp. 43–4.

jealous of Mrs Harmanszoon's privileged position and complained about how men were shut out at this prudish Muslim court.[109]

In 1684, two EIC representatives from the Madras Council, Ralph Ord and William Cawley, went to Aceh to negotiate for an English fortified settlement in Aceh. During their second audience with Sultanah Zakiatuddin, she asked the two Englishmen to sit nearer to her "… the Queen was pleased to order us to come nearer, where Her Majestye was very inquisitive into the use of our wearing perrywigs".[110] She was fascinated by them and asked the Englishmen about their use. Then the sultanah requested that Ord, if it was of no inconvenience to him, take off the wig so that she could see how he looked without it, to which the English gentleman kindly obliged. It is safe to say that discussions with envoys' wives and children about European fashion and an interest in wigs would be unique to women rulers!

Politics of Entertainment

One tradition the sultanahs did continue, following their male predecessors' court protocol, was receiving diplomats, envoys, important merchants and guests of the kingdom. Under Iskandar Muda and Iskandar Thani, Aceh had established an elaborate procedure, the ceremony of which was comparable to the ones at the Ottoman and Mughal courts. European sources from the second half of the seventeenth century are unanimous in their praise of the sultanahs' impeccable hospitality.

VOC envoys, such as Sourij and Vlamingh, reported at length on how Sultanah Safiatuddin treated them. In the balai, they were served on silver and gold dishes meals of seven to nine courses. The foreign missions and local guests were seated on fine carpets in the palace courtyard before the sultanah's lodgings, entertained and served with a large golden box of betel leaves, fruits and areca nuts. The whole ceremony continued with merrymaking, dancing and feasting. To sweeten the palate, sweetmeats, delicacies and excellent fruits were served. The queen's eunuchs placed the presents brought by the foreign ambassadors on golden vessels or trays,

---

[109] NA, VOC 1157, Dagh-Register gehouden bij den Arnold Vlamingh, 1644, f. 578V.
[110] Farrington, "Negotiations at Aceh in 1684", p. 27.

over which were carried gilded pavilions to flank and protect them. If there was an official letter from any of the foreign representatives, it was placed on a silver plate covered with yellow silk cloth and carried on an elephant with great ceremony, attended by the sultanah's favourites. The mission bringing the letter would accept gifts, and the envoy was given a suit of silk clothes and a turban. On taking leave, the envoy would ride on a richly-decorated elephant back to his dwelling or factory, accompanied by orang kaya and other important men of the court. This was a grand procession with music from pipes and drums, and flags carried by footmen who, according to Bowrey, would lance any native who did not move out of the way after being told to do so. As the grand procession passed the city, many other merchants would sprinkle rosewater on them as a mark of honour and respect. When the parade finally ended at the foreign diplomat's house or the factory, they alighted from the elephants and exchanged ceremonial compliments and good wishes, before the orang kaya took their leave.

Entertainment for the guests was as varied as the food and drink, and included elephant and tiger fights over which the queen presided.[111] Vlamingh recounted the magnificent spectacle of these fights staged to welcome VOC officials, describing how the sultanah appeared from the palace accompanied by her female maidens to sit on a stone building in the palace square to watch the fight.

The sultanahs' reigns were also characterised by frequent festivities and amusements, including hunting, which could be as elaborate as the court ceremonies. Sourij described an excursion to a *speelhoff* (a place for amusement) headed by Sultanah Safiatuddin, where members of the elites and foreign delegates took part in the singing, dancing and bathing activities, not to mention the sumptuous seven-course meals.[112] On another occasion, the sultanah, the elites and foreign guests went to a beautiful field with a lake where there was bathing and fishing. Willemszoon mentioned an expedition the sultanah led to a place called Indrapuri about three hours from the palace. The elaborate procession

---

[111] NA, VOC 1157, Dagh-Register gehouden bij den Arnold Vlamingh, 1644, ff. 598R–598V.
[112] NA, VOC 1143, Dagh-Register gehouden bij den Pieter Sourij, 1642, ff. 566V–567R.

involved all the sultanah's horses, elephants and royal ornaments. After arriving at a great river near a village, they settled at a very entertaining *speelhuis* (a place for amusement), where the orang kaya wives and the eunuchs went fishing, and musicians played gold and silver trumpets.[113] The sultanah was also fond of singing and dancing, and invited the Dutch to join the Acehnese in enjoying these pleasures. The Dutch were not too happy that they had to add dancers and entertainers to their lists of gifts. Nevertheless, these relaxed occasions, numerous under female rule, provided excellent opportunities for the Acehnese elites to forge friendships and alliances with these foreign representatives and merchants.

For these outings and festivities, not only were the foreign envoys, important merchants and the orang kaya invited, but so were the other courtiers and ladies at court. Sourij, who joined one of her fishing trips, described the merry ceremony with lots of dancing and feasting where her majesty's ladies-in-waiting served him fish they had caught themselves.[114] Vlamingh reported that on another of the queen's fishing trips, he was served fish caught by her majesty![115] On another occasion, the sultanah invited the Dutch envoys to a celebration organised by one of the sultanah's officials to honour her. Vlamingh described the festive atmosphere vividly when he related that special small paper houses filled with various types of delicacies were laid out, but alas the festivities had to stop abruptly because of pouring rain. Once the Dutch envoy described how the whole palace was lit with candles: one could just imagine the whole spectacle.

While the sultanahs were impeccable hosts to foreigners and guests, they did not forget their subjects during festivities. Throwing huge parties for the public was part of sharing the kingdom's bounty with its subjects. It reflected the monarch's generosity and increased the subjects' loyalty and allegiance to the throne. In his study of Malay court rituals, A.C. Milner suggested that ceremonial functions, public processions and state

---

[113] NA, VOC 1143, Dagh-Register gehouden bij den Oppercoopman Hr Pieter Willemszoon, 1642, ff. 523V–524R.
[114] NA, VOC 1143, Dagh-Register gehouden bij den Pieter Sourij, 1642, ff. 568V–569R.
[115] NA, VOC 1157, Dagh-Register gehouden bij den Arnold Vlamingh, 1644, ff. 604V–605R.

festivities were not meant for the rulers to enjoy, but were part and parcel of a raja's work.[116] Thus, attending these monarch-sponsored festivities to enjoy themselves (*bersuka-suka*) was part of a subject's duty.[117] Sultanah Safiatuddin's preparations for and organisation of her husband's funeral was one of the first tasks she undertook when she became queen.[118] The *Bustan* describes in detail how this procession successfully completed the extremely important task of ensuring the king's proper burial rites were carried out. The *Bustan* also details seemingly unimportant aspects of the funeral procession in which spectators took delight in the ceremony's almost carnival atmosphere, which featured floats and giant puppets of mythical animals and monsters. Many people came from great distances to witness this grand spectacle. Alms in the form of gold and silver foil and jewels were strewn on the streets in such large amounts that subjects who collected them could actually become rich. According to Reid, the popular enjoyment of royal festivals was another indication of the power and cosmic beneficence of a great ruler, or simply subjects having a great time when a generous ruler was on the throne. The multitude of subjects who attended these state-sponsored festivities demonstrated how populous the realm was, but more important, it testified to the ruler's skill and greatness.[119]

Conclusion

It is not possible to demonstrate conclusively that power and leadership style are gendered. Piety, prudence, benevolence and collaboration may be prominent features of female rule, but were not unique to women rulers. However, there is enough evidence to show that there are significant differences between the leadership styles of the Acehnese sultanahs and their male predecessors. As "stranger-queens" in their own land, these female rulers stood apart from the male orang kaya, and royal-elite relations were markedly different under male and female rulers. The

---

[116] Milner, *Kerajaan*, p. 45.
[117] Ibid., pp. 23–4.
[118] See Chapter 2 for details of the funeral procession.
[119] Reid, *Southeast Asia*, Vol. 1, p. 182.

sultanahs' advantage was that they had a unique arbiter-mediator role and their relationships with the elites were free from macho rivalries. Establishing a network of powerful women confidants and eunuchs, a keen interest in fashion, and showing care to envoys' wives and children were distinctively feminine traits. It appears that there is an institution of "queenship" that differs from "kingship".

Indeed, at the time "queenship" was actually recognised, and it appears to have been firmly established in the kingdom after a few decades of female rule. In the 1670s, Bowrey observed that Aceh had, for a considerable amount of time, been governed by a queen and the very title of king proved to be nauseous to them.[120] In the 1680s, Dampier noted the English residents were of the opinion that "a queen had ruled Aceh since the beginning, from the antiquity of the present constitution, it was believed that the Queen of Sheba was the queen of this country".[121]

The male elites, both local and foreign, had a positive view of the sultanahs, especially Safiatuddin, the longest reigning queen. The VOC official Jacob Compostel once described her as having more royal worth than her predecessors.[122] Al-Raniri in the *Bustan* echoed this positive view and stated that she demonstrated exemplary conduct, being merciful to her subjects and a blessing to the indigent. She loved her subjects as a mother would her children. She loved and respected the ulama and all the descendants of the Prophet, and she accorded them with rewards and gifts.[123] It is rare praise indeed that both men, so culturally distant, could come to a similar assessment of a female sovereign in an era when it was not fashionable to discriminate in favour of women.

---

[120] Bowrey, *A Geographical Account*, pp. 295–6.
[121] Dampier, *Voyages and Discoveries*, p. 99.
[122] Chijs, *Dagh-Register*, 1641–42, p. 123.
[123] This is my translation of the text. See Salleh, ed., *Bustan al-Salatin*, p. 43; Iskandar, ed., *Bustan us-Salatin*, p. 59.

chapter

7 The End of Female Rule and Its Legacy

Safiatuddin's Death and Her Three Female Successors

A single short sentence in the *Generale Missiven* reports that Sultanah Safiatuddin died in 1675. It appeared that she died peacefully from old age (she would have been 63 years old by then), and her death was not accompanied by crisis or chaos at court, unlike with the passing of Iskandar Thani. The election of the second queen, Sultanah Naqiatuddin, was smooth. This testified to the level of political stability in the kingdom at the time. She ruled for three years until her death.[1] Sultanah Inayat Syah Zakiyyat al-Din Syah followed, again with no opposition from the orang kaya and ruled a decade before her death in 1688.[2] After her death, the last of the four queens, Kamalat Syah, was installed; however, by this time there was opposition to another female on the throne, which is detailed below. Although she managed to stay on the throne until 1699, unlike her three predecessors she was deposed by a male challenger of Arab descent, Sultan Badr al-Alam Syariff Hashim Jamal al-Din (r. 1699–1702).[3]

---

[1] Lombard's study stops at the first Sultanah Taj al-Alam; Djajadiningrat, "Critisch", p. 214.
[2] Ibid.
[3] Ibid., p. 192.

The Last Female Ruler of Aceh—Kamalat Syah

Contemporary indigenous and European records are silent on how Kamalat Syah stepped down from the throne in 1699. Did she abdicate willingly, was she forced or was she deposed? The only passing mention of a possible deposition is found in the *Adat Aceh*, which states that "she is deposed by all the Ministers and all the people because of a letter from Mecca from the Qadhi Malik al-Adil stating that a female raja is not within the laws".[4] In view of the long acceptance of female rulers, and the broad convergence of customs and traditions in favour of their legitimacy, this contention requires examination.

According to P.J. Veth, there had been opposition to female rule from a group influenced by Arabs in Aceh who believed that female rule was against the tenets of Islam. He called them the *priester partij/ Arabische partij*. Against this group was the orang kaya faction who, according to Veth, acted as protectors of ancestral institutions whom he referred to as the *nationale partij*.[5] In 1688, with the death of Inayat Syah, the *nationale partij* immediately chose a young female from the royal family as her successor. The *priester partij*, though in the minority, was joined by some orang kaya to protest against another female successor and called for a return to male rule. An armed struggle ensued between these two parties, with the *nationale partij* gaining the upper hand. Kamalat Syah was installed and ruled for 11 years. The *priester partij* did not give up, however, and sought other means to achieve their goal. The weapon they sought was the letter from the Kadhi Malik al-Adil from Mecca stating that female rule was illegal. Armed with this in writing they went to the people of Aceh to inform them that female rule was against Islamic law. The *nationale partij* could not withstand this opposition any longer, and Kamalat Syah was deposed.[6]

---

[4] "Baginda itupun dimakzulkan oleh segala wazir dan segala rakyat kerana sebab datang surat dari Makkah dikirim oleh Kadhi Malikul Adil tiada sampai hukum sebab raja perempuan". Gani and Harun, *Adat Aceh*, p. 29.
[5] Veth, "Vrouwenregeeringen", p. 368.
[6] Ibid., p. 369.

Although Veth did not mention which orang kaya joined the Arab group, it is probable that they were the uleebalang from the hinterland. Jacob de Roy related that now and then the highlanders would come from their mountains to Aceh with about 3,000 to 4,000 men to demand a king.[7] Thomas Bowrey mentioned the inhabitants up-country were not happy with a female ruler and would rather a king ruled over them. They believed that the true heir was still alive, and they would obey him. In all probability, this "true heir" refers to the queen's illegitimate half-brother, Panglima Polem, a descendant of the illegitimate son of Iskandar Muda. Bowrey, however, did not see him as a serious rival to the queen. "It is and will be," he wrote, "past his reach or skill ever to obtain the government of Achin".[8] More serious opposition happened during the selection of the fourth queen, Kamalat Syah, which Dampier described as a "civil war" in Aceh. Dampier related that four orang kaya living in a more remote part of the country took up arms to oppose the new queen and the rest of the orang kaya. They managed to amass 5,000 to 6,000 men to march against the capital. They stayed near the landing place by the river close to the city. The queen's party, under the shahbandar, set up tents, kept a small guard of soldiers and placed two or three brass guns on the opposite bank. Dampier's "civil war" turned out to be a mere skirmish: he related that these soldiers were calling out to each other, discussing why they were fighting rather than actually engaging in conflict. They did this the whole night, and the next morning everyone went about their usual business. The process was repeated the next night.[9] The hinterland group left without success.

There was another reason for this group of agriculture-based uleebalang to oppose the trading-based, port city-dwelling orang kaya. Marsden mentioned that in the 1680s agriculture had suffered considerably, owing to the general licence given to all inhabitants to search for gold in the rivers and mountains, whereas prior to this, only authorised people could seek gold, while the rest were obliged to farm.[10] Whether this group of disaffected inlanders cooperated with the Arabs cannot be ascertained,

---

[7] "Voyage Made by Jacob Janssen de Roy to Borneo and Atcheen, 1691", p. 367.
[8] Bowrey, *A Geographical Account*, p. 313.
[9] Dampier, *Voyages and Discoveries*, pp. 100–1.
[10] Marsden, *The History of Sumatra*, p. 450.

but it is unlikely that the small and remote threat posed by the inlanders alone could unseat Sultanah Kamalat Syah, who still had the support of the mercantile city orang kaya at court.

Veth did not mention who comprised this *Arabische partij*, but as an Arab succeeded Kamalat Syah, it is probable that he was part of an Arab group who opposed female rule. Whether they were native-born or foreign Arabs, however, remains a mystery. Arabs migrating to Aceh as merchants, religious scholars and *sayyids* (a title referring to the descendants of the prophet Muhammad), in particular, enjoyed a high degree of prestige and were welcomed by Acehnese society.[11] Given that the ulama and the orang kaya had accepted the first three female rulers, it is somewhat curious that the appointment of the fourth would cause opposition then deposition after 11 years. A possible explanation is that those who opposed Kamalat Syah's rule were foreign-born Arabs. In 1683, a Meccan delegation sent by Sharif Barakat arrived in Aceh.[12] As opposition to female rule became louder in the 1680s, it is possible that the *priester partij* Veth mentioned refers to these visitors from Mecca. According to one source, (which this book's author cannot verify) when the delegation returned in September 1683, two delegates remained in Aceh where they were quickly accepted into court circles, and one was appointed as the kadhi.[13] In the 1680s, the opposition to female rule was not strong enough, but the situation changed in the 1690s. The death of the moderate local ulama, Abdul Rauf

---

[11] Snouck Hurgronje, *The Achehnese*, p. 155.

[12] Snouck Hurgronje based his account on Ahmad Dahlan's *Khulasat al-Kalam* (pp. 146–7), but provided no other reference details, nor does he shed more light on this delegation and their activities in Aceh. Snouck Hurgronje, "Een Mekkaansch Gezantschap naar Atjeh in 1683", p. 553. Azyumardi Azra mentioned this same delegation. In addition to citing Snouck Hurgronje's article, he quoted Ahmad Zayni Dahlan, *Khulasat al-Kalam fi Bayan Umara al-Balad al-Haram* (Cairo: n.p., 1305/1888), pp. 104–5; Azra, *The Origins of Islamic Reformism*, p. 181. Not reading Arabic, I am unable to verify this Arab source.

[13] One of them, Sayyid Ibrahim Syarif Hasyimsyah al-Jamalullail, was appointed as the Kadhi Malik al-Adil. See Pocut Haslinda Syahrul, *Silsilah Raja-Raja Islam di Aceh dan Hubungannya dengan Raja-Raja Islam Nusantara* [Genealogy of Muslim Kings in Aceh and their Relations with Muslim Kings in the Nusantara] (Jakarta: Pelita Hidup Insani, 2008). Quoted in Suzana Hj Othman and Muzaffar Dato' Hj Mohamad, *Ahlul-Bait Rasulullah SAW dan Kesultanan Melayu* [The Family of the Prophet (pbuh) and the Malay Sultanate] (Kuala Lumpur: Crescent News, 2006), p. 158.

al-Singkel, in 1693 might have enabled the Arabs to gain more influence. In the 1690s, the arrival of a letter from Mecca stating that female rule was against Islam strengthened the Arabs' hand, and Kamalat Syah had to step down.

It is beyond my purpose to determine exactly who the last sultanah's Arab successors were, but it is possible to venture that the members of this Arab group had risen to positions of prominence at court and may have established ties with the royal family. The potent mix of prestige, kinship ties to the royal family, plus the letter from Mecca finally secured the throne for Sultan Badrul Alam Syariff Hashim Jamal-al-Din in 1699.[14] This ended the 59-year-long run of female sovereigns in Aceh.

It is difficult to ascertain why Kamalat Syah was deposed in 1699, but we can venture that the political and religious situation in Aceh at the time did not favour female rule. By the 1680s, religious sentiment was on the increase in both Aceh and the surrounding territories of the SWC. The comment on female rule by Ibn Muhammad Ibrahim, a Persian diplomat in Aceh in 1685, reflected a view more representative of notions of female status in the Muslim heartland. The appeal of women was sexual, real power belonged in men's hands, and only the weakness and effeminacy of the orang kaya could explain the unorthodox situation:

> Thus, the councillors kept the reins of power in their own hands and governed the island without any problem. Their hypocrisy did not balk at this unmanly solution. They simply hid their heads under a female kerchief of shamelessness and disloyalty. These women-hearted men of state seated the maiden of their virgin thought on the throne of deception and from that time on this kingdom ... has been given to Houri-like beauties, women as charming as angels.[15]

---

[14] Even their family names were uncertain. The *Adat Acheh* gives the name as Paduka Seri Sultan Badrul Alam Syarif Hasyim Jamalullail: *Adat Acheh*, p. 24. Djajadiningrat used both Sultan Badr al-alam Sjarif Hasjim Djamal ad-din and Djamal al-leil: Djajadiningrat, *Kesultanan Aceh*, p. 60. Veth mentioned that he was Badroel-alam Scherief Haschim Djamaloed-din: Veth, "Vrouwenregeeringen", p. 83.

[15] *The Ship of Sulaiman*, trans. John O'Kane, Persian Heritage Series No. 11 (London: Routledge and Kegan Paul, 1972), pp. 174–8, quoted in *Witnesses to Sumatra*, ed. Reid, p. 92.

In Aceh, the arrival of the Meccan delegates stimulated and reflected such sentiments. By the 1690s, the group hostile to female rule had become powerful thanks to their prestige and political ties to royalty. Aceh's connectedness with the Islamic world, and its desire to emulate and be part of this network brought a reworking of politics that emphasised a more patriarchal interpretation of Islam. Patriarchy justified by religion sealed the sultanah's deposition. While the letter from Mecca was used to justify removing Kamalat, I argue that the real reason for her deposition had more to do with the politics of power rather than religion.

1641–99: Why Female Rule and Never Again

Why and how the tradition of kingship in Aceh was broken in the seventeenth century is the focus of this study. The phenomenon of queenship in Aceh occurred over six decades—a long time indeed—but only once in the kingdom's history. Was it an accident of history? Half a century is rather a long time for an "accident" to take place. Was it an experiment? Perhaps—it had never been tried before. If so, it was an experiment that lasted. In any case, it generally takes an unusual confluence of conditions to produce a turn or a twist that sets historical events on a new path. I suggest that the beginning of female rule in Aceh was a function of a unique situation in the Acehnese kingdom in 1641.

In Chapter 1, on the succession of Sultanah Safiatuddin Syah, I argued that there were no fixed laws of succession in Aceh. However, one necessary condition to ensure the accession and acceptance of a ruler was the consensus of the orang kaya. So why did the elites agree to accept a woman on the throne in 1641? I favour an explanation rooted in the political realities of the time. Sultanah Safiatuddin Syah's lineage was impeccable: she was the widow of Iskandar Thani and daughter of Iskandar Muda by a royal wife. The dearth of royal males in 1641 was another factor. Iskandar Muda and Iskandar Thani had contributed to this problem by killing those they deemed as royal rivals. Iskandar Muda ensured that no orang kaya or orang kaya faction would be strong enough to challenge his rule, and the orang kaya remained deeply factionalised and weak. The succession of Iskandar Thani was an aberration: uniquely—for Aceh—the existing ruler designated him. This procedure, however, was common in other Malay kingdoms, and was one of the preconditions recognised in the *Sejarah Melayu* for legitimate succession. Iskandar Muda's despotic style, an exception rather than the rule in Acehnese history, allowed him to choose his own successor without opposition from his orang kaya. However, because the elites did not choose Iskandar Thani, they did not support him. At the time of Iskandar Thani's death, no orang kaya or a faction of the elites had regained enough power to impose a candidate of their choice. Furthermore, owing to the lack of a strong, credible, royal, male candidate, no aspirants could stand without the backing of a strong orang kaya faction, nor could they be accepted by the majority. In those circumstances, a candidate with a chance of election had to be neutral, uninvolved with any orang kaya faction and, of course, be of royal blood, which conferred legitimacy.

In Aceh's genealogy of kings up to 1641, three sultans were of foreign origin: Sultan Ala al-Din, known as Mansur Syah (1577–86), was from Perak, Sultan Mahkota Buyung (1586–88) from Inderapura and Iskandar Thani (1636–41) from Pahang. The former two were killed and Iskandar Thani is believed to have been poisoned. This reveals or at least reflects the anti-foreign sentiment of the Acehnese elites. Iskandar Thani was remembered without love because he was a foreigner. The anti-foreigner sentiment was intense enough to spur the Acehnese elites to make a pact never again to allow foreign kings to rule over them. Therefore, the next successor had to be locally born and chosen from Aceh's own dynasty.

By process of elimination, Safiatuddin was the most suitable candidate. She was closest, by consanguinity or marriage, to both male predecessors. She was an adult, whereas the nearest male might be a minor; she was healthy, not handicapped; and she was native. But she was female. There were surely discussions on the issue of her sex as this was a new element in the history of Aceh's dynastic succession. Nevertheless, her contemporaries overlooked her sex to preserve the larger principles of legitimacy. Acehnese adat and historical antecedent allowed women to be in powerful positions, and Islamic doctrines, as interpreted by the ulama of the time, did not ban a woman from leadership. Externally, the strengthening Dutch power after the conquest of Melaka had swung the power balance against the Acehnese. Owing to the circumstances and the willingness of the majority of the elites to take a chance on a female ruler, she was elected, but not *because* she was female.[16]

Still, being a woman had its advantages. It made the sultanah neutral and placed her apart—even a stranger—from the rest of the male elites.[17] The combination of neutrality and legitimacy enabled her to be elected and accepted by the majority of the orang kaya. The orang kaya must have seen the advantages of having a young and inexperienced female ruler needing their instruction and guidance, though marriage might introduce a source of unwelcome influence. Hence, the elites jealously guarded her widowhood and chastity.[18] This was revealed during the episode in which the head ulama was killed for an alleged sexual liaison with Sultanah Safiatuddin. The truth of this allegation could not be ascertained, but it was certain that no one could or would be allowed to capture her heart and, therefore, open the way to the throne.

I suggest the second, third and fourth female sovereigns were chosen *because* they were female. The practice of electing a female after Sultanah Safiatuddin's death in 1675 was a deliberate effort on the part of the orang kaya, following the successful experiment with the first female ruler. The jewel affair illustrates that the first sultanah was not an absolutist, but neither was she a weakling. Not as deferential as the orang kaya would have hoped, she ruled in her own right, making some fancy political manoeuvres of her own that at times derailed some of the orang kaya's plans. Most significantly, she had instituted a successful and beneficial cooperative relationship with her elites, one in which diversity was not eliminated but balanced. It was a workable system, one that even the orang kaya wished to perpetuate. Thomas Bowrey wrote:

---

[16] For a discussion on female succession in Europe see Armin Wolf, "Reigning Queens in Medieval Europe: When, Where and Why", in *Medieval Queenship*, ed. Parsons, pp. 169–88. No such study has been undertaken on female succession in the Southeast Asian context.
[17] Fernández-Armesto, "The Stranger-Effect in Early Modern Asia", pp. 181–202.
[18] Veth, "Vrouwenregeeringen", pp. 367–8.

> Achin now and hath for a considerable time been governed by a Queen ... in soe much that the very name of a Kinge is longe since become nautious unto them, first caused through the tyrannicall Government of theire last Kinge.[19]

Female rule provided some solutions to the perennial conflict between an all male royalty and nobility. Marsden wrote "the people being now accustomed and reconciled to female rule which they found more lenient than that of their kings, acquiesced in general in the established mode of government".[20]

Female candidates became a deliberate choice for the orang kaya after the death of Safiatuddin Syah. However, new criteria became more important in selecting female candidates, such as age and marital status. Marsden pointed out that the initial opposition to the election of the last female ruler, Kamalat Syah, was because she did not meet criteria that were "esteemed essential" in a female ruler: besides being a royal, "she should be a maiden advanced in years". Bowrey mentioned "the Queen should never marry or know the use of man".[21] Although the ages and marital status of the second, third and fourth queens are unknown, the second and third queens were probably rather old. Sultanah Naqiatuddin died after a two-year reign in 1678—which would be consistent with advanced age at her accession. Bowrey, Dampier, Ord and Cawley described Sultanah Zakiatuddin as an old maid. It is likely that Kamalat Syah did not remain queen until her death because she was young, and there is a strong probability that she got married. Femininity in power can be self-subverting. While the three other sultanahs were able to use their womanhood advantageously and were successful in overcoming its limitations, the last sultanah became its victim. Being young she committed what for a virgin queen is often a fatal error—she married. For a king, marriage to a powerful spouse meant strengthening the political alliance, wealth and even legitimacy. For a queen, marriage itself might have compromised her freedom of action regardless of whether she married royalty, nobility, native or someone from outside the realm. As mentioned

---

[19] Bowrey, *A Geographical Account*, pp. 295–6.
[20] Marsden, *The History of Sumatra*, p. 449.
[21] Bowrey, *A Geographical Account*, p. 298.

above, it is quite likely Kamalat Syah did not last as queen because she married one of the delegates or a family member belonging to the sharif of Mecca residing in Aceh. This group—Arab, foreign, ignorant of or indifferent to the peculiarities of Acehnese political traditions—captured power, justifying their action by reference to a belief that Islam forbids a female at the helm of a Muslim kingdom.

Women in Power: Why Female Rule Lasted for Six Decades

Contrary to the popular belief that the male elites were homogeneous and generally preferred female rulers—who allowed them more freedom and more say in matters of government—there was sporadic opposition to female rule during the accessions of the third and fourth female monarchs. Overall though, female rule was generally accepted and supported, as Aceh witnessed prolonged peace under female sovereigns.[22] As illustrated in Chapter 5, in the Acehnese tradition women's rule was not problematic in Islam. Similarly, adat, or local Malay ideas of political leadership, did not consider the sex of the ruler as a determinant factor for succession or effective leadership.

According to Milner, traditional Malay adat ideas of political leadership, as found in indigenous chronicles and hikayat, demonstrate that the ruler was more valued for his manners than his practical skills.[23] The mark of a true king lay in his behaviour. An exemplary raja should exhibit excellent manners (*baik budi bahasanya*), and speak in a graceful/ sweet (*manis*), gentle (*lemah lembut*) and polite way. One of the most important duties of a raja was to bestow titles, gifts and honours on his subjects according to their rank.[24] Milner may have underestimated the political and practical roles of the raja. For instance, he asserted that

---

[22] In his study of the Patani queens, Amirell found a similar response from contemporary observers who saw female rule as desirable and sustainable for long periods of time. Amirell, "The Blessings and Perils of Female Rule", p. 303.

[23] Like the ruler portrayed in the *Hikayat Pahang*, he was valued more for his manners than his practical skills. Milner, "The Malay Raja", p. 198.

[24] Ibid., p. 196.

the raja's authority as presented in the *Hikayat Deli* was not specifically political in nature as the ruler could offer his subjects little more than titles and audiences. However, Milner went on to argue that titles and ceremonies were not subsidiary aspects of government but precisely what subjects sought from their raja. Titles were not empty rewards, and the festive events organised for subjects were part of a raja's duties. The true marker of a good ruler lies in good manners and the ability to treat his subjects in the appropriately formal way.

Milner's study showed that from the adat perspective, sex does not factor into the Malay conception of leadership. A female could be as well suited to being an exemplary raja as a male. Indeed, judging from most contemporary observers' descriptions of female rule in Aceh as gentle, generous and graceful, the female sovereigns were the epitome of good leadership. The generosity of Sultanah Safiatuddin and Sultanah Zakiatuddin to subjects and foreign envoys alike, and the justice meted out through a more humane penal system illustrate a leadership style influenced by adat, which also sanctioned the practice of decision making through musyawarah. Female rulers promoted muafakat, which created an environment where power and wealth sharing was possible, turning the relationship between nobility and royalty from one of conflict to cooperation. The queens, by virtue of their sex, remained separate and neutral from the masculine jealousies, egos and rivalries that characterised relations between the male king and his elites.

The writings of the ulama in Aceh, as reflected in the *Taj* and *Bustan*, did not view female rule as a contravention of Islamic law. The ruler's moral attributes rather than his sex-determined good leadership. Nevertheless, how leadership and female roles and status were contested, conceived, defined and practised in a Muslim society depended on how the power holders of the time interpreted Islamic tenets. There was no eternally or universally established model of Islamic political, social and cultural forms as such forms were historically contingent.[25] Thus, while Aceh tolerated female rule, Muslim communities in places, such as Mughal

---

[25] As in the Islamic world, in the Christian world and other world traditions as well, differing views exist on the roles of women in politics: Brenda Meehan-Waters, "Catherine the Great and the Problem of Female Rule", *Russian Review* 34, 3 (1975): 306.

India and Ottoman Turkey, considered even women's influence at court as disastrous.[26] Even in Aceh, as we have seen, the alleged fatwa from Mecca forbade female rule in 1699. It will be interesting to see how the debate on female leadership develops in modern Aceh, if an opportunity were to arise, given the current popular calls for the implementation of sharia law. How will the present elites negotiate between adat and religion?

Generally, despite the peculiar scope for gynaecocracy in the Malay world, and in Aceh in particular, Islamic tradition viewed political and public realms as male by default. A female had little or no place in civic life. On the rare occasion a female became sovereign, she was deemed to have been placed on the throne and tolerated by the male elites, to whom she would have to defer as, being a woman she would have very little knowledge in the art of governance, war, trade or religion. In Muslim kingdoms, elite women were generally secluded and their mobility was severely limited. Unlike a male king, a female monarch would not have the opportunity to forge alliances by marrying princes and sons from noble families or by taking them as concubines. Worse, a female ruler would be more susceptible to sexual scandals and liaisons, which could easily threaten her position and the stability of the kingdom. Marriage itself could compromise her position.

Given these limitations, how did the female sovereigns last for six decades? The discussion of the jewel affair in Chapter 2 illustrated how, through a deliberate deference to her elites and with a dash of feminine softness to sooth ruffled tempers when needed, Sultanah Safiatuddin was able to get her own way and successfully steered her kingdom out of troubled waters through peaceful diplomacy. Her rule was indeed collaborative and deliberately shaped to keep the rival factions of her orang kaya in balance. Compromise balanced the interests of the throne, elites and kingdom. The authority of the orang kaya was respected and their rights honoured. Final authority, however, as demonstrated in the jewel affair, lay in the sultanah's hands. Unlike the reigns of her male

---

[26] Ruby Lal, *Domesticity and Power in the Early Mughal World* (Cambridge: Cambridge University Press, 2005), pp. 220–5; Sunullah Effendi and Ahmad Refik saw the "sultanate of women" in Turkey as harmful. See Hambly, *Women in the Medieval Islamic World*, p. 9.

predecessors, which were characterised by conspicuous consumption and extravagant spending on jewels to enhance charisma, prowess and status, her reign saw more pragmatic spending and conservation of the kingdom's resources. Instead of prowess, she emphasised piety and her moral attributes to inspire devotion from her subjects. To other kings and governors she exhorted peace and goodwill in diplomatic relations, without high rhetoric and virile antics.

Chapter 3 showed how the sultanah survived two coups that threatened not only her position but possibly even her life. She also managed to survive a sex scandal and still maintain her position on the throne. She endured these trials by balancing the orang kaya factions, giving favours to her supporters and withholding rewards to weaken the factions that opposed her. When the need arose, for example, at the height of tensions during the Perak affair, she astutely manoeuvred to please the laksamana, who was against her policy of accommodating the Dutch. Meanwhile, she continued to strengthen the faction under the Maharaja, who supported her policy. In the end, her policy towards the Dutch prevailed.

Chapter 5 illustrated how seclusion did not entail isolation. It was a function of royalty rather than sex, an important element to enhance the exclusivity and mystique of royal power. Nevertheless, as a female ruler in a largely patriarchal court, the sultanah had to devise means to stay abreast of court happenings, be they rumours or real events. In this context, the sultanah's numerous and trustworthy eunuchs, especially Maharaja Adonna Lilla, and powerful court ladies assumed important roles when they acted as intermediaries between the sultanah and her orang kaya. Maharaja Adonna Lilla was the perfect conduit for engaging the male sex and to serve as her eyes and ears in a largely male court. Indeed, gendered perceptions, such as the queen being inaccessible and inconsistent because she was a woman, were cleverly turned to an advantage. The "inaccessibility problem" during negotiations proved valuable as her actions, seen as unfathomable to others, gave her room for manoeuvre. Her "inconsistencies" bought time for the Acehnese during periods of difficult negotiations.

Benevolent and pious, female rule met the criteria of both adat and Islam, which helps explain why the sultanahs were able to remain power for six decades. Perhaps their greatest achievement after their male predecessors' harsh and despotic rule was to do as Catherine the Great of Russia did, "to soften autocracy without emasculating it".[27]

Did Aceh Decline under Female Rule?

The received view regarding female rule was that royal power declined under the women sovereigns and this, in turn, precipitated Aceh's decline. A more detailed study of Aceh during this period, using contemporary Dutch, English and indigenous sources does not support this assessment. Accounts by private merchants, such as Bowrey, Dampier and De Roy, residing in Aceh towards the end of the seventeenth century, reveal a politically stable and peaceful kingdom. They described a thriving and cosmopolitan entrepôt attractive to private merchants. Aceh remained a centre of Islamic learning and a training centre for would-be ulama.[28]

As demonstrated in Chapter 4, descriptions of Aceh as a busy and thriving port with numerous ships from Europe, India and Southeast Asia throughout the latter half of the seventeenth century appear frequently in VOC records and other travellers' accounts. Company officials' frequent complaints in the 1640s and 1650s regarding the tough competition between them and the English, and the other "Moorish traders" testify to this.[29] In the 1670s, Bowrey described numerous traders and craftsmen, such as the English, Dutch, Danes, Portuguese, Chinese, Malabarese, Bengalis, Gujaratis, Javanese, Malays, Makassarese and others, frequenting the port of Aceh.[30] In the two years Dampier was in Aceh (1688–89), he found it to be the largest, richest and most populous of all the isles of Sumatra. He noted about 7,000 to 8,000 houses in the

---

[27] Nikolai M Karamzin described the greatest achievement of Catherine the Great of Russia, in *"Karamzin's 'Memoir on Ancient and Modern Russia": A Translation and Analysis* by Richard Pipes (Cambridge, MA: Harvard University Press, 1959), p. 130.

[28] Likewise, under Raja Ijau in Patani, external trade increased, bringing greater economic prosperity. Patani also saw a period of high cultural achievement where it was a leading centre for music, dance, drama and handicraft production, including metal works and wood carving. Amirell, "The Blessings and Perils of Female Rule", pp. 311–2.

[29] In around 1640, Surat had four times the trade of Goa. Michael N. Pearson, *The Indian Ocean* (London: Routledge, 2003), p. 135.

[30] Bowrey, *A Geographical Account*, p. 286.

city alone.³¹ Aceh's harbour was seldom without at least 10 to 15 ships from many nations. Food was abundant and cheap, and he mentioned the cultivation of rice—which was previously imported—had recently been introduced.³² Aceh was rich in natural resources; the goldmines, especially, attracted many foreigners. Aceh's capital was a cosmopolitan city thronging with people of many diverse origins, such as the English, Danes, Portuguese, Gujaratis, Chinese and many more. Dampier made a special note of the Chinese traders whom he described as "remarkable". Some Chinese lived in Aceh all year long, while others made annual voyages. The Chinese came in June in about 10 or 15 ships and settled at the end of town, called the China Camp, where they lived and traded: in addition to merchants and sailors there were also carpenters, painters and musicians. For two months they transformed the whole camp into a fair selling all sorts of goods including Chinese toys.³³

In the 1690s, Jacob de Roy wrote about the thriving port city of Aceh where some one hundred European vessels came each year as well as a great number of native vessels. De Roy rated Aceh as the best place in the East Indies to make one's fortune.³⁴ Anthony Reid argued that critical military encounters with Europeans brought about a collapse of local ethnic shipping, trade and revenue decline, and the failure of Islamic commerce's last stand by 1680. Although this may be true for some areas of the archipelago, the case of Aceh shows a resilient regional network of Muslim and non-Muslim traders. More recent studies have shown that Ottoman decline in the eighteenth century is no longer universally accepted; nor is India's as Mughal successor states were still commercially viable.³⁵ European private merchants flocked to Aceh and profited by participating in the regional network of trade. Aceh remained the port of call for Muslim traders from India and the region, and though Muslim

---

[31] Dampier, *Voyages and Discoveries*, pp. 84–9.
[32] Likewise, Admiral Van Neck, commenting on Raja Ijau, said "all her subjects considered her government better than that of the dead king", and "all the necessities that now are very cheap there were in the days of the king (so they say) one half more expensive because of the great taxes that then were imposed". Quoted in Amirell, "The Blessings and Perils of Female Rule", p. 312.
[33] Ibid., p. 95.
[34] "Voyage Made by Jacob Janssen de Roy to Borneo and Atcheen, 1691", pp. 356, 363.
[35] Pearson, *The Indian Ocean*, p. 118.

trade was disrupted by VOC blockades and the pass system, this ancient trade survived. Although the pepper trade fluctuated in the last two decades of the seventeenth century, Aceh still profited from its gold and elephant trades. The descriptions of Aceh during that time by the likes of Bowrey, Dampier and De Roy do not paint a picture of a declining kingdom succumbing to the pressures of European incursions, but one that was remarkably resilient.

Contemporary indigenous and Dutch assessments of the women sovereigns were positive. Jacob Compostel noted that Sultanah Safiatuddin had more royal worth than her male predecessors. Pieter Sourij commented that the sultanah's rule was gentle but awe-inspiring. Al-Raniri related that because of the sultanah's excellent attributes, Aceh remained peaceful and prosperous. The twists and turns of the jewel and Perak affairs revealed a queen who was well able to manage both her local male elites and those from other nations. By facilitating a more inclusive and collaborative style of government and administering justice based on the laws of the land, the sultanah certainly dismantled her father's despotic, personal and arbitrary approach. Collaborative rule meant a reduction in or a limitation of royal power, rather than its deterioration or decline. On the contrary it strengthened the institution of royalty, as Iskandar Muda's personal rule had been fragile and arbitrary. The royal monopoly on power was now broken and distributed among the orang kaya, especially those who shared her policies. Promoting her half-brother from the position of kali to the highest-ranking position of Maharaja Sri Maharaja is one such example. This showed also that royalty and nobility were never totally distinct, and the royalty-nobility balance of power was never a zero-sum game, but one which was negotiated. The limitation of monarchical power and return to state institutions ushered in by the first sultanah brought about a more stable institutionalisation of power sharing, which was a key to the kingdom's continued stability and prosperity until the century's last decade. Her immediate successors continued this style of government; however, as there are no first-hand accounts of the court audiences during their reigns, it is rather difficult to ascertain the degree of power sharing, and how the balance of power between royalty and nobility played out. It is possible to speculate that by the fourth female ruler, the orang kaya—especially the Arab group—had gradually accumulated more power, at least enough to depose Sultanah Kamalat Syah. It is unfortunate that the style and substance of limited monarchy instituted under these female rulers did not survive their reigns. The reign of Kamalat Syah's successor, Badr al-Alam Syariff Hasyim Jamal al-Din, marked a return to the style of the sultanah's male predecessors, as he accumulated more royal wealth at the expense of the orang kaya and foreign merchants. It was a period of political crisis in Aceh in the eighteenth century that paved the way for the monarchy's decline, not during the queens' reigns as this study shows.

This book has presented a different picture of Aceh under female sovereigns. The assertion that Aceh experienced a downturn in its fortunes after a "golden age" during the reign of Iskandar Muda must be revisited. What are the criteria of this golden age? Expansion in trade, territories, manpower and the codification of laws are some indicators of progress. These took place under Iskandar Muda, and he ostentatiously displayed his wealth and power to inspire awe and fear in his allies and enemies alike. Nevertheless, this "progress" was achieved at a high cost. The golden age of Iskandar Muda relied on coercion—the threat of force—and the ruler's tyranny and cruelty tarnished its lustre. Thousands of lives were lost as a result of conquests and resettlements; the sultan's profligate nature drained the kingdom's resources. Dismantling this arbitrary power and institutionalising law to protect the rights of both subjects and foreigners were key features of female rule. In this regard, the adverse course Iskandar Muda began was actually reversed by his female successors. It is time to recognise their work and its positive effects.

Aceh and Other Malay Polities

Another assertion re-examined in this book is that female rule was responsible for the loss of Aceh's power over its vassal states. A closer examination of the evidence in Chapters 3 and 4 regarding relations between Aceh, its vassals, the VOC and EIC revealed a more complex picture than the generalisation that with European ascendancy the indigenous polities declined. I suggest that overlord-vassal relations, as conducted by their male predecessors, were not sustainable and these ties had already frayed during their reigns.

Iskandar Muda and Iskandar Thani maintained the hierarchical traditional ties of vassal—overlord relations by binding these states to Aceh through a mixture of military intimidation, charisma, divinely sanctioned power and legitimacy through conquest and kinship ties. They demanded tribute and loyalty but provided less patronage and protection in return and, at times, especially under Iskandar Muda, these relations were more exploitative and destructive.

Overlord-vassal relations based on coercion or hard power, rather than protection or soft power, without regard to local loyalties were unsustainable. If an opportunity arose, vassals would switch allegiances to new overlords deemed better at meeting the vassals' needs. In a fluid political environment of impermanent hierarchies, comparable polities would compete for the position of overlord. Despite its subjugation since 1613, Johor's aristocracy did not see themselves as vassals or "slaves" of Aceh's royal house, but as the legal and moral successors to the Melaka Sultanate that once ruled the Malay world.[36] Sultan Abdul Jalil Riayat Shah (r. 1623–77) and the laksamana of Johor were to play an instrumental role in re-establishing Johor as a paramount Malay power.[37] They actively sought out allies in Patani and Pahang, and even among the Portuguese, to counter Aceh's influence. In 1629, when the Acehnese fleet attacked Melaka, Johor, Pahang and Patani came to the aid of the Portuguese. In 1639, Johor initiated the renewal of the Treaty of Friendship and Alliance signed in 1606 with the Dutch in an attempt to outflank Aceh.

Sultanah Safiatuddin did not lose two of Aceh's vassal states, Johor and Pahang, in the first year of her reign. Johor did not see itself as a vassal of Aceh in the first place, and though Iskandar Thani was a son of Pahang, Johor competed with Aceh to be overlord in the Strait and environs, including Pahang. Iskandar Thani's attempt to subjugate militarily both these kingdoms in 1638 failed.[38] A few months after she came to power, in a diplomatic volte-face, Safiatuddin signed a written contract of peace with Johor with Dutch mediation. Regarding Pahang,

---

[36] Borschberg, "Luso-Johor-Dutch Relations in the Straits of Malacca and Singapore", p. 17.
[37] He was the son of Sultan Ala'ud-din, who escaped Aceh's capture in 1613. He succeeded Sultan Ma'yat Shah.
[38] For full details on Aceh-VOC-Johor and Pahang relations during this period, see Sher Banu, "Ties That Unbind", pp. 303–21.

she saw the situation there as almost a fait accompli as the laksamana who Iskandar Thani sent to Pahang had betrayed him, offering his allegiance to Johor instead. Unlike her husband, who was obsessed over the "cursed boedjangh" turned traitor and devised military means to return Pahang to his fold, Sultanah Safiatuddin reversed her husband's policy. In her letter to Antonio van Diemen, she explained:

> [S]ince all the Great Men and inhabitants in Pahang have rebelled against me ... and ... the Bendahara of Pahangh has handed over the country to Johor ... Pahangh is now a land over which the Captain will dispose as he likes.

She requested only that her weapons, ammunition and people to be sent back to Aceh.[39]

Johor and Pahang may have gone their own ways, but Sultanah Safiatuddin was successful in maintaining Aceh's traditional overlord-vassal relations in Perak and the SWC, but by emphasising a more symbiotic relationship grounded on ties of kinship and religious loyalty. The Perak affair revealed the resilience of the traditional vassal-overlord system working to the advantage of local polities. The VOC failed to engross the tin trade and execute its monopolistic policies in the northern part of the Strait of Melaka. The company officials also failed to bring the Perak murderers to justice and, in the end, the company had to cancel Perak's reparation debts.

The VOC's increased involvement on the SWC was not so much the result of either the company's growing power in the Strait of Melaka or Aceh's decline. Rather it was because of the local leaders' initiative, seeing that the company presented new opportunities for them to change allegiance, and rework political and commercial networks to their benefit. Acehnese-appointed panglimas were chased out of the SWC, and the revenue to which Aceh was entitled was lost. The system of tributary control Iskandar Muda erected along the west coast was dismantled because new patrons were available. Aceh, however, did not lose its

---

[39] NA, VOC 1141, Copie translaet missive der Coninginne van Attchin aen den Gouverneur Generael [Translated letter from the Queen of Aceh to the Governor General], 1642, f. 147V.

traditional commercial and political links with the coastal polities. Aceh continued to receive pepper and gold brought directly by the Minangkabau inhabitants from both the east and west coasts of Sumatra. Unhappy with the company's one-sided commercial policy of price fixing and attempts at monopolising trade, these traders continued to frequent Aceh rather than the VOC commercial base in Padang. Deli and Asahan on the east coast, which supplied a substantial amount of rice to Aceh, had defected to the company in the 1660s. However, they maintained commercial links by continuing to export rice to Aceh, despite the VOC.[40]

VOC officials became embroiled in local political factions from the 1660s to the mid-eighteenth century. The Dutch never enjoyed more than half a year's peace, and the numerous wars frustrated the enforcement of contracts. The Dutch were not able to control the island's pepper and gold trade as small planters and traders carried their harvests through jungles and across rivers to places all over the coast. It was impossible to close off more than 4,500 kilometres of the Sumatran coastline to rivals.[41] In 1670, the VOC decided to take up gold production, and imported experts and equipment to mine the gold from the Barisan Mountains. However, European mining methods did not suit local conditions, and European miners could not survive the tropical working conditions. In the 1680s, with the beginnings of a religious revivalism of sorts, partly as a response to increased incursions from the Christian West, spiritual ties were rekindled between Aceh and these west coast polities. Polities, such as Oelakkan and Barus, looked to Aceh for spiritual leadership. Indeed, in the amorphous and fluid political culture of the Malay world in the pre-modern era, when territorial and physical control was never the norm, these cultural, religious and commercial ties were truly the ones that bound patron-client loyalty.

---

[40] NA, VOC 1200, Origineel advijs van d'E. Arnold de Vlamingh van Oudtshooren [Original Advice from Arnold de Vlamingh van Oudtshooren], 1653, ff. 227R–227V, 228V. Quoted in Andaya, "A Very Good-Natured but Awe-Inspiring Government", pp. 74–5.
[41] Els M. Jacobs, *Merchant in Asia: The Trade of the Dutch East Indies Company during the Eighteenth Century* (Leiden: CNWS Publications, 2006), p. 60.

Aceh-VOC Encounters: Interactive Emergence

Sultanah Safiatuddin's desire to establish a friendship and alliance with the VOC was clear. The new ruler decided to make use of the treaty system to effect new kinds of relations. Aceh's interests would now have to be pursued and safeguarded by using new tools of diplomacy in which relations were based on mutual interest. The sultanah and her elites realised that in the context of the new realities facing them, supernatural and sacrosanct powers of legitimacy, royal lineage and kinship ties, though important, were in themselves insufficient to order interstate relations. New bases of legitimacy, peace and order were needed to regulate international relations and conduct trade.

Aceh retained its political and commercial autonomy, and it was not subjected to unequal trading relations with European companies. The accommodating and conciliatory stance the female sovereigns adopted in response to VOC blockades and pressures ensured that Aceh did not become embroiled in wasteful and dangerous wars. Sultanah Safiatuddin concluded many treaties and contracts with the VOC and EIC, thereby fully embracing these new instruments of peace in international diplomacy. The sultanah signed away some trade privileges and revenues, but she ensured that customs duties and tolls for her vassals were protected. The sultanah granted limited toll-free privileges and only for definite periods. In Perak, she allowed equal sharing of tin between the VOC and Aceh, but she excluded Dutch company officials from Aceh's lucrative elephant trade with Indian merchants.

The Perak affair resonated with the new noise of East-West encounters. They demanded adjustments, sometimes creative, at other times clumsy, in what John Wills called "interactive emergence".[42] As the Perak affair illustrated, these encounters happened at many levels and junctures, from personal relations between the envoys and the orang kaya, ranging from intense hate to genuine friendships to commerce, politics, language and legal structures. The VOC had limited success in using the legal instruments of diplomacy, such as contracts and treaties. According to Hugo Grotius, the Dutch jurist and diplomat, Europeans and

---

[42] Wills, "Maritime Asia", p. 83.

Asians were bound by the same legal agreements as both cultures were equal. However, when did this system, laid down by Europeans and initially confined to Europe, become universal? In many cases Europeans did not treat other non-Europeans and non-Christians equally, and vice-versa. China saw Dutch merchant-ambassadors as tribute bearers, and the Chinese viewed the limited trade they allowed the Dutch as a grant or privilege.[43] The legalistic, letter-of-the-law approach the VOC adopted to signing contracts and treaties contrasted with the personal, spirit-of-the-law approach preferred by Asian monarchs. While VOC officials viewed contracts as inviolable and permanent, local rulers saw them as transient and mutable, depending on changing circumstances. Similarly, in Aceh, the instructions granting Dutch trade privileges in the form of firman, estemie or kurnia could be viewed as unilateral grants, given and taken at will, as a royal prerogative. Indeed the word kurnia literally means grant. By no stretch of the imagination was this seen as mutually obligatory, nor was it meant to be a permanent contract.

The contrasting approaches led to many misunderstandings and misperceptions. The Acehnese saw VOC officials as too demanding and rude in forcing rulers to accede to their ways rather than being satisfied and thankful for the grants based on the ruler's benevolence. The officials, in contrast, felt that they were only demanding what were their rights bound by treaties. This, in turn, led to company officials stereotyping Acehnese as treacherous and untrustworthy, and the Acehnese viewing company officials as essentially merchants robed in ambassadorial clothing. They constantly questioned the company's sincerity in its friendship with them: the exchanges between Arnold de Vlamingh and the laksamana during the jewel affair vividly illustrate these misunderstandings. Furthermore, with these contrasting perceptions, ambassadorial language usually got lost in translation. In medieval and renaissance Europe, diplomatic exchanges between east and west required eloquence in both Greek and Latin, the preferred languages of international diplomacy. As these became ever more complex,

---

[43] Jurrien van Goor, "Merchants as Diplomats: Embassies as an Illustration of European-Asian Relations", in *Prelude to Colonialism: The Dutch in Asia*, ed. Jurrien van Goor and Foskelien van Goor (Hilversum: Uitgeverij Verloren, 2004), pp. 10–1.

drafting legal and political documents, mastery of public speaking and ambassadorial business became prized skills.[44] In Southeast Asia in the seventeenth century, there were neither languages of international diplomacy nor ambassadorial skills or protocol yet in existence. This is why the likes of Truijtman, Vlamingh and Sri Bidia Indra, the long term Acehnese envoy to Batavia, faced so many problems. Even the English and the Dutch could disagree on what constituted legal commercial practice in their rivalry with each other and their relations with indigenous local powers in Asia.[45]

Not all these encounters were negative, however, as one reads with delight how Truijtman or Vlamingh enjoyed their pleasurable moments, savouring the exotic delights of local food, fruits and cultural entertainments. One is reminded that Europe was not so different after all when one compares how Sultanah Safiatuddin welcomed her Christian ambassadors with how Queen Elizabeth welcomed Muslim envoys from Turkey and Morocco.[46] In terms of hospitality and accommodating intercultural exchanges, both queens were impeccable.[47]

Safiatuddin had her share of favourites among the Dutch envoys. She had a soft spot for Justus Schouten and Balthazar Bort and did not hesitate to write to the governor general in Batavia requesting the return of these men. European men may have taught her about commerce and diplomacy, but Sultanah Safiatuddin also learnt about European fashion from Mrs Harmanszoon, and Sultanah Zakiatuddin about men's wigs from Messrs Ord and Cawley. In the course of the long period of interactions between European officials and locals, friendships were also struck. Sri Bidia Indra's friendship with the VOC's envoy to Aceh, Johan Truijtman, is one such example.

---

[44] Jerry Brotton, *The Renaissance Bazaar: From the Silk Road to Michelangelo* (Oxford: Oxford University Press, 2002), p. 86.
[45] E.B. Sainsbury, *A Calendar of the Court Minutes etc., of the East India Company, 1668–1669* (Oxford: The Clarendon Press, 1929), p. 225.
[46] Nabil Matar, *Turks, Moors and Englishmen in the Age of Discovery* (New York: Columbia University Press, 1999), p. 34.
[47] Ibid., pp. 66, 70.

The diversity of responses to European intrusions and the different degrees of impact on indigenous polities by the end of the seventeenth century show that though East and West might no longer interact as equals, European ascendancy was far from uniform or uninterrupted. By the end of the century, Aceh was no longer an expanding empire as it had been at the beginning and, relative to the gradual strengthening of the VOC's territorial and commercial empire, neither was Aceh a backwater nor a subject state. Partly thanks to the good governance of its women rulers and their creative and accommodative diplomacy, Aceh remained an independent kingdom, an important regional port of call with its own autonomous commercial networks, and it continued to serve as the "Veranda of Mecca" for the region. The VOC was not successful in dominating the northern part of the Strait of Melaka, even by the end of the eighteenth century. Aceh remained independent for another two hundred years, even after the demise of the Dutch East Indies Company in 1802. Long after the rest of the East Indies had been divided into colonies, Aceh remained a thorn in the side of the Dutch, whose colonial government had to fight a 30-year war (1873–1903) to bring this last frontier within its colonial borders.

Revisiting Kingship in the Malay/Muslim World

To what extent is leadership gendered rather than a function of personality? This question remains without definite answers, and this debate will, of course, continue. However, this study of women sovereigns in the Acehnese context shows that there are distinctive features in the leadership style that differentiate women from their male counterparts, and these could be owing to their sex. Safiatuddin's network of elite women and eunuchs, her close confidant in the eunuch Maharaja Adonna Lilla, her unique ways of dealing with her errant orang kaya—in one instance by making one sit with his hands on his head asking for forgiveness— and the rumours and slander of adultery she faced were unique to her sex. Raja Ijau of Patani threw her golden scarf to the Bendahara Kayu Kelat as a way of asking him to spare her life. He immediately caught it and wrapped it round his head, then placed his kris on the ground, kneeling before her to signal that he not only wished to grant her life but accepted her as his ruler.[48]

The reigns of Aceh's sultanahs constituted a model of rule based on moral force and a consensual style of decision making that depended on musyawarah and was sanctioned by adat and Islamic tenets. It was in clear contrast to the prowess model of kingship characteristic of the charismatic men who preceded them. The women rulers also provided a model of royal-elite relations differing from the masculine or male-centred approach of Iskandar Muda and Iskandar Thani, largely characterised by the rulers' jealousies, rivalries, competition, hierarchical relations and arbitrary control. However, more research needs to be undertaken on other women rulers in the region and beyond to compare their styles of leadership before there is any conclusive answer to the existence of such a thing as "female leadership" or "queenship".

More research needs to be done to determine and understand the relationship between female rule and "the age of commerce" in Southeast Asia. Did the preponderance of Muslim female rulers in this region from 1500 to 1800 facilitate the "age of commerce" and if so, how? The female model of leadership studied in this book shows that female rule was better suited to facilitating peace, commerce and diplomacy, and it was a key reason that Aceh was able to remain stable internally, and independent and economically autonomous in the seventeenth century. It also helps support Reid's postulation that the preponderance of female rulers in this region over these three centuries was a factor explaining the "age of commerce".[49]

Apart from the few studies mentioned in the introduction, most writing on leadership in Southeast Asia has centred on charisma and prowess as criteria for effective leadership, neglecting other forms of power, such as that based on social and moral capital. And yet, given the fluid political environment of the Malay world where relations between polities were based on personal ties of loyalty, soft power was more effective than military might. There is also the tendency to view the nature of power in the early modern era as personal, absolute or ceremonial. However,

---

[48] Salleh, ed., *Hikayat Patani*, pp. 29–31.
[49] Reid, "Female Roles in Pre-Colonial Southeast Asia", p. 640.

as this study shows, law codes and institutional structures based on adat and Islam had already been established, though the extent to which these laws and institutions were deployed depended on the leadership style of the rulers concerned. Thus, there is a need to rethink the different criteria of leadership and success in the Malay world, and the diverse picture of statehood and governance during the early modern period.

Patriarchally dominant and mainstream views in Islamic history, tradition and scholarship perceive religious and political leadership as necessarily male. This view was challenged by Fatima Mernissi's study on female rulers in mainland Islamic areas. In Ottoman Turkey, Sunullah Effendi, the foremost guardian of Islam, publicly lamented and described the increase in women's influence at the Ottoman court in the seventeenth century as harmful and disruptive to the empire. Women, he believed, should have nothing to do with government and sovereignty. In contrast, Safavid Iran held both royal men and women with an air of sanctity and elevated them almost to sainthood. Both men and women were believed to be blessed with divinely bestowed charisma, and Safavid women, such as Pari-Khan Khanum and Shahzadeh Sultanum, are considered to have wielded considerable authority. This again contrasts with Mughal India, where imperial women were not only unmentioned in the chronicles, but they were "profoundly invisible".[50]

Despite these diversities and the importance of studying women's leadership roles in Islam, there is very little study on Muslim women rulers in the more "peripheral" areas of Islam. For example, India and the Malay world of Southeast Asia had a greater preponderance of women rulers. Why are there more queens ruling in their own right in this region? This book's study of the Acehnese queens has discussed the importance of localisation, and the interpretation and practice of Islam in the context of local cultures and the worldviews of the power holders. It is important to show that past Muslim queens were accepted and explain why they were so, to change mind sets now about the possibilities and advantages of having women in leadership positions, even if not necessarily at the highest positions of authority. More research needs to be done though, to show the diversity of interpretation of

---

[50] Lal, *Domesticity and Power in the Early Mughal World*, pp. 220–5.

female religious and political leadership in the Muslim world in different epochs as such forms were historically constituted.

Indeed female political leaders are not a rarity even in contemporary Muslim Southeast Asia as represented by Megawati Soekarno Putri and Wan Azizah Ismail. This long tradition of having women at the helm is no mere historical accident, but reflects Reid's thesis on an indigenous political culture of female autonomy. However, it is important to note that there are other factors enabling or limiting female leadership, namely male attitudes and the way religion—in this case, Islam—is being interpreted. Safiatuddin ascended the throne not just because of her impeccable lineage as the daughter of Iskandar Muda and widow of Iskandar Thani, but because the orang kaya reached a consensus about accepting her appointment. The local ulama's acceptance of female leadership as not contravening Islamic law enabled Safiatuddin to ascend the throne, but opposition from the Meccan ulama led to Kamalat's deposition. Female rule, however, could not have lasted for 59 years without the sultanahs' political acumen and leadership style.

Contributions of This Book: Uses and Limitations

This book has not answered all the questions posed at the beginning. It is not yet possible to ascertain much about the identities and origins of the second, third and fourth female rulers, indeed, sources at times suggest more questions than answers. These same sources, however, have provided enough evidence to challenge popular claims about Aceh under the rule of the female sultanahs. The willingness of the male elites to accept a woman on the throne in 1641, though not a deliberate choice, paid off: this prevented Aceh from meeting the same fate as the many other Malay polities that had succumbed to Dutch power, such as Banten and Makassar. The female rulers, especially Sultanah Safiatuddin, showed that they could be as capable and successful as their male counterparts. In this regard, present-day Acehnese women could draw some inspiration and confidence that they too can play important roles and contribute to the making of a new and more successful Aceh in the future.

A balanced assessment of the sultanahs' reigns is possible. Rather than universalising stereotypes of "female rule" or "female rulers" or making cosmic generalisations about them, this book presents a particular case study of a succession of women rulers—their representations and their lived realities—in a certain place at a specific time in history. To take the scope of the conclusions further, more research would be needed on other female sovereigns in the context of female rule in Southeast Asia, across the Dar al-Islam and the world. Nevertheless, the achievements of and the interest in the queenly phase of Aceh's history would surely compare favourably to any of the other women rulers.

Glossary

adat	customary practice
bahar	1 bahar is roughly between 210 to 230 kg
balai	audience hall
balai furdah	council in charge of commerce and finance
balai gadeng	an arm of the legislative branch
balai laksamana	military, naval council
balai majelis mahkamah rakyat	an arm of the legislative branch consisting of representatives from the *mukim*s
balai musyawarah	legislative branch
balai rungsari	an arm of the legislative branch
bendahara	treasurer or, at times, first ranking member of the court after the ruler
berdalaut	sovereign
binthara	court official
boedjangh	royal messenger
burgher	free Dutch citizen
caliph	Muslim civil and religious ruler
capado	eunuch
chakravartin	Hindu concept of the universal, ideal universal ruler
chap	seal

coopman	trader
dagh-register	day book, diary, journal
dalam	inside/private (domain); palace quarters
darurat	crisis
daulat	sovereignty, power (mystical) and authority of ruler
derhaka	disobedience; treason, the highest sin one could commit against a ruler
dewa-raja	king with divine powers
estemie	the ruler's order bearing the royal seal
fatwa	religious decree
generale missiven	general correspondence
grooten priester	high priest
hadith	sayings of the Prophet
hajj	pilgrimage to Mecca prescribed as a religious duty for Muslims; one who has made such a pilgrimage (often used as a title or honorific)
hakim	judge
Heren Zeventien/XVII	the Board of Directors of the VOC forming the supreme decision-making authority, generally convened in Amsterdam; English "Seventeen Gentlemen"
hikayat	folklore; long story, written as prose or poetry in Malay, often anonymous
hukumat	laws
imam	head of congregational prayers
jawi	Malay in Arabic script
jihad	holy war
Kadhi Maliku'l Adil; Qadi Malik al-Adil	religious judge
kadhi (kali)	Muslim judge (Acehnese version of *kadhi*)

kanun/qanun	canonical laws
kati	Malay measure of weight: 1 *kati* is about 625 g; 1 *kati* = 16–20 *tael*s = 1⅓ pounds = 6 hectograms = about 625 g; monetary unit = 112.8–144 *guilder*s
kerajaan	the state of having a king
keuchik	village head
khalifah	God's shadow or representative on earth
khatun	women who hold political authority
khutbah	religious sermon
kitab	religious text
kling	ethnic group from India
kris	dagger
kurnia	grant; (permission to) grant
laksamana	admiral of the navy
Maha Mulia	His/Her Highness
manis	graceful/sweet manner
mas	Acehnese coin
muhrim/mahram	unmarriageable kin with whom sexual intercourse would be considered incestuous, a punishable taboo
mukim	collection of villages
musyawarah	consensus-building
naeleer	captain
nanggroe/negeri	district
ondercoopman	junior merchant
oppercoopman	senior trader
opperhooft	head resident
orang kaya	rich nobles who were also state officials
panglima	governor
penghulu kawal	official at court in charge of policing
peteh	Malay currency

Glossary

puji-pujian	compliments
putri	princess
Raad van Indië	Council of the Indies (VOC)
raja	prince; chief; ruler
real, reals/reales	former Spanish monetary unit
real, reals/reis	former Portuguese monetary unit
resident	head of the VOC's local office, ranking lower than an *opperhoof*
rijksdaalder	Dutch silver coin: 1 *rijksdaalder* = 3 *guilder*, florin = 60 *stuiver*s
rijxraad/rijxraaden	state council member(s)
ruba	customary dues
sagi	literally means a three-point or triangular sieve to separate rice from husks; here it refers to the three provinces comprising a confederation of districts
sakti	magical
sarakata	court document without bearing the ruler's seal
saudagar raja	king's merchant
sayyid	descendants of the Prophet Muhammad
sembah	obeisance
Serambi Mekah	veranda of Mecca
shahbandar	administrative official or representative of a merchant group in a port
sharia	Islamic law based on the Qu'ran
sharif	descendant of Muhammad through his daughter Fatima
sheikh (sheik)	Arab chief; honorific
Sheikh al-Islam	highest religious judge
silsilah	geneology
speelhoff; speelhuis	place for amusement
spetie	ready money, cash

sri	auspicious
state-juffrouwen	ladies-in-waiting
stuiver	Dutch coin: 60 *stuiver*s = 1 *rijksdaalder*
suassa	copper and gold alloy
sultan	male Muslim sovereign
sultanah	female Muslim sovereign
tandil	bodyguard
tael	unit of weight and a monetary unit used in China, Japan, Tonkin, Cambodia, Siam, Aceh, Makassar, etc. As a unit of weight, one *tael* is about 37.5 g. The worth of one *tael* as a monetary unit varied from place to place. In Aceh, the *tael* was usually measured in gold: 1 *tael* was worth 4 *rijksdaalder*s, or 16 golden *mas*. If in silver, it was worth about 60 *stuiver*s or 8 silver *mas*.
tariqat	schools of Sufism
temenggong	chief of public security
teungku	religious village head
ulama	a body of Muslim scholars or religious leaders; and a member of this body
uleebalang	local leaders holding political and military authority
ummah	community of believers
ureueng tuha	man of wisdom
vrouwenregeeringen	government by women
wakil raja	deputy *raja*
wali	legal guardian of a bride
wayang	shadow puppet theater
wazir	vizier

Bibliography

Primary Sources

Dutch Archival Records, Manuscripts

Nationaal Archief (NA) [Dutch National Archives], The Hague, the Netherlands.
Overgekomen Brieven en Papieren uit Indie (OBP) [Briefs and Papers Received from the Indies] (papers from Aceh and Melaka to Batavia, 1640–1700), the Archives of the Dutch East India Company (VOC).

Dutch Archival Records, Published

Chijs, J.A. van der et al., ed. *Dagh-Register Gehouden int Casteel Batavia vant Passerende daer ter plaetse als over Geheel Nederlandts-India Anno, 1640–1682* [The Daily Journals of Batavia Castle]. 's-Gravenhage and Batavia: Martinus Nijhoff and G. Kolff, 1887–1928.

Coolhaas, W.Ph., ed. *Generale Missieven van Gouveneurs-Generaale en Raden aan Heren XVII der Verenigde Oostindische Compagnie* [General Correspondence of the Governor Generals and the Seventeen Gentlemen of the Dutch East Indies Company], Vols 1–4. 's-Gravenhage: Martinus Nijhoff, 1960–71.

Heeres, J.E. and P.A. Tiele, ed. *Bouwstoffen voor de Geschiedenis der Nederlanders in den Maleischen Archipel* [Information for the History of the Dutch in the Malay Archipelago], Vols 1–3. 's-Gravenhage: Martinus Nijhoff, 1886–95.

Heeres, J.E. and F.W. Stapel, eds. *Corpus Diplomaticum Neerlando-Indicum*, Vols 1–6. 's-Gravenhage: Martinus Nijhoff, 1907–55.

Jonge, J.K.J. de, ed. *De Opkomst van het Nederlandsch Gezag in Oost-Indie* [The Origins of Dutch Power in the East-Indies], Vols 1–8. 's-Gravenhage: Martinus Nijhoff, 1862–88.

English Archival Records and Manuscripts

British Library, India Office Records.
Factory Records.
G/21 Java, 1595-1827 London, Recordak Microfilm Service, 1956.
G/35 Sumatra, 1615-1825 London, Recordak Microfilm Service, 1960.
India Office MSS Eur/Mack (1822)/5.

English and Dutch Sources, Published

Bastin, John. *The British in West Sumatra (1685-1825): A Selection of Documents, Mainly from the East India Company Records Preserved in the India Office Library, Commonwealth Relations Office, London.* Kuala Lumpur: University of Malaya Press, 1965.

Beaulieu, Augustine de. "Memoirs of Admiral Beaulieu's Voyage to East Indies (1619-1622), drawn up by himself", in *Navigantium atque Itinerarium Bibliotheca. Or a Compleat Collection of Voyages*, trans. M. Thevenot, ed. John Harris. London: printed for T. Bennet, 1705, pp. 228-335.

─────── "The Expedition of Commodore Beaulieu to the East Indies", in *Navigantium atque Itinerarium Bibliotheca. Or a Complete Collection of Voyages*, ed. John Harris. London: printed for T. Woodward et al. Revised ed., 1744, pp. 717-49.

Best, Thomas. The *Voyage of Thomas Best to the East Indies, 1612-14*, ed. Sir William Foster. London: The Hakluyt Society, 1934.

Bort, Balthasar. "Report of Governor Balthasar Bort on Malacca: 1678", trans. M.J. Bremner, intro. and notes C.O. Blagden, *Journal of the Malayan Branch of the Royal Asiatic Society* 5, 1. Singapore: Methodist Publishing House, 1927.

Bowrey, Thomas. *A Geographical Account of Countries Round the Bay of Bengal, 1669 to 1679*, ed. Lt-Col. Sir Richard Carnac Temple. London: The Hakluyt Society, 1905.

Braddell, T. "On the History of Acheen", *Journal of the Indian Archipelago and Eastern Asia* 5 (1851): 15-25.

─────── . "Adat Atjeh", *Journal of the Indian Archipelago and Eastern Asia* 4 (1858): 598-606 and 728-33; 5 (1858): 6-31.

Dam, Pieter van. *Pieter van Dam's Beschrijvinge van de Oostindische Compagnie* [Description of the East India Company], Vols 1-7, ed. Frederik Willem Stapel and C.W.Th van Boetzelaer van Dubbeldam. 's-Gravenhage: Martinus Nijhoff, 1927-54.

Dampier, William. *A New Voyage Round the World*, ed. N.M. Penzer, intro. Sir Albert Gray. London: The Argonaut Press, 1927.

———. *Voyages and Discoveries*, ed. N.M. Penzer, intro. and notes Clennell Wilkinson. London: The Argonaut Press, 1931.

Danvers, F.C. and W. Foster. *Letters Received by the East India Company from Servants in the East, 1602-1617*, Vols 1-6. London: Sampson Low, Marston, 1896-1902.

East India Company. *Records of Fort St. George: Diary and Consultation Book of 1686, Vol. II*. Madras: Superintendent, Government Press, 1913.

———. *Despatches from England [to Fort St. George] 1681-86*. Madras: Superintendent, Government Press, 1916.

Fawcett, C.R. *The English Factories in India 1670-1684*, Vols 1-4. Oxford: The Clarendon Press, 1936-55.

Foster, W. *The English Factories in India 1618-1669: A Calendar of Documents in the India Office, British Museum and Public Record Office*, Vols 1-3. Oxford: The Clarendon Press, 1906-27.

Graaff, Nicolaus de. *Reisen van Nicolaus de Graaff: gedaan naar alle gewesten des werelds beginnende 1639 tot 1687 incluis*. [The Travels of Nicolaus de Graaff around the World from 1639-1687], ed. J.C.M. Warnsinck. 's-Gravenhage: Martinus Nijhoff, 1930.

Hamilton, Alexander. *A New Account of the East Indies*, ed. Sir William Foster. London: The Argonaut Press, 1930.

———. *A Scottish Sea Captain in Southeast Asia, 1689-1723*, ed. Michael Smithies. Chiang Mai: Silkworm Books, 1997.

Houtman, Frederick de. *Cort Verhael vant' gene wedervaren is Frederick de Houtman; tot Atchien* [A Short Account of What Happened to Frederik de Houtman; to Aceh]. Gouda: G.B. van Goor Zonen, 1880.

Leeuw, W.J.A. de. *Het Painansch Contract*. Amsterdam: H.J. Paris, 1926.

Markham, A.H., ed. *The Voyages and Works of John Davis the Navigator*. London: The Hakluyt Society, 1880.

Marsden, William. *The History of Sumatra*, intro. John Bastin. Singapore: Oxford University Press. 3rd ed., 1986.

Mundy, Peter. *The Travels of Peter Mundy in Europe and Asia, 1608-1667*, ed. Lt-Col. Sir Richard Carnac Temple, Vols 1-5. Cambridge: The Hakluyt Society, 1907-25.

Nieuhof, Johannes. *Voyages and Travels into Brasil, and East-Indies...* London: Awnsham and John Churchill, 1703.

———. *Voyages and Travels to the East Indies, 1653–1670*. Singapore and New York: Oxford University Press, 1988.

Pires, Tome. *The Suma Oriental of Tome Pires: An Account of the East, from the Red Sea to Japan...* Vol. 1, ed. Armando Cortesao. London: The Hakluyt Society, 1944.

Roy, Jacob Jansz de. *Hachelijke reis-togt van Jacob Jansz de Roy, Na Borneo en Atchin, In sijn vlugt van Batavia, dewaards ondernomen in Het Jaar 1691* [The Precarious Journey by Jacob Jansz de Roy to Borneo and Aceh in his Vessel from Batavia in 1691]. Leiden: Pieter van der Aa, 1887.

Sainsbury, E.B. *A Calendar of the Court Minutes, etc. of the East India Company, 1635-1679*, Vols 1-11. Oxford: The Clarendon Press, 1907-38.

Schouten, Wouter. *De Oost-Indische Voyagie van Wouter Schouten*, ed. Michael Breet with Dr Marijke Barend-van Haeften. Zutphen: Walburg Press, 2003.

Valentijn, François. *Oud en Nieuw Oost-Indiën* [Old and New East-India], Vols 1-5. Dordrecht and Amsterdam: J. van Braam, G. onder de Linden, 1724-26.

———. "Valentyn's Account of Malacca (Cont.)", trans. D.F.A. Hervey, *Journal of the Straits Branch of the Royal Asiatic Society* 22 (1890): 225-46.

"Voyage Made by Jacob Janssen de Roy to Borneo and Atcheen, 1691". Completed in 1698 in Batavia at the order of William van Oudtschoorn, Governor General of Netherlands East Indies. Translated from the Dutch into English in 1816, British Library, India Office MSS Eur/Mack (1822)/5 (orig. publ. Holland, ed. Johannes Oosterwijk, 1716).

Malay Sources, Manuscripts

Tun Sri Lanang Library, Universiti Kebangsaan Malaysia [The National University of Malaysia].

Malay Manuscript Archive.

MS 1, Salasilah keturunan Sultan-Sultan dalam negeri Aceh; iaitu keturunan anak cucu Sultan Iskandar Zulkarnain.

MS 2, Kesultanan dan pemerintahan di zaman kegemilangan kerajaan Aceh.

MS 3, Kanun Syarak Kerajaan Aceh di zaman pemerintahan Sultan Alaudin Mansur Syah.

MS 4, Peta Aceh dan susunan kabinet pemerintahan Aceh.

MS 5, Salasilah taraf hulubalang serta hukum laut dan dagang.

MS 6, Hukum menenggala sawah; hukum hutang piutang emas, gelaran resmi menteri-menteri kerajaan Aceh dizaman pemerintahan Sultan Iskandar Muda Mahkota Alam.

MS 10, Hukum hak milik tanah dan perintah kerajaan Aceh kepada rakyat supaya belajar dan mengajar ilmu dunia dan akhirat.
MS 11, Hukum kapal-kapal yang belayar diperairan negeri Aceh dan hukum memahalkan harga makanan dan pakaian.

Malay Sources, Published

Abdul Rahman. *Syair Puteri Hijau (Soeto Tjerita jang Benar Telah kejadian di Tanah Deli)* [The Poem of Princess Green (A True Story that Happened in the Land of Deli)]. Weltervreden: Balai Pustaka, 1927.
Abdul Samad Ahmad, ed. *Sulalatus Salatin: Sejarah Melayu* [Malay Annals]. Kuala Lumpur: Dewan Bahasa dan Pustaka, 1984.
Cheah Boon Keng, ed. *Sejarah Melayu: The Malay Annals*. Kuala Lumpur: Malaysian Branch of the Royal Asiatic Society, 1998.
Drewes, G.W.J. and P. Voorhoeve, ed. *Adat Atjeh*. 's-Gravenhage: Martinus Nijhoff, 1958.
Hill, A.H. "Hikayat Raja-raja Pasai" [The Chronicles of the Kings of Pasai], *Journal of the Malayan Branch of the Royal Asiatic Society* 33, 2 (1960): 1–215.
Iskandar, Teuku, ed. *De Hikayat Atjeh*. 's-Gravenhage: Martinus Nijhoff, 1958.
———, ed. *Bustan us-Salatin*. Kuala Lumpur: Dewan Bahasa dan Pustaka, 1966.
Khalid M. Hussain, ed. *Taj us-Salatin*. Kuala Lumpur: Dewan Bahasa dan Pustaka, 1992.
Muhammad Haji Salleh, ed. *Sulalat al-Salatin Ya'ni Perteturun Segala Raja-raja* [Geneology of Rulers]. Kuala Lumpur: Yayasan Karyawan dan Dewan Bahasa dan Pustaka, 1997.
Ras, J.J., ed. *Hikayat Bandjar: A Study in Malay Historiography*. 's-Gravenhage: Martinus Nijhoff, 1968.
Siti Hawa Haji Salleh, ed. *Bustan al-Salatin*. Kuala Lumpur: Dewan Bahasa dan Pustaka, 1992.
———, ed. *Hikayat Patani*. Kuala Lumpur: Dewan Bahasa dan Pustaka, 1992.
Teeuw, A. and D. Wyatt, trans. and ed. *Hikayat Patani: The Story of Patani*. 's-Gravenhage: Martinus Nijhoff, 1970.
Tjut Rahmah M.A. Gani and Ramli Harun. *Adat Aceh*. Jakarta: Departemen Pendidikan dan Kebudayaan, 1985.

Tuanku Abdul Jalil, ed. *Adat Meukuta Alam*. Banda Aceh: Pusat Dokumentasi dan Informasi Aceh, 1991.

Winstedt, R.O., ed., "The Malay Annals or *Sejarah Melayu*", *Journal of the Malayan Branch of the Royal Asiatic Society* 16, 3 (1938): 1–222.

Portuguese Sources, Archival Records

Instituto dos Arquivos Nacionais Alameda da Universidade, Lisbon, Portugal.

Letter from Sultanah Safiatuddin Tajul Alam to the Viceroy of the Estado da India, 1668 (Portuguese copy), Ministério dos Negócios Estrangeiros, 558, n. 119.

Secondary Literature

Abbott, Nabia. "Women and the State in Early Islam", *Journal of Near Eastern Studies* 1, 1 (1942): 106–26.

(Haji) Abdul Malik Karim Amrullah [Hamka]. "Dewan Perwakilan Rakjat Atjeh Diabad Ketujuhbelas" [Aceh's House of Representatives in the 17th Century], *Gema Islam*, No. 36-37 (1963): 11-2.

Abdullah Sani Usman. *Nilai Sastera Ketatanegaraan dan Undang-undang dalam Kanun Syarak Kerajaan Aceh dan Bustanus Salatin* [The Value of Literature on Governance and Law in the Canon Law of the Kingdom of Aceh and Garden of Kings]. Bangi, Selangor: Penerbit Universiti Kebangsaan Malaysia, 2005.

Abu Talib Ahmad and Tan Liok Ee, ed. *New Terrains in Southeast Asian History*. Athens, OH: Ohio University Press, 2003.

Adnan Abdullah et al. *Kedudukan dan Peranan Wanita Pedesaan Daerah Istimewa Aceh* [The Position and Role of Women in the Aceh Special Region Countryside]. Jakarta: Departemen Pendidikan dan Kebudayaan Proyek Inventarisasi dan Dokumentasi Kebudayaan Daerah, 1986.

Affan Seljuq. "Relations between the Ottoman Empire and Muslim Kingdoms in the Malay-Indonesian Archipelago", *Der Islam* 57 (1980): 301–10.

Ahmad Daudy. *Syeikh Nuruddin ar-Raniri*. Jakarta: Penerbitan Bulan Bintang, 1978.

———. *Allah dan Manusia dalam Konsepsi Syeikh Nurudin al-Raniri* [God and Man in Sheikh Nurudin al-Raniri's Conception]. Jakarta: C.V. Rajawali, 1983.

Ahmad, Leila. *Women and Gender in Islam: Historical Roots of a Modern Debate*. New Haven: Yale University Press, 1992.

Al-Attas, Syed Muhammad Naguib. "Raniri and the Wujudiyyah of 17th Century Acheh", *Monographs of the Malaysian Branch of the Royal Asiatic Society*, No. 3, ed. Wang Gungwu. Singapore: Malaysia Printers, 1966.

Al-Ghazali. *Nasihat al-Muluk: Nasihat Kepada Raja-raja* [Advice for Kings], translit. Jelani Harun. Kuala Lumpur: Dewan Bahasa dan Pustaka, 2006.

Ali Hasjmy. "Wanita Aceh dalam Pemerintahan dan Peperangan" [Acehnese Women in Government and in War], in *Wanita Indonesia Sebagai Negarawan dan Panglima Perang* [Indonesian Women as Statesmen and Military Commanders], ed. Emi Suhaimi. Banda Aceh: Yayasan Pendidikan Ali Hasjmy, 1953.

———. *Iskandar Muda Meukuta Alam.* Jakarta: Bulan Bintang, 1975.

———. *59 Tahun Aceh Merdaka di bawah Pemerintahan Ratu* [59 Years of Aceh's Independence under Female Rule]. Jakarta: Penerbitan Bulan Bintang, 1977.

Alves, Gorge Manuel dos Santos. "Princes contre marchands au crepuscule de Pasai, 1494-1521", *Archipel* 47, 1 (1994): 125-46.

Amina Wadud. *Qu'ran and Woman: Rereading the Sacred Text from a Woman's Perspective.* New York: Oxford University Press, 1999.

———. *Inside the Gender Jihad: Women's Reform in Islam.* Oxford: Oneworld Publications, 2006.

Amirell, Stefan, "The Blessings and Perils of Female Rule: New Perspectives on the Reigning Queens of Patani, c. 1584-1718", *Journal of Southeast Asian Studies* 42, 2 (2011): 303-23.

Amirul Hadi. *Islam and State in Sumatra: A Study of Seventeenth-Century Aceh.* Leiden: E.J. Brill, 2004.

Andaya, Barbara W. *Perak, the Abode of Grace: A Study of an Eighteenth Century Malay State.* Kuala Lumpur: Oxford University Press, 1979.

———. "Melaka under the Dutch, 1641-1796", in *Melaka: The Transformation of a Malay Capital c. 1400-1980*, ed. K.S. Sandhu and P. Wheatley. Kuala Lumpur: Oxford University Press, 1983, pp. 195-241.

———. "The Changing Religious Role of Women in Pre-Modern South East Asia", reprinted in *Representations of Gender, Democracy and Identity Politics in Relation to South Asia*, ed. Renuka M. Sharma. New Delhi: Sri Satguru Publications, 1996, pp. 105-29.

———, ed. *Other Pasts: Women, Gender and History in Early Modern Southeast Asia.* Honolulu: Center of Southeast Asian Studies, 2000.

Andaya, Leonard Y. and B.W. Andaya, "Southeast Asia in the Early Modern Period; Twenty-Five Years on", *Journal of Southeast Asian Studies* 26, 1 (1995): 92-8.

Andaya, Leonard Y. *The Kingdom of Johor, 1641–1728.* Kuala Lumpur: Oxford University Press, 1975.

———. "The Structure of Power in 17th Century Johor", in *Pre-Colonial State Systems in Southeast Asia: The Malay Peninsula, Sumatra, Bali-Lombok, South Celebes*, ed. Anthony Reid and Lance Castles. Kuala Lumpur: Monograph 6 of the Malaysian Branch of the Royal Asiatic Society, 1975, pp. 1–11.

———. *The Heritage of Arung Palakka: A History of South Sulawesi (Celebes) in the Seventeenth Century.* 's-Gravenhage: Martinus Nijhoff, 1981.

———. "Aceh's Contribution to Standards of Malayness", *Archipel* 61, 1 (2001): 29–68.

———. "The Seventeenth-Century Acehnese Model of Malay Society", in *Reading Asia: New Research in Asian Studies*, ed. Frans Husken and Dick van der Meij. Richmond, Surrey: Curzon Press, 2001, pp. 83–109.

———. "'A Very Good-Natured but Awe-Inspiring Government': The Reign of a Successful Queen in Seventeenth-Century Aceh", in *Hof en Handel. Aziatische Vorsten en de VOC, 1620–1720* [Court and Trade: Asian Rulers and the VOC, 1620–1720], ed. Elsbeth Locher-Scholten and Peter Rietbergen. Leiden: KITLV Press, 2004, pp. 59–84.

———, "The Stranger-King Complex in Bugis-Makassar Society", paper at the Stranger-Kings in Southeast Asia and Elsewhere Workshop, Jakarta, Indonesia, 5–7 June 2006.

Arasaratnam, S. "The Use of Dutch Materials for Southeast Asia's Historical Writing", *Journal of Southeast Asian History* 3, 1 (1962): 95–105.

———. "Some Notes on the Dutch in Malacca and the Indo-Malayan Trade, 1641–1670", *Journal of Southeast Asian History* 10, 3 (1969): 480–90.

———. *Maritime Trade, Society and European Influence in Southern Asia, 1600–1800.* Brookfield, VT: Ashgate Variorum, 1995.

Ardener, Shirley, ed. *Perceiving Women.* London: Malaby Press, 1975.

Auni Luthfi. "Decline of the Islamic Empire of Aceh, 1641–1699", MA thesis, McGill University, 1993. Available at http://digitool.library.mcgill.ca/R/?func=dbin-jump-full&object_id=26066&local_base=GEN01-MCG02 [accessed 24 June 2015].

Azra Azyumardi. *The Origins of Islamic Reformism in Southeast Asia: Networks of Malay-Indonesian and Middle Eastern 'Ulama' in the Seventeenth and Eighteenth Centuries.* Honolulu: Allen and Unwin, University of Hawai'i Press, 2004.

Barendse, Rene J. *The Arabian Seas: The Indian Ocean World of the Seventeenth Century*. Armonk, NY: M.E. Sharpe, 2002.

Barnard, Timothy P. *Multiple Centres of Authority: Society and Environment in Siak and Eastern Sumatra, 1674–1827*. Leiden: KITLV Press, 2003.

Bartlett, Robert. *England under the Norman and Angevin Kings, 1075–1225*. New York: Oxford University Press, 2000.

Basel, J.L. van. "Begin en Voortgang van onzen Handel en Bezittingen op Sumatra's Westkust", *Tijdschrift voor Neerlands-Indie* 9, 2 (1847): 1–57.

Bassett, D.K. "The Factory of the English India Company at Bantam, 1602–1682", PhD thesis, University of London, 1955.

———. "European Influences in Southeast Asia, c 1500–1630", *Journal of Southeast Asian History* 4, 2 (1963): 134–65.

———. "Early English Trade and Settlement in Asia, 1602–1690", in *Britain and the Netherlands in Europe and Asia*, ed. J.S. Bromley and E.H. Kossmann. London: Macmillan, 1968, pp. 83–109.

———. "British 'Country' Trade and Local Trade Networks in the Thai and Malay States, c. 1680–1770", *Modern Asian Studies* 23, 4 (1989): 625–43.

———. *The British in Southeast Asia during the 17th and 18th Centuries*. Occasional Paper No. 18. University of Hull: Centre for Southeast Asian Studies, 1990.

———. "Early English Trade and Settlement in Asia, 1602–1690", in *Trade, Finance and Power*, ed. Patrick Tuck. London and New York: Routledge, 1998, pp. 1–25.

Beck, Lois and Nikki R. Keddie, ed. *Women in the Muslim World*. Cambridge, MA: Harvard University Press, 1978.

Black, Jeremy. *Europe and the World, 1650–1830*. Oxford and New York: Routledge, 2002.

Blake, Stephen P. *Shahjahanabad: The Sovereign City in Mughal India, 1639–1739*. Cambridge: Cambridge University Press, 1991.

Blussé, Leonard, F.P. van der Putten and Hans Vogel, ed. *Pilgrims to the Past: Private Conversations with Historians of European Expansion*. Leiden: CNWS Publications, 1996.

Blussé, Leonard and K. Zandvliet. *The Dutch Encounter with Asia, 1600–1950*. Amsterdam: Rijksmuseum, 2002.

Blussé, Leonard and Felipe Fernández-Armesto, ed. *Shifting Communities and Identity Formation in Early Modern Asia*. Leiden: Leiden University Press, 2003.

Borschberg, Peter, "Luso-Johor-Dutch Relations in the Straits of Malacca and Singapore, c. 1600–1623", *Itinerario* 28, 2 (2004): 15–33.

———. "Hugo Grotius' Theory of Trans-Oceanic Trade Regulation: Revisiting Mare Liberum (1609)". *IILJ Working Paper* 2005/14 Series. History and Theory of International Law. Available at http://www.academia.edu/4302946/Grotius_Theory_of_Trans-Oceanic_Trade_Regulation_Revisiting_Mare_Liberum_1609_ [accessed 20 Oct. 2016].

Boxer, Charles. "A Note on Portuguese Reactions to the Revival of the Red Sea Spice Trade and the Rise of Aceh, 1540–1600", *Journal of Southeast Asian History* 10, 3 (1969): 415–28.

Bradley, Francis. "Piracy, Smuggling and Trade in the Rise of Patani, 1490–1600", *Journal of the Siam Society* 96 (2008): 27–50.

———. "Moral Order in a Time of Damnation: The *Hikayat Patani* in Historical Context", *Journal of Southeast Asian Studies* 40, 2 (2009): 267–93.

Brakel, L.F. "State and Statecraft in 17th Century Aceh", in *Pre-Colonial State Systems in Southeast Asia*, ed. Reid and Castles. MBRAS, 1975, pp. 45–55.

Brotton, Jerry. *The Renaissance Bazaar: From the Silk Road to Michelangelo*. New York: Oxford University Press, 2002.

Bruijn, J.R. and I. Schoffer. *Shipping of the Dutch East Indies Company between the Dutch Republic and Southeast Asia*. Leiden: Leiden University, 1968.

Bruijn, J.R., F.S. Gaastra and I. Schoffer, ed. *Dutch-Asiatic Shipping in the 17th and 18th Centuries*, Vols 1-3. 's-Gravenhage: Martinus Nijhoff, 1987.

Cameron, Averil. "The Construction of Court Ritual: The Byzantine *Book of Ceremonies*", in *Rituals of Royalty: Power and Ceremonial in Traditional Societies*, ed. David Cannadine and Simon Price. Cambridge: Cambridge University Press, 1987, pp. 106–36.

Chambert-Loir, Henri. "Chronique: Rapport de Mission à Aceh", *Bulletin de l'Ecole Française d'Extrême-Orient* 64, 1 (1977): 303–10.

Chaudhuri, K.N. "The East India Company and the Export of Treasure in the Early 17th Century", *Economic History Review* 16, 1 (1963): 23–38.

———. *The Trading World of Asia and the English East India Company, 1660–1760*. Cambridge: Cambridge University Press, 1978.

———. *Trade and Civilization in the Indian Ocean: An Economic History from the Rise of Islam to 1750*. Cambridge: Cambridge University Press, 1985.

Chaudhury, S. and M. Morineau. *Merchants, Companies and Trade, Europe and Asia in the Early Modern Era*. Cambridge: Cambridge University Press, 1999.

Cheah Boon Keng, "Power behind the Throne: The Role of Queens and Court Ladies in Malay History", *Journal of the Malaysian Branch of the Royal Asiatic Society* 66, 1 (1993): 1–21.

Chutintaranond, Sunait and Chris Baker, ed. *Recalling Local Pasts: Autonomous History in Southeast Asia.* Chiang Mai: Silkworm Books, 2002.

Clarence-Smith, William G. "Elephants, Horses, and the Coming of Islam to Northern Sumatra", *Indonesia and the Malay World* 32, 93 (2004): 271–84.

Colombijn, Freek. "The Volatile State in Southeast Asia: Evidence from Sumatra, 1600–1800", *Journal of Asian Studies* 62, 2 (2003): 497–529.

Crecelius, D. and E.A. Beardow. "A Reputed Acehnese *Sarakata* of the Jamal Al-Lail Dynasty", *Journal of the Malaysian Branch of the Royal Asiatic Society* 52, 2 (1979): 51–66.

Daftary, Farhad. "Sayyida Hurra: The Isma'ili Sulayhid Queen of Yemen", in *Women in the Medieval Islamic World: Power, Patronage and Piety,* ed. Gavin Hambly. New York: St. Martin's Press, 1998, pp. 117–30.

Dasgupta, Arun Kumar. "Acheh in the Seventeenth Century Asian Trade", *Bengal Past and Present* 81, 151 (1962): 37–49.

———. "Aceh in Indonesian Trade and Politics 1600–1641", PhD thesis, Cornell University, 1962.

Disney, Anthony, ed. *Historiography of Europeans in Africa and Asia, 1450–1800.* Brookfield, VT: Ashgate Variorum, 1995.

Djajadiningrat, Raden Hoesein. "Critisch overzicht van de in Maleische werken vervatte gegevens over de geschiedenis van het Soeltanaat van Atjeh", *Bijdragen tot de Taal-, Land- en Volkenkunde* 8, 1 (1911): 135–265.

———. *Kesultanan Aceh (Suatu Pembahasan Tentang Sejarah Kesultanan Aceh Berdasarkan Bahan-bahan Yang Terdapat Dalam Karya Melayu)* [Aceh Sultanate (A Debate on its History Based on Malay Sources)], trans. Teuku Hamid of "Critisch..." No. 12. Aceh: Departemen Pendidikan dan Kebudayaan: Proyek Pengembangan Permuseuman, 1982–83.

Drakard, Jane. "An Indian Ocean Port: Sources for the Earlier History of Barus", *Archipel* 37 (1989): 53–82.

———. *A Malay Frontier: Unity and Duality in a Sumatran Kingdom.* Ithaca, NY: Southeast Asia Program Publications, Cornell University, 1990.

———. *A Kingdom of Words: Language and Power in Sumatra.* London: Oxford University Press, 1999.

Drewes, G.W.J. "De Herkomst van Nuruddin ar-Raniri", *Bijdragen tot de Taal-, Land- en- Volkenkunde* 111 (1955): 137–51.

———. "Nur al-Din al Raniri's Charge of Heresy against Hamzah Fansuri and Shamsuddin from an Internal Point of View", in *Cultural Contact and*

Textual Interpretation: Papers from the Fourth European Colloquim on Malay and Indonesian Studies, ed. C.D. Grijns and S.O. Robson. Dordrecht: Foris Publications, 1986, pp. 54–9.

Duby, G. and M. Perrot, ed. *A History of Women in the West.* Cambridge, MA: Belknap Press, 1992–94.

Eagly, A.H. and M.C. Johannesen-Schmidt. "The Leadership Styles of Women and Men", *Journal of Social Issues* 57, 4 (2001): 781–97.

Esterik, Penny van, ed. *Women of Southeast Asia.* Detroit, MI: North Illinois University, Centre for Southeast Asian Studies, 1982.

Farrington, A. "Negotiations at Aceh in 1684: An Unpublished English Document", *Indonesia and the Malay World* 27, 77 (1999): 19–33.

Fatima Mernissi. *Women and Islam: A Historical and Theological Enquiry.* Oxford: Basil Blackwell, 1987.

———. *The Veil and the Male Elite: A Feminist Interpretation of Women's Rights in Islam*, trans Mary Jo Lakeland. Cambridge, MA: Perseus Books, 1991.

———. *Forgotten Queens of Islam*, trans. Mary Jo Lakeland. Minneapolis: University of Minnesota Press, 1993.

———. *Hidden from History: Forgotten Queens of Islam.* Lahore: ASR Publications, 1994.

———. *Women's Rebellion in Islamic Memory.* London: Zed Books, 1996.

Fernández-Armesto, Felipe. "The Stranger-Effect in Early Modern Asia", in *Shifting Communities*, ed. Blussé and Fernández-Armesto. Leiden, 2003, pp. 181–202.

———. *Pathfinders: A Global History of Exploration.* Oxford: Oxford University Press, 2006.

Fleschenberg, Andrea and Claudia Derichs, ed. *Women and Politics in Asia: A Springboard for Democracy?* Singapore: Institute of Southeast Asian Studies, 2012.

Forbes, Duncan, trans. *The Adventures of Hatim Tai: A Romance.* London: printed for the Oriental Translation Fund, 1830.

Francis, E. "De Vestiging der Nederlanders ter Westkust van Sumatra" [The Establishment of the Dutch on the Sumatra West Coast], *Tijdschrift voor Indische Taal-, Land- En Volkenkunde* 5, 2 (1856): 8–33.

Fredricksmeyer, E.A. "The Origins of Alexander's Royal Insignia", *Transactions and Proceedings of the American Philological Association* 127 (1997): 97–109.

Geertz, Clifford. *Negara: The Theatre State in 19th Century Bali.* Princeton, NJ: Princeton University Press, 1980.

Glamann, Kristof. *Dutch-Asiatic Trade, 1620–1740*. Copenhagen: Danish Science Press, 1958.
Gonda, J. *Ancient Indian Kingship from the Religious Point of View*. Leiden: E.J. Brill, 1969.
Goor, Jurrien van. "Sea Power, Trade and State-Formation: Pontianak and the Dutch, 1780–1840", in *Trading Companies in Asia, 1600–1830*, ed. Jurrien van Goor. Utrecht: HES Utigevers, 1986, pp. 83–106.
———. "Merchants as Diplomats: Embassies as an Illustration of European-Asian Relations", in *Prelude to Colonialism: The Dutch in Asia*, ed. Jurrien van Goor and Foskelien van Goor. Hilversum: Uitgeverij Verloren, 2004, pp. 27–46.
Grinter, Catherine Anne. "Book IV of the *Bustan us-Salatin* by Nuruddin ar-Raniri: A Study from the Manuscripts of a 17th Century Malay Work Written in North Sumatra", PhD thesis, University of London, 1979.
Gullick, John M. *Malay Society in the Late Nineteenth Century*. Singapore: Oxford University Press, 1987.
H.M. Zainuddin. *Tarich Atjeh dan Nusantara* [History of Aceh and the Archipelago]. Medan: Pustaka Iskandar Muda, 1961.
Haan, F. de. "Naar Midden Sumatra in 1684", *Tijdschrift voor Indische Taal-, Land- en Volkenkunde* 39 (1897): 327–66.
Hall, Kenneth R. "The Opening of the Malay World to European Trade in the Sixteenth Century", *Journal of the Malaysian Branch of the Royal Asiatic Society* 58, 2 (1985): 85–107.
Hambly, Gavin, ed. *Women in the Medieval Islamic World: Power, Patronage, Piety*. New York: St. Martin's Press, 1998.
Harfield, Alan G. *Bencoolen: A History of the Honourable East India Company's Garrison on the West Coast of Sumatra, 1685–1825*. Barton-on-Sea, Hampshire: A and J Partnership, 1995.
Harriden, Jessica. *The Authority of Influence: Women and Power in Burmese History*. Copenhagen: NIAS Press, 2012.
Hasan, Zoya, ed. *Forging Identities: Gender, Communities and the State*. New Delhi: Kali for Women, 1994.
Healey, Robert M. "Waiting for Deborah: John Knox and Four Ruling Queens", *Sixteenth Century Journal* 25, 2 (1994): 371–86.
Henley, David. "Conflict, Justice, and the Stranger-King Indigenous Roots of Colonial Rule in Indonesia and Elsewhere", *Modern Asian Studies* 38, 1 (2004): 85–144.
Herrin, Judith. *Women in Purple: Rulers of Medieval Byzantium*. Princeton, NJ: Princeton University Press, 2001.

Hill, Barbara. *Imperial Women in Byzantium, 1025-1204: Power, Patronage and Ideology.* Harlow: Pearson Education, 1999.

Hodgson, Marshall G.S. *The Venture of Islam: Conscience and History in a World Civilisation*, trans. Mastuti Haji Isa and Rosiah Abdul Latiff as, *Kebangkitan Islam*, Vol. 1. Kuala Lumpur: Dewan Bahasa dan Pustaka, 2004.

Hurgronje, C. Snouck. *Mekka I. Die stadt und ihre Herren; II: Aus dem heutigen Leben* [Mecca I. The City and it Men; II: From the Present-day Life]. 's-Gravenhage: Martinus Nijhoff, 1888.

———. "Een Mekkansch Gezantschap naar Atjeh in 1683" [A Meccan Delegation to Aceh in 1683], *Bijdragen tot de Taal-, Land- en Volkenkunde (BKI)* 5, 3 (1888): 545-54.

———. *De Atjehers. Uitgegeven op last der Regeering.* Leiden: E.J. Brill, 1893-94.

———. *The Achenese*, trans. A.W.S. O'Sullivan with index by R.J. Wilkinson. Leiden: E.J. Brill, 1906.

Ibrahim Alfian. *Mata Uang Emas Kerajaan-Kerajaan di Aceh* [Gold Coins of the Aceh Kingdom]. Banda Aceh: Proyek Rehabilitasi dan Perluasan Museum Daerah Istimewa Aceh, 1979.

Irwin, G.W. "The Dutch and the Tin Trade of Malaya in the Seventeenth Century", in *Studies in the Social History of China and Southeast Asia: Essays in the Memory of Victor Purcell*, ed. Nicholas Tarling and Jerome Ch'en. London: Cambridge University Press, 1970, pp. 267-87.

Ismail Sarbini. "Wanita Sulalatus-Salatin Menangis Sepanjang Zaman?" [Women of the Malay Annals Crying through the Ages?], *Dewan Sastera* 20, 4 (1990): 44-8.

Ismail Sofyan, M. Hasan Basry and Ibrahim Alfian, ed. *Wanita Utama Nusantara dalam Lintasan Sejarah* [Prominent Women of the Archipelago in the Course of History]. Jakarta: Jayakarta Agung Offset, 1994.

Ito, Takeshi and Anthony Reid, "From Harbour Autocracies to 'Feudal' Diffusion in Seventeenth-Century Indonesia: The Case of Aceh", in *Feudalism: Comparative Studies*, ed. E. Leach, S.N. Mukherjee and J. Ward. Sydney: Sydney Association for Studies in Society and Culture, 1985, pp. 197-213.

Ito, Takeshi. "Why did Nuruddin Al-Raniri Leave Aceh in 1054 A.H.?", *Bijdragen tot de Taal-, Land- en Volkenkunde (BKI)* 134, 4 (1978): 489-91.

———. "The Elephant Trade of Aceh in the 1640s-60s", *Journal of East-West Maritime Relations* 3 (1994): 1-11.

———. "The World of the Adat Aceh: A Historical Study of the Sultanate of Aceh", PhD thesis, Australian National University, 1984. Available at https://digitalcollections.anu.edu.au/handle/1885/10071 [accessed 24 June 2015].

Jackson, Peter. "Sultan Radiyya Bint Iltutmish", in *Women in the Medieval Islamic World*, ed. Hambly. New York, 1999, pp. 181-97.

Jacobs, Els M. *Merchant in Asia: The Trade of the Dutch East Indies Company during the Eighteenth Century*. Leiden: CNWS Publications, 2006.

Jacobsen, Trudy. *Lost Goddesses: The Denial of Female Power in Cambodian History*. Denmark: NIAS Press, 2008.

Jay, Jennifer W. "Imagining Matriarchy: 'Kingdoms of Women' in Tang China", *Journal of the American Oriental Society* 116, 2 (1996): 220-9.

Johns, A.H. "Malay Sufism as Illustrated in an Anonymous Collection of 17th Century Tracts", *Journal of the Malayan Branch of the Royal Asiatic Society* 30, 2 (1957): 1-111.

Jolliffe, J.E.A. *Angevin Kingship* London: Adam and Charles Black, 1955.

Kammen, Douglas. "Queens of Timor", *Archipel* 84 (2012): 149-73.

Kathirithamby-Wells, J. and J. Villiers. *The Southeast Asian Port and Polity: The Rise and Demise*. Singapore: Singapore University Press, 1990.

Kathirithamby-Wells, J. "Acehnese Control over West Sumatra up to the Treaty of Painan 1663", *Journal of Southeast Asian History* 10, 3 (1969): 453-79.

———. "The Inderapura Sultanate: The Foundations of its Rise and Decline from the Sixteenth to the Eighteenth Centuries", *Indonesia* 21 (1976): 65-84.

———. "Royal Authority and the *Orang Kaya* in the Western Archipelago, c. 1500–1800", *Journal of Southeast Asian Studies* 17, 2 (1986): 256-67.

———. "Forces of Regional and State Integration in the Malay Archipelago, c. 1500–1700", *Journal of South East Asian Studies* 18, 1 (1987): 24-44.

———. "The Johor-Malay World, 1511-1784: The Ideology of Kingship in the Context of Change", *Sejarah* 1 (1988): 35-62.

———. "Restraints on the Development of Merchant Capitalism in Southeast Asia before c. 1800", in *Southeast Asia in the Early Modern Era: Trade, Power and Belief*, ed. Anthony Reid. Ithaca, NY: Cornell University Press, 1993, pp. 123-50.

———. "Forms and Concepts of Courtly Wealth in 17th Century Aceh, Ayutthaya and Banten", *Sejarah*, Special Issue (1994): 57-69.

———. "Ethics and Entrepreneurship in Southeast Asia, c. 1400–1800", in *Maritime Asia Profit Maximisation, Ethics, and Trade Structure c. 1300-1800*, ed. Karl Anton Sprengard and Roderich Ptak. Wiesbaden: Harrassowitz Verlag, 1994, pp. 171-87.

Khan, Shaharyar M. *The Begums of Bhopal: A Dynasty of Women Rulers in Raj India*. London: I.B. Tauris, 2000.
Kobkua Suwannathat-Pian. *Thai-Malay Relations: Traditional Intra-Regional Relations from the Seventeenth to the Early Twentieth Centuries*. Singapore: Oxford University Press, 1988.
———. "Thrones, Claimants, Rulers and Rules: The Problem of Succession in the Malay Sultanates", *Journal of the Malaysian Branch of the Royal Asiatic Society* 66, 2 (1993): 1–27.
Kroeskamp, Hendrick. *De Westkust en Minangkabau (1665–1668)*. Utretch: Drukkerij Fa. Schotanus and Jens, 1931.
Laderman, Carol. "Putting Malay Women in Their Place", in *Women of Southeast Asia*, ed. Van Esterik. Northern Illinois, 1996, pp. 79–99.
Laffan, Michael. "Dispersing God's Shadows–Reflections on the Translation of Arabic Political Concepts into Malay and Indonesian", paper for the project, 'History of Translations into Indonesian and Malaysian Languages' (n.d). Ian Proudfoot, *Malay Concordance Project*. Available at http://mcp.anu.edu.au/papers/laffan_apc.html [accessed 10 Oct. 2015].
Lal, Ruby. *Domesticity and Power in the Early Mughal World*. Cambridge: Cambridge University Press, 2005.
Lambton, Ann K.S. *State and Government in Medieval Islam: An Introduction to the Study of Islamic Political Theory: The Jurists*. Oxford: Oxford University Press, 1981.
Langen, K.F.H. van. *De Inrichting van het Atjehsche Staatsbestuur onder het Sultanaat* [The Organisation of the Aceh State Administration under the Sultanante]. 's-Gravenhage: KITLV Monograph, 1888. Trans. Aboe Bakar as *Susunan Pemerintahan Aceh Semasa Kesultanan*. Banda Aceh: Pusat Dokumentasi dan Informasi Banda Aceh, 1997.
Lee Kam Hing. "Foreigners in the Achehnese Court, 1760–1819", Paper No. 106, *International Conference on Asian History*. Kuala Lumpur, 1968.
———. *The Sultanate of Aceh: Relations with the British, 1760–1824*. Kuala Lumpur: Oxford University Press, 1995.
Lee, Patricia-Ann. "Reflections of Power: Margaret of Anjou and the Dark Side of Queenship", *Renaissance Quarterly* 39, 2 (1986): 183–217.
Lee, Stephen J. *The Reign of Elizabeth I: 1558–1603*. London: Routledge, 2007.
Lenman, Bruce. "The Exiled Stuarts and the Precious Symbols of Sovereignty", *Eighteenth Century* 25, 2 (2001): 185–200.
Lerner, Gerda. *The Creation of Patriarchy*, Vol. 1. *Women and History*. New York: Oxford University Press, 1986.
———. *Feminist Consciousness: From the Middle Ages to 1870*, Vol. 2. *Women and History*. New York: Oxford University Press, 1993.

Leupe, P.A. "The Siege and Capture of Malacca from the Portuguese in 1640–1641: Extracts from the Archives of the Dutch East Indies Company", trans. Mac Hacobian from "Berigten van het Historisch Genootschap te Utrecht, 1859", *Journal of the Malayan Branch of the Royal Asiatic Society* 14, 1 (1936): 128–429.

Leur, Jacob Cornelius van. *Indonesian Trade and Society, Essays in Asian Social and Economic History.* 's-Gravenhage: W. van Hoeve, 1955.

Lieberman, Victor B. "Wallerstein's System and the International Context of Early Modern South East Asian History", *Journal of Asian History* 24, 1 (1990): 70–90.

———. "An Age of Commerce in Southeast Asia? Problems of Regional Coherence: A Review Article", *Journal of Asian Studies* 54, 3 (1995): 796–807.

———, ed. *Beyond Binary Histories: Re-imagining Eurasia to c. 1830.* Ann Arbor, MI: Michigan University Press, 1999.

———. *Strange Parallels: Southeast Asian Global Context, c. 800–1830*, Vol. 1. *Integration on the Mainland.* Cambridge: Cambridge University Press, 2003.

Locher-Scholten, Elsbeth and Anke Niehof, ed. *Indonesian Women in Focus: Past and Present Notions* Dordrecht: Foris Publications, 1987.

Lombard, Denys. *Le Sultanate d'Atjeh au temps d'Iskandar Muda 1607–1636.* Paris: l'Ecole Française d'Extrême-Orient, 1967.

———. *Kerajaan Aceh: Jaman Sultan Iskandar Muda (1607–1636)* [Aceh Sultanate: Reign of Sultan Iskandar Muda (1607–1636)], trans. Winarsih Arifin. Jakarta: Balai Pustaka, 1986.

———. "The Malay Sultanate as a Socio-economic Model", in *Asian Merchants and Businessmen in the Indian Ocean and the China Sea*, ed. Denys Lombard and Jean Aubin. Oxford: Oxford University Press, 2000, pp. 113–20.

Manguin, Pierre-Yves. "Of Fortresses and Galleys: The Acehnese Siege of Melaka 1568 Following a Contemporary Bird's Eye View", *Modern Asian Studies* 22, 3 (1988): 607–28.

———. "The Merchant and the King: Political Myths of Southeast Asian Coastal Polities", *Indonesia* 52 (1991): 41–54.

———. "The Amorphous Nature of Coastal Polities in Insular Southeast Asia: Restricted Centres, Extended Peripheries", *Moussons* 5 (2002): 73–99. Available at https://moussons.revues.org/2699 [accessed 20 Oct. 2015].

Matar, Nabil. *Turks, Moors and Englishmen in the Age of Discovery.* New York: Columbia University Press, 1991.

Mclaren, Anne. "Elizabeth I as Deborah: Biblical Typology, Prophecy and Political Power", in *Gender, Power and Privilege in Early Modern Europe:*

1500–1700, ed. Jessica Munns and Penny Richards. Harlow: Pearson Education, 2003, pp. 90–107.

Meehan-Waters, Brenda. "Catherine the Great and the Problem of Female Rule", *Russian Review* 34, 3 (1975): 293–307.

Meersman, Achilles. *The Franciscans in the Indonesian Archipelago, 1300–1775*. Nauwelaerts: Lovain, 1967.

Meilink-Roelofsz, M.A.P. *Asian Trade and European Influence in the Indonesian Archipelago between 1500 and about 1630*. 's-Gravenhage: Martinus Nijhoff, 1962.

Miles, Rosalind. *Women and Power*. London: Macdonald, 1985.

Miller, Joseph C. "Nzinga of Matamba in New Perspective", *Journal of African History* 16, 2 (1975): 201–16.

Milner, A.C. "Malay Raja: A Study of Malay Political Culture in East Sumatra and the Malay Peninsula in the Early Nineteenth Century", PhD thesis, Cornell University, 1977.

———. *Kerajaan: Malay Political Culture on the Eve of Colonial Rule*. Tucson, AZ: University of Arizona Press, 1982.

Modern Humanities Research Association. *MHRA Style Book: Note for Authors, Editors, and Writers of Theses*, ed. Glanville Price et al. London: Modern Humanities Research Association. 6th ed., 2002. Available at http://eprints.um.edu.my/11584/ [accessed 20 Oct. 2015].

Monique Zaini-Lajoubert. "Imej Wanita dalam Beberapa Karya Sastera Melayu Tradisional dari Abad-abad ke 17 dan 19" [The Image of Women in Several Works of Traditional Malay Literature from the 17th to the 19th Centuries], *Alam Melayu* 2 (1994): 29–55. Available at http://www.mhra.org.uk/Publications/Books/StyleGuide/download.shtml [accessed 20 Oct. 2015].

Mohammad Dahlan Mansoer et al. *Sejarah Minangkabau*. Djakarta: Bhratara, 1970.

Mohammad Said. *Atjeh Sepanjang Abad* [Aceh through the Century], Vol. 1. Medan: Pengarang Sendiri, 1961.

Muhammad Akram Nadawi. *Al-Muhaddithat: The Women Scholars in Islam*. Oxford: Interface Publications, 2007.

Muhammad Gade Ismail and Rusdi Sufi. "Ratu Nurul Alam, Inayat Syah dan Kamalat Syah", in *Wanita Utama Nusantara dalam Lintasan Sejarah*, ed. Sofyan et al. Jakarta, 1994, pp. 62–75.

Mulaikka Hijjas. "The Woman Raja: Female Rule in Seventeenth Century Aceh", M. Phil thesis, University of Oxford, 2001.

Munns, Jessica and Penny Richards, ed. *Gender, Power and Privilege in Early Modern Europe, 1500–1700*. Harlow: Pearson Education, 2003.

Nagtegaal, Luc. "The Dutch East India Company and the Relations between Kartasura and the Javanese North Coast, c. 1680 to c. 1740", in *Trading Companies*, ed. Van Goor. Utrecht, 1986, pp. 51–81.

———. *Riding the Dutch Tiger: The Dutch East Indies Company and the Northeast Coast of Java, 1680–1743*, trans. Beverly Jackson. Leiden: KITLV Press, 1996.

Necipoglu, Gulru. "Suleyman the Magnificent and the Representation of Power in the Context of Ottoman-Hapsburg-Papal Rivalry", *The Art Bulletin* 71, 3 (1989): 401–27.

Newbury, Colin. *Patrons, Clients and Empire: Chieftaincy, and Over-rule in Asia, Africa, and the Pacific*. Oxford: Oxford University Press, 2003.

Nieuwenhuijze, C.A.O. van. *Samsu 'l-din van Pasai. Bijdrage tot de Kennis der Sumatraanse mystiek* [Samsu 'l-din from Pasai: A Contribution to the Knowledge of the Sumatran Mystique]. Leiden: E.J. Brill, 1945.

Nisriwani Yahya and Syed Zulflida S.M. Noor, ed. *101 Puteri Dunia Melayu: Sejarah dan Legenda* [101 Princesses in the Malay World: History and Legends]. Kuala Lumpur: Jabatan Muzium dan Antikuiti, 2003.

Ong, Aihwa and Michael G. Peletz, ed. *Bewitching Women, Pious Men: Gender and Body Politics in Southeast Asia*. Los Angeles, CA: University of California Press, 1995.

Pagden, Anthony, ed. *Facing Each Other: The World's Perception of Europe and Europe's Perception of the World*, Vol. 1. Brookfield, VT: Ashgate Variorum, 2000.

Pamenan, Iljas Sutan. *Rentjong Aceh Ditangan Wanita* [Aceh's Dagger in a Woman's Hand]. Jakarta: D.J. Waringin, 1959.

Parsons, John Carmi. "Family, Sex and Power: The Rhythms of Medieval Queenship", in *Medieval Queenship*, ed. John Carmi Parsons. New York: St. Martin's Press, 1993, pp. 1–11.

Pearson, Michael N., ed. *Spices in the Indian Ocean World*. Brookfield, VT: Ashgate Variorum, 1996.

———. *The Indian Ocean*. London: Routledge, 2003.

Penth, Hans Georg. "An Account in the Hikayat Atjeh on Relations between Siam and Atjeh", in *Felicitation Volumes of Southeast-Asian Studies. Presented to his Highness Prince Dhaninivat Kromamun Bidyalabh Bridhyakorn on the Occasion of his Eightieth Birthday*, Vol. 1. Bangkok: The Siam Society, 1965, pp. 55–69.

Pinto, Fernão Mendez. *The Voyages and Adventures of Ferdinand Mendes Pinto, the Portuguese*, trans H. Cogan with intro. A. Vambery. London: T.F. Unwin, 1891.

Pinto, Paulo J. de Sousa. "Captains, Sultans and Liasons Dangereuse: Melaka and Johor in the Late Sixteenth Century", in *Iberians in the Singapore-Melaka Area and Adjacent Regions (16th to 18th Century)*, ed. Peter Borschberg. Wiesbaden: Harrassowitz Verlag, 2004, pp. 131–46.

Pipes, Richard. *"Karamzin's Memoir on Ancient and Modern Russia": A Translation and Analysis*. Cambridge, MA: Harvard University Press, 1959.

Prakash, Om. "Asian Trade and European Impact: A Study of the Trade from Bengal, 1630-1720", in *The Age of Partnership, Europeans in Asia Before Dominion*, ed. Blair B. Kling and M.N. Pearson. Honolulu: University of Hawai'i Press, 1979, pp. 43–70.

———, ed. *European Commercial Expansion in Early Modern Asia*. Brookfield, VT: Ashgate Variorum, 1997.

Radermacher, J.C.M. "Beschrijving van het Eiland Sumatra, in zoo Verre Hetzelve tot nog toe Bekend is" [A Description of the Island of Sumatra to my Knowledge], *Verhandelingen van het Bataviaasch Genootschap van Kunsten en Wetenschappen* No. 3. Batavia: Te Lands Drukkerij, 1824, pp. 1–103.

Ramusack, Barbara and Sharon Sievers. *Women in Asia: Restoring Women to History.* Bloomington, IN: Indiana University Press, 1999.

Raychaudhuri, Tapankumar. *Jan Company in Coromandel, 1605-1690. A Study in the Interrelation of European Commerce and Traditional Economies.* 's-Gravenhage: Martinus Nijhoff, 1962.

Reid, Anthony and Takeshi Ito. "A Precious Dutch Map of Aceh, c. 1645", *Archipel* 57 (1999): 191–208.

Reid, Anthony. "16th Century Turkish Influence in Western Indonesia", *Journal of Southeast Asian History* 10, 3 (1969): 395–414.

———. "Trade and the Problem of Royal Power in Aceh, c. 1550–1700", in *Pre-Colonial State Systems in Southeast Asia*, ed. Reid and Castles. MBRAS, 1975, pp. 45–55.

———. "The Structure of Cities in Southeast Asia in the 15th to 17th Centuries", *Journal of Southeast Asian Studies* 11, 2 (1980): 235–50.

———. *Southeast Asia in the Age of Commerce, 1450-1680*, Vol. 1: *The Lands Below the Winds*. New Haven: Yale University Press, 1988.

———. "Elephants and Water in the Feasting of Seventeenth Century Aceh", *Journal of the Malaysian Branch of the Royal Asiatic Society* 62, 2 (1989): 25–44.

———. ed. *Southeast Asia in the Early Modern Era: Trade, Power and Belief.* Ithaca, NY: Cornell University Press, 1993.

———. *Southeast Asia in the Age of Commerce, 1450-1680*, Vol. 2: *Expansion and Crisis*. New Haven: Yale University Press, 1993.

———, ed. *Witnesses to Sumatra, A Travellers' Anthology*. Singapore: Oxford University Press, 1994.

———. "Female Roles in Pre-Colonial Southeast Asia", *Modern Asian Studies* 22, 3 (1998): 629–45.

———. *Charting the Shape of Early Modern Southeast Asia*. Singapore: ISEAS, 2000.

———. "Charismatic Queens of Southern Asia", *History Today* 53, 6 (2003): 30–5.

———. *An Indonesian Frontier: Acehnese and Other Histories of Sumatra*. Singapore: Singapore University Press, 2004.

———. "Understanding Melayu (Malay) as a Source of Diverse Modern Identities", in *Contesting Malayness: Malay Identity Across Boundaries*, ed. Timothy Barnard. Singapore: Singapore University Press, 2004, pp. 1–24.

———. "The Pre-Modern Sultanate's View of its Place in the World", in *Verandah of Violence: The Historical Background of the Aceh Problem*, ed. Anthony Reid. Singapore: Singapore University Press, 2006, pp. 52–71.

Rhodes, Nicholas, Michael Goh Han Peng and Vasilijs Mihailovs. "The Gold Coinages of Samudra Pasai and Aceh Dar As-Salam, the Islamic Sultanantes of Northern Sumatra, c. 1280–1760", unpublished document, Singapore, 2007.

Ricklefs, Merle Calvin. *A History of Modern Indonesia since c. 1300*. Basingstoke, Hampshire: Macmillan Press. 2nd ed., 1993.

Riddell, Peter G. *Islam and the Malay-Indonesian World: Transmission and Responses*. London: C. Hurst, 2001.

———. "Aceh in the Sixteenth and Seventeenth Centuries: 'Serambi Mekkah' and Identity", in *Verandah of Violence*, ed. Reid. Singapore, 2006, pp. 38–51.

Roded, Ruth, ed. *Women in Islam and the Middle East: A Reader*. London: I.B. Tauris, 1999.

Rusdi Sufi. "Sultanah Safiatuddin Syah", in *Wanita Utama Nusantara dalam Lintasan Sejarah*, ed. Sofyan et al. Jakarta, 1994, pp. 42–59.

Ruzy Suliza Hashim. *Out of the Shadows: Women in Malay Court Narratives*. Bangi, Selangor: National University of Malaysia, 2003.

Schrieke, Bertram Johannes Otto. *The Effect of Western Influence on Native Civilisations in the Malay Archipelago*. Java: G. Kolff, 1929.

———. *Indonesian Sociological Studies*, Vol. 1. *Selected Writings of B. Schrieke*. 's-Gravenhage: W. van Hoeve, 1955.

Sears, Laurie J., ed. *Fantasizing the Feminine in Indonesia*. Durham: Duke University Press, 1996.

Sharifah Zaleha Syed Hassan and Rashila Ramli, ed. *Kedudukan dan Citra Wanita dalam Sumber-sumber Tradisional Melayu* [Women's Position and Self-Image in Traditional Malay Sources]. Bangi, Selangor: Institut Alam dan Tamadun Melayu, 1998.

Sher Banu A.L. Khan. "A Glimpse of the Invisible: Queens and Ladies of the Court as Seen through the Eyes of the Malay Chronicles", unpublished manuscript, 1999.

———. "The Sultanahs of Aceh, 1641-99", in *Aceh: History, Politics and Culture*, ed. Arndt Graf, Susanne Schroter, Edwin Wieringa. Singapore: Institute of Southeast Asian Studies, 2010, pp. 3-25.

———. "Ties That Unbind: The Abortive Aceh-VOC Alliance for the Conquest of Melaka, 1640-1641", *Indonesia and the Malay World* 38, 111 (2010): 303-21.

———. "The Jewel Affair: The Sultana, Her *Orang Kaya* and the Dutch Foreign Envoys", in *Mapping the Acehnese Past*, ed. R. Michael Feener, Patrick Daly and Anthony Reid. Leiden: KITLV Press, 2011, pp. 141-62.

———. "What Happened to Sayf al-Rijal?", *Bijdragen tot de Taal-, Land- en Volkenkunde (BKI)* 168, 1 (2012): 100–11.

Siapno, Jacqueline Aquino. *Gender, Islam, Nationalism and the State in Aceh: The Paradox of Power, Co-optation and Resistance*. London: Routledge Curzon, 2002.

Siegel, James T. *The Rope of God*. Berkeley: University of California Press, 1969.

———. *Shadow and Sound: The Historical Thought of a Sumatran People*. Chicago: University of Chicago Press, 1979.

Siti Hawa Haji Salleh. "Pengaruh Citra Wanita dalam Sastera Tradisional ke atas Sastera Moden" [Women's Self-Image in Traditional Literature and its Influence on Modern Literature], *Dewan Sastera* (1992): 8-15.

Smail, John. "On the Possibility of an Autonomous History of Modern Southeast Asia", *Journal of Southeast Asian History* 2, 1 (1961): 72-102.

Spellberg, Denise A. *Politics, Gender and the Islamic Past: The Legacy of A'isah Bint Abi Bakr*. New York: Columbia University Press, 1994.

Spellman, W.M. *Monarchies 1000-2000*. London: Reaktion Books, 2001.

Stearns, Peter N. *Gender in World History*. London: Routledge, 2000.

Steenbrink, Karel. *Dutch Colonialism and Indonesian Islam: Contacts and Conflicts, 1596-1950*, trans. Jan Steenbrink and Henry Jansen. Amsterdam: Rodopi. 2nd ed., 2006.

Stowasser, Barbara F. *Women in the Qu'ran, Traditions and Interpretation*. New York: Oxford University Press, 1994.

Struys, Jan Jansz. *De schriklijke reis van Jan Jansz. Struys, 1668–1673*, ed. D.J. Douwes. Zaandijk: Klaas Woudt, 1974.

Stutterheim, W.F. "A Malay Sha'ir in Old-Sumatran Characters of 1380 A.D.", *Acta Orientalia* 14 (1936): 268–79.

Subrahmanyam, S. *The Portuguese Empire in Asia, 1500–1700: A Political and Economic History*. London: Longman, 1993.

Sunderland, Jane. *Gendered Discourses*. Basingstoke, Hampshire: Palgrave Macmillan, 2004.

Suzana Hj Othman and Muzaffar Dato' Hj Mohamad. *Ahlul-Bait Rasulullah SAW dan Kesultanan Melayu* [The Family of the Prophet (pbuh) and the Malay Sultanate]. Kuala Lumpur: Crescent News, 2006.

Tambiah, Stanley Jeyaraja. *Culture, Thought, and Social Action: An Anthropological Perspective*. Cambridge, MA: Harvard University Press, 1985.

Taufik Abdullah. "Kepemimpinan Wanita dalam Perspektif Sejarah" [Women Leaders from the Historical Perspective], *Sejarah: Pemikiran, Rekonstruksi, Persepsi* 5 (1994): 65–75.

Taylor, Jean G. *The Social World of Batavia: Europeans and Eurasians in Dutch Asia*. Madison, WI: Wisconsin University Press, 1983.

Teh Gallop, Annabel and Bernard Arps. *Golden Letters: Writing Traditions of Indonesia*. London, Jakarta: British Library, Yayasan Lontar, 1991.

Teh Gallop, Annabel. "Musings on a Piece of Wallpaper: Some Thoughts on Early Royal Letters from Aceh", paper presented at the International Workshop on Malay Manuscripts, Leiden University Library, 16–18 March, 1998.

———. "Malay Seal Inscriptions: A Study in Islamic Epigraphy from Southeast Asia", PhD. thesis, University of London, 2002.

———. "Gold, Silver and Lapis Lazuli: Royal Letters from Aceh in the 17th Century", in *Mapping the Acehnese Past*, ed. Feener et al. Leiden, 2011, pp. 105–40.

Thomaz, Luis Filipe F.R. "Sumatra's Westcoast in Portuguese Sources of the Mid 16th Century", in *Regions and Regional Developments in the Malay-Indonesian World*, ed. Bernhard Dahm, Sixth European Colloquium on Indonesian and Malay Studies (ECIMS). Wiesbaden: Harrassowitz Verlag, 1992, pp. 23–32.

———. "The Image of the Archipelago in Portuguese Cartography of the 16th and Early 17th Centuries", *Archipel* 49 (1995): 79–124.

Thornton, John K. "Legitimacy and Political Power: Queen Njinga, 1624–1663", *Journal of African History* 32, 1 (1991): 25–40.

Tichelman, G.L. "Een Atjehsche Sarakata (Afschrift van een besluit van Iskandar Muda)", in *Tijdschrift voor Indische Taal, Land, en Volkenkunde uitgegeven*

door het Bataviaasch Genootschap van Kunst en Wetenschappen 73 (1933): 368–73.
Tiele, P.A. *De Europeërs in den Maleischen Archipel. Negende gedeelte 1618–1623.* 's-Gravenhage: Martinus Nijhoff, 1887.
Tuck, Patrick J.N., ed. *The East India Company: 1600–1858*, Vol. 4. New York: Routledge, 1998.
Veen, Ernst van and Leonard Blussé, ed. *Rivalry and Conflict: European Traders and Asian Trading Networks in the 16th and 17th Centuries.* Leiden: CNWS Publications, 2005.
Veltman, T.J. "Nota over de geschiedenis van het Landschap Pidie" [Notes on the History of Pidie], *Tijdschrift voor Indische Taal-, Land- en Volkenkund* 58 (1919): 15–157.
Veth, Pieter Johannes. "De geschiedenis van Sumatra" (in 3 parts), *De Gids* 13, 2 (1849): 437–60, 529–600, 677–704.
———. "Vrouwenregeeringen in den Indischen Archipel" [Government by Women in the Indies Archipelago], *Tijdschrift voor Nederlandsch Indie* 2 (3 & 4) (1870): 354–69.
———. *Atchin en zijne betrekkingen tot Nederland, topographisch-historische beschrijving* [Aceh and its Relations with the Netherlands: A Description of its Topographical History]. Leiden: Gualth Kolff, 1873.
Villiers, John. "Trade and Society in the Banda Islands in the Sixteenth Century", *Modern Asian Studies* 15 (1981): 743–9.
———. "Doing Business with the Infidel: Merchants, Missionaries, and Monarchs in Sixteenth Century Southeast Asia", in *Maritime Asia*, ed. Sprengard and Ptak. Wiesbaden, 1994, pp. 151–70.
Vlekke, Bernard Hubertus Maria. *Nusantara: A History of Indonesia.* Cambridge, MA: Harvard University Press, 1945.
Voorhoeve, P. "Van En Over Nuruddin Ar-Raniri", *BijdragenTaal-Land-En-Volkenkunde* 107, 4 (1951): 353–68.
Warren, James Francis. *The Sulu Zone, 1768–1898: The Dynamics of External Trade, Slavery, and Ethnicity in the Transformation of a Southeast Asian Maritime State.* Singapore: Singapore University Press, 1981.
Wazir Jahan Karim. *Women in Culture: Between Malay Adat and Islam.* Boulder, CO: Westview Press, 1992.
Wills, John E. "Maritime Asia, 1500–1800: The Interactive Emergence of European Domination", *American Historical Review* 98, 1(1993): 83–105.
Winstedt, Richard Olaf and R.J. Wilkinson. "Perak under the Achinese" (from "A History of Perak"), *Journal of the Malayan Branch of the Royal Asiatic Society* 12, 1 (1934): 18–77.

Winzeler, Robert. "Amok: Historical, Psychological and Cultural Perspectives", in *Emotions of Culture: A Malay Perspective*, ed. Wazir Jahan Karim. Singapore: Oxford University Press, 1990, pp. 96–122.

Wolf, Armin. "Reigning Queens in Medieval Europe: When, Where and Why", in *Medieval Queenship*, ed. Parsons. New York, 1998, pp. 169–88.

Wolters, Oliver William. *Early Indonesian Commerce: A Study of the Origins of Srivijaya*. Ithaca, NY: Cornell University Press, 1967.

———. "Southeast Asia as a Southeast Asian Field of Study", *Indonesia* 58 (1994): 1–17.

———. *History, Culture and Region in Southeast Asian Perspectives*. Singapore: Institute of Southeast Asian Studies, 2nd ed., 1999.

Wormser, Paul. *Le* Bustan al-Salatin *de Nuruddin ar-Raniri: Réflexions sur le Rôle Culturel d'un Étranger dans le Monde Malais au XVIIe Siècle*. Paris: Cahiers d'Archipel, 2012.

Yamani, Mai, ed. *Feminism and Islam: Legal and Literary Perspectives*. Reading, Berkshire: Garnet Publishing for Ithaca Press, 1996.

Yang, Lien-Sheng. "Female Rulers in Imperial China", *Harvard Journal of Asiatic Studies* 23 (1960–61): 47–61.

Index

Abdul Jalil, Sultan, 38
Abdurrahman, Habib, 223
Aceh Canonical Laws, 27, 35, 46, 56, 191
   writing of, 27n1
Aceh Council, 136
Aceh Dar al-Salam, Islamic kingdom of, 1
   from "absolute" to limited monarchy, 221–7
   conquest of Perak, 94
   corroboration of sources of information on, 26
   coup and counter-coup, 124–6
   decentralisation of, 216–21
   decision making in, 215, 223
   decline of, 8, 18, 141–2, 216–21
   under female sovereigns, 20–3
   defeat against Portuguese, 144
   Dutch blockade in 1647–50, 20
   Dutch VOC documents on, 23–4
   English East India Company (EIC) documents on, 24–5
   European interventions in, 2
   female rulers and the practice of Islam in, 172–5
   foreign-born rulers, 30
   founder and first sultan of, 28
   "golden age" under the rule of Iskandar Muda, 1, 1n2
   Indian trade with, 132, 134, 134n13
   Islam and State in seventeenth-century, 183–5
   Malay writings on, 25
   military encounters with Europeans, 20
   origins of, 28
   and other Malay polities, 264–7
   Perak, treaty of (1655), 136
   perceptions of power and rulers, 46–8
   political succession, criteria for, 27–39
   recentralisation of, 216–21
   reception of foreign Muslim traders, 152
   regional balance of power, 33
   relations with
      Ottoman Empire, 172
      Portuguese, 176
      Sumatra West Coast, 144–5
   struggle with VOC over Perak, *see* Aceh-VOC struggle, over Perak
   sultanate of, 28
   travellers' accounts on, 25–6
   and vassals on Sumatra West coast, 141–4
   VOC officials in Perak, massacre of, 112–15
   women rulers of, 2

Aceh-Dutch War (1873–1903), 223
Acehnese *Berdaulat* (the Sovereign One), 177
Acehnese forces, reconstruction of, 233
Aceh-Perak-SWC-VOC relations, 18–19
Aceh-Portuguese War in 1560s, 232
Aceh-VOC encounters, 268–71
Aceh-VOC struggle, over Perak, 129–31
  dilemma for or against waging war, 132–5
  overlord-vassal relations, affect on, 130
  Schouten's mission to Aceh and, 136
  tussle for tin, 136–40
act of treason, 58
adat (customs)
  as basis of legitimacy, 48–51
  beliefs and practices, 11
  and Islamic religion, 10–12
  role of, 2
Adat Aceh, 45, 177, 188–9, 191, 216, 224
Adat Meukuta Alam (a code of laws), 222
Adonna Lilla, Maharaja, 63–4, 75–6, 79, 81, 84–7, 92, 125, 159, 194, 238, 240, 260, 271
adultery, punishment for, 186
"age of commerce", 16, 272
  rise of female rule in, 51
Ahmad Syah, Sultan, 32, 160
al-Adil, Qadhi Malik, 249, *see also* qadhi; Maliku'l Adil, Kadhi
al-Alam, Jamal, 219n31, 221, 227
al-Din, Badr al-Alam Syariff Jamal, Sultan, 28, 34, 189, 190, 248, 252, 264
al-Din, Salah, 29
al-Din, Shams, Sheikh, 59, 189
Alfian, Ibrahim, 50
al-Jauhari, 46, 204

al-Raniri, Nuruddin, 7–8, 43–4, 46, 59–60, 124, 159, 189–91, 214, 247
al-Singkel, Abdul Rauf, 43–5, 48, 181, 188, 190–1, 251–2
  death of, 207
Amina Todijn, Sultanah, 136
Andaya, Barbara, 11, 11n36, 14, 17, 119, 130, 203
Andaya, Leonard, 2, 2n4, 20, 72, 240
Anglo-Dutch war (1674), 133, 139
Aru, 144

bahar, 70, 95–6, 107–10, 118, 123, 137–9, 147–9, 153, 228
balai furdah, 222
balai gadeng, 222
balai laksamana, 222
balai majelis mahkamah rakyat, 222
balai musyawarah, 222
balai rungsari, 222
balance of power, 217, 255
  royalty-nobility, 263
Bandar Sepuloh, 152
Barakat, Sharif, 194, 251
Barus, 141, 144, 157, 159, 161, 267
Batahan, 144
Bencoolen, 161, 168–9
Bendahara of Pahang, 266
bendahara, 136–9, 199, 235
Binthara, Maharaja, 100–2, 115, 148
*boedjangh*s (royal messengers), 99, 109, 112–13, 116–17, 156
Bort, Balthasar, 130, 139, 149–50, 200, 241
Bowrey, Thomas, 7, 26, 187, 198, 201, 225, 241, 244, 250, 255–6, 263
Bradley, Francis, 14, 234
Bruyl, Gabriel, Resident, 138, 150, 156
Bustan us-Salatin, 8, 15, 33, 36, 40, 45, 56, 58, 62, 172, 177, 188, 191–2, 199, 230, 233, 246

capado, see eunuchs
capitalism, development of, 227
Cawley, William, 166–8, 170, 201, 224, 243, 270
Cbpab Srei (Code of Conduct for Women), 14
chakravartin, concept of, 172–3, 176
chap sikureueng (seal), 182
Charles II, King, 24, 155
China Camp, 262
coins, minting of, 234
collaborative rule, model of, 227–8
colonial societies, formation of, 235
Commentary on Forty Hadiths, 191
Commissar
    Croocq, Paulus, 70, 70n39
    de Meere, Jan, 73, 98, 223, 232
    de Vlamingh, Arnold, 84, 241
    Schouten, Justus, 63, 73
    Sourji, Pieter, 72, 74–80
    Truijtman, Johan, 97
    van Deutecom, Jochum Roelofszoon, 70, 96
Compostel, Jacob, 40, 44, 63–5, 72, 75, 247, 263
coopman (trader), 149, 150
Corneliszoon, Jacob, 158
Corpus Diplomaticum, 162
Council of the Indies in Batavia, 152
"Crown Jewels", 66
Curre, Michiel, 113–14, 120, 122

Dagh-Register, 103, 105–6, 125, 139, 238
dalam (inside/private) domain, 77, 79, 204, 223
Dampier's "civil war", 250
Dampier, William, 7, 26, 54, 187, 191, 201–3, 225, 231, 250, 261, 263
Dar al-Kamal dynasty, 28, 31, 35, 55
Dato' Bendahara, 135–6
Dato' Temenggong, 116

Daudy, Ahmad, 59
daulat (sovereignty or authority of a ruler), 48, 147, 211
Davis, John, 25, 51
Daya, 28, 144
de Beaulieu, Augustine, 25, 228
de Christo, Bento, Father, 180
decision making, practice of, 215, 223, 225
de Graaff, Nicolaus, 25, 39–41, 61
Delfshaven (Dutch ship), 99, 103
De Castro, Francisco de Souza, 185
Deli, 68, 122, 125, 144, 214, 258, 267
de Meere, Jan, Commissar, 73, 98, 223, 232
De Remedie (ship), 151
derhaka (treason), 125, 211
de Roy, Jacob, 7, 26, 225, 233–4, 240, 250, 261–3
de Salengre, Philips Carel, 97, 125
dewa-raja, Hindu concept of, 172–3
diamonds, 70–3, 73n56, 83, 86
Di Hulu, Raja, 161
Drakard, Jane, 160–1
Dutch capture of Melaka (1641), 18, 33, 41, 89, 94, 141
Dutch East Indies Company, *see Veerinigde Ooost-Indische Compagnie* (VOC)

early years, of Safiatuddin Syah, 57–92
    accomplishments in, 60
    alms distribution, 62
    Commissar Arnold Vlamingh and, 80–8
    and Commissar Pieter Sourij, 74–80
    conflict over paying for the jewels, 73–4
    dealing with Sultan Iskandar Thani's legacy, 58–60
    Dutch foreign envoys and, 66–74

funeral procession of Iskandar Thani, 61–2
jewel affair, 66–74
leadership style, 66
rapprochement with Sourij, 90
support of orang kaya, 60, 62–5
Effendi, Sunullah, 273
Eid al-Adha, 195, 197
Eid al-Fitr, 195–6
elephant trade of Aceh, 153, 232
growth of, 229
with India, 105, 268
profits from, 263
royal monopoly for, 127
VOC and, 21, 229
Elizabeth I, Queen, 54, 207, 270
English East India Company (EIC), 2, 4, 171
documents relating to Aceh, 24–5
Madras Council, 166–7, 169, 243
and Sumatra West Coast, 164–70
entertainment, politics of, 243–6
estemie, 99, 109–10, 116–8, 120, 122–3, 147, 156, 269
eunuchs, 7, 63–4, 90, 204–5, 219, 243, 245, 247, 260
gifts for, 242
network of women and, 237–41
Safiatuddin's network of, 271
European fashion, in Aceh, 241–3, 270
European hegemony, in Asia, 19

Fansuri, Hamzah, 43n70, 59, 159, 189, 214
Fatimid dynasty (909–1171), 206
fatwa (religious decree), 43–4, 59, 202, 208, 259
female *laksamana* (admiral of the navy), 51
female leadership, *see* queenship
female rule, in Aceh Dar al-Salam
in 1641, 51–6

in "age of commerce", 16, 51
decline of kingdom under, 20–3, 261–4
entertainment, politics of, 243–6
in Islam, 41–6
leadership under, 16–17
legal ruling allowing, 44
network of women and eunuchs under, 237–41
opposition to, 251
origin, nature, and impact of, 2, 3–10
political opposition to, 217
political power and state formation, issue of, 15
preference for, 4
promotion of, 7
reasons for end of, 10
reasons for lasting six decades, 257–61
reasons of, 253–7
relations between queen and male elite, 9, 15, 17
religious debate over, 43–4
Taj caveats to, 47
ties that unbind, 17–19
tolerance of, 44
trade under, 227–34
traditional and religious values of, 15
women rulers, 2
female rulers
absence from Islamic rituals and festivities, 197–8
accumulation of weaponry during reigns of, 233
in Aceh Dar al-Salam, 2
administration of law and justice under, 185–7
attributes of, 191–4
collaborative rule, 227–8
degree of visibility, 198–206
and European fashion, 241–3
in Islamic history, 41–3

Index

versus male rulers, 198–9
origins of, 37n52
and practice of Islam in Aceh, 172–5
relations with male elites, 9, 15
stranger-queens, 234–7
succession of
    circumstances leading to, 39–41
    legality in Islam for, 40, 46–8
    opposition for, 40
traditional and religious values of, 15
and ulama, 188–91
see also queenship
female slaves, stately procession of, 241–2
Fernández-Armesto, Felipe, 235
fiqh (laws pertaining to ritual obligations), 191
firman (ruler's order), 142
First Blast of the Trumpet, The, 54
fortifications, in Aceh, 165n133, 233
Fort St. George, 165
freedom of women, to appear in public, 203

gampong, administration of, 223
Gary, Henry, 137, 155
gender and power, in Middle Ages, 13
Generale Missiven, 111, 132, 248
genealogy, 28, 216, 254
God's shadow on earth, concept of, 178
gold trade, 19, 152–3, 160, 170, 234, 263, 267
Governor General, 76, 78, 82, 98, 99
  in Batavia, 9, 23, 24, 80, 83, 85, 89, 100
  Maetsuyker, Joan, 111, 124, 133, 134, 135, 152, 158, 179, 181
  Reniers, Carel, 123
  van der Lijn, Cornelis, 97, 103
  van Diemen, Antonio, 72, 73, 95, 266

Grantham, Thomas, 165
Grijpskerken (yatch), 113
Groenewegen, Jan, 150–2, 155–8
Groll (ship), 146
grooten priester (high priest), 125, 181
Grotius, Hugo, 268
Gujarat, 43, 59, 183, 190, 193
Gujarati, 99–100, 146, 228–30
gynaecocracy, 259

Hadi, Amirul, 2, 6, 34, 44–5, 47–8, 183, 188–9
hajj (Islamic pilgrimage to Mecca), 239
Harmanszoon, Jan, 84–5, 95, 228, 242
Harmanszoon, Willem, 241
Harriden, Jessica, 12
Hashim/Hasyim, *see* al-Din, Badr al-Alam Syariff Jamal, Sultan
Hatim Tai, *see* Tai, Hatim
Heren Zeventien, 103, 109, 111, 117, 134–5
hijab, 203, 205
Hijab al-Amir, 205–6
Hijjas, Mulaika, 3, 8
hikayat (folklore), 25, 29, 49
Hikayat Aceh, 25, 29–30, 68, 172, 213
Hikayat Pahang, 49
Hikayat Patani, 42, 235
holy war, idea of, 176, 232
hpoun, Burmese notions of, 14
Hurgronje, Snouck, 5, 183, 216, 223, 251n12

Ibn Battuta, 174
Ibrahim, Raja, 161
Ijau, Raja, *see* Raja Ijau of Patani
imam, 40, 43, 45, 182, 196–7, 207, 222
Inderapura, 30, 37, 55, 144–7, 150, 152, 157, 159, 161–2, 254

Indra, Sri Bidia, 80, 98, 100, 102, 116, 148, 241, 270
Irwin, G.W., 21
Iskandar Muda, Sultan, 1–2, 17, 20, 32, 35–6, 38, 52, 94, 144, 150, 171–2, 205, 218, 264, 272
  defeat of, 210, 232
  diplomatic missions and alliances with Turkey, 173
  execution of justice, 188
  expansion of Aceh's power, 22
  "golden age" in Aceh's history, 22, 264
  idea of a universal king, 176
  as "King of Kings", 68
  letter of 1615 to England's James I, 175, 205
  overlord-vassal relations, 213
  training for war-elephants, 232
Iskandar Thani, Sultan, 1, 7, 17, 31, 88, 145, 176, 205, 248, 264
  attempted murder of, 58–9
  death of, 38, 58
  depiction of his own powers, 178
  diplomatic missions and alliances with Turkey, 173
  enemies of, 59
  execution of justice, 188
  fascination with precious stones, 69–72
  funeral procession of, 60–1
    described by European travelers, 62
  relation with Dutch, 73
  succession of, 254
  succession to the throne, 58
  treasures and jewels of, 68–9
Islamic court of Aceh, 203
  for arbitration, 188
Islamic learning and literature, proliferation of, 191
Islamic trading system, 173

Islam, practice of
  female rulers and, 172–5
  rituals and festivities, 195–8
    female ruler's absence from, 197–8
  in seventeenth-century Aceh, 183–5
Islam, tenets of, 249
Ito, Takeshi, 2, 7–9, 183–4, 188, 217, 223, 230–1, 235

Jacobsen's *Lost Goddesses*, 12, 14
"jewel affair", 57, 66–74, 89, 93, 174, 204, 223, 232, 238
jewels and the aura of kingship, 66–9
  as symbols of sovereignty and power, 67
  visual display of, 69
Johor, 1, 22, 33, 38, 41, 68, 89, 98, 131, 139, 147, 155, 213, 265, 266

Kadhi Malik al-Adil, *see* Maliku'l Adil, Kadhi
kadhi (religious judge), 45, 58, 222, 251
kali, 63, *see also* Lebai Kita Kali
Kamalat Syah, Sultanah, 2, 10, 34, 171, 220, 225, 263
  deposition of, 208, 252
  as last female ruler of Aceh, 249–53
Kanun Syarak Kerajaan Aceh, *see* Aceh Canonical Laws
Kathirithamby-Wells, Jeyamalar, 18, 141–5, 152, 227
Kattaun, 169
Kayu Kelat, Bendahara, 235, 271
keuchik (village head), 222–3
khalifah (God's shadow), 12, 45, 172, 178, 188
*khatun*s, 42, 174–5
khutbah (Friday sermon), 182

"kingship" in Southeast Asia, 13–17, 176, 247, 253
   Acehnese conceptions of, 48–51
   jewels and the aura of, 66–9
   in Malay/Muslim world, 271–4
   theories of, 46
"kings of kings", 173, 208
*kitab*s (religious texts), 190
Kling (ethnic group from India), 62, 113, 117, 122–3, 132
Knox, John, 54
Kota Raja (Banda Aceh), 144, 159
Kota Tengah, 157–9
kris (dagger), 71, 72, 110, 118, 125, 235, 271
Kulup, Panglima, 140
kurnia (permission to grant), 116, 148, 269

Labu, 144
laksamana, 81–3, 90, 101, 104–5, 120, 124, 148, 218
   duties of, 230
   responsibility of, 231
Latiff, Abdul, 135
law and justice under sultanahs, administration of, 185–7
leadership style, of female rulers, 16–17, 58, 65–6, 93, 171, 218, 237, 246, 272, 274
Lebai Kita Kali, 63, 75, 78, 81, 87, 100, 180, 186, 189–90, 219, 232
Lella, Sri Maharaja, 99
Lockyer, Charles, 169
Lombard, Denys, 2, 227
Luthfi, Auni, 2–3, 6

Macareel (Dutch ship), 99, 103
Maetsuyker, Joan, 111, 124–5, 133–4, 152, 158, 179, 181

Maharaja Adonna Lilla, *see* Adonna Lilla, Maharaja
Maharaja Binthara, *see* Binthara, Maharaja
Maharaja di Raja, 124, 194
Maharaja Sri Maharaja, 77–8, 81, 85, 100, 104, 112, 115, 147–8, 181, 185, 219, 263
Mahkota Alam dynasty, 35
Malay leadership, ideal of, 226
Malay Peninsula, map of, 129
Maliku'l Adil, Kadhi, 10, 58, 183, 189, 231, 249
Mangbangh, Manuel, 63–4
Manjutta, 161
Marsden, William, 4, 8
massacre, of VOC officials in Perak, 112–15, 131
Masulipatnam, 105, 133, 134, 146, 149, 229
Mataram, 96, 164
Melaka, siege of (1629), 144, 232, 255
"men of prowess", 13–17, 174
Mergui massacre (July 1687), 169
Mernissi, Fatima, 10, 42, 182, 206, 273
Meulek, Tengku di, 27n1
Miller, Dean, 48
Minangkabau kingdom, 160, 163
Mir'at al-Tullab, 45, 191
misogyny, 52–3
Moedeliar, Radia, 102, 148
Moessady (ship), 239
Mohun, Richard, 166, 170
Mongol Empire, 174–5
muafakat, custom of, 223, 258
Mughals, 49, 72, 172, 240, 243, 262, 273
Mughayat Syah, Ali, 28–9, 31, 35
Muhammad Syah, Sultan, 34, 36, 152, 159
Mundy, Peter, 36, 58, 69, 205

Muslim women leaders, tradition of, 11
musyawarah (consensus building), 17, 222, 226, 258, 272
Mutahir, Tun, 199
Muzaffar Shah, Sultan, 99, 108, 116, 119, 131, 136

narcissistic, 71, 178
Naqiatuddin Syah, Nur Alam, Sultanah, 2, 33, 36, 171, 220
nationale partij, 249
Newbury, Colin, 143
nine-stone jewel, 67, 68
Njinga, Queen, 53, 55

Oelakkan, 158, 159, 267
oligarchic monopoly, 227
oppercoopman (senior trader), 40, 44, 85, 97, 98, 117, 148, 150
orang kaya (state officials), 3–4, 32, 41, 57, 151, 167
    anti-Dutch faction, 63–4, 90, 97, 101–2, 104–6, 110, 112, 116, 120, 122–4, 126, 131, 137–9, 147, 158, 160, 218–9, 231, 238
    disputes over the jewels, 83
    factional struggles, 120
    opschudding (state of commotion) among, 39
    power struggles amongst, 236
    preference for women rule, 4
    pro-Dutch faction, 79, 101, 105–6, 120, 131, 139, 156, 219
    promotion of women rule, 7
    rise of, 6
    Sultanah Safiatuddin Syah and her, 62–5
Ord, Ralph, 166–7, 224, 243
Ottoman Turks, 232, 273

overlord-vassal relationship, 18, 93, 130, 140, 163–4, 213, 218, 264–6

Padang, 1, 144, 146, 150–3, 157, 161, 267
    troubles in, 157–9
Paduka Tuan, 63, 81, 84, 86, 101, 104, 125–6, 231
Paduka Sri Sultanah, 181, 182
Pahang, 32, 33, 36, 38, 254, 265, 266
Painan, Treaty of (1663), 18, 141, 143, 152, 154–5, 160, 163
Palawan, Raja, 158–9
panglima bandar, post of, 167, 218, 231
panglima dalam, *see* laksamana
Panglima Polem, 35, 217, 220, 250
*panglima*s (governors), 143–5, 148, 150, 156, 220–1, 266
Pasai, 28, 50, 144
Pasaman, 144
Patani, 5, 11, 14, 38, 42, 51, 149, 215, 226
patriarchal, 2, 6, 15, 92, 207, 253, 273
patron-client relationship, 15, 18, 141, 163, 267
penghulu (village head), 151
penghulu kawal, 186, 217, 230
Pegu, 12, 132, 149, 229
pepper trade, 141, 145, 147–9, 165, 168, 173, 231, 263, 267
Perak affair, 93, 94–7, 100, 140–1, 174, 260
Perak River, blockade of, 93, 95–7, 99, 101, 104, 113, 136
Perak, treaty of (1655), 136
Persian, 61, 70, 72, 172, 204, 252
Pidir, 144
piety *versus* pageantry, 175–81
Pits, Jacob, 158–60
political conservatism, in Islam, 55

political leadership, Malay ideas of, 49, 88, 257, 273–4
political opposition, to female rule, 59, 202, 213, 217, 220, 248–9, 251, 257
political succession in Aceh
    Acehnese lineage and, 34–5
    criteria for, 27–39
    factors governing, 28
    female factor in, 35, 41–6
    Islamic paradigm for, 34
    by marriage, 37
    practice of, 35
    royal male heirs, 36
    rules of, 34
politicisation of religion, 175
port bureaucracy, 230
Portuguese Melaka, 4, 33, 73, 144–5
power and rulers, perceptions of, 46–8
Priaman, 144–9, 151, 153–4, 158, 161, 168, 214
priester partij (a group of ulama), 10, 249, 251
primus inter pares, status of, 173
Pryaman Company, 169
puji-pujian (compliments), 24
Pulau Chinco, 151, 156, 162
Putih, Bendahara, 161

qadhi, 63, 189
Qanun al-Asyi Darussalam, 221, 238
queen mother, phenomenon of, 49
queenship, 174, 272
    Acehnese conceptions of, 48–51
    under Acehnese sultanahs, 16–17
    concept of, 16
    construction of, 202
    gender-based construct on, 199
    institution of, 13, 16
    from *Ira et Malevolentia* to *Pax et Custodia*, 210–15
    Islamic doctrine of, 47
    and Islamic kingship, 16
    legality of, 46
    and participation in politics and governance, 46
    phenomenon of, 253
    positions of high authority, 175
    stranger-queens, 234–7
    Taj us-Salatin's explication of, 47
Qu'ran, 193, 195, 203

Raja Macatta, Bendahara (Mahkota), 159
Raja Ijau of Patani, 14, 42, 230n68, 234–5, 271
Raja Ungu of Patani, 215
reals (Spanish silver coin), 70–1, 83, 91, 132, 136–8, 147, 149
regular audiences, practice of, 224
Reid, Anthony, 2–3, 20–1, 51–2, 173, 210–11, 216–17, 262
religious localisation, process of, 174
religious scholars, attitude towards leadership and women, 46
religious tolerance, 180
Riayat Shah, Abdul Jalil, Sultan, 37, 94, 265
Rijal, Syaiful, Sheikh al-Islam, 124, 124n91, 181, 189, 190
rijksdaalders (Dutch silver coins), 146
royal absolutism, period of, 210–12
royal-elite relations, model of, 17, 212, 214–15, 227, 228, 235, 272
royal letters, 175–81
royal power
    decline of, 221, 233
    limitation of, 222
ruba (customary dues), 152
ruler's attributes, 191–4

Sablat, 169
sacral kingship, 173

Safavid Iran, 273
Safiatuddin Syah, Sultanah, 1–2, 6, 21, 39, 45, 52, 55, 135
  Aceh's relations with Sumatra West Coast under, 145–51
  adoption of the title khalifah, 175, 177, 188
  allegation of sexual liaison, 124–5, 260
  balancing of pro- and anti-Dutch factions, 110, 131
  on blockade of the Perak River, 99
  challenges from the VOC, 94
  correspondences with the Dutch in Batavia and Melaka, 179
  coup and counter-coup, 124–6, 260
  daily audience at the *balai* (audience hall), 15
  dealing with Johan Truijtman, 97–103, 118
  death of, 164, 248, 256
  early years, *see* early years, of Safiatuddin Syah
  efforts to
    accommodate Dutch demands, 131
    curb Dutch encroachments on the SWC, 155–6
  firman (ruler's order) of 1641, 142
  fixing of price of cloth in exchange for pepper, 148
  and her three female successors, 248
  jewel affair, 57, 66–74, 89, 93, 174
  leadership style, 57, 66, 93
  loss of Sumatra West Coast vassal states, 162–4
  maturing years of, 93–128
  and more crises at Aceh's court, 124–6
  patron-client relationship, 18
  Perak affair, 94–7, 99, 100, 174
  policy of accommodation with an external power, 164
  politics of consolidation, 93–128
  rejection of VOC's demands for new privileges, 105–7
  relations between royalty and elite, 9
  religious tolerance, 180
  response against VOC's interference in SWC, 154–7
  role of moderator and arbiter, 237
  royal decree, 237
  Taj al-Alam, title of, 33, 177, 181, 182
  on tin trade in Perak, 107
  treatment of the Dutch, 98–9
  ulama's support to, 188
  vassals' rights to collect tolls, 229
  welcoming traders, policy of, 230
sakti (magical), 67, 173
Saphier (yacht), 123
sarakata, 218
Sas, Johannis, 161
Sassanid, 204, 206
saudagar raja, 139
sayyids, 251
Schouten, Dirk, 136
  mission to Aceh, 136
Schouten, Justus, 73, 270
seals and coins, 7, 79, 99, 182
  minting of, 234
  rijksdaalders (Dutch silver coins), 146
  of sultanah of Aceh Dar al-Salam, 181
Sejarah Melayu, 47, 67, 199, 240, 254
Serambi Mekah (Veranda of Mecca), 10, 62
sexual scandals and liaisons, 259
shahbandars (administrative officials), 7, 75–6, 83, 90, 114, 116–17, 120, 123, 135–7, 167–8, 228, 250
Shah Jahan, Emperor, 229

sharia (Islamic law), 27, 55, 184, 188, 190, 259
sharif (governor), 194, 257
Sheikh al-Islam, 43, 45–6, 59, 124–5, 180, 182, 189–90, 195
Siam, 133, 155, 169, 206, 215
Silebar, 168, 169
Sillida, 147, 149, 152–4
  factory, 151
  Sillida, Treaty of (1660), 150
silsilah, 28
Singkel, 144
Sourij, Pieter, 74–80, 146–7, 180, 185–6, 189, 200, 218, 225, 232
sovereignty and power, symbols of, 67, 182
speelhuis (place for amusement), 245
Spellman, W.M., 213
Sri Sultan Perkasa Alam, 182
stadthouder, 160
stranger-hood, concept of, 235
stranger-kings, concept of, 234n84
stranger-queens, concept of, 234–7
Sufism, 189
Sulalat-us-Salatin, 47
Suleyman the Magnificent, 67
Sumatra, map of, 129
Sumatra West Coast (SWC), 18, 21, 115
  Aceh and her vassals on, 141–4
  Aceh's relations under Sultanah Safiatuddin Syah with, 145–51
  Dutch encroachment on, 152
  early relations between Aceh and, 144–5
  east-west interactions on, 163
  Sultanah Zakiatuddin Syah and the EIC on, 164–70
  VOC and, 151–4, 163
Surat, 96, 100–1, 103, 134, 137, 149, 165, 229, 239
symbols of sovereignty, *see* sovereignty and power, symbols of

Tai, Hatim, 178
Taj al-Alam, title of, 33, 177, 181, 182
Taj us-Salatin, 46, 56, 175, 191, 196, 198, 204
  caveats to female succession, 47
  on construction of female leadership, 202
  explication of female leadership theories, 47
tariqat (schools of Sufism), 189–90
Tazkirah Tabakah, 216
Teh Gallop, Annabel, 68, 175–6
teungku (religious village head), 223
Thijssen, Jan, 96
Tiku, 68, 141, 144–54, 156, 158, 161, 168, 214
tin trade, 94–6, 102, 107, 153, 228
  Aceh-VOC tussle for, 136–40
trade, under female rule, 227–34
  in weaponry system, 232
Triamang, 169
Truijtman, Johan, 114, 147, 193, 270
  assessment of the sultanah, 110
  Dagh-Register, 103, 105–6
  excuses regarding Dutch patrol ships, 101
  indignities suffered by, 102, 132
  investigation of Perak murders, 121
  laksamana's rude treatment of, 98
  missions to Aceh and Perak (1649–52), 97–103
  mission to Perak and Aceh for the Perak murders, 115–20
  and more trouble at Aceh's court, 111–12
  trouble at Perak river, 120–4
  trouble in Acehnese court, 103–11

ulama (religious scholar), 8, 54
  sultanahs and, 188–91
  writings of, 258
ummah (community of believers), 172

United East India Company, *see Veerinigde Ooost-Indische Compagnie* (VOC)
universal king, idea of, 68, 172, 176
ureueng tuha (man of wisdom), 223

van der Lijn, Cornelis, 96–7, 103
van Deutecom, Jochum Roelofszoon, 96
van Diemen, Antonio, 72–4, 95, 266
van Goor, Jurrien, 142
van Langen, K.F.H., 216–17, 220
van Voorst, Coopman, 149
vassal states, 107
    Aceh, 18, 93–4, 141–4, 162–4, 173, 213
    Johor, 33, 89, 98, 213
    kings relation with, 173
    Pahang, 33
    Perak, 17, 119, 128, 140–1
    rights to control tolls, 174, 229
    suzerainty over, 93
    vassal-overlord relations, 18, 93, 119, 130, 140, 163–4, 213, 218, 264–6
Veerinigde Ooost-Indische Compagnie (VOC), 2, 7, 17–18, 233, 271
    blockade of the Perak River, 93, 95–7, 99, 101, 104, 136
    closure of factory in Aceh, 162
    commercial base in Padang, 267
    conquest of Melaka (1641), 18, 33, 41, 89, 94, 141
    control of tin trade, 94
    covert actions in dealing with Aceh's SWC vassals, 154
    defeat in monopolising Perak's tin, 139
    documents relating to Aceh, 23–4
    drawing of VOC factory at Aceh, 65
    exclusion of English and Asian traders from the SWC, 164
    harassment of Indian traders, 100
    influence and intervention in the SWC polities, 19
    as the new overlord, 160–2
    officials in Perak, massacre of, 112–15
    Perak, treaty of (1655), 136
    relations with Perak, 138
    struggle with Aceh over Perak, *see* Aceh-VOC struggle, over Perak
    and SWC polities, 151–4, 163
    territorial and commercial empire, 271
    trading privileges, 148
    troubles in Padang, 157–9
    unfair trading practices, 98
veiling and seclusion, idea of, 203–4
Verspreet, Abraham, 158, 160
    plan to suppress religious opposition, 160
Villiers, John, 227
visibility, degree of, 198, 203
visibility and space of female rulers, delineation of, 198–206
vizier, 47, 67, 222
Vlamingh, Arnold, 80–8, 95–6, 238, 241
VOC officials in Perak, massacre of, 112–15
vrouwenregeeringen (government by women), 4–5

wakil raja (deputy raja), 160
wali (bride's legal guardian), 40
war-elephants, training of, 232
weaponry system
    accumulation of, 232–3
    import of, 232
    during reigns of female rulers, 233

West Java, map of, 129
Willemszoon, Pieter, 193, 228, 237–9, 244
Wills, John, 140, 268
Wolters, Oliver William, 15–16, 174
women
  of piety, 13–17
  position in Islam, 10–12
  in power, 257–61
  roles and positions of, 16
Wujudiyyah wihdatul wujud, 59, 189
Wu Zetian, Empress, 53, 207

Zakiatuddin Syah, Inayat, Sultanah, 2, 33, 164–70, 171, 191, 248

www.ingramcontent.com/pod-product-compliance
Lightning Source LLC
Chambersburg PA
CBHW030521230426
43665CB00010B/716